Christian Spirituality

An Introduction to the Heritage

CHARLES J. HEALEY, SJ

ALBA·HOUSE NEW·YORK

SOCIETY OF ST. PAUL, 2187 VICTORY BLVD., STATEN ISLAND, NEW YORK 10314

ST PAULS

Excerpt from *John Donne, Selections From Divine Poems, Sermons, Devotions, and Prayers.* Edited and introduced by John Booty. Copyright © 1990, Paulist Press. Used with permission.

Excerpt from *John and Charles Wesley, Selected Writings and Hymns.* Edited and with an introduction by Frank Whaling. Copyright ©1981, Paulist Press. Used with permission.

Library of Congress Cataloging-in-Publication Data

Healey, Charles J.
   Christian spirituality: an introduction to the heritage / Charles J. Healey.
      p.   cm.
   Includes bibliographical references.
   ISBN 0-8189-0820-3
   1. Spirituality — History of doctrines. 2. Church history.
   I. Title.
   BV4501.2
   248'.09—dc21   98-25703
                                         CIP

Imprimi Potest:
Robert J. Levens, SJ
Provincial, New England Province, Society of Jesus
January 12, 1998

Produced and designed in the United States of America by the
Fathers and Brothers of the Society of St. Paul,
2187 Victory Boulevard, Staten Island, New York 10314,
as part of their communications apostolate.

ISBN: 0-8189-0820-3

Printing Information:

Current Printing - first digit   1   2   3   4   5   6   7   8   9   10

Year of Current Printing - first year shown

1999   2000   2001   2002   2003   2004   2005   2006   2007   2008

Table of Contents

Preface

For a number of years I have had the privilege of teaching a course in history in the summer graduate program in Christian Spirituality at Creighton University in Omaha, Nebraska. The students have been an ideal group to teach. They were engaged in various aspects of pastoral ministry (retreat directors, spiritual directors, teachers, pastors, vocation directors etc.), and they brought to their studies a sincere interest and a strong motivation. They were committed Christian men and women who were seeking to deepen their own awareness of God's presence in their lives and to broaden their knowledge of Christian spirituality so that they might more effectively assist others in their pastoral work.

A personal appropriation of the rich legacy of Christian spirituality was certainly intended, but not merely in the sense of increasing one's knowledge of people, movements, and dates. A desired goal was the attaining of a framework or overall view that would enable a person to recognize and understand the various schools, movements, and spiritual writings in their relationships with one another. Thus, more of an analytical introduction was intended. Building upon this framework or overview, students could continue to expand their knowledge and understanding with further reading and study according to their own needs and desires.

This book flows from that teaching. It is intended as a one-volume introduction to the rich legacy of Christian spirituality. It begins with the writings of the Apostolic Fathers — the earliest writings after New Testament times — and concludes with the Second Vatican Council (1962-65).[1] Plentiful footnotes and bibliographical references are provided to facilitate further study. Although there have been many recent publications dealing with the history of Christian spirituality, most are more focused and specialized in nature and a sense of continuity is easily lost. There still remains the need of an introductory study and it is hoped that this present work fills that need.

Much has been written in recent times on the meaning of the term *Christian spirituality*. This is not the place to explore the various ways it has been used and is being used today.[2] It can be an elusive term. In seeking to clarify the scope and content of a history of Christian spirituality, I have always found helpful the question posed by Urban Holmes, "How has Christian humanity throughout its history understood what it is to seek God and to know him?"[3] An historical study of Christian spirituality seeks to give an answer to that question. As the following pages indicate, the response has been articulated in various ways and has taken many different forms. But all of them focus on God, the human person, and the way, the means, or the journey by which the human is united with the divine. Christ must be at the center of this response for we are treating here of *Christian* spirituality. It can be said that Christian spirituality focuses on "the particular ways in which Christian men

---

[1] Some recent writers are not comfortable with this chronological approach on the grounds that it often favors a more organic, linear development and does not do justice to the complexities of the tradition and the voices of those who have been marginalized. Such, however, does not always have to be the case. For this question and others regarding Christian spirituality and history see Philip Sheldrake, *Spirituality and History, Questions and Interpretation and Method* (New York: Crossroad, 1992).

[2] See *Ibid.*, pp. 32-56; and Michael Downey, *Understanding Christian Spirituality* (New York: Paulist Press, 1997).

[3] Urban T. Holmes, *A History of Christian Spirituality, An Analytical Introduction* (New York: The Seabury Press, 1980), p. 3.

and women have come to understand, value, and direct their lives as disciples of Jesus of Nazareth in their own worlds."[4] In this particular study, the Roman Catholic perspective will come more to the fore, since my whole background has been in this tradition. But a sincere attempt has been made to do justice to the Orthodox, Protestant, and Anglican contributions to the history of Christian spirituality.

There are many valid and good reasons to respond to the above question and take the time to study and reflect upon the legacy of Christian spirituality. It has long been recognized that history is an excellent teacher and one that helps us to avoid making the same mistakes that have been made earlier. Knowledge of the Christian tradition broadens the limitations of our own horizons. It enables us to recognize the rich variety and complexity of Christian spirituality; it can free us to seek a way in prayer and spiritual practice which responds best to God's grace and is most suitable to our particular vocation. It helps us to develop the skills to be more competent guides for others and it enables us to help others without demanding that they be like us and follow our particular way. It brings us in contact with many wonderful teachers, spiritual guides, and holy persons who can inspire and enlighten us as we seek to know and love God in the present circumstances of our lives. The past has a way of shedding light on the present.

The distinguished historian, John Tracy Ellis, understood so well the delicate balance and relationship that should be present and operative when one considers the past and the present. He writes:

> Contemporary trends have always been a strong factor in swaying the human mind, but the tendency in our time would seem to be especially powerful if not irresistible. There is need, therefore, for salutary counteraction, and history is one of the most effective of all counteractions, for

---

[4] See Richard Woods, *God's Presence in History* (Chicago: Thomas More Press, 1989), p. 4.

Owen Chadwick has said, "History ... does more than any
other discipline to free the mind from the tyranny of present
opinion."[5]

The relationship between the past and the present, however,
should not be oversimplified. A healthy tension must be maintained. On one hand, we must let the past speak for itself and not
try to impose our contemporary answers or solutions upon it. On
the other hand, we approach the past from our present perspective
and we see it from our contemporary viewpoint. We are able to recognize more clearly today the cultural and historical factors and
influences that were operative in the past. A discerning and critical
frame of mind must accompany an appreciative awareness of the
riches of the legacy. We seek to discern that which is of perennial
and lasting value and significance from that which is historically and
culturally conditioned. We seek to ascertain what is of continuous
value to us today.

Since this present work seeks to bring out the similarities, differences, and other relational aspects of the various movements,
schools, and writers that are treated, some categories and terms can
be helpful in this process. The contrast between the *kataphatic* and
the *apophatic* approaches to prayer has become fairly well known.
The *kataphatic* is generally referred to as the way of light. It advocates the use of images and various aspects of created reality in
speaking about one's relationship and union with God. Included in
this approach would be such spiritual writers as St. Bernard of
Clairvaux, Julian of Norwich, St. Teresa of Avila, and St. Ignatius
Loyola. The *apophatic* way is that of darkness, emptiness, and the
negation of images. Associated with this approach are Pseudo-
Dionysius, the anonymous author of the *Cloud of Unknowing*, and
St. John of the Cross. The speculative/affective scale can also be
used to indicate whether the emphasis is being placed on the mind

---

[5] John Tracy Ellis, Foreword to James Hennesey, S.J., *American Catholics* (New York: Oxford University Press, 1981), xi.

or the heart. For example, the writers in the Greek mystical tradition are generally speculative, while St. Bernard of Clairvaux and many other medieval writers are more affective. These two scales, the kataphatic/apophatic and the speculative/affective can be variously joined so as to bring out differences and contrasts between schools, writers, and trends.[6] The use of these categories will be clarified in the pages that follow but it seems good to highlight them at this point.

I have also found helpful the categories developed by Friedrich von Hügel in his work, *The Mystical Element of Religion.* He speaks of three essential elements that are required for a fully developed and living religion — the institutional, the intellectual, and the mystical. All three elements have an important place and all three must be held together in a healthy tension. Each must be attentive to the other and there has to be interaction, harmony, and balance among them. They cannot go their separate ways or develop apart from the others. These categories and insights of von Hügel can be easily applied and can help us to understand the strengths and limitations of various movements, currents, and forms of spirituality.

In conclusion, I wish to express my sincere appreciation to those who have been so helpful to me in bringing this work to a conclusion. I am indebted to Sr. Mary Sweeney, S.C.H., Harvey D. Egan, S.J., Paul P. Gilmartin, S.J., and John R. Willis, S.J. for reading the text and for their helpful suggestions. I am grateful to Pope John XXIII National Seminary for granting a sabbatical that allowed me to concentrate on this project. Finally, it is a distinct pleasure for me to dedicate this book to those who are and have been associated with the Christian Spirituality Program at Creighton University. My long association with this program has indeed been a gift.

---

[6] See Holmes, *op. cit.*, pp. 4-5.

1 Spiritual Writers of the Early Church

1. The Apostolic Fathers

The earliest Christian manuscripts after New Testament times are usually referred to as the writings of the Apostolic Fathers. These would include such diverse second-century writings as the Epistle of Clement of Rome, the *Didache,* the Epistle of Barnabas, the *Shepherd* of Hermas, the Letters of Ignatius of Antioch, the second Epistle of Clement and the writings of the apologists, Justin the Martyr and Irenaeus of Lyons. They are precious documents that provide us with important information about the concerns, hopes, and desires of the early Christians.

The content of these writings varies a great deal. For example, Clement's letter is sent from Rome to settle some of the difficulties, frictions and schisms that were afflicting the Church of Corinth. The *Didache* (or *The Teaching of the Twelve Apostles*), discovered at Constantinople in 1875, contains teaching on the two ways (the way of life and the way of death), liturgical directives, practices of Church discipline, and an exhortation to watchfulness and sobriety with reference to the end of the world. The Epistle of Barnabas also treats the two ways and gives a Christian interpretation of the Old Testament against a Jewish interpretation. The well-known Letters of St. Ignatius of Antioch were sent to various Christian communities while the saintly bishop was traveling to Rome to face his martyrdom. The visionary *Shepherd* of Hermas is primarily a call to repentance, while the Second Epistle of Clement is a homily delivered during the Liturgy. It is one of the earliest Christian sermons that has been preserved, apart from the New Testament.

Some distinctive themes emerge from these early writings. There is clearly a call to preserve unity in the face of the external persecutions and the internal conflicts that challenged the early Church as it struggled to clarify its identity and to remain faithful to the teachings of the Gospel. This is particularly evident in the letters of St. Ignatius of Antioch. We find him writing to the Ephesians: "Make of yourselves a choir, so that with one voice and one mind, taking the keynote of God, you may sing in unison with one voice through Jesus Christ to the Father, and He may hear you and recognize you, in your good works, as members of His Son. It is good for you, therefore, to be in perfect unity that you may at all times be partakers of God."[1] And to the Magnesians he writes: "Let there be nothing among you to divide you; but be at one with the bishop and with those who are over you, thus affording a model and lesson of immortal life."[2]

These writings also attest to the presence of charisms in the early Church, similar to those found in the Acts of the Apostles and the letters of St. Paul. This is true of prophecy and visions but even more so of *gnosis*. Gnosis is a charism, a gift of the Holy Spirit that enables us to know Christ in Scripture. It finds its source in the prayerful meditation of Scripture and centers on Christ and his Cross. It is much more than an intellectual activity, for it brings about a living grasp of the realities of Christ's saving work. Christian gnosis is "first and always the understanding of the Scriptures, but wholly illuminated and absorbed in Christ."[3]

---

[1] Letter to the Ephesians, 4. See *The Apostolic Fathers*, The Fathers of the Church Series (New York: CIMA Publishing, 1947), p. 89.

[2] *Ibid.*, pp. 97-98.

[3] Louis Bouyer, *The Spirituality of the New Testament and the Fathers* (New York: Desclee, 1963), p. 183.

The Two Ways and Simplicity

The two ways, with its roots in Jewish catecheses and the Sermon on the Mount, is a prominent theme in the writings of the Apostolic Fathers. It is the main theme in the first part of the *Didache*, where we read in the opening words: "There are two ways, one of life and one of death; and great is the difference between the two ways."[4] This theme is also taken up in the Epistle of Barnabas where it is taught:

> There are two ways of Teaching and of Power: that of Light and that of Darkness; and there is a great difference between the two ways. Over the one are stationed the light-bringing angels of God; over the other, the angels of Satan. And the first is Lord from eternity to eternity; the latter is the ruler of the present world of lawlessness.[5]

Between these two ways, the person of faith must choose with a clear and definitive decision.

Closely connected with this theme of the Two Ways is the important notion of *aplotes*, the Greek word for simplicity or purity of heart. This is a response and a choice that comes from a heart that is pure and united. The opposite of this would be the divided heart, the response of duplicity that tries to avoid the choice of the two ways. The Greek word that sums up this divided heart and duplicity is *dipsuchia*. Bouyer emphasizes that "this teaching is one of the most remarkable constants to be found in the most different apostolic Fathers."[6] For example, we find Clement writing in his epistle: "The Father pours out His graces with sweetness on those who come to him with a simple heart, having no duplicity."[7] This theme of *aplotes* or purity of heart will reappear often in the history

---

[4] Cf. *The Apostolic Fathers, op. cit.* p. 171.

[5] Chapter 18; *Ibid.*, pp. 218-219.

[6] Bouyer, *op. cit.*, p. 189.

[7] Epistle of Clement to the Corinthians, chapter 23; see *The Apostolic Fathers, op. cit.*, p. 29.

of spirituality. It will have a prominent part in the thought of such writers as Evagrius Ponticus, John Cassian and many others as we shall see in the course of this study.

For these early apostolic writers, there was a very close connection between purity of heart and asceticism. The various ascetical practices had as their goal the ongoing growth in purity of heart. These practices sought to nourish and preserve a heart that was focused on the Lord and His way. Thus, asceticism in all its forms was not an end in itself but a means to prevent the heart from becoming divided. Problems arose once this was forgotten. For example, it was not long before a group known as the Encratites emerged in the early Church. They advocated a form of exaggerated asceticism that made it an end in itself rather than a means of preserving purity of heart. This resulted in their claims that one must renounce marriage and abstain from meat and wine if one was to be saved. Encratism is a deviation from the true purpose of asceticism.

2. Martyrdom in the Early Church

Martyrdom has played an important role in the history of spirituality, an importance that is often overlooked. Bouyer writes with emphasis:

> The importance of martyrdom in the spirituality of the early Church would be difficult to exaggerate. But it did not have this exceptional importance merely for the particular period when the majority of martyrdoms took place. After the elements of New Testament, certainly no other factor has had more influence in constituting Christian spirituality.[8]

For Christians during the first three centuries, martyrdom was always a possibility. This imminent threat could not help but have a

---

[8] Bouyer, *op. cit.*, p. 190.

powerful effect and influence on the early followers of Christ. Before the time of Constantine and the Edict of Milan, Christianity was an unrecognized and illegal religion, and martyrdom was always something that the Christian might have to face.

There was present in the early Church a large and significant amount of written documents focusing on martyrdom. They vary a great deal, but they all make their contributions to our understanding of martyrdom in these early centuries. First, there were various accounts of the martyrdoms that did take place. One form took its origin from the official records that were kept for archival purposes. There were also the accounts of eyewitnesses that recorded the event shortly after it took place. In many ways, these accounts are similar to the narration of the martyrdom of St. Stephen, given to us in the Acts of the Apostles (chap. 7). *The Martyrdom of St. Polycarp*, bishop of Smyrna, is one of the oldest and most familiar, written shortly after his death in 156. There is also the moving account of *The Passion of Saints Perpetua and Felicitas*; this narrates the martyrdom of the twenty-two year old Vibia Perpetua and the slave girl Felicitas in Carthage, Africa on March 7, 203, along with four other young catechumens.[9] Perpetua was the mother of a baby boy, and Felicitas was pregnant at the time of her arrest and gave birth before the execution. This narration is enhanced by Perpetua's own reflections, taken most likely from some notes she wrote in prison before her actual martyrdom.

There were also the written documents about the martyrdoms that blended many elements of literary fiction with the official reports and the accounts of eyewitnesses. These literary elements tended to increase as the time lengthened from the actual events, becoming in the process more expressions of popular piety than historical accounts.

The context of martyrdom also inspired writings of a more theological nature. The best known examples of this type would be

---

[9] Both of these accounts can be found in *The Fathers of the Primitive Church*, edited by Herbert Musurillo, S.J. (New York: Mentor-Omega Books, 1961).

the Letters of St. Ignatius of Antioch. These valuable documents were composed early in the second century when the saintly bishop of Antioch was journeying to Rome to face his condemnation and death. He wrote to the various Christian communities that extended hospitality and support to him during the course of his journey. He also wrote ahead to the Church of Rome, beseeching the Christians there not to hinder his making the ultimate sacrifice of his life in witness to the faith. He expresses his desire for martyrdom with great feeling, writing:

> I am writing to all the Churches to tell them all that I am ready, with all my heart, to die for God — if only you do not prevent it. I beseech you not to indulge your benevolence at the wrong time. Please let me be thrown to the wild beasts; through them I can reach God. I am God's wheat; I am ground by the teeth of the wild beasts that I may end as the pure bread of Christ.[10]

Finally, there were the *Exhortations to Martyrdom* which prominent spiritual writers composed to inspire and support Christians in times of persecution and danger. Examples of this type would be the exhortations of St. Cyprian of Carthage and the great Origen. At a later date both of these men would be called upon to give witness to their teaching in the concrete example of their own suffering for the faith.

3. Gnosis — True and False

It is important to keep in mind that there was both an orthodox use of the term *gnosis* and a usage that was associated with the heresy of Gnosticism that emerged in the early centuries. Thus we can speak of a true gnosis and a false gnosis. We will first look at

---

[10] Letter to the Romans, 4. *The Apostolic Fathers, op. cit.*, p. 109.

the rich orthodox tradition and then at its deviation in the heretical Gnosticism that was such a threat to the early Church.[11]

The biblical roots of the true gnosis are clearly delineated in the writings of St. Paul and St. John. Finding his inspiration in the Jewish tradition, Paul sees gnosis as a knowledge of Christ and the Scriptures, and an understanding of the secrets of God concerning ultimate ends. It is a gift of the Spirit that brings a gnosis of the mystery, the mystery that is revealed to us in the gnosis of Christ and His Cross. This is summed up so well in the third chapter of the Letter to the Ephesians where Paul prays in those beautiful words:

> May Christ dwell in your hearts through faith, and may charity be the root and foundation of your life. Thus you will be able to grasp fully, with all the holy ones, the breadth and length and height and depth of Christ's love, and experience this love which surpasses all knowledge so that you may attain to the fullness of God himself (Ephesians 3:17-20).

Paul echoes these words in so many other places. We find him writing in the same letter, "May the God of our Lord Jesus Christ, the Father of glory, grant you a spirit of wisdom and insight to know him clearly. May he enlighten your innermost vision that you may know the great hope to which he has called you" (Ephesians 1:17-19). And finally, he proclaims: "I wish to know Christ and the power flowing from his resurrection; likewise to know how to share in his sufferings by being formed into the pattern of his death" (Philippians 3:10-11).

In the Johannine writings the noun *gnosis* is not used but the Greek verb *gignosko* (to know) is used over and over again in the

---

[11] Bouyer has two chapters on this subject. The first is "The Problem of Gnosis: Christian Gnosis and Hellenism" (pp. 211-236); the second focuses on the tradition of true gnosis and is entitled "The Development and Continuity of Gnosis From its Origins to St. Irenaeus" (pp. 237-255).

context of knowing God or Christ. For example, in response to Jesus' question, "Will you also go away?", Peter proclaims: "We have believed and have come to know that you are the Holy One of God" (6:69). In Jesus' priestly prayer, he prays to his heavenly Father, "Eternal life is this: to know you, the only true God, and him whom you have sent, Jesus Christ" (17:3).

The Apostolic Fathers built on this biblical foundation. For them gnosis was a gift of the Holy Spirit that found its focus in meditation on the Scriptures, centering on Christ and his cross. We find in the *Didache* the following descriptions: "We give Thee thanks, Our Father, for the life and knowledge which Thou hast revealed to us through Jesus thy Son" (9,3). And, "We thank Thee, Holy Father, for Thy holy name, which Thou has caused to dwell in our hearts, and for the knowledge and faith and immortality, which Thou hast made known to us through Jesus Thy Son" (10,2). Echoing St. Paul, St. Ignatius of Antioch writes in his Letter to the Ephesians (17): "Why do we not all become wise by accepting the knowledge of God which is Jesus Christ?" In the Epistle to the Corinthians of St. Clement of Rome and the Epistle of Barnabas there are further developments of this concept.[12]

Gnosis would only become a problem when Christianity began to come in contact with Hellenism, the syncretist culture that emerged around the Mediterranean where the Greek language and culture mingled with native cultures. The patristic writers of the second and third centuries applied the term "Gnosticism" to the false Christian teachers and sects that emerged in this context. The term "Gnosticism" was limited to these heretical groups, many of which persisted until the seventh century. Discoveries of various other Gnostic texts in recent times have led scholars to recognize the wider roots and complexities of Gnosticism, many of which had no link to Christianity.

Keeping in mind, then, that the term "Gnosticism" does not refer to one particular sect, but to a number of diverse heresies, there

---

[12] See Bouyer, *op. cit.*, pp. 247-251.

are still common characteristics and teachings that can be recognized in all of them. Heading the list would be the distinguishing traits of dualism, emanationism, and salvation through esoteric knowledge.

Gnosticism is basically dualistic, positing an absolute cleavage between God and the universe. Matter is evil and prevents any contact with God. There is, however, a divine spark in human persons by which they are able to ascend to the good God and to free themselves from the evil world of matter through knowledge. Thus salvation and redemption come through gnosis, through knowledge of one's original state. It is a knowledge that comes from a revelation from God. It is an esoteric knowledge; it is not available to everyone, but only to those who are capable of being saved by it.

Christ's essential role in this plan of redemption is to come among human persons, to reveal to them this saving knowledge, and to awaken them to a knowledge of their original state. But he does not become truly Incarnate; he merely takes on the appearance of being human. He has not come to save the world but to save human beings from the world by awakening in them a true knowledge of themselves. This, of course, strikes at the heart of the mystery of the Incarnation and Christ's saving activity through his death and resurrection. The early Christian writers, particularly St. Irenaeus, were quick to expose this false gnosis and restore Christ's true role in God's plan of salvation.

4. St. Irenaeus of Lyons

St. Irenaeus (c. 140 - c. 202) is the most important of all the Christian writers of the second century. He was born in Asia Minor and was a disciple of St. Polycarp of Smyrna. In a moving letter of Irenaeus, we have a wonderful description of his boyhood memories of hearing Polycarp speaking of his relationship with the Apostle John and the others who had seen the Lord.[13] After migrat-

---

[13] Found in Eusesbius' *Ecclesiastical History*, 5, 20 (cf. Bouyer, pp. 225-226).

ing to Gaul for unknown reasons, Irenaeus became a priest at Lyons and later its bishop. He wrote in Greek, but of all his written works only two complete ones survive. The most important is his work *The Detection and Overthrow of the Pretended but False Gnosis*, usually referred to as *Adversus Haereses (Against Heresies)*, extant in its complete version only in a Latin translation of perhaps the fourth century. The second is the *Proof of the Apostolic Tradition*, extant only in an Armenian version. This is a work of apologetics that provides us with a good summary of basic Christian teaching.

Adversus Haereses is comprised of five books. Book 1 summarizes the teachings of heretical Gnostics and is thus a valuable source for the history of Gnosticism. The next three books contain Irenaeus' refutation of Gnostic teaching with arguments drawn from reason (Book 2), from the teachings of the Apostles and Christian tradition (Book 3), and from the sayings of the Lord (Book 4). Book 5 deals almost exclusively with the resurrection of the body since this was denied by all the Gnostics.

Irenaeus will have no part of the ontological dualism of the Gnostics and their pessimism about creation and the human person. Visible creation is good, not evil, and the body will rise again. He shows himself to be one of the first Christian humanists, and his well-known description of the human person sums up much of his thought: "The glory of God is the human person fully alive" (*gloria Dei, vivens homo*).[14] Christ has taken on our human condition in order to destroy sin, do away with death, and bring us eternal life.

Since the Gnostics drastically limited the role of Christ in the plan of salvation and denied the reality of His Incarnation, Irenaeus emphasizes the true nature of Christ and the importance of His death in the work of redemption. Salvation comes through Christ's Incarnation and through the Cross. Following the teaching of St. Paul on the recapitulation of all things in Christ, Irenaeus emphasizes that what was lost through the sin of Adam was restored by

---

[14] See *Adversus Haereses*, Book IV, chapter xxxiv (cited in Bouyer, p. 225).

Christ. Christ is the recapitulation of all things and the restorer of what was lost. Irenaeus writes:

> When the Son of God was incarnated and became man, He recapitulated in Himself the long history of men, bringing us salvation in a universal way, in such a way that what we lost in Adam: existence to the image and likeness of God, we regained in Jesus Christ.[15]

With his spirited defense against the heresies that seriously threatened the Church and his clear exposition of Christian teaching and the apostolic tradition, Irenaeus contributed much to the early Church. Because of the important role he played at this critical time, he is rightly looked upon as the founder of Christian theology. Although the evidence is not conclusive, it is believed that Irenaeus died a martyr, and thus he most likely gave up his life for the faith he defended so powerfully in his writings.

5. The Influence of Alexandria

When we speak of the school of Alexandria and its influence, we are primarily interested in the contributions of Clement and the towering figure of Origen. Alexandria was an important intellectual center at this time, and it did not take long for the spreading new religion of Christianity to come into contact with many of its intellectual currents. Both Clement and Origen would have significant influence on the future Christian spiritual tradition. But before passing on their own distinct contributions, they incorporated certain ideas and concepts that were flourishing in the thriving intellectual center that Alexandria was. Two important influences were those of the person of Philo and the philosophy of Neo-Platonism.

Philo (c. 20 BC - c. 50 AD) was a Jewish theologian and Hel-

---

[15] *Ibid.*, pp. 227-228.

lenistic philosopher from a wealthy and influential Alexandrian family. He himself was drawn to a life of study and contemplation, but much of his time was also given to defending the legal rights of his fellow Jews in Alexandria and to working to strengthen them in the practice of their faith. There were two aspects of his spiritual teaching that would have an important influence on later Christian mystical thought: his teaching on *theoria* and his use of the allegorical method in biblical interpretation.

Philo reflects his Jewish background with his strong emphasis on the transcendence of God. His teaching on *theoria* (theory) can be briefly described as an experience of the transcendent God that involves the communication of the divine Spirit. The *pneuma* (spirit) of God somehow takes the place in us of our own spirit, an experience that finds expression in the mind or *nous*. Philo speaks of this experience as ecstasy, and he also uses the term "sober intoxication" to describe it, a term that will appear later in the writings of St. Gregory of Nyssa and others. This experience must be preceded by an ongoing moral purification, particularly through a life of piety and virtue. This is the way that leads to gnosis, the knowledge of God.

Philo's second significant contribution was through his allegorical interpretation of Scripture. This method, also referred to as the mystical or spiritual sense, seeks to draw out the deeper, spiritual meaning that is found in the biblical text. Philo employs this method in his studies on the life of Moses. It is a method that would greatly influence Origen and other later Christian writers in the Greek mystical tradition.

The influence of Alexandrian Judaism upon Christianity through the writings of Philo has often been noted. Louis Bouyer does not hesitate to write that "the fact remains that through Philo in particular, Alexandrian or, more generally 'hellenized' Judaism, played a role perhaps no less important in the development of Christian spirituality than the Judaism of Palestine."[16]

Neo-Platonism, a philosophical system with many religious

---

[16] *Ibid.*, p. 34.

overtones, was developing in Alexandria around the same time Christian philosophical thought was establishing itself in the same city. Its beginnings lie with the Alexandrian philosopher and teacher Ammonius Sacca, but it would find its clearest exposition in the writings of Plotinus. Plotinus was born in Egypt in 205, studied with Ammonius Saccas for a number of years, and then taught in Rome where he died in 270. Our main source for his thought is the *Enneads*, the posthumous compilation of his writings.

According to Plotinus, the first substantial principle or hypostasis is the One or the Good. Created reality proceeds from the One through a series of emanations. *Nous* or Intellect comes forth first through a necessary process of emanation. It is also referred to as the Divine Mind, in which the whole world of Ideas or Forms in the Platonic sense is contained. Soul, in turn, comes forth from Intellect; at its higher level, the Soul belongs to the world of the Intellect, and at its lower level it acts as a principle of life and growth, animating all created things. Each principle not only proceeds from the previous principle but also turns back in contemplation of it in order to be fully constituted according to a law of abiding procession and reversion.[17]

Plotinus stresses that human happiness and salvation will come about through a return to a union with the One, through an ascent back through the emanations to the source of unity. As there is a procession from the One into matter and multiciplicity, so there is a return to the One and to unity. This calls for a conversion and a process of purification. This process requires a separation from matter and the practice of virtue that makes possible the flight to the One and the regaining of that pure Intellectuality by which it resembles God. The ascent is motivated through *eros*, a natural love that brings about the desire for unity with the One; the final outcome of the return is the ecstatic union in love with the One. This union with the One takes place at the level of the *Nous* or Intellect and in this life it can only happen intermittently.

---

[17] See the article on Plotinus by W.H. O'Neill in the *New Catholic Encyclopedia* (New York: McGraw-Hill, 1967), vol. 11, p. 443.

Although the thought of Plotinus is not easy to summarize, one can readily recognize the seeds of the threefold way — the purgative, illuminative and unitive — that will become the classic formulation in the writings of later Christian mystical writers.

A brief word on the so-called Hermetic literature will conclude this treatment of the background currents that were present in Alexandria when the early Christian writers began their work. The Hermetic literature comprises eighteen treatises on such diverse subjects as magic, astrology, alchemy and spirituality, thus reflecting the broad syncretism that was so much a part of the Alexandrian intellectual scene. Among other things, these writings reflect the influence of the Platonic tradition as well as the influence of Philo. Two of the treatises are more religious in content; the first treatise gives the revelations of Poimandres, the "shepherd of men" and the thirteenth those of Hermes Trismegistus to his son, Tot. The opposition between the physical world and the intelligible world is stressed.

6. Clement of Alexandria

The information about Titus Flavius Clement and the beginnings of the catechetical school at Alexandria is scanty. According to tradition, he was born at Athens of pagan parents around 150. After his conversion to Christianity, he traveled extensively, seeking instruction from famous Christian teachers. He finally settled in Alexandria in Egypt and studied with Pantaenus, the first director of the catechetical school in that city. In a well-known passage from the *Stromata* Clement writes appreciatively of Pantaenus' influence as a teacher: "The last that I met, but the first in power, I discovered in Egypt where he was hidden.... He was a true Sicilian bee; he gathered flowers in the field of the prophets and the apostles and brought forth in the souls of his hearers a pure honey of gnosis."[18]

---

[18] *Stromata*, I, 12. cf. Bouyer, p. 263.

Clement remained in Alexandria for about twenty years. He succeeded Pantaenus as head of the catechetical school and was active as a teacher and lecturer in the city. He had to leave Egypt during the persecution of Septimius Severus in 202 or 203 and most likely found refuge in Cappadocia with his former pupil, Bishop Alexander. Very little is known about his last years. It seems he never returned to Alexandria and died in Cappadocia around 215.

Clement was a cultivated Greek philosopher and Christian apologist and a man of vast learning. He did not hesitate to support and explain Christian beliefs with categories from Greek philosophy, particularly Platonism and Stoicism. He was optimistic about the compatibility of faith and secular learning and was one of the first to see philosophy in the role of the servant of theology. His three major writings clearly reflect this orientation: *The Exhortation to the Greeks* (the *Protrepticus*); *The Tutor* (*Pedagogus*); and the *Stromata*.

The *Exhortation to the Greeks* is a work of Christian apologetics and an exhortation to conversion. Clement seeks to lead the pagans to whom it is addressed to an acceptance of the true religion and the teaching of Christ. *The Tutor* (*Pedagogus*) is a sequel to the *Exhortation* and is addressed to those who have accepted the Christian faith. Clement now has Christ, the Logos, come forth as an educator who seeks to instruct the newly baptized in the virtuous life. It is in the path of love that the Logos educates His children.

In his third major work, the *Stromata,* Clement makes use of a free flowing style of writing that enables him to write on a number of different subjects in a non-systematic way. The word *Stromata* means tapestries or carpets. This work, consisting of eight books, emphasizes such subjects as the relationship of Christianity to Greek culture and philosophy, the true Christian gnosis as opposed to the false, and the Christian's search for ways to know God and to achieve union with Him.

Two themes of Clement's religious thought that call for particular attention are those of *gnosis* and *apatheia*. The theme of gnosis, as we have seen, was very much a part of the early Christian tradition. In his writings, particularly the *Stromata*, Clement emphasizes the importance of gnosis and the qualities and virtues that characterize the true gnostic. For Clement, gnosis is the gift of God, the gift of Christ. The gnostic is called to know God, to see God, to possess him.[19]

Clement was the first to introduce into Christian usage the term *apatheia*. This is a word that will be taken up later by the Cappadocians and Evagrius Ponticus and will have an important, although at times controversial, role to play at a later period. Clement is precise in the way he uses the term. For him it is "a domination acquired, by the grace to which our liberty yields itself, over everything in us which is opposed to the radiance of charity."[20] *Apatheia*, then, is the calming of all disordered tendencies by their complete submission to a love that is fully possessed. The link between *apatheia* and love is an essential one.

At the end of Clement's *Pedagogus* there is a beautiful Greek hymn to Christ the Educator. Even if it was added to the manuscript at a later date, it sums up very well the spirit and thought of Clement of Alexandria. It goes in part:

> Rein of indomitable steeds, wing of birds
> Secure, fast tiller of ships, O Shepherd
> Of royal sheep! Wake up your pure children
> To praise and hymn you in all holiness
> With chaste lips, leader of your offspring, Christ!
>
> Christ's footprints are the path to heaven. Eternal
> Word, everlasting Aeon, unending Light,
> Spring of pity, accomplisher of valor
> Through the sober lives of those who sing to God,
>
> Christ Jesus! heavenly milk — your Wisdom's grace —
> From a young bride's sweetest bosom. We tender babes
> Drink with innocent lips as it is pressed forth,
> Filled with the draught of the Spirit from a mystic breast.

---

[19] *Ibid.*, p. 271.
[20] *Ibid.*, p. 273.

Let us all sing together our chaste praise,
Our blameless hymns to Christ the King. Let us sing
Of the mead of his life's teaching. Let us sing
Of the mighty Son. Those born of Christ are a choir
Of peace, a prudent gathering. Let us all
Then sing together of the God of peace.[21]

7. Origen

With Origen (c. 185 - c. 253), the school of Alexandria reached its greatest importance. A remarkably gifted man, he was the most eminent teacher and scholar of the early Church, a man of deep faith and outstanding virtue, and a truly creative and seminal thinker who would have a great influence on the development of Christianity. He can rightly be considered the first biblical exegete, the first systematic theologian, and the first mystical theologian in the Christian tradition.

There was a certain amount of controversy surrounding Origen during his own lifetime and even more so after his death. The charge was often made by his opponents that he was more of a Platonic philosopher than a Christian theologian. Long after his death and after much controversy, he was condemned at the Fifth General Council of Constantinople in 553. In this regard, one must keep in mind the distinction between Origen's own writings and the writings and teachings of many of his disciples who became known historically as Origenists. It should also be kept in mind that Origen was writing as a pioneer and expressing himself on points that were not yet settled by the Church. Finally, it is well known that Origen himself desired only to be a true Christian nourished by the Word of God and living faithfully within the Church. He writes in one of his homilies: "I wish to be a man of the Church, not the founder of heresy; I want to be named with Christ's name and bear the name

---

[21] See Musurillo, *op. cit.*, pp. 189-190.

which is blessed on earth. It is also my desire to do this in deed as well as in Spirit" (Homily on Luke, 16).[22]

A good deal of biographical information is available to us about Origen because of the work of the early historian, Eusebius. Much of the sixth book of Eusebius' *Ecclesiastical History* focuses on Origen's life. He was born in Egypt — most likely Alexandria — around the year 185, the eldest son in a devout Christian family. His father, Leonidas, died as a martyr for the faith during the persecution of Septimius Severus in 202. Eusebius reports that the young Origen was only prevented from going forth to share his father's martyrdom by his mother's hiding of his clothes.

Origen had received an excellent education in Scripture and various secular subjects from his father and so was able to support himself and his family by his teaching. At the age of eighteen, this brilliant youth was appointed director of the catechetical school at Alexandria by Bishop Demetrius. His teaching met with great success, for many were attracted to him by the quality of his teaching and even more so by the witness of his life. Eusebius tells us that Origen lived a very ascetical life while teaching at Alexandria. This same source reports that Origen's youthful ardor led him to castrate himself, taking literally the passage in Matthew's gospel about those who make themselves eunuchs for the kingdom of God (Matthew 19:12).

Origen would remain teaching for many years in Alexandria. After some years, he turned over the teaching of the preparatory subjects to an assistant, and he himself set up an advanced school for Christians, introducing these students to philosophy, theology, and Sacred Scripture. As Origen became more and more known throughout the Church, he also made a number of journeys throughout the empire. He visited Rome, preached in Caesarea in Palestine, and on one occasion was invited by Julia Mamaea, the

---

[22] See the preface by Hans Urs von Balthasar in *Origen, An Exhortation to Martyrdom, Prayer and Selected Works*, translation and introduction by Rowan A. Greer (New York: Paulist Press, 1979), p. xi ff.

mother of the emperor Alexander Severus, to come to Antioch and speak about the Christian faith.

At a later visit to Caesarea, Origen was ordained to the priesthood. This caused problems with his own bishop in Alexandria, Demetrius, who claimed that Origen could not be ordained because he was a eunuch. Demetrius later called two synods in Alexandria, which declared Origen's ordination illicit and banished him from the Church of Alexandria. Origen took refuge in Caesarea in Palestine and continued his teaching, writing, and many other activities for the Church. At the request of the bishop of Caesarea, Origen founded a theological school there and was active in this work for the next twenty years. Among his disciples in Caesarea was Gregory Thaumaturgus (the wonder-worker), who paid great tribute to Origen in a farewell address before leaving for his missionary work in Cappadocia.

The persecution of the emperor Decius in 250 brought his many activities to a halt. He was imprisoned and cruelly tortured to see if he would apostatize, but he continued to profess the faith with great courage. He was released after the death of the emperor, but his health was broken from his suffering, and he died shortly afterwards at Tyre in 253 or 254.

The amount of writing brought forth by Origen during his lifetime was prodigious. Unfortunately, most of what now remains has been preserved in Latin translations rather than the original Greek. His chief works and the main part of his literary output focus on Sacred Scripture. He composed scholia (brief explanations of difficult passages), homilies, and commentaries on various books of Scripture. There are also the apologetical works such as his *Against Celsus*, and doctrinal and speculative writings like his important *First Principles (De Principiis)*. There are also the more practical and pastoral writings such as the *Treatise on Prayer* (a work which contains one of the first methodical explanation of the Lord's Prayer), and the *Exhortation to Martyrdom*.

The Bible always held the principal place in all of Origen's writings. It was constantly the basis for his other writings, for he saw it as the reflection of the invisible world. He can rightly be called the founder of biblical science, since he was the first to attempt to establish a critical text of the Old Testament (the *Hexapla*). He made a clear distinction between the historical or literal sense of Scripture and the spiritual or allegorical sense. The latter was always his preferred method of interpreting the Bible, for he was convinced that the prayerful and reflective reading of Scripture led to the knowledge of deeper spiritual realities. The knowledge of God and his purposes was revealed through the devout reflection and study of Scripture. This was particularly true for his ascetical and mystical writings. It is only in recent years that Origen's great importance in this area of Christian spirituality has been restored and recognized anew.

Origen's Spirituality

Hans Urs von Balthasar emphasizes that the central aspect of Origen's spirituality is "an absolute and passionate love for the Logos, which has taken on personal lineaments for us in Jesus Christ, suffusing the total cosmos of men and angels." He goes on to add:

> The Logos becomes intelligible to us in a threefold incarnation of God's Spirit, Reason, and Word: in His historical, resurrected, and eucharisted body, in His ecclesiological body (whose members we are), and in His body of Sacred Scripture whose letters are animated by His living Spirit. For Origen these three forms of incarnation are inseparable from one another. They constitute a vast and all-encompassing sacrament. Hence he can look upon and converse with the Written Word as sacred, and as much deserving of reverence as converse with the consecrated elements.[23]

According to Origen, the purpose of the Incarnation was to bring about the union of human persons with the Logos. This union

---

[23] *Ibid.*, p. xii.

would be complete in heaven, but it could be glimpsed in this life through mystical experience.

Origen conceives the spiritual life as a journey back to God in which the image and likeness to God is restored. Human persons were created in the image of God, in the image of the Logos, but this likeness was lost through sin. Since the Word became flesh for our salvation, it is possible for us to recover the likeness to the Word by choosing to turn to him. Thus, the spiritual life begins with the awareness and knowledge of our true nature and our kinship with the divine.

Origen develops this theme of the soul's journey back to God in his homilies on the Old Testament books of Exodus and Numbers. Philo had done this earlier in his *Life of Moses*, and Gregory of Nyssa would later do the same in his work of the same title. Origen develops this theme particularly in his Homily 27 on the book of Numbers, where he parallels the journey through the desert of the Israelite people from Egypt to the Promised Land with the various stages of the soul's return to God. Origen describes the successive stages of the spiritual journey and the various stops and resting places, as well as the temptations and challenges against faith and virtue that have to be faced.[24]

The early stages are marked by a stripping away process that begins with the renunciation of sin. The struggle against sin is followed by the struggle against the passions as well as against the demons who lay their snares. It is important to keep in mind that this process of detachment and struggle for Origen must take place in conjunction with the imitation and participation in the life of Christ, particularly the cross. The attainment of *apatheia* and spiritual freedom come with the practice of detachment. This is followed by further insights that result from various gifts of the Spirit, including the important gift of the discernment of spirits. The taste for the things of God increases as the taste for the things of the earth is less-

---

[24] For a good account of the stages of the journey, see Jean Daniélou, *Origen*, translated by Walter Mitchell (New York: Sheed and Ward, 1955), p. 297 ff.

ened. This leads to gnosis, the knowledge of the things of God, and passage to the final stages of contemplation.

Origen's treatment of this higher stage of contemplation is found in his important *Commentary on the Canticle of Canticles* (Song of Songs). Although he was not the first to write a commentary on this Scriptural text (Hippolytus of Rome had done so before him), this work of Origen would have great influence on subsequent mystical writers. Origen was the first to interpret the Song of Songs as the intimate union of the soul with the Logos, but he never separated this interpretation from the union of Christ with the whole Church.

In this work Origen develops his theory of the threefold stages of the spiritual life, a concept that would have far-reaching influence in the later Christian mystical tradition as the purgative, illuminative, and unitive ways. Finding his inspiration in the division the Greeks employed of dividing the abstract sciences into the categories of ethics, physics and theory, Origen speaks about the threefold stages of morals, physics and contemplation. He turns to three books of the Bible to illustrate these stages, Proverbs, Ecclesiastes, and the Song of Songs. The Book of Proverbs teaches morals and virtues and the rules for living a good life. Ecclesiastes teaches physics or the natural contemplation of the world, by which we see things as they really are and come to an awareness of the transient nature of all things. It is only after the soul has been purified morally and attained a true understanding of the things of nature that it can move on to the contemplation of the God-head.

For Origen, the Song of Songs develops this stage of union with the Logos. The subject of the poem is spiritual love, the marriage of the soul to the Logos. It speaks of the soul whose "one desire is to be made one with God's Word: to go to the heavenly Bridegroom's room — to the mysteries, that is, of his wisdom and knowledge — on her wedding-night."[25] Thus, for Origen, this contem-

---

[25] *Commentary on the Canticle*, 91. See Daniélou, p. 306.

plation is a knowledge of God that is made possible by the light received from the Logos. By contemplation one is divinized. In contemplation the mind, the soul's highest part, rediscovers its true nature and is reunited to its source. The Bridegroom's kiss is God's enlightening the mind so that what was obscure and unknown is now clear. Origen develops his teaching on the spiritual senses to clarify this knowledge of the things of God. The spiritual senses are those aspects of God's grace that enable one to taste, touch, and contemplate the divine realities. Origen writes in the *Commentary on the Canticle*: "In comparison with the satisfaction that that flavor gives him, all else will seem unappetizing.... If a man becomes fit to be with Christ, he will taste the Lord and see how pleasant he is."[26]

By way of summary, we can speak of two images used in Origen's spiritual ascent: (1) the growth of the Logos in the soul; and (2) the marriage of the Logos with the soul.[27] The first is developed in connection with Luke 2:52: "Jesus grew in stature and grace." The growth of Christ in the Christian takes place with progress in the virtues and the expansion of gnosis. There is always an outward thrust for Origen, for this purity of soul is manifested in the love of one's neighbor. As indicated earlier, the second image, the marriage of the Logos with the soul fills the pages of the *Commentary on the Canticle*.

We can leave Origen with the reminder that he was indeed a pioneer. He opened up new ground that would be developed, amplified, and corrected as needed by those who would come after him. His influence would be great and much is owed to him by his successors in the history of spirituality and mystical thought. This influence would be particularly evident in the writings of Gregory of Nyssa and Evagrius Ponticus. Through Evagrius Ponticus he would influence monasticism in the East, and through Cassian, monasticism in the West.

---

[26] *Ibid.*, p. 308.
[27] See Bouyer, *op. cit.*, p. 294.

8. The Church in North Africa

Before leaving these early Christian writers, some brief account should be taken of the North African writers, Tertullian and St. Cyprian of Carthage. With the exception of St. Augustine, Tertullian is the most important of the ecclesiastical Latin writers. His writings have had an important and lasting influence on Christian theology. Although a large body of his writings has been preserved, we do not have a great deal of information about his life. He was born around 155 in Carthage, a city that was part of the Roman province in Africa. After his conversion to Christianity around 193, he settled in Carthage and at a later date migrated to Rome. The year of his death is unknown, but it is believed to be after 220.

Tertullian was a man of great energy with a strong, somewhat intemperate personality. He developed a deep passion for truth and a polemical tone is present in most of his writings. With his great concern for the purity of the Church, he gradually become more and more influenced by Montanism. Around 207, he joined the Montanist sect and became the leader of the group known as the Tertullianists. Montanism originated in Phrygia in Asia Minor and later spread to other parts of the Roman empire. Rigorist and ascetical in its outlook, its followers believed that they alone received the Holy Spirit and thus belonged to the true Church.

Among Tertullian's voluminous writings, there is a general treatise on prayer, known as the *De Oratione*. Written around 199 and addressed to catechumens, it contains the earliest surviving explanation of the Lord's Prayer. It is much more practical in its format than Origen's treatise on prayer, and it has a number of suggestions and counsels about prayer and some interior and exterior attitudes that should accompany it.

St. Cyprian of Carthage possessed a much calmer and more serene temperament than Tertullian. He was, however, greatly influenced by the theological writings of Tertullian, and Jerome tells us that he referred to Tertullian as 'the Master.' As bishop of Carthage, he was a man of action and his writings are marked more by a practical and pastoral bent than by an interest in theological speculation. His writings enjoyed great popularity in early Christian times and also during the Middle Ages.

Cyprian was born in Africa, most likely in Carthage, somewhere between 200 and 210. After his conversion to Christianity, he became a priest and then bishop of Carthage around 248-249. He had to take refuge during the fierce persecution of Decius which broke out in the year 250, but he was able to keep in touch with his clergy and people. Eight years later he himself suffered martyrdom at a time of renewed persecution as is recorded in the *Proconsular Acts of Cyprian*. He was the first African bishop to be martyred.

Cyprian's writings reflect many of the concerns he had to face as bishop during difficult times. Among his chief writings are the *De Lapsis (The Lapsed)* and the *De Ecclesiae Unitate (The Unity of the Church)*. The former sets out guidelines for the reconciliation of those who had compromised themselves in varying ways during the Decian persecution. The second work was an important treatise on the Church, stressing the great need for unity and the evil of schism. Cyprian also has a treatise on the Lord's Prayer (*De Oratione Domenica*), thus following in the footsteps of Tertullian. However, there is this important difference. In Tertullian's work, the commentary on the Our Father formed only a part of the writing, whereas in Cyprian the interpretation of the Our Father becomes the central theme.

For Further Reading

Bouyer, Louis, *The Spirituality of the New Testament and the Fathers.* New York: Desclee Company, 1963, pp. 167-302.

The Apostolic Fathers. Translated by F. Glimm, J. Marique, S.J. and G. Walsh, S.J., The Fathers of the Church Series, New York: CIMA Publishing, 1947.

Early Christian Fathers. Edited by Cyril C. Richardson. New York: Macmillan, 1970.

Daniélou, Jean, *Origen*. Trans. by Walter Mitchell. New York: Sheed and Ward, 1955.

Musurillo, Herbert A., *The Fathers of the Primitive Church*. New York: Mentor-Omega Book, 1966.

Origen, *An Exhortation to Martyrdom, Prayer and Selected Works*. Trans. and Introduction by Rowan A. Greer. New York: Paulist Press, 1979.

Quasten, Johannes, *Patrology*, vol. II. Westminster, MD: The Newman Press, 1953.

2 *Eastern Monasticism*

1. Origins and Developments

The late third century and the beginning of the fourth saw the rise of a remarkable movement among Christians in the eastern part of the Roman empire. It seemed to spring up spontaneously and independently in various parts of the East. Egypt would become the most prominent location, although the movement would also take root in Syria, Asia Minor, and Palestine. It was a movement that was characterized by a desire for a solitude that found expression in the withdrawal to the desert regions. It developed into a distinct style of life with strong ascetic elements as a vital part of its makeup.

Many factors played a part in the emergence of Eastern monasticism. There was certainly the strong desire on the part of many to respond generously to Christ's words found in Luke's Gospel, "If anyone wishes to come after me, let him deny himself, take up his cross, and follow me." The gospel ideals of sacrifice, renunciation, and discipleship would always play a prominent part in leading men and women to embrace this way of life. There were also links to earlier Christian times. The Acts of the Apostles describes the "apostolic life," the life of the early Christians united in prayer, charity, and the sharing of goods. There is also a link to the early ascetics, virgins, and others who lived the celibate life. They were always held in a position of honor and esteem in the early Church.

The conditions of the times must also be kept in mind. The rise of monasticism roughly coincided with the end of the persecutions of the Christians and the subsequent peace and accommodation that took place between Church and State. Martyrdom was no longer the ever present possibility that it had always been in earlier days, and many would now find an equivalent or substitution for it in the flight from the world and the ascetic practices of the desert monks. Christianity now was no longer the enemy of the state but an accepted and even respected religion. With this profound change in status, there would inevitably take place some lowering of the earlier ideals and practices that many would find distasteful and unacceptable. Thus, an element of countercultural protest played a part in the rise of the monastic movement. Perhaps many asked themselves the question: "How can I in these present circumstances give the supreme witness the martyrs did in their self-renunciation and their following of Christ and His Cross?"

Other key characteristics of early monasticism should be kept in mind. It was marked, especially in the early stages, by a strong individualistic thrust. This would account in part for some of the exaggerations and excesses in ascetic practices that were found at times, particularly in the deserts of Syria. The early monks did not become part of a structured and organized way of life. People embraced this new form of life primarily as solitaries. These desert ascetics were lay persons seeking to find God in prayer and solitude apart from the normal life of Church and society. At a later date, the movement would be significantly influenced by St. Basil's *Rule for Monks* and become more a part of the mainstream life of the Church, but this was not the case with its beginnings. It can thus be described as a populist, evangelical movement that began on the grass root level. There was nothing of an intellectual movement connected with monasticism in its beginnings. The early monks were devout, unlettered persons who sought God in a very simple and uncluttered way of life. It would be a mistake, however, to conclude that they were seeking only peace and tranquillity and an escape from worldly concerns. The desire and willingness to engage in a spiritual combat was very much a part of the life. This combat would involve the struggle to overcome their own disordered tendencies, and to do battle against the evil demons that sought to turn them away from this life and prevent them from their desired union with God in prayer.

As Eastern monasticism developed, it gradually assumed two main forms, the eremitic and the cenobitic. The eremitic refers to the life of the solitary or the hermit, the monk who lives alone. This type of life is best exemplified by St. Anthony, the father of Eastern monasticism, whose life had such a widespread fame and influence. As time went on, the hermit's complete solitude gave way in some places to a loosely organized grouping of solitaries or hermits that could be considered semi-eremitical. They lived in separate huts but came together for some common activities. There sprang up in some places in the desert small villages of such monks. For example, in the desert of Nitria in Egypt, there was a community that grew to over 5,000 under the leadership of Ammon, one of Anthony's followers.

The cenobitic form of monasticism refers to the fully communal life. The monks would live together in community and pursue their lives of prayer, work, and asceticism in common. St. Pachomius was largely responsible for this development in the early stages. Later, St. Basil's *Rule for Monks* would greatly influence this type of monasticism and provide a firm organizational basis for it.

It was not a question of one form supplanting the other. Both eremitic and cenobitic forms flourished at the same time in various locations. It was not uncommon for one particular area to be dominated by one form. For example, eremitic monasticism developed in the more remote areas of lower Egypt, while Pachomian cenobitic monasticism flourished in the regions of upper Egypt.

2. Early Monastic Writings

Among the early writings were the immensely popular *Life of Anthony*, the early lives of Pachomius, and the well-known *Sayings of the Fathers*. These writings, particularly the *Sayings*, provide us with a good sense of the spirit, content, and main thrust of early monasticism.[1]

St. Athanasius (c. 295-373), bishop of Alexandria and staunch defender of the faith against the Arian heresy, wrote the *Life of Anthony* shortly after the death of the famous monk in 356. This spiritual classic is the oldest of the monastic biographies and a work that had a very widespread circulation and an important role to play in the spread of primitive monasticism. It was soon made available in translation far and wide to those who did not read Greek. Many read this life and were inspired to follow in the footsteps of Anthony, for it provided the reader not only with a model, but also with a road map and guide for the life of the anchorite. For example, St. Augustine in his *Confessions* (8,6) relates how Ponticanus made Anthony known to him; he narrated the story of the two young men who were so moved at reading the *Life of Anthony* that they left their positions and careers at the emperor's court and embraced the monastic life.

We know from Athanasius' *Life* that Anthony was born in Egypt of Christian parents around 251. His parents were prosperous and left him in good circumstances after their deaths. Shortly after this, Anthony entered church one day and heard the Gospel being read with Christ's words to the rich young man: "If you would be perfect, go, sell what you possess and give to the poor, and you will have treasure in heaven" (Mt 19:21). These words struck him to the heart and he began to put them into practice. He first made provisions for his younger sister and then gave away all his possessions. Then, after seeking counsel and direction from an elderly

---

[1] These early writings can be supplemented by such later writings as Palladius' *Historia Lausiaca* and John Cassian's *Institutes* and *Conferences*.

solitary, he began to live in a hut outside the village and to live a life of discipline and asceticism. Anthony would have been between eighteen and twenty at this time.

Anthony lived poorly and gave himself to manual work, for work was to be an essential component of the solitary's life. He provided for his own needs and then gave away what was extra. He prayed constantly, with his prayer nourished by the reading of Scripture. His life was also one marked by such various ascetic practices as night vigils, fasting, and sleeping on the ground. He sought out those experienced in this way of life in order to learn from them and to grow in the virtues and desirable qualities they manifested in their lives. At this stage he had not lost contact with others; that would only come at a later time.

The spiritual combat with the demons was the next major challenge for Anthony. It came only after they saw his firm resolve and constancy in the early stages. The devil revealed himself indirectly at first. Anthony was besieged with doubts about the wisdom of his course of actions and greatly troubled by various temptations. But he remained firm in his resolve, fortified by faith and constant prayer, and finding his strength not in himself but in the grace of Christ. The devil next revealed himself directly with no better results, for Anthony rejected him with the words of the Psalmist, "The Lord is my helper and I shall look down upon my enemies." The *Life* concludes this important initial encounter with the words: "This was Anthony's first contest against the devil — or rather, this was in Anthony the success of the Savior."[2]

Anthony continued his life of penance and prayer, but at this point he sought greater solitude. He first took refuge in some tombs that were situated some distance from the village, with a friend supplying him with bread from time to time. The attacks of the demons intensified with this move to greater solitude; Anthony suffered greatly, but he remained faithful and constant in naked faith and

[2] Life, 6. See *Athanasius, The Life of Anthony and the Letter to Marcellinus,* translation and introduction by Robert C. Gregg (New York: Paulist Press, 1980), p. 35.

trust. When Anthony was later consoled by a heavenly presence, he entreated the vision that appeared, "Where were you? Why didn't you appear in the beginning, so that you could stop my distresses?" And the answer came to him: "I was here, Anthony, but I waited to watch your struggle."[3]

A little later, Anthony sought greater solitude much further in the desert, ultimately taking refuge in a deserted fortress. He remained there for almost twenty years, leaving only when some friends came and forcefully removed the fortress door. Anthony came forth willingly, for he was now a changed man, fully possessed by the Spirit of God and ready to share with others the fruits of his solitude and the victories he had won through the power of God. As his biographer writes: "Through him the Lord healed many of those present who suffered from bodily ailments; others he purged of demons, and to Anthony he gave grace in speech. Thus he consoled many who mourned, and to others hostile to each other he reconciled in friendship, urging everyone to prefer nothing in the world above the love of Christ."[4]

The rest of the *Life* relates Anthony's deeds, teachings, and accomplishments after this return to the world. He continually encouraged the many disciples who revered him and sought to learn from him. The biography contains a long discourse of Anthony that seems to summarize a great deal of his teaching and counsel. He made some trips to Alexandria to assist those in need, but for the most part his last years were spent in the desert, helping those who sought him out and continuing the prayer and the way of life he had lived so long and so faithfully. Death came to this holy man of God, rightly known as the father of monasticism, at an advanced age in 356 at his beloved "inner mountain" near the Red Sea.

Some final points should be noted. First, there is the element of ongoing growth in the spiritual life that marks Anthony's quest for holiness. Traditional monastic holiness will always favor the

---

[3] *Life*, 10, *Ibid.*, p. 39.
[4] *Ibid.*, p. 42.

image of the ladder in speaking about the spiritual ascent. It calls for human discipline and effort and struggle. But ultimately it is the grace of Christ, the power of God working in Anthony that is essential. In the *Life of Anthony*, St. Athanasius reflects a favorite theme of his and of all the Greek Fathers, that of our divinization in Christ. Through the power and grace of Christ, the human person is divinized by sharing in the life of the Triune God. By assuming our humanity, Christ made it possible for us to share in his divinity.

Secondly, it is evident that demonology plays a central role in the *Life of Anthony* and in all of the literature of early Eastern monasticism. Some of the accounts may sound strange to the contemporary ear, but one must recognize the important role the struggle with demons has in primitive monasticism.[5] In the course of his long spiritual quest, Anthony became very adept in the discernment of spirits and he shared this knowledge in the insightful counsels given in his long discourse that is found in the *Life*.

Finally, the outward thrust of Anthony's life must be kept in mind. The ongoing desire for solitude and the constant practice of discipline were not ends in themselves. Their purpose was to give rise to the interior freedom that made it possible for Anthony to surrender completely to the Spirit of God. He then would be in a position to share the fruits of his victories by guiding and leading others to God. He was ready and willing to assist the steady stream of visitors that sought him in the desert for direction, healing, and encouragement. He had reached the point where he was indeed the Father of all.

While it is Anthony who is so closely connected with the eremitic form of monasticism, it is St. Pachomius (c. 290-346) who plays the major role in the development of cenobiticism, that is the monastic life lived in a communal setting. With Pachomius, we have the beginnings of the institutionalizing of monasticism.

---

[5] For a helpful treatment of this, see Louis Bouyer, *The Spirituality of the New Testament and the Fathers* (New York: Desclee, 1963), pp. 312 -313.

A number of biographies of Pachomius by his contemporaries have survived, and they provide us with a good deal of information about his life and accomplishments. He was born and raised in Egypt from a pagan background, and he entered the military as a young man. He was greatly impressed by the charity of some Christians he met at Thebes when he was a young military recruit. After his release from the army, he was baptized and then embraced the solitary life under the direction of a neighboring hermit, Palemon. He lived this life for six or seven years and then felt called to establish a community of monks. A man of vision and purpose, he recognized the inherent risks involved in the solitary life as well as the need of establishing spiritual and material supports for the life of the monk.

His first attempt at establishing a community met with little success, for his early disciples were apparently reluctant to accept any authority imposed upon them. Learning from this experience, he drew up a rule or way of life before establishing his second foundation at Tabennisi in the area of Egypt known as the Thebaid. This undertaking met with great success and the numbers increased rapidly. Their way of life was based on a rule, to which all the monks submitted, that regulated a common life of prayer and work. The monks were divided into separate houses (usually grouped according to the same trade or work), and each house had its own superior who in turn was under the authority of Pachomius.

After this monastic community was firmly established, Pachomius set up and organized a monastery for women, at the request of his sister, Mary. Before his death, he founded a total of nine monasteries in the Thebaid region of Egypt, seven for men and two for women. All of them followed the rule he had drawn up and formed a large and closely knit congregation. Pachomius' *Rule for Monks* came to a final form over a number of years. St. Jerome provided a Latin translation of the *Rule*, the only version that is still extant in its complete form. This *Rule* of Pachomius would have great influence on later monastic rules both in the East and the West.

Although this cenobitic form of monasticism met with great

success, it did not supplant the eremitical or semi-eremitical form in the East. Both continued to flourish as separate ways of life. The Pachomian rule provided for a much more structured and organized way of life, with obedience to the recognized superior of the community and to the rule playing a central role. Obedience did play a part in the life of the anchorite but on a much lesser scale. Obedience in this way of life was to the elder or spiritual master, whom the monk had freely selected and consulted for individual guidance.

Sayings of the Fathers

The *Apophthegms* or *Sayings of the Fathers* have always been a popular form of early monastic writings, and they provide us with a good flavor of the desert spirituality.[6] Most of the *Sayings* have their origin in the eremitical or semi-eremitical forms of monasticism. They are brief sayings that were originally given to an individual monastic by the spiritual father or abba in response to a particular request or need. The request was usually made in such words as: "Father, give me a word that I may live." The monk would then return to his cell to pray over the word or saying that had been given and to take it to heart. As Thomas Merton puts it so well: "Always simple and concrete, always appealing to the experience of the men who had been shaped by solitude, these proverbs and tales were intended as plain answers to plain questions."[7]

Later, the various sayings were written down and preserved in collections. Often, groups of monks would preserve the many sayings of their spiritual master or some other revered holy person. They were never intended to be a systematic presentation of the spirituality of the desert, but with them we are closest to the wisdom of the desert. They were of great help to the hermits who were

---

[6] For some available collections, see Benedicta Ward, *The Desert Christian, The Sayings of the Desert Fathers* (New York: Macmillan, 1975); and Thomas Merton, *The Wisdom of the Desert* (New York: New Directions, 1960). Both of these works have helpful introductions.

[7] Cf. Merton, *op. cit.*, p. 12.

striving for purity of heart and engaged in the ongoing quest for growth in love and prayer. Even today, one is struck by the plain, direct, commonsense approach of these sayings and their capacity to move the heart.[8]

It would be a mistake to conclude that monasticism was all that was going on in the area of Christian spirituality at this time. The momentous changes that took place in Church-State relations after the peace of Constantine brought about important developments in the more populated areas of the Eastern empire. Large churches were now built, where Christians could carry out liturgical worship with a freedom and a ceremonial splendor that was impossible during the time of persecutions. Devotion to the Blessed Virgin Mary and to the saints rapidly developed. There was also the growing desire to undertake pilgrimages.

Two women exemplify this developing interest in the religious practice of pilgrimages, St. Helena and the nun known as Egeria.[9] St. Helena, the mother of the first Christian emperor Constantine, became a Christian in 312. Shortly after her son moved the capital from Rome to Constantinople, she undertook an extended pilgrimage to the Holy Land. There she was able to oversee the important restoration and building program that Constantine had undertaken in the Holy Land. After her death, Helena's name was intimately connected with the legend of the finding of the true cross.

In 1884, an Italian scholar announced the discovery of a manuscript that described a three year pilgrimage of a devout woman to Jerusalem and various other places in the Near East. This valuable work, composed in Latin, has been usually referred to as *Egeria's Travels*.[10] Little is known of Egeria (or Etheria) herself, but it seems

---

[8] For an effective application to contemporary spirituality, see Henri Nouwen, *The Way of the Heart, Desert Spirituality and Contemporary Ministry* (New York: The Seabury Press, 1981).

[9] See the chapter on pilgrims in Lawrence Cunningham, *The Catholic Heritage* (New York: Crossroad, 1983), pp. 47-63.

[10] For a good summary of the scholarly investigations about Egeria, see the introduction to *Egeria: Diary of a Pilgrimage*, translated and annotated by George E. Gingras (New York: The Newman Press, 1970).

she was a member of a religious community of women from either Gaul or Spain. She wrote accounts of her journeys that took place in the late fourth or early fifth century and sent them back as letters to the members of her community. Egeria's work comprises two major sections. The first part is devoted to her pilgrimages to various monastic centers in Egypt, Syria, and Asia Minor, and her return to Constantinople. The second part focuses on her extended stay in Jerusalem and provides a great deal of important information about the liturgical worship and religious practices that took place there. She describes in great detail the daily order of the divine liturgy, the Sunday liturgy, the liturgy of Holy Week and the other great liturgical feasts, the instruction of catechumens in preparation for receiving baptism, and concludes with an account of the feast of the Dedication of the Basilica of the Holy Sepulcher.

3. The Cappadocian Fathers

During the fourth century, St. Basil the Great, St. Gregory Nazianzen, and St. Gregory of Nyssa were towering figures. They are commonly referred to as the Cappadocian Fathers, since they all came from the part of Asia Minor known as Cappadocia. Basil and Gregory Nazianzen were lifelong friends, and Gregory of Nyssa was Basil's younger brother. The older sister of Basil and Gregory was St. Macrina, to whom her brother Gregory paid great tribute in one of his works, the *Life of St. Macrina.*

All of the Cappadocians were men of great faith and learning who put their many gifts at the service of the Christian faith. Basil was the man of action, the organizer and legislator; Gregory Nazianzen was more the eloquent orator and poet; and Gregory of Nyssa was the religious philosopher and spiritual master. The contributions of the Cappadocians to the development of doctrinal theology should be kept in mind, particularly their defense of the teaching of the Council of Nicea against Arianism and their writings on the Holy Spirit. As a group they also made a distinct contribution

to the development of monasticism. Bouyer writes that they ushered in "a new transformation of monasticism, by which from an
essentially popular and evangelical movement, it was to become a
school of learned spirituality, wholly permeated with the heritage
of Alexandria and, above all, of Origen."[11] They would take the
thought of Origen and rethink, rectify and broaden it.

St. Basil the Great (c. 330 - c.379) came from a distinguished
Christian family in Cappadocia. He received an excellent education,
studying rhetoric and law at Caesarea, Constantinople, and Athens. He first met St. Gregory Nazianzen when they were students
together at Athens. After finishing his studies and teaching rhetoric for a period, Basil was drawn to the monastic life. He visited
many of the monastic centers in Egypt and Syria and then returned
to Caesarea; he gave his goods to the poor and settled in the valley
of Iris in his native land. Gregory Nazianzen joined him there for a
period, and they gave themselves to prayer and the study of Scripture. They also composed together a *Philocalia*, an anthology of
Origen's spiritual writings. Ever the man of action and initiative,
Basil also founded a number of monasteries during this period.
Around 364, he was ordained to the priesthood by Eusebius, the
bishop of Caesarea who recognized his many gifts. In 370, Basil
succeeded Eusebius as bishop of Caesarea.

Basil was a man of great energy and pastoral zeal, and his work
and accomplishments as bishop were far reaching. He played a
major role in the struggle against the spread of Arianism, organized
the monastic life in his diocese, and established hospitals for the sick,
homes for the poor, and hospices for travelers. Even with these
many activities and concerns, he found time to compose a considerable body of theological and spiritual writings.

Basil's *Rule for Monks* is considered the most important of his
ascetic and spiritual writings, but there are other significant writings in this area. His many letters are excellent sources for his life

---

[11] See Bouyer, *op. cit.*, p. 330. Bouyer entitles his chapter: "Erudite Monasticism: The
Cappadocians."

and teachings, as well as for the history and practices of the Eastern Church in the fourth century. There are also his homilies, sermons, and various other ascetic treatises. Finally, there is the very influential *Liturgy of St. Basil*, by which he contributed so much to the reform and revision of the liturgy of Caesarea. One writer insightfully notes: "Perhaps the simplest and most direct way to characterize the spiritual teaching of Basil, and a way that recalls that he was the author (or reviser) of the Liturgy that bears his name, is to say that it is essentially *eucharistic*: that is, humanity's relationship to God is to be one of thanksgiving."[12]

Basil's *Rule for Monks* made a very significant contribution to the development of monasticism. This *Rule*, which we have in a longer and a shorter version, was an important work of monastic legislation that would greatly influence and modify the main thrust of monasticism in the East.[13] It is a monastic rule that clearly favors the cenobitic way of life over that of the solitary. For Basil, it is only in a life shared with others that the Christian commandment of love can be lived out in practice. It is in companionship with others that the monk can fulfill the Lord's commandment to love and serve the other, as well as benefit from the mutual sharing of spiritual gifts. Basil sees the mutual support and correction that is provided only in community as essential to the life of the monk.

There were other distinct contributions made by Basil in his *Rule*. He would want the size of the monastery to be smaller than the very large numbers that comprised the Pachomian monasteries. This smaller size would help to preserve a spirit of silence and recollection and also assist in bringing about a more personal relationship between the monk and his superior. The Basilian monastery would be austere, with a strong spirit of asceticism, but it would not have the severe practices often found among the solitaries in the

---

[12] See Andrew Louth, "The Cappacocians" in *The Study of Spirituality*, edited by Jones, Wainwright and Yarnold (New York: Oxford University Press, 1986), p. 163.

[13] For an English translation of Basil's *Rule* (the long rule), see St. Basil, *Ascetical Works*, translated by Sr. M. Monica Wagner, C.S.C. (Washington, DC: Catholic University Press, 1962), pp. 223-337.

desert. Obedience to the superior would play a central role, and the monk's day would be carefully regulated by a life of prayer in common and by work. Everything was to lead to a life of charity carried out in obedience. Finally, it should be stressed that Basil's *Rule for Monks* did much to integrate monasticism into the mainstream life of the Church. The Basilian monasteries would include schools and orphanages and would be places of hospitality for the sick and the needy. There would be times of silence and solitude for the monk, but there would also be times for outward reach and involvement.

St. Gregory Nazianzen (c. 330-389), like his lifelong friend Basil, was from a distinguished family in Cappadocia, who also received an excellent education as a young man. However, he greatly differed from Basil in temperament and personality. Of a sensitive nature, he was drawn much more to solitude and contemplation than to the active life of a bishop and churchman. He was, however, often called to assume important ecclesiastical positions, with the result that his entire life was marked by a succession of flights and returns to the world.

After his studies, he spent some time in monastic retirement with Basil. Later, at the urging of his father, who was bishop of Nazianzus, he was ordained a priest around 362. He immediately regretted this move and withdrew, but after a period of retirement and reflection, he returned to his priestly duties in the diocese. He was consecrated bishop of Sasima by Basil in 371, and he later succeeded his father as bishop of Nazianzus in 374. After only a year, he again sought to lead a life of retirement and contemplation. This, too, was interrupted when he was called in 379 to reorganize the church at Constantinople that had suffered so much from Arian emperors and archbishops. His fame spread at this time, due primarily to his eloquent sermons. It was at Constantinople that he preached the famous *Five Orations on the Divinity of the Logos* that did so much to earn him the title "the Theologian." The Second Ecumenical Council that met at Constantinople in 381 recognized him as bishop of the capital city. After some controversy over his appointment, he resigned and returned to Nazianzus and served there as bishop for the next two years. In 384 he was finally able to retire and devote his last years to prayer, study and writing. Gregory's literary output is in the forms of sermons, poems and letters. All of his writings are marked with an elegance of form and style that earned him a great popularity during his own lifetime and in later generations. It is in his poems, particularly, that much of his spirituality is expressed. A number of his poems are of an autobiographical nature, in which he expresses his own personal experiences, thoughts, and feelings with such power and eloquence that they have been compared to the *Confessions* of St. Augustine.[14]

In his spirituality, Gregory placed great stress on our identification with Christ. One must be willing to separate oneself from everything that would hinder this union with Christ. He writes: "Indeed, I desire to die with Christ so as to rise with Him, bearing everything that He bore: the Word, the body, the nails, the resurrection"; and "For me, Christ is the reward of everything. And I carry the poverty of His cross in richness."[15] Following St. Athanasius, Gregory emphasized our divinization in Christ, a theme that was dear to the Greek Fathers. Christ took on our humanity that we might share in his divinity. The response of the Christian to this should be the generous giving of oneself to Christ. This is the goal of all ascetic practices; this is the goal of the monastic life. Gregory writes with great feeling: "I must be buried with Christ, rise with Him, inherit heaven with Him, become son of God, become God.... This is what is the great mystery for us, this is what God incarnate is for us, become poor for us."[16]

St. Gregory of Nyssa

Gregory of Nyssa (c. 335 - c. 394) did not have the great administrative gifts of his older brother Basil, nor the oratorical or

---

[14] See Quasten, *Patrology*, vol. III (Westminster, MD: The Newman Press, 1953), p. 245.

[15] See Bouyer, *op. cit.*, pp. 344-345.

[16] *Ibid.*, p. 348.

poetical gifts of Gregory Nazianzen, but he surpassed both of them as a speculative theologian and mystical writer. Recent scholarly studies have recognized the far-reaching contributions he has made in his many writings. Bouyer notes that "it is beginning to be recognized that Gregory of Nyssa was one of the most powerful and most original thinkers ever known in the history of the Church."[17] His writings in the area of Christian mysticism have been so significant that he is sometimes known as the "Father of Christian mysticism."

Gregory of Nyssa was educated by his older brother, Basil the Great, and later married and pursued a career as a rhetorician. Although it is not certain, he may have lived for a period after the death of his wife at the monastery his brother Basil founded in Pontus. He became bishop of Nyssa in 371 and was a staunch defender of Nicene orthodoxy during the troubled times of the Arian controversies. After the death of Basil in 379, he continued his brother's work as a churchman and writer, and he played a very significant role in church affairs in the East. He had a prominent part in the Second Ecumenical Council which met at Constantinople in 381.

Among Gregory's voluminous writings are doctrinal treatises, biblical commentaries, monastic and ascetic works, and orations and sermons. One of his earliest ascetic treatises is his *On Virginity*. Other treatises that develop his spiritual teaching include *On What it Means to Call Oneself a Christian*, *On Perfection*, and *On the Christian Mode of Life (De Instituto Christiano)*. There is also *The Life of Saint Macrina*, a little biography of his beloved and saintly sister who contributed much to the development of women's religious communities. One of the most significant contributions in his spiritual writings was to give a mystical orientation to the monastic life. This thrust would be developed in such writings as his *Life of Moses*, and his *Commentary on the Canticle of Canticles*.

Gregory's teaching on the image of God in the human person is very important for his spiritual doctrine. The image of God is

---

[17] *Ibid.*, p. 351. Werner Jaeger and Jean Daniélou have contributed much to the study of Gregory of Nyssa.

reflected in the human soul, not only in the rational part (the *nous*), as Clement and Origen stressed, or the free will, as Irenaeus emphasized, but also in a life of goodness and virtue.[18] Created in the image of God, the human person was separated from God through the exercise of free will. For Gregory, the spiritual life constitutes an ongoing ascent to God in which the image of God in the human person is progressively restored.

Gregory follows Origen's lead and speaks of three stages in this ascent to God. However, there is this important difference between the two. Origen emphasizes a movement of increasing light; the soul moves from darkness to light and then on to greater light. For Gregory, however, the journey begins in light and moves towards lesser light and then into darkness. With Gregory, this apophatic way, the way of darkness, will take on great importance and significance for the first time.

The first stage is a way of light, and it is characterized by the purification of the soul and the restoration of the image of God.[19] This stage involves a struggle against the perverted passions and leads to *apatheia*, greater unification, and purification. The second stage is characterized by a greater knowledge of God that involves a closer awareness of hidden things. "And this awareness is a kind of cloud, which overshadows all appearances, and slowly guides and accustoms the soul to look towards what is hidden."[20] In this awareness, there is a knowledge of God that comes about by an experience of his presence. For Gregory, the basis of this awareness is the indwelling of the Trinity within the soul.

This experience can satisfy at first, but as it makes progress, the soul realizes that God infinitely transcends all that it can ever know of Him. The divine essence remains inaccessible, even to the

---

[18] See Quasten, *op. cit.*, vol. III, p. 292.

[19] For a good description of these stages, see the introduction by Jean Daniélou, *From Glory to Glory, Texts from Gregory of Nyssa's Mystical Writings*, selected and with an introduction by Jean Daniélou, translated and edited by Herbert Musurillo, S.J. (New York: Charles Scribner's Sons, 1961), p. 23 ff.

[20] *Ibid.*, p. 247.

mind that has been enlightened by grace. And so it must pass on to the third stage, that of the darkness. Gregory writes: "The true vision and the true knowledge of what we seek consists precisely in not seeing, in an awareness that our goal transcends all knowledge and is everywhere cut off from us by the darkness of incomprehensibility."[21] The soul can grasp the transcendent Godhead only in the obscurity of faith. This knowledge of God in the darkness (*theognosia*) is a true experience of the presence of God. The intensity of the divine presence in the darkness causes the soul to go out of itself. Gregory usually uses the term *ecstasy* to describe this experience of God's presence. But he also uses such paradoxical expressions as "sober inebriation," "luminous darkness" and "watchful sleep" to bring out the idea that one sees God by not seeing and knows God by not knowing. Bouyer writes: "*Theognosia* tends to become a particular psychological experience, of an ecstatic nature, in which the presence of God is apprehended, in a manner at once luminous and obscure, by the new spiritual senses which are developed or, perhaps, revived in the soul."[22]

Gregory was fond of seeing in the life of Moses a symbol of the spiritual journey of the Christian to God. In his *Life of Moses*, he speaks of the revelation at the burning bush, and Moses' ascents of Mt. Sinai, first into the cloud, and then into the darkness. Gregory also writes in his *Commentary on the Canticle:* "Moses' vision of God began with light; afterwards God spoke to him in a cloud. But when Moses rose higher and became more perfect, he saw God in the darkness."[23]

Another important contribution of Gregory of Nyssa is his teaching that the soul's movement towards God and the quest for sanctity involve one in a process of perpetual progress. A person never arrives but continues to make further progress. He uses the Greek word *epectasis* to describe this movement of perpetual ascent and infinite growth. He writes:

---

[21] *Ibid.*, p. 118.
[22] Bouyer, *op. cit.*, p. 362.
[23] *From Glory to Glory*, p. 247.

...let us change in such a way that we may constantly evolve towards what is better, being *transformed from glory to glory*, and thus always improving and ever becoming more perfect by daily growth, and never arriving at any limit of perfection. For that perfection consists in our never stopping in our growth in good, never circumscribing our perfection by any limitation.[24]

For Gregory, every ending is a beginning, and every arrival is a new departure. Jean Daniélou emphasizes: "This notion of a perpetual beginning, that is not merely a repetition but something always new and fresh, is one of Gregory's most germinal ideas."[25]

Gregory's spiritual doctrine owed much to those who preceded him in the development of the Greek mystical tradition, particularly Origen. What he inherited, however, was stamped with his own originality and creativity. His teaching, in turn, would have widespread influence upon the later mystical tradition. Through the author who has come to be known as Pseudo-Macarius, it would take a more popular form. Through Evagrius Ponticus, a form of Origenism would spread to many monastic centers in Egypt; and through the influential Pseudo-Dionysius, it would be the seed of a newer development.

4. Evagrius Ponticus, Pseudo-Macarius, and Pseudo-Dionysius

It is only in recent years that the name of Evagrius Ponticus (345-399) has come to the fore as an important person in the history of Christian spirituality. His name was embroiled in controversy after his death because of some of his Origenist views. The Fifth Ecumenical Council that met at Constantinople in 553 condemned him, mainly for the Origenist views found in his specula-

---

[24] *Ibid.*, p. 84.
[25] *Ibid.*, p. 69.

tive work *Kephalaia Gnostica*. His influence waned considerably after this, although his orthodox spiritual writings lived on in the thought and writings of various other spiritual masters. Recent studies have restored a number of his writings and have recognized the influence he has had in the development of Christian spirituality. Bouyer writes: "No one today still doubts that Evagrius is one of the most important names in the history of spirituality, one of those that not only marked a decisive turning point but called forth a real spiritual mutation."[26]

Evagrius was born in Ibora in Pontus near the Black Sea in 345.[27] He was ordained a lector by Basil the Great and later a deacon by Gregory Nazianzen. He accompanied Gregory to Constantinople and assisted him at the Ecumenical Council that met there in 381. When the council ended, he remained at Constantinople and ably assisted the new bishop, Nectarius, as his archdeacon. A crisis arose when Evagrius fell in love with the wife of a prominent member of the highest society at Constantinople. Threatened by the situation, he fled the capital and took refuge at the monastery founded by the Roman matron, Melania the Elder, at Jerusalem. Melania was a holy and learned woman who was well acquainted with the thought of Origen. After a period of study, healing and discernment in Jerusalem, Evagrius settled in Nitria in the Egyptian desert and embraced the monastic life.

Evagrius gave himself wholeheartedly to this way of life. He became a disciple of the revered Macarius the Egyptian, and also came to know the other Macarius known as Macarius the Alexandrian. After spending two years with the monks at Nitria, he took up a life of greater solitude and austerity with the monks at Cellia, about twelve miles south of Nitria. He became the most in-

---

[26] Bouyer, *op. cit.*, p. 381.

[27] For very helpful information on the life and teaching of Evagrius, see the introduction by John Eudes Bamberger in Evagrius Ponticus, *The Praktikos and Chapters on Prayer*, translated with an introduction and notes by John Eudes Bamberger, O.C.S.O. (Kalamazoo, MI: Cistercian Publications, 1981).

fluential teacher of the Origenist school through his extensive writings, and he became well known for his gifts as a spiritual guide. His fame for holiness and learning had spread far and wide at the time of his death in 395.

Evagrius was the great synthesizer of the spirituality of the desert. His extensive writings took the form of short aphorisms or sentences that enabled the desert ascetics to digest his teaching easily and even commit it to memory. The *Praktikos* and *The Chapters on Prayer* are very important for his spiritual teaching. The *Kephalaia Gnostica* is his major speculative work and contains his teaching on cosmology and anthropology. The ideas for which he was condemned are found principally in this speculative work.

The spiritual life for Evagrius is divided into two main groupings. The first involves the person in the ascetic struggle against temptation and vice and the quest for the life of virtue; this is the stage of *praktikos* (practice). The second is the life of prayer and growth in contemplation; this is the stage of *gnosis* or *theoria*.

Evagrius carefully outlines and systematizes the stage of *praktikos*. He distinguishes eight basic vices: gluttony, impurity, avarice, sadness, anger, acedia, vainglory and pride. Acedia is the disgust of spiritual things that is brought on by weariness and boredom with the ongoing struggle. Evagrius' penetrating description of this demon is well known. He writes:

> The demon of acedia — also called the noonday demon — is the one that causes the most serious trouble of all. He presses his attack upon the monk about the fourth hour and besieges the soul until the eighth hour. First of all he makes it seem that the sun barely moves, if at all, and that the day is fifty hours long. Then he constrains the monk to look constantly out the windows, to walk outside the cell, to gaze carefully at the sun to determine how far it stands from the ninth hour, to look now this way now that to see if perhaps one of the brethren appears from his cell. Then too he instills in the heart of the monk a hatred for the place, a hatred for his very life itself, a hatred for manual labor. He

leads him to reflect that charity has departed from among the brethren, that there is no one to give encouragement....[28]

Evagrius also carefully shows the development that takes place in the growth in virtue, tracing out its progression from the beginning in faith, through patience and hope and *apatheia* to love (*agape*). Apatheia assumes a very important role in this development. For Evagrius, apatheia "is simply the domination of the passions in us that are opposed to charity. It withdraws us from the domination of demons to give us back to that of God."[29] Signs of its presence are the capacity to pray without distractions and a deep peace of soul that permeates all levels of consciousness. Apatheia prepares the way for charity and flowers only in charity. The second stage of gnosis can only begin when charity flourishes.

Evagrius' language in speaking about this second stage of gnosis or contemplation tends to be very intellectual and abstract, reflecting the influence of Origen upon his thought; however, he is less biblical and more philosophical in his treatment than either Origen or Gregory of Nyssa. He distinguishes two stages of this gnosis. The first he refers to as a knowledge of divine reason (*physike theoria*); it is a knowledge conformed to the divine reason, the Logos who created all things. In the second stage of this gnosis, the apophatic or way of darkness is stressed, for one goes beyond all thoughts and ideas to contemplate God. For Evagrius, this is the supreme gnosis, and he refers to it as the knowledge of the Trinity. Evagrius also calls this "pure prayer."[30]

Evagrius remained a controversial figure after his death, and his direct influence waned with his condemnation in 553. Indirectly, however, his spiritual teaching would continue to have great influence as it passed through such orthodox spiritual writers as Basil the Great, Palladius, John Climacus, and Maximus the Confessor.

---

[28] *Praktikos*, no. 12. See Bamberger, *op. cit.*, pp. 18-19.

[29] Bouyer, *op. cit.*, p. 386.

[30] *Ibid.*, p. 384; for a fuller treatment, see p. 387 ff.

It would be through John Cassian that Evagrius would exercise a great influence on Western monasticism and spirituality. As mentioned earlier, a number of Evagrius' writings have been recovered in recent years.

The Macarian Homilies

The authorship of the *Spiritual Homilies* has occasioned a great deal of scholarly research and speculation. Until the nineteenth century, the work was attributed to the revered Egyptian monk, Macarius the Egyptian, also surnamed the Elder or the Great. This belief has been abandoned and, in general, the author is now believed to have been a monk living in northeast Syria (Mesopotamia) between the middle of the fourth and the middle of the fifth centuries. He is often referred to as the Pseudo-Macarius. In his writings, he shows that he knows the monasticism and spirituality of the Cappadocian Fathers, especially Basil and Gregory of Nyssa.

Some scholars have found a connection between these homilies and the heresy known as Messalianism. Messalianism comes from the Syriac word *messalleyane*, which means "those who pray." It was a monastic movement in Syria in the late fourth century that put a great emphasis on constant prayer, while neglecting other ascetic practices, the sacraments, the institutional Church, and manual labor. It was condemned at the Third Ecumenical Council at Ephesus in 431. Some speculate that at a later time, the *Spiritual Homilies* were expunged of any Messalian errors and then, under the name of the respected Macarius the Egyptian, they were regarded as unobjectionable and gained great acclaim. Other scholars, however, deny any significant connection between Messalianism and the *Spiritual Homilies*, and so the question remains inconclusive at the present time.[31]

---

[31] For further information on this complex question, see Quasten, vol. III, pp. 162-165; Bouyer, 370-371; and the introduction by George Maloney, S.J. to *Pseudo-Macarius, The Fifty Spiritual Homilies and the Great Letter* (New York: Paulist Press, 1992).

The *Spiritual Homilies* are exhortations or conferences that were given to monks in order to help them grow in their spiritual lives. There is a clearly intended practical thrust and orientation to the subjects treated. The spirituality of these conferences is basically a spirituality of the heart. There is a strong emphasis on the role of experience in prayer, on an ever-increasing experience of the indwelling Trinity through the power of the Holy Spirit.

The teaching found in these conferences also reflects a profound awareness of the effects of sin. The Christian life is seen as an ongoing spiritual combat between the power of grace and the power of sin, between the presence of the Spirit and the presence of evil. Sin and grace coexist in us, and it is with grace that we must side. Sin is foreign to our nature and must be expelled. But only God can rid us of sin, and so we must pray and pray unceasingly. Constant prayer is essential for all believers. The struggle is never ended, for grace and sin continue to be present together. It is in this context that the loving grace of God's Spirit continues to heal, save and divinize us. Although the emphasis is definitely on the action of the Holy Spirit and interior growth, an outward thrust is not lacking. We find in Homily 15, no. 8: "For this is purity of heart, that, when you see the sinners and the weak, you have compassion and show mercy toward them."[32]

The image and theme of light is also stressed in the Macarian *Homilies* to such an extent that we can speak of a mysticism of light. The author speaks of God's indwelling presence in the purified Christian as a transforming light. With this transforming light of the risen Lord through His Spirit, the Christian shares in the light that transformed Christ on Mt. Tabor. Macarius writes in the first homily:

> For the soul that is deemed to be judged worthy to participate in the light of the Holy Spirit by becoming his throne and habitation, and is covered with the beauty of ineffable

---

[32] Homily 15, 8. See Maloney, *op. cit.*, p. 111.

glory of the Spirit, becomes all light, all face, all eye. There is no part of the soul that is not full of the spiritual eyes of light. That is to say, there is no part of the soul that is covered with the darkness but is totally covered with spiritual eyes of light.[33]

Various letters are also considered part of the Macarian writings, of which the most important is known as *The Great Letter*. Its connection with Gregory of Nyssa's *De Instituto Christiano* has been a great source of scholarly research and speculation.[34] In this letter, Macarius writes about the monastic life and its ideal, and also many aspects of the life itself that were discussed in the *Homilies*.

The Macarian writings enjoyed much popularity in subsequent times. They influenced such important spiritual writers in the East as Diadochus of Photice, Mark the Hermit, Symeon the New Theologian, Gregory Palamas and the other Hesychastic writers of Mt. Athos. The *Homilies* were translated into Slavonic and became well known in the Slavic Churches. In the West, many of the Protestant reformers were drawn to them, particularly Johann Arndt, John Wesley, and the seventeenth-century Pietists. John Wesley wrote in his diary, "I read Macarius and sang." Quasten writes of this influence: "These *Homilies* entitle their author to a preeminent position in the history of early Christian mysticism and have proved a source of inspiration to modern mystics."[35]

Pseudo-Dionysius

Dionysius (Denis) the Areopagite is the name assumed by the unknown author of four Greek treatises on liturgical and mystical

---

[33] Homily 1, 2. cf. *Ibid.*, p. 37.

[34] Werner Jaeger argues that the original work is Gregory of Nyssa's *De Instituto Christiano* and that *The Great Letter* of Macarius is a popularization and a paraphrasing of this work. Cf. *Two Rediscovered Works of Ancient Christian Literature: Gregory of Nyssa and Macarius* (Leiden, 1954). Others have disagreed with his conclusions. See Maloney, p. 28; and pp. 249-250.

[35] Quasten, *op. cit.*, vol. III, p. 162.

theology that have had a tremendous influence on the development of Christian mysticism. The works were attributed to the Areopagite mentioned in the Acts of the Apostles who listened to a sermon of St. Paul at Athens (Acts 17:34). Later traditions identified the author as the first bishop of Athens in the second century and the martyred first bishop of Paris in the third century. During the Middle Ages in the West, Dionysius, assumed to be the Areopagite, enjoyed a widespread reputation and popularity. It wasn't until the fifteenth and sixteenth centuries that this identity began to be challenged. Recent scholarly investigations have completely dismissed the apostolic claim. It is now commonly conjectured that the author was a sixth-century Syrian monk.

The four treatises that comprise the Dionysian writings are *The Divine Names, The Celestial Hierarchy, The Ecclesiastical Hierarchy,* and *The Mystical Theology.* There are also ten letters of Dionysius.[36] All of the writings reflect a strong Neoplatonist influence in both content and terminology. Since he is such a speculative thinker, the writings themselves are challenging for the reader and require careful study. "Enigmatic" is a word that has often been used to describe Pseudo-Dionysius as a writer.

As is clear from his titles, *The Celestial Hierarchy* and *The Ecclesiastical Hierarchy,* the theme of *hierarchy* is a central one in Dionysius' understanding of the world. For him a "hierarchy is a sacred order, a state of understanding and an activity approximating as closely as possible to the divine.... The goal of a hierarchy, then, is to enable beings to be as like as possible to God and to be at one with him."[37] It is through the hierarchies that the Trinitarian life is shared, and it is through the hierarchies that the process of divinization takes place. The hierarchies proceed from the Trinity and descend in threes through the nine angelic orders, "thence to

---

[36] For English translations of all his works, see *Pseudo-Dionysius, The Complete Works,* translated by Colim Lubheid, foreword, notes, and translation collaboration by Paul Rorem; and Introduction by J. Pelikan, J. Leclercq, and K. Froehlich (New York: Paulist Press, 1987).

[37] *Ibid.,* pp. 153-154.

the ecclesiastical organ of bishops, priests, and deacons charged with initiating the monks, saints, and purified in a divine way of life through the process of purification, illumination, and perfection or union with the divine Being."[38]

The Mystical Theology is a relatively short treatise, but its importance and significance in the Christian mystical tradition has been monumental. In this work, Dionysius first develops his teaching on the two types of theology and then develops the nature of mystical contemplation. According to Dionysius, God can be known in Two Ways: by reason and by mystical contemplation. He calls the first demonstrative or apodictive theology and the second mystical theology. Demonstrative or rational theology can be either affirmative or negative. We can affirm of God all the good that is found in his creation, saying for example that He is kind, good, and holy. Theology by negation recognizes that all our concepts of God fall far short of the God who is so unlike us, that they are more expressive of what God is not than what He is.

Although reason does bring us to some knowledge of God, there is a higher way of knowing and this is the way of mystical theology, a way that is supernatural and intuitive. This knowledge is a divine gift. It cannot be obtained through human effort; one can only be open to receive it through prayer and purification. Since our senses and our intellect are so limited, we must leave all created things behind and find God in the darkness. Dionysius' moving prologue to *The Mystical Theology* provides us with a good sense of his radical apophatic thought.

> O Trinity
> beyond essence and
> beyond divinity and
> beyond goodness
> guide of Christians in divine wisdom,
> direct us towards mysticism's heights

---

[38] See the article on Pseudo-Dionysius by F.X. Murphy in the *New Catholic Encyclopedia, op. cit.*, vol. 11, p. 944.

beyond the unknowing
beyond light
beyond limit,
there where the
unmixed and
unfettered and
unchangeable
mysteries of theology
in the dazzling dark of the welcoming silence
lie hidden, in the intensity of their darkness
all brilliance outshining,
our intellects, blinded — overwhelming, with the intangible and
with the invisible and
with the illimitable,
Such is my prayer.
And you, beloved Timothy,
in the earnest exercise of mystical contemplation, abandon
all sensation and
all intellection and
all objects or sensed
or seen and
all being and
all non-being and
in unknowing, as much as may be,
be one with the beyond being and knowing. By the ceaseless
and limitless going out of yourself and
out of all things else you will be led in utter pureness,
rejecting all and
released from all
aloft to the flashing forth,
beyond all being, of the divine dark.[39]

Dionysius' influence would be significant in both the East and
the West. St. Maximus the Confessor would synthesize much of his
thought in the seventh century, and medieval Europe held him in

---

[39] Translation by Elmer O'Brien, S.J. in his *Varieties of Mystic Experience* (New York: New
American Library, 1965), pp. 69-70.

high esteem. He remains today a mysterious figure from the past whose contribution to the history of Christian mysticism, especially its apophatic strain, has been great. As one Dionysian scholar concludes:

> The Pseudo-Dionysius style and message may both perplex and enchant. Patience, small doses, and frequent review of *The Mystical Theology* can help smooth the way. In any case, a perplexed reader is in good company, for the history of Christian doctrine and spirituality teems with commentators and general readers who have found the Areopagite's meaning obscure, and yet his mysterious appeal irresistible.[40]

5. The Antiochene School — St. John Chrysostom

The approaches taken to theology, scripture, and spirituality on the parts of the so-called Alexandrian school and Antiochene school have often been compared. For example, with the writers connected with the Antiochene school of thinking, there was little interest in the mystical tradition that was so much a part of the Alexandrian heritage. The emphasis was more on what Bouyer refers to as a moralistic asceticism.[41] Biblical interpretation in the Antiochene school also focused on the literal meaning, and there was little concern with the allegorical interpretation that had developed so extensively in the Alexandrian tradition. Some important writers connected with the school of Antioch include Diadore of Tarsus, Theodore of Mopsuestia, Theodoret of Cyr and St. John Chrysostom. Among these writers, the name of John Chrysostom stands out.

---

[40] See Paul Rorem's Foreword to *Pseudo-Dionysius, The Complete Works, op. cit.,* p. 3.
[41] Bouyer, *op. cit.,* p. 436.

St. John Chrysostom (c. 347-407) is included when tradition lists the four great Fathers of the East. He was born in Antioch of a noble and prosperous Christian family and received a very good education. As a young man, he was attracted to the monastic life; he lived with an old hermit in the neighboring mountains for five years and then as a solitary for two years. The austerity of the life he led caused health problems, and he was forced to return to Antioch. He was ordained a deacon there in 381 and then a priest in 386. During the years 386 to 397, he preached regularly in the main church of the city. He fulfilled this ministry with such zeal and success that his fame as a preacher and orator spread far and wide. Because of his great preaching ability, he was later given the name *Chrysostom,* that is Golden Mouth. In 397 he was chosen to be the patriarch of the capital city, Constantinople, an appointment that ushered in a very difficult period in his life. His plans for the reform of the clergy and the laity and his fearless preaching and fiery temperament led to much opposition and to an ultimate exile from Constantinople in the year 404. After much suffering, he died in exile in September of 407.

John Chrysostom has left a very large literary legacy, most of which is in sermon form. There are a number of exegetical homilies on various books of the Old and New Testaments. There is also the *Baptismal Catecheses* that is based on the instructions he gave to those preparing for Baptism while he was a priest at Antioch. He also authored the very popular *On the Priesthood,* and other treatises such as those on the monastic and ascetic life, on virginity and widowhood, and on suffering. There are also about 236 extant letters.

A strong ascetic bent was always present in the life of John Chrysostom, although he was far more severe with himself than others. A growth in compassion and an understanding of human nature did take place over the course of his life. This was due in no small measure to his priestly ministry. Bouyer writes of the movement he inspired: "The exercise of the ministry, responsibility for souls, had made of a rather dried up ascetic inclined towards a disquieting fanaticism, the precursor if not the initiator of a spirituality for the laity, full not only of understanding but of sympathy."[42] The trials and sufferings in his own life had also played a role in this movement. This is brought out in one of the letters that he wrote to the widow and deaconess, Olympias, from his place of exile:

> Nothing, Olympias, is worth so much in commending us to God as patience in sufferings. This is the queen of blessings, the most beautiful of crowns and, as it is superior to the other virtues, so in it the form of the others shines out the more resplendently.[43]

6. Later Monastic Developments

Various writings emerged from the monastic circles of the East in the fifth and sixth centuries, but in a certain sense there were no further creative developments. For the most part, the writings of this period would deepen and solidify the tradition that was inherited. They would take various forms. There were the collections of the *Apophthegms* or *Sayings of the Fathers* that were grouped either alphabetically according to the particular names of the holy persons or according to the topics treated. There also emerged historical studies of monasticism that gave detailed accounts of the lives, deeds, and ascetic practices of many of the famous figures in this history. These would include the famous *Historia Lausiaca* of Palladius, a disciple of Evagrius, and the *History of the Monks* of Theodoret of Cyr, a work that focused on the ascetic practices of the monks of Syria.

There were also the treatises, conferences and letters of important figures of the monasticism of the fifth and sixth centuries. St. Nilus, superior of a monastery near Ancyra in Galatia, has left a

---

[42] *Ibid.*, p. 446.
[43] *Ibid.*, p. 448.

number of letters and treatises on various aspects of the monastic life. It was under his name that Evagrius' treatise, *On Prayer*, was preserved. Mark the Hermit, the abbot of another monastery at Ancyra, was also the author of a number of ascetic treatises. Barsanuphius and John were two hermits who lived close to a monastery near Gaza. They gave spiritual guidance and direction to the monks of the monastery and to many visitors who approached them. Their direction was given in the form of written answers to the questions that were submitted to them in writing. Their *Questions and Answers* provide some good insights about the ministry of spiritual direction in the early Church. Dorotheus, one of their disciples who founded a monastery near Gaza, followed their practical approach in his work, the *Instructions*.[44]

A work which crystallized and synthesized much of this monastic tradition was the *Ladder of Divine Ascent* of John Climacus (c. 579-649).[45] This book became so popular that the author was given the name Climacus (Ladder). He lived the hermit's life for forty years in the Sinai desert, not far from the great monastery of Mt. Sinai, and afterwards became abbot of the monastery itself. It was while he was abbot that he wrote the *Ladder* for other monks, at the request of the superior of a nearby monastery. The structure of the book centers around the image of the ladder stretching from earth to heaven. There are thirty steps or rungs in this ascending ladder, one for each year in the hidden life of Christ. The thirty chapters can be divided into three main parts. The first three chapters focus on the break with the world and the spirit of renunciation that is required. The longer second section, steps 4-26, treats the active life, that is the practice of the virtues and the struggle against the passions. The emphasis here is not on external ascetic practices but on growth in humility and purity of heart. The last

---

[44] See *The Study of Spirituality, op. cit.*, pp. 178-180.

[45] For a good treatment of the work see the introduction by Kallistos Ware in *John Climacus, The Ladder of Divine Ascent* (New York: Paulist Press, 1982), pp. 1-70. See also the essay by Thomas Merton, "The Spirituality of Sinai," in *Disputed Questions* (New York: Farrar, Straus and Giroux, 1976), pp. 83-93.

four steps are given to the contemplative life with chapters on stillness, prayer, and the love of God. In the entire ascent, the imitation of Christ is a central theme. John Climacus writes in the first step: "A Christian is an imitator of Christ in thought, word, and deed, as far as this is humanly possible, and he believes rightly and blamelessly in the Holy Trinity."[46]

Over the years, the *Ladder* of John Climacus has enjoyed great popularity. Few works in the Eastern Christian Church have been studied, copied and translated more than this. It has always been held in high esteem in Eastern Orthodox monasteries, and it has been widely read by lay people in the East. Although the two books differ greatly in style and character, it can be said that the *Ladder* has enjoyed the popularity in the East that *The Imitation of Christ* by Thomas à Kempis has had in the West.

One does not find in these spiritual writers of the fifth and sixth centuries the strong interest in mystical prayer that was present in such earlier writers as Evagrius Ponticus and Pseudo-Dionysius. There was certainly a great interest in prayer, but it focused more on the ordinary forms of prayer. For various reasons, such as the presence of the Messalian heresy in some monastic circles as well as the Origenist controversies that also took place, there was a gradual ebbing away of the mystical tradition.[47] Two writers, however, who continued to integrate this earlier tradition in a fruitful way in their own writings were Diadochus of Photice and Maximus the Confessor.

Diadochus was bishop of Photice in Epirus, and he was present at the Council of Chalcedon in 451. But outside of these points, little is known about his life. He probably died around 468. His most important work, the *Hundred Chapters on Spiritual Perfection*, is of great importance for the history of Christian spirituality and mysticism, and it is a work that had significant influence on

---

[46] *Ibid.*, p. 74.
[47] See Bouyer, *op. cit.*, p. 427 ff.

later spiritual writers. It clearly shows the influence of Evagrius Ponticus and Pseudo-Macarius.

St. Maximus the Confessor (580-662) was the last great theologian of Greek patristics and a writer whose contributions to doctrinal developments and spirituality have been extremely significant. He was heir to the fullness of the Alexandrian and Cappadocian traditions, but he infused them with his own creative insights and a rich Trinitarian and Christological orientation. Among his spiritual writings are *The Four Hundred Chapters on Love*, the *Commentary on the Our Father*, the *Chapters on Knowledge*, *The Ascetic Life*, and *The Church's Mystagogy*. [48]

St. Maximus is an heroic figure from the past. After receiving an excellent education and working as the first secretary at the court of the emperor Heraclius at Constantinople, he embraced the monastic life. He was a monk at the monastery of Chrysopolis on the Asiatic coast across from Constantinople and then at the monastery of St. George at Cyzicus (modern Erdek). Because of the Persian invasion in 626, he was forced to leave for North Africa where he continued to live the monastic life for many years. He played an important role in the Christological controversies of the times, holding against the Monothelites a human as well as a divine will in Christ. In 653 he was arrested along with Pope Martin I, at the order of emperor Constans II, tried for treason and banished in 655. He was arrested again in 662 for his continued opposition to the Monothelite heresy and brought back to Constantinople. He was condemned once more, and after his tongue was torn out and his right hand cut off, he was banished again, dying in exile in 662. He was completely vindicated at the Sixth Ecumenical Council held at Constantinople, and subsequent ages have recognized his great courage and constancy by bestowing on him the name Maximus the Confessor.

---

[48] For an introduction to Maximus and these writings, see *Maximus the Confessor, Selected Writings*, translated by George C. Berthold and introduction by Jaroslav Pelikan (New York: Paulist Press, 1985).

In his writings, Maximus was very successful in synthesizing many important strands of thought that he inherited from the earlier tradition. Among his many contributions, the theme of *deification* or *divinization* has a very important place. The goal of the spiritual life for Maximus is the divinization of the person, the progressive sharing in the life of the Triune God. This begins for the Christian with the grace of baptism, and the goal of the Christian life is to bring this baptismal grace to perfection through an ongoing cooperation with the grace of the Holy Spirit. The basis of all this is the love of God that has been manifested in the Incarnation of His Son. As one writer summarizes so well: "The spirituality of Maximus is a rich synthesis within which many apparently conflicting traditions find a place, but a synthesis which is based on a profound understanding of the mystery of God's love for us in the incarnation of his Son."[49]

7. The Syriac Tradition

In addition to the Greek writings of the patristic period in the East, there is also the body of writings that have been composed in the Syriac language. Syriac is a dialect of Aramaic that was used in an area that stretched eastwards from Syria, across the Roman empire into Mesopotamia and parts of the Persian empire. With the exception of St. Ephrem, who always enjoyed a great popularity outside of this area, little was known of this literature until fairly recent times. It is only in this present century that scholars have begun to do justice to the extensive writings of Syriac-speaking Christianity.[50]

---

[49] See the article by Andrew Louth in *The Study of Spirituality, op. cit.*, p, 195.

[50] For further information on the Syriac school, cf. the article by Sebastian Brock, "The Syriac Tradition" in *The Study of Spirituality, op. cit.*, pp. 199-215. See also the article by Roberta C. Bondi, "The Spirituality of Syriac-speaking Christians" in *Christian Spirituality, Origins to the Twelfth Century*, edited by Bernard McGinn, John Meyendorff, and Jean Leclercq (New York: Crossroad, 1989), pp. 152-161.

The Syriac Christian literature includes both the early writings that give clear witness to its Semitic sources, and also spiritual treatises that clearly show a Greek influence. In the fifth and sixth centuries, Greek influence on Syriac writers was at its strongest. Syriac translations were made from a number of the monastic writings from Egypt. The writings of Evagrius Ponticus came to have a special place of importance in Syriac spirituality, but translations were also made of the Macarian *Homilies*, the Dionysian corpus, and many of the other monastic writings.

St. Ephrem the Syrian (c. 306-373) is a very important figure in the Syriac school of spirituality. He was the foremost writer in this tradition, and his writings were widely translated and circulated after his death. He was born in Nisibis, a flourishing commercial and political center in northeastern Mesopotamia, close to the borders of the Persian empire. In his early years, he was very active in serving the Church there, teaching and writing hymns, homilies, and biblical commentaries. Nisibis fell to the invading Persian army in 363, and Ephrem and all the other inhabitants were forced to take refuge further west in the Roman empire. He settled in Edessa and remained there for the rest of his life. Ordained to the diaconate at Edessa, he taught at a school of biblical and theological studies that he most likely founded, and he continued to bring forth his rich writings. He is said to have founded women's choirs to sing the hymns he composed. Death came while he was ministering to the sick during a plague in 373.[51]

The majority of Ephrem's writings are in the form of hymns. There are various series such as the *Hymns on the Nativity*, *Hymns on the Epiphany*, *Hymns on the Church*, *Hymns on Paradise*, *Hymns on Virginity and the Symbols of the Lord*, and *Hymns against Julian*. One finds in the hymns of Ephrem, and in much of the later Syriac writings, a strong emphasis on a sacramental view of the Christian

---

[51] For further information on the life and times of Ephrem and translations of some of his hymns, see *Ephrem the Syrian, Hymns*, translated and introduced by Kathleen E. McVey, preface by John Meyendorff (New York: Paulist Press, 1989).

life. Through the eyes of faith, the hidden spiritual realities are seen that are concealed within the visible, physical world. Baptism is a point of entry into this way of seeing, and the mystery of the Incarnation plays a central role. For Ephrem, the created world is a vast system of symbols or mysteries. It is interesting to note that in some of his hymns, Ephrem uses feminine imagery in speaking about God. In this he follows what is found in the earlier Syriac poems, *The Odes of Solomon.*[52]

Another important figure in the Syriac tradition who came much later is Isaac of Nineveh, also known as Isaac the Syrian (d. c. 700). Very little is known about his life. Shortly after he was consecrated bishop of Nineveh, he withdrew to live a life of solitude. He lived the monastic life and composed for his disciples a number of treatises on the monastic life. He was heir to the earlier writings of Evagrius, Macarius and Pseudo-Dionysius, as well as those within his own Syriac tradition, but he writes on the traditional themes with such a simplicity and warmth that his writings were widely translated and enjoyed great popularity.

For Further Reading

Bouyer, Louis, *The Spirituality of the New Testament and the Fathers.* New York: Desclee Company, 1963, pp. 303-454.

Quasten, Johannes, *Patrology*, vol. III. Westminster, MD: The Newman Press, 1953.

Athanasius, The Life of Anthony and The Letter to Marcellinus. Translation and Introduction by Robert C. Gregg. New York: Paulist Press, 1980.

The Desert Christian, Sayings of the Desert Fathers. Translated with a foreword by Benedicta Ward, S.L.G. New York: Macmillan Publishing Co., 1975.

Merton, Thomas, *The Wisdom of the Desert.* New York: New Directions, 1960.

---

[52] For these themes see Bondi, pp. 157-160 and Sebastian Brock, "The Poet As Theologian," *Sobornost* 7:4 (1977), pp. 243-250.

Chitty, Derwas J., *The Desert A City, An Introduction to the Study of Egyptian and Palestinian Monasticism under the Christian Empire*. Oxford: Basil Blackwell, 1966.

Louth, Andrew, *The Origins of the Christian Mystical Tradition, From Plato to Denys*. Oxford: Clarendon Press, 1981.

From Glory to Glory, Texts from Gregory of Nyssa's Mystical Writings. Selected and with an Introduction by Jean Daniélou, S.J., Translated and Edited by Herbert Musurillo, S.J. New York: Charles Scribner's Sons, 1961.

Evagrius Ponticus, *The Praktikos and Chapters On Prayer*. Translated, with an introduction and notes, by John Eudes Bamberger, O.C.S.O. Kalamazoo, Michigan: Cistercian Publications, 1981.

Pseudo-Macarius, The Fifty Spiritual Homilies and the Great Letter. Translated, Edited with an Introduction by George Maloney, S.J. New York: Paulist Press, 1992.

Pseudo-Dionysius, The Complete Works. Translation by Colm Lubheid. Foreword, Notes and Translations Collaboration by Paul Rorem. New York: Paulist Press, 1987.

John Climacus, The Ladder of Divine Ascent. Translation by Colm Luibheid and Norman Russell. Introduction by Kallistos Ware. New York: Paulist Press, 1982.

Maximus Confessor, Selected Writings. Translation and Notes by George C. Berthold. Introduction by Jaroslav Pelikan. New York: Paulist Press, 1985.

John Chrysostom, *The Priesthood*. Translated by W.A. Jurgens. New York: The Macmillan Co., 1955.

Ephrem the Syrian, Hymns. Translated and Introduced by Kathleen E. McVey. New York: Paulist Press, 1989.

3 Early Western Spirituality

1. Western Asceticism — St. Ambrose and St. Jerome

Developments in the Western part of the Roman empire would be much slower than they were in the East, and spiritual writings in the West in Patristic times would never equal what came forth in the East. But there were still rich contributions. St. Augustine of Hippo was the greatest of the Latin Fathers, and before him there were the significant contributions of St. Ambrose and St. Jerome.

St. Ambrose (c. 337-397) was born into an aristocratic and Christian family at Trier, where his father was serving as Prefect of Gaul. After his father's early death, the family moved to Rome where Ambrose studied law and rhetoric. Ambrose was in Rome in 353 when his sister, Marcellina, received the veil as a virgin in a papal ceremony at the Basilica of St. Peter. Around 370, he was appointed *consularis* or governor of the province of Aemilia and Liguria in northern Italy, and he took up residence at Milan. In this capacity he was called upon to oversee the election of a new bishop in Milan in 374. The opposing factions recognized his many gifts, and he himself was elected bishop of the city by acclamation, even though he was only a catechumen at the time.

After his baptism and consecration as bishop, Ambrose devoted himself to a profound study of Scripture and the Greek Fathers under the direction of the learned priest, Simplicianus. This helped to prepare him for his new pastoral responsibilities and also brought about the result that much of Greek thought was transmitted to the West through the writings of Ambrose. For the next twenty-three years, Ambrose was an outstanding bishop during times that saw much change and turmoil in Church and society. The Arian problem was always a constant preoccupation for him, and he was a staunch defender of the Church during times of political upheaval in the empire.

Most of Ambrose's extensive writings took their origin from his pastoral concerns and the many homilies that he preached over the years. Later, he edited and revised many of the homilies, and they were published as treatises. In his many scriptural commentaries, he followed the methodology of Philo and Origen and often employed an allegorical exegesis. Among his other writings is the *De officiis ministrorum*, a work on Christian morals written primarily for his priests and one that follows the format of the *De officiis* of Cicero. The *De mysteriis* is based on his homilies given to catechumens and explains the symbolism of the rites of Baptism and the Eucharist by using Scripture. Ambrose's *De sacramentis* is based on similar homilies and instructions to catechumens. His ninety-one extant letters provide us with a good deal of information about his own life and the religious and political conditions of the times. He also composed a number of hymns, although only a few of them have survived.

Ambrose's writings on virginity are important in the development of Christian spirituality. Among his treatises are five that focus on the theme of virginity. The first and the fullest treatment is his *De Virginibus*, completed in 377 as a letter to his sister, Marcellina, who was a consecrated virgin. While developing a spirituality and theology on virginity, he maintains a balanced and positive view of marriage. The influence of Origen's *Commentary on the Canticle of Canticles* is very much in evidence, and there are many other scriptural citations. The Blessed Virgin Mary, St. Agnes, John the Baptist and other scriptural figures are given as models of virginity.

The presence of Christ within us as a foretaste of eternal life is often emphasized in Ambrose's writings on virginity. For example, he has this beautiful passage in the *De Virginitate* that foreshadows the tender thought of St. Bernard:

> Thus we have everything in Christ… everything is within Christ's power, and Christ is everything to us. If you wish to be healed of your wound, He is the healer; if you burn with fevers, He is the fountain; if you are laden with iniquity, He is justice; if you have need of help, He is strength; if you fear death, He is life; if you desire heaven, He is the way to it; if you flee from darkness, He is the light; if you seek food, He is nourishment…. "Taste, then, and see how good is the Lord: happy the man who hopes in Him."[1]

It has often been noted that St. Ambrose manifests in his life and in his writings a sensitivity, delicacy, and human touch that proved to be very attractive to others. As Bouyer writes of him: "This aristocrat, this man of affairs, whose ecclesiastical policy was of an uncompromising rigor, as soon as he touches on the things of the soul and on human feelings, reveals to us, in the gentleness of his Christian urbanity, as very few and perhaps no other writers of antiquity, the *humanitas et benignitas Salvatoris*."[2]

St. Jerome

St. Jerome's temperament and character differed greatly from that of Ambrose. There was little of the serenity that marked the latter's life. Jerome expressed his likes and dislikes very strongly, and his life was marked by many controversies and disagreements. It seems that it was hard for him to avoid the elements of intemperance and excessive aggressiveness in many of his undertakings.

---

[1] See Louis Bouyer, *The Spirituality of the New Testament and the Fathers* (New York: Desclee, 1963), p. 458.

[2] *Ibid.*, pp. 458-459.

Jerome (c. 345-c. 420) was born of Christian parents in Stridon, Dalmatia, near the border of Pannonia (modern Croatia). As a young man he studied grammar, rhetoric, and the liberal arts in Rome. After his baptism there around 366, he began to devote himself to the practice of the ascetic life. He became acquainted with many of the practices and ideals of Eastern monasticism while traveling through Gaul, and this led him to begin his own undertaking of this way of life in various experimental forms.

He first returned to his homeland and lived in an ascetic community that formed itself around Valerian, bishop of Aquileia. Later he traveled to the East and lived as a hermit for two years in the Syrian desert (373-375). It was there that he began the study of Hebrew, and it was also during this time that he had his famous dream where he was charged with being more of a Ciceronian than a Christian because of his love of secular literature. From 376-382 he was at Antioch in Syria, where he was ordained a priest, and during these years he devoted himself to his biblical studies and writings. He accompanied Bishop Paulinus to Constantinople in the year 380 where he met Gregory Nazianzen. This meeting increased Jerome's enthusiasm for Origen and led to his undertaking the translations of some of Origen's works. In 382, Jerome accompanied Bishop Paulinus to Rome.

Jerome's stay in Rome lasted for only three years, but it set the course for the rest of his life. He became secretary to Pope Damasus, and with his encouragement, Jerome began his monumental translation of the Bible into Latin from the original languages. His reputation for learning and his ascetic lifestyle opened many doors for him in Rome. The two areas that particularly occupied his interest and enthusiasm were biblical studies and asceticism. He became very popular among the high-born Roman ladies, and he gave regular biblical instructions to the noble women who gathered at the homes of the pious widows, Marcella and Paula, on the Aventine Hill. He was also sought after as a spiritual director, and his guidance was marked by a strong ascetic bent. This apostolate in the city and some of his writings aroused a certain amount of controversy and critical reaction. Shortly after the death of Pope Damasus in 384, Jerome left the city that had grown hostile to him.

He made a pilgrimage to many of the holy places and monastic centers in Egypt and Palestine with a group of Roman women and then settled in Bethlehem in 386. Here he founded, with the help of the Roman lady, Paula, a double monastery similar to what Melania the Elder and Rufinus had founded on the Mount of Olives in Jerusalem. Jerome remained here for the rest of his life and continued his immense literary activity and study. Even here his life was not free from some controversies and polemical writings such as the unfortunate disagreement over the writings of Origen with his long time friend, Rufinus.

Jerome's main writings are in the area of Scripture, and his great contributions in biblical studies have been deservedly recognized by subsequent generations. But he also did much to make known in the West the ascetic ideals and practices of the East. His *Letters* are a particularly rich source for this, and there are also his own ascetic treatises and the many translations he made from Greek sources.[3]

2. Dissenting Voices

The treatises of St. Ambrose on virginity and the *Letters* of St. Jerome that propagated ascetic ideals and practices met with much success and led to many conversions in both Milan and Rome; but they also aroused much criticism and discontent in certain quarters. Many reacted strongly to this ascetic emphasis, and many advocates against it soon came to be heard. "I shall give up my religion," said one of them, "if these retirements into the desert go on increasing!"[4]

---

[3] For a treatment of his various writings, see Johannes Quasten, *Patrology,* vol. IV, edited by Angelo Di Beradino (Westminster, MD: Christian Classics, 1986), pp. 219-242.

[4] Quoted in P. Pourrat, *Christian Spirituality* (London: Burns Oates and Washbourne, 1922), vol. I, p. 150.

One of the first dissenting voices was that of Helvidius, a layman from Milan. Around 384, he took issue with Ambrose's use of Mary as a model of virginity and undertook to prove from Scripture that Mary, after the virgin birth of Jesus, had other children by Joseph. Jerome was in Rome at this time and he was asked to respond to these charges. He did so in his treatise, *Against Helvidius, On the Perpetual Virginity of Holy Mary.*

Another dissenting voice was that of the former monk, Jovinian, in Rome. He too sought to minimize the value of virginity by calling into question the Virgin Birth. But he went further than Helvidius by also challenging the efficacy of many ascetic practices and disciplines. He taught that the grace of baptism gave an assurance of salvation that ruled out any need of such practices as fasting or other forms of discipline or penance. In his treatise, *Against Jovinian*, Jerome referred to him as "the Christian Epicurean." Jovinian and his followers were excommunicated by Pope Siricius and compelled to leave Rome.

The third voice of dissent came from Vigilantius in Spain. Around the year 405, he emerged as the leader of those who argued against obligatory celibacy for the clergy. It wasn't until the fourth century that priestly celibacy began to be required.[5] Before that time, there was a fairly common custom for the clergy not to marry after they were ordained. If they were married before their ordination, they were allowed to continue to function as married priests. The rule of obligatory priestly celibacy came to be more established at the beginning of the fourth century. In the West it was required for those who were ordained to the diaconate and priesthood, and those who were married had to give up the married life before being ordained. The East retained the earlier custom, although celibacy was required for bishops.

Vigilantius, a priest of Barcelona in Spain, began to attack various Church practices and institutions such as the monastic life,

---

[5] Here I am following the treatment of Pourrat; see p. 153 ff.

the veneration of the relics of the martyrs, fasts, vigils, and voluntary poverty. Priestly celibacy came under special attack. He believed that chastity was impossible and claimed that the teaching that counseled virginity was a heresy. He went so far as to require that ordination to the priesthood be limited only to the married. Again St. Jerome was called upon to respond to Vigilantius who had made a number of converts, and he responded from Bethlehem with his treatise *Against Vigilantius*.

3. St. Augustine and his Significance

St. Augustine of Hippo (354-430) is certainly one of the greatest of the Fathers and one of those true geniuses of humanity whose contributions have been immense. His writings are of tremendous importance and significance, and his influence on posterity has been profound. Many different gifts and talents came together in this person who was a philosopher, theologian, mystic, poet, orator, polemicist, writer, and pastor. As the Patristic scholar Berthold Altaner writes of him:

> The great bishop united in himself the creative energy of Tertullian and the breadth of spirit of Origen with the ecclesiastical sensitivity of Cyprian; the dialectical acumen of Aristotle with the soaring idealism and speculation of Plato; the practical sense of the Latins with the spiritual subtlety of the Greeks. He was the greatest philosopher of the patristic era and, without doubt, the most important and influential theologian of the Church in general. Since his own time, his works have found enthusiastic admirers.[6]

Unlike many of the figures of antiquity, we do know a great deal about the life of Augustine, for there is a personal stamp on so much of his writings. His *Confessions* are an invaluable source for

---

[6] Quoted in Quasten, *op. cit.*, vol. IV, p. 351.

details about his youth, early manhood, and the ongoing search for truth and wisdom that culminated in his conversion and baptism in 387. His many sermons and letters also reveal a great deal about the man himself.

Augustine was born at Thagaste in Northern Africa in 354 of a pagan father, Patricius (who became a Christian before his death), and a devout Christian mother, Monica. He profited from a good education, first at Madaura and then at Carthage. As a young man at Carthage, he began to live with the unnamed woman who would be his companion for the next fifteen years and the mother of his son, Adeodatus. As a student at Carthage, Augustine abandoned Christianity and joined the Manicheans, the gnostic, dualistic sect that would claim his allegiance for a number of years. It was also at Carthage during these student years that he read Cicero's *Hortensius*, a work that aroused in him an abiding passion for the study of philosophy.

Augustine taught rhetoric at Carthage from 376 to 383, and then for a year at Rome before moving to Milan in 384. By this time he had become disillusioned with Manichean teaching, and he began a serious study of Greek philosophy, particularly Neoplatonism. The preaching of St. Ambrose, the bishop of Milan at this time, had a positive influence, and Augustine slowly grew in his knowledge of the Christian faith and teaching. His long search culminated in the struggle and conversion that he describes so powerfully in Book 8 of his *Confessions*. After a period of prayer and reflection with friends at Cassiciacum, north of Milan, Augustine returned to Milan and was baptized by St. Ambrose at the Easter Vigil Liturgy in 387.

Augustine returned to his native Africa in 388. He established a monastery at Thagaste with a number of the friends who were with him at Cassiciacum, including his son Adeodatus. This was a time of quiet growth, and he gave himself to the practice of the monastic life and to much writing. In 391, he was somewhat reluctantly ordained to the priesthood at Hippo by Bishop Valerian, and here too he founded and directed a monastery. This monastery would become a center of study and learning, where a number of African priests and bishops received their training and formation. Around 395 he succeeded Valerian as bishop of Hippo and for the next 34 years he generously served the local Church of Hippo, the larger African Church and the Church universal as creative thinker, writer and spiritual leader. Among other things, he was very involved in the defense of the faith against the Manicheans, Donatists, and Pelagians. Death came to this great bishop and doctor of the Church in 430, while the Vandals were laying siege to the city of Hippo.

Among Augustine's spiritual writings, the *Confessions* hold a very special and prominent place. This is the first example of spiritual autobiography, and it is a work that has always enjoyed the reputation of being one of the great spiritual classics of all times. It is not only a confession of his sins, but also his confession of faith and praise in the God who had worked so powerfully and lovingly in his life. He marvels at the grace of God in his life, for he realizes that it is by God's grace that he finds God, and it is by God's grace that he is united to God. He never grows weary of proclaiming this, and many have been moved by his well-known and lofty words. We find him writing at the beginning: "You are great, O Lord, and greatly to be praised: great is your power and to your wisdom there is no limit... you have made us for yourself, and our heart is restless until it rests in you" (Book I, c. 1). And much later in the work, he writes so poignantly: "Too late have I loved you, O Beauty so ancient and so new, too late have I loved you!" (Book 10, c. 27).[7]

In the first nine of the twelve books of the *Confessions*, Augustine gives an account of his life from infancy up to the time of his conversion. Book Nine concludes with the death of his mother, Monica, at Ostia, as they were preparing to return to Africa. His focus throughout this narration is primarily on his interior life and his long spiritual journey rather than on the external events and deeds of his life. His style is that of an extended prayer or song of

---

[7] Cf. *The Confessions of St. Augustine*, translated with an Introduction by John K. Ryan (New York: Doubleday Image Books, 1960), p. 43 and p. 254.

praise that is addressed to the God who has filled his life with His grace. In Book 10, Augustine contemplates his present state and ponders the power of the faculty of memory that enables him to reflect back on his past. The last three books are more speculative in nature, as Augustine philosophizes about such matters as time, eternity, and creation.

Among Augustine's scriptural commentaries and homilies, the *Exposition of the Psalms* is a particularly rich source for his spiritual doctrine. This is the longest of his writings and a work that occupied many years of his life. His writings on the psalms came from two main sources: first, the homilies and sermons on the psalms that he gave on various occasions; and secondly, the written expositions or explanations that came from his prayerful study of the psalms.

Augustine's influence on Western Christian spirituality has been great, for he did much to lay the theological foundations for the spiritual life, particularly in the area of grace.[8] It is a spirituality that is ordered to the worship and love of the Trinity, as is shown so clearly in his *De Trinitate*. It is a spirituality that focuses, too, on Christ as the way, guide, and savior for the Christian on the ascent to the Triune God. The restoration of the image of God in the human person is an ongoing and essential task in the ascent to God. It is the action of the Holy Spirit that heals, renews and restores the image of God that has been deformed and obscured by sin. One must move from the land of unlikeness to the land of likeness. Augustine's spirituality has a strong ecclesial dimension, for it must be inserted into the life of the Church. He writes in his commentary on John: "We are convinced, brothers, that one possesses the Holy Spirit to the extent which he loves the Church of Christ" (32, 8). Finally, it is a spirituality that draws its life and ongoing sustenance from the prayerful meditation of Scripture. Thus we can

---

[8] I am indebted here to the treatment of Augustine's spiritual doctrine in Quasten, *op. cit.*, vol. IV, pp. 453-460.

speak of Augustine's spirituality as being Trinitarian, Christological, ecclesiological, anthropological, and biblical.

Looking at the essential elements of Augustine's spirituality, it is clear that for him charity and its development in the human person is at the very heart of Christian life and holiness. This is a constant theme in his writings and he approaches it from different perspectives over and over again. But he is no less insistent in stressing that humility is the indispensable condition for the development of love. Our complete dependence upon God's grace and the teaching and example of Christ form the basis for this necessary stance of humility before God. The genuine ascent to God comes by imitating the humble Christ. Growth in charity also calls for an ongoing practice of purification and the growth of the other virtues. As he writes in one of his sermons: "All our striving in this life consists in healing the eye of the heart in order that it may see God" (Serm. 88, 5).

Prayer and contemplation are also at the heart of Augustine's spiritual thought, and his writings in this area have exercised a lasting influence on succeeding generations. In his *De quantitate animae*, one of his earliest treatises and one which reflects the strong emphasis of Neoplatonism, Augustine writes of the seven stages or steps involved in the ascent to the knowledge and contemplation of God. The first three stages are concerned with the ascent of the soul above the vegetative, sensitive and intellectual aspects of human life. The fourth stage is that of moral effort, purification, and virtue. The fifth stage is called tranquillity because of the peace that comes from the process of purification and the practice of virtue. This prepares the soul for the ascent to the sixth stage, the entrance into the divine light. In the seventh and final stage there is the repose or resting in the light where the soul is caught up in the contemplation and vision of truth.[9]

In many respects, we have a good example of the above stages of contemplation in the account Augustine gives in the *Confessions*

---

[9] For a fuller treatment of these stages, cf. Pourrat *op. cit.*, vol. I, pp. 209-215.

(Book 9, c. 10) of the vision he experienced at Ostia with his mother, Monica. Much has been written about this passage in which he so vividly describes the progressive purification of the soul moving upward to contemplation and the experience of contemplation itself.

It is important to recognize that as Augustine's knowledge of Scripture deepened in later years, his writings on contemplation took on a much more biblical orientation. This is very evident in his *Exposition of the Psalms*. In these commentaries, there is a strong emphasis on the centrality of the heart's desires that help us to understand the reality of heaven. Christ has descended from heaven in order to help us in our ascent. He writes: "Let us sing, then, my Brothers, this 'Song of Steps,' resolved to ascend in heart; for Christ descended to us so that we might ascend."[10] The homily on Psalm 41 brings out the desire of the human heart for God in an ecclesial context, showing clearly the ecclesial dimension of Augustine's mystical thought. He writes:

> "As the deer longs for the water springs, so, O my God, my soul longs for You." Who is it, then, who speaks in this way? If we wish it, it is we ourselves who speak this language. And what need have you to ask who is speaking, when it is within your power to be him whom you ask about? Yet it is not one man alone: it is one body, the body of Christ, the Church. Now, this holy desire is not found in all who enter into the Church; yet, let those who have tasted the sweetness of God and who, in this chant, recognize this sweetness that they love — let them not believe themselves alone in tasting it, and let them be persuaded that a like seed is spread throughout the field of the Lord, through the whole world, and that this word: "As the deer longs for the water springs, so, O my God, my soul longs for You" is that of a certain Christian unity.[11]

---

[10] See Augustine of Hippo, *Selected Writings*, translation and Introduction by Mary T. Clark (New York: Paulist Press, 1985), p. 202.

[11] See Bouyer, *op. cit.*, p. 475.

Finally, Augustine's reflections about the relationship between the active life and the contemplative life should be briefly noted. He makes use of various biblical figures to contrast the two modes of Christian life: Martha and Mary; Peter and John; Rachel and Leah, the wives of Jacob. He does hold for the primacy of the contemplative life, but he also recognizes the value in faith of the active life and the mixed life of action and contemplation, particularly when the needs of the Church call for it. There are tensions, to be sure, between these ways of life but one should never be lived apart from the other. As he writes in Book 19 of *The City of God*, "No one ought to be so entirely contemplative as not to consider his neighbor's benefit, nor so active as to neglect the contemplation of God."[12]

4. Western Monasticism — Early Traces

The ideals of Eastern monasticism and asceticism found their way to the West by means of many different paths and sources. For example, St. Athanasius spent some time in Rome while in exile from his episcopal see in Alexandria because of the Arian controversy. It is very likely that he wrote the *Life of Anthony* during the period of his second exile in Rome, before returning to Alexandria. The subsequent popularity of this work in the East has already been noted, but it was also translated into Latin not long after its publication, and soon it became very well known in the West. St. Augustine, as noted earlier, wrote in his *Confessions* of his discovery of the *Life of Anthony* through his friend Ponticianus. St. Jerome, it will be recalled, lived as a monk in Syria before coming to Rome in 380, where he did much to make known Eastern ascetic practices. St. Jerome also translated the *Rule of Pachomius* into Latin, and his onetime friend, Rufinus, translated the *Rule of St. Basil* into Latin.

Various forms of the monastic life sprung up in Italy and Gaul

---

[12] *Selected Writings, op. cit.*, p. 465.

that reflected, to some extent, the influence of Eastern monasticism. While he was bishop of Milan, St. Ambrose sponsored a monastic community of men near Milan. His sister, Marcellina, lived the life of a consecrated virgin first at Rome and later at Milan. Eusebius, the bishop of Vercelli in northern Italy from 344 to 371, inaugurated the monastic life for the clergy in his diocese. St. Paulinus of Nola also did much to propagate the monastic life in the West. He and his wife both embraced the monastic life after many years of marriage. He was held in great respect by such contemporaries as Jerome, Ambrose and Augustine. It was at Paulinus' request that St. Augustine began to write his *Confessions,* shortly after he became bishop of Hippo.

St. Augustine's own contributions to the development of monasticism in the West were very significant. From the time of his conversion in 387, he was personally drawn to monastic living. He spent a period of prayer and solitude at Cassiciacum with a number of friends, shortly before his baptism in Milan in 387. After his return to Africa, he established and directed a monastic community at Thagaste that became a center for prayer and study. As a priest at Hippo, he also established a monastery that subsequently prepared priests and bishops for pastoral work in the African Church. Then, as bishop of Hippo, he developed a monastic community with the priests of his diocese and a way of life that included celibacy, obedience and poverty. It was a new type of monasticism, for in this case, pastoral service was intimately connected with the monastic life.

Augustine's writings on monasticism were to have a significant influence on the development of monasticism in the West. Over the course of history, a number of rules were attributed to him that have come down to us in different forms. For many years it was believed that the original text of Augustine's Rule was contained in the *Letter to Nuns* (Letter 211), written in 423 to a community of nuns he had founded. Recent research, however, has established that the original text was a rule for men that Augustine wrote around 397, after he had become bishop and had established a monastery for clerics in the bishop's house at Hippo. Later, a rule for women was adapted from this Rule; this is the one contained in Letter 211, a text that is basically the same as the original one.[13] The Rule itself is a relatively short one with few specific regulations and detailed legislation. It is possible that the Rule was a summary of oral conferences that St. Augustine gave to his monks. The ideas are presented in a concise way that seems to presume they are familiar and well known. The fundamental ideas are based on the example of the Jerusalem community as described in the Acts of the Apostles 4:32, for here "the whole group of believers was united, heart and soul." Augustine writes at the beginning of the Rule: "Above all, live together in harmony (Ps 67:7), having one mind and one heart (Acts 4:32), intent on God, since that is why you have come together."[14]

Many later rules of religious communities of men and women were based on the Rule of Augustine, particularly among the groups founded in the eleventh and twelfth centuries. Among the numerous communities of men are the Canons Regular of St. Augustine; the Norbertines; the Crosiers; the Trinitarians; the Dominicans; the Augustinian Hermits or Friars; and the Servites. Among the foundations of women religious that based their rule on Augustine's are the Brigittines; the Ursulines; the Canonesses of St. Augustine; the Visitation Order of Francis de Sales; the Sisters of the Good Shepherd founded by Jean Eudes; and many communities that devote themselves to nursing and the care of the sick, such as the Hawthorne Dominicans.

---

[13] The main work in establishing the critical Latin text of the Rule of Augustine was done by the Augustinian scholar, L. Verheijen, O.S.A. in his two volume work, *La Règle de Saint Augustin* (Paris, 1967). An English translation of this rule can be found in *Augustine of Hippo, Selected Writing, op. cit.*, pp. 485-493. See also *The Rule of St. Augustine*, with introduction and commentary by Tarsicius J. Van Bavel, O.S.A. (New York: Image Books, 1986). This contains both the masculine and feminine versions of the Rule.

[14] *Selected Writings, op. cit.*, p. 485.

5. Monasticism in Gaul — John Cassian

The early monastic establishments in Gaul (France) reflected in many ways the form and practices of early Eastern monasticism. They were monasteries of lay persons who had little contact with an intellectual culture or setting. The flourishing of a particular monastery was often due to its holy and charismatic leader.

St. Martin of Tours (317-397) was a good example of such a monastic leader. A former soldier before embracing the monastic life, he became after his death a very popular and much venerated saint. An ancient story tells how Martin the Roman soldier gave half his cloak to a beggar, and then in a dream that night saw Christ wearing it. He first lived the monastic life at Poitiers with St. Hilary, where there was a semi-eremitical community. After he became bishop of Tours, Martin continued to establish a number of monasteries, including those at Ligugé and Marmoutier. His fame as a monastic leader continued after his death, and many monasteries were named after him and dedicated to him.

A monastery was founded on the island of Lerins in Southern Gaul shortly after the year 400. Many of the monks here were from an educated and upper class, and in time this monastery became a center for learning and culture and a place that provided many bishops for the Church in Gaul. St. Cesarius first lived as a monk at Lerins. When he became bishop of Arles in 502, he founded a monastery there and wrote his *Regula Monachorum*, a rule for men. Ten years later he founded a monastery at Arles for women that soon flourished under the leadership of his sister, Cesaria. He wrote a rule for women, the *Regula ad virgines*, for this community.

It would be John Cassian (c. 360-c. 432) who would have the greatest influence on monasticism in Gaul through his very significant writings.[15] He was a fascinating person in many ways and proved to be the ideal person to transmit much of the practices of Eastern monasticism to the West. He had the ability not only to

---

[15] For a good overall study of Cassian, see Owen Chadwick's *John Cassian* (Cambridge: Cambridge University Press, 1968).

make the necessary adaptations for an area far different from that of the Egyptian desert, but also to distill from the teachings of the Egyptian monks that which would be most helpful and appropriate for the monks in the West.

John Cassian was most likely from a Latin-speaking community of a Roman province in what is now Rumania. As a young man he went to Palestine with his friend, Germanus, and entered a cenobitic monastery in Bethlehem. He and Germanus later visited many of the well known monastic centers in Egypt, attracted by the eremitic monasticism that was so popular in that area. There Cassian became a devoted disciple of many of the famous leaders of the monastic movement in Egypt; he also become heir to much of the tradition associated with Origen and Evagrius. The Origenist controversy and crisis that later developed in Egypt led to his move to Constantinople around 399. St. John Chrysostom, the patriarch of Constantinople, ordained Germanus a priest and John Cassian a deacon. After John Chrysostom was deposed and sent into exile, the clergy loyal to him sent Germanus and Cassian to Rome to appeal to the pope on his behalf.

Cassian arrived in Rome in 405 and remained there for the next ten years. During this period he became friends with the future Pope Leo the Great. He then set out for Gaul, probably at the request of some who had heard of his monastic experience in the East and sought his assistance for the growing monastic movement in Gaul. He was ordained to the priesthood either at Rome or at the time of his arrival in Southern Gaul. He founded two monasteries at Marseilles, one for men and one for women. At the request of Bishop Castor of Apt, he wrote the *Institutes,* a work that described the way of life and the various religious practices of Eastern monasticism. Cassian then set about composing his *Conferences,* twenty four in all, that were based on the teachings of the famous monastic leaders of such Egyptian centers as Scete and Panephysis. Cassian was able to transmit a synthesis and assimilation of this teaching with great prudence, moderation, and discretion, while at the same time preserving the richness and depth of this tradition in a clear and readable style of writing. He clearly recognized the stronger emphasis on the cenobitic form of monasticism that was found in the West, and so he adapted many of the practices of the eremitic tradition to this community setting. Cassian was also careful to avoid any terms that could be misunderstood or found objectionable. For example, even though he transmits much of Evagrius' teaching, he avoids the controversial term *apatheia* and uses instead the more biblical term of *purity of heart*.

In the first of his conferences, Cassian emphasizes that the monk's primary goal is to seek the kingdom of God. This cannot be attained, however, without a purity of heart. All the ascetic practices and renouncements are in vain unless they foster that purity of heart that leads to the fullness of love. Asceticism must lead to the perfection of charity. Cassian writes with great insight:

> This is why we see many who, having given up the greatest wealth not only in gold and silver but also in splendid estates, nevertheless become very upset over a knife, a scraper, a needle, or a pan. If they had looked unwaveringly to the purity of their hearts they would never have become involved with such trifles and they would have rejected these just as they did great and valuable possessions. There are some who guard a book so jealously that they can barely endure to have someone else read it or touch it. Such a situation, instead of gaining them the reward of gentleness and love, turns for them into occasions of impatience and even death....
>
> Everything we do, our every objective, must be undertaken for the sake of this purity of heart. This is why we take on loneliness, fasting, vigils, work, nakedness. For this we must practice the reading of the Scripture, together with all the other virtuous activities, and we do so to trap and to hold our hearts free of the harm of every dangerous passion and in order to rise step by step to the high point of love.[16]

---

[16] Conference One, numbers 6 and 7. See John Cassian, *Conferences*, translation and preface by Colm Lubheid, introduction by Owen Chadwick (New York: Paulist Press, 1985), p. 41.

Cassian is particularly helpful with his suggestions for prayer, a subject that receives much attention in his writings. Conferences Nine and Ten are devoted entirely to this subject. For Cassian, the purpose and goal of the monk's life is a total and uninterrupted dedication to prayer. The ascetic practices and the pursuit of the virtues provide the foundation upon which prayer builds, and it is prayer that draws all of them firmly together. Thus, there is an intimate connection between prayer and the practice of all the virtues. Without the ongoing quest for purity of heart, there will be no true spirit of prayer. Cassian also insightfully recognizes the link between the time of prayer and the time that precedes it. If persons are not prayerful to some extent during their daily lives, they will be less able to pray when they turn to explicit prayer. One's thoughts, words, and actions before prayer are very important, for as Cassian writes: "It is an inexorable fact that the condition of the soul at the time of prayer depends upon what shaped it beforehand. The soul will rise to the heights of heaven or plunge into the things of earth, depending upon where it lingered before the time of prayer."[17]

Cassian recognizes that individuals pray in different ways and that an individual might pray in different ways at different moments, according to present circumstances. Following St. Paul, however, he speaks of four basic types of prayer. First, there is the prayer of supplication that seeks pardon for sins, a prayer that is especially appropriate for beginners. Second, there is the form of prayer that makes good resolutions to God, appropriate for those making progress in the practice of virtue. Third, there is intercessory prayer for others on the part of those who have grown in charity and love of one's neighbor. Finally, there is the prayer of thanksgiving that comes from the contemplation of God's goodness, greatness, and faithfulness.

From these forms of prayer there can come moments of great unity and intensity that Cassian refers to as "the prayer of fire." This is the highest state of prayer, a wordless form of prayer in which "our

---

[17] Conference Ten, 4. *Ibid.*, pp. 139-40.

spirit is moved by measureless joy to pour out wordless thanksgiving to God." The heart is rapt in the burning prayer which human words can neither grasp nor utter. It is the gazing on God alone, a great fire of love. These moments of intense and fervent prayer can spring forth from various sources through the movement of the Holy Spirit: from a verse of a psalm; from the reading of the Word; from the encouragement and words of a holy person; from the death of a dear friend.

Although the prayer of fire is wordless, Cassian is insistent that the source and foundation of this prayer is the continuous reading of Scripture. It is the food that nourishes the prayerful spirit. Scripture should be penetrated so deeply that its words become one's own. The monk must always be ruminating on some part of Sacred Scripture. The Book of Psalms is particularly important for prayer, for it was written as a book of prayers; it contains prayers of supplication, resolution, petition and gratitude. Cassian strongly encourages the method of choosing a particular verse or formulation from the psalms that speaks to the heart, and then returning to it over and over again. The constant repetition of the verse helps to keep the thought of God constantly in one's mind. The verse that Cassian himself chooses is: "Come to my help, O God; Lord, hurry to my rescue" (Ps 69:2).

John Cassian's involvement in the grace and free will controversy (Conference Thirteen) did mar his subsequent reputation to some extent, but in general his influence on Western monasticism and spirituality has been great.[18] An unknown author drew up a rule that was based on the first four books of the *Institutes*, and this became known as the Rule of Cassian. Cassian clearly influenced the rule that came to be known as the *Rule of the Master* (*Regula Magistri*). St. Benedict highly esteemed the writings of Cassian, and in his influential Rule he recommends the reading of Cassian. Thus, Cassian's popularity spread with the wide dissemination of the Rule

---

[18] For Cassian's role in the grace controversy, see Chadwick, *op. cit.*, p. 110 ff. and Quasten *op. cit.*, vol. IV, 520-522.

of St. Benedict. Among the many subsequent admirers of Cassian were Alcuin, Saints Peter Damian, Dominic, Thomas Aquinas, Ignatius of Loyola, Teresa of Avila, and Francis de Sales.

6. The Rule of St. Benedict — Benedictine Spirituality

St. Benedict of Nursia (c. 480-c. 547) would become the most famous monastic legislator in the West. His Rule built upon previous monastic rules and reflects the wisdom and the experience of the tradition that he inherited. In time, the summary that he made of this tradition came to be recognized as the most significant, and gradually it came to supplant all the other monastic rules that were written in the sixth and seventh centuries in the West.

The only source for an account of the life of St. Benedict is the second book of the *Dialogues* of Pope Gregory the Great. This work supplies us with the basic outline of Benedict's life, but it has to be read with some caution. It is not a biography in the modern sense of the term, for in many instances Gregory is moved more by an interest in drawing lessons and inspiration from the life of Benedict than by historical considerations. There is a strong interest in Benedict's gift of prophecy and his power of working miracles. For Gregory, Benedict is a wonderful example of God working in a person's life and the person advancing towards God.

According to the *Dialogues*, Benedict was born in the region of Nursia, northeast of Rome, the son of a prosperous family. He went to Rome as a young man to continue his studies, but he soon became disillusioned and threatened by the vice and sophistication that he encountered there. Abandoning his studies, he embraced the ascetic life and began to live as a hermit on Mt. Subiaco. For three years he lived in solitude in a cave, his needs met by a kind monk from a neighboring monastery. He lived this life of prayer, penance, and solitude for three years, until his hiding place was eventually discovered by shepherds. His subsequent fame attracted many visitors and disciples, who came seeking his advice and spiritual guidance. Later, the monks of the monastery at Vicovaro asked him to come and be their superior. This union proved to be a disastrous one, for these monks had no desire to follow Benedict's serious way of life. They grew rebellious and, as the *Dialogues* relate, their attempt to poison him was thwarted by a miracle.

Benedict returned to Subiaco and devoted himself to the new disciples that came in large numbers. He established twelve monasteries of twelve monks, each with its own superior. It seems that he himself directed another that was set up for the formation of the novices. After a number of years at Subiaco, the hostility of a parish priest in the neighborhood led to his decision to leave Subiaco and travel south with some of his disciples. On the mountain rising above the town of Cassino, about eighty miles south of Rome, he leveled the remains of a pagan temple and replaced it with a church dedicated to St. Martin of Tours. He established on this mountain a fully cenobitic monastery that would in time become the most famous monastery in the Western world. Benedict remained at Monte Cassino for the rest of his life, and it was there that he most likely composed his famous *Rule for Monks*. A neighboring monastery was built for women and governed by his sister, St. Scholastica. A third monastery was built at Terracina, about thirty miles from Cassino.

In the *Dialogues*, St. Gregory the Great testifies that Benedict composed a monastic rule that was "notable for its discernment and its clarity of language." Much has been written of this Rule that would become so famous and prominent in Western monasticism.[19] Much research and study has been done on the *Rule of Benedict* (RB) and its relationship with other Latin monastic rules, particularly the one known as the *Rule of the Master* (RM). Formerly it was thought that Benedict's Rule was the earlier of the two, but recent studies are in general agreement that the *Rule of the Master* came first and

---

[19] For English translations of Benedict's Rule, see *RB 1980, The Rule of St. Benedict in Latin and English with Notes,* Timothy Fry, O.S.B., editor (Collegeville: The Liturgical Press, 1981); and *The Rule of St. Benedict,* translated, with introduction and notes by Anthony C. Meisel and M.L. del Mastro (New York: Image Books, 1975).

that Benedict made use of it in the composition of his Rule.[20]

There is no question that the RB is a monastic document and guide that has had great historical influence and significance. What accounts for its special place in the history of Western monasticism? First of all, it is an excellent expression and synthesis of the monastic tradition that developed before Benedict in different places and in different ways. It can rightly be said that "the disparate branches of the monastic tradition are brought together and harmonized, correcting and completing one another, so that the richness of the whole deposit may be preserved without loss."[21] Second, although it is a relatively short document (only one-third the length of the much longer RM), it is a very practical and workable guide for all aspects of monastic activity. It expresses clearly and directly a wealth of spiritual wisdom that can guide the abbot and monks in their day by day search for God. Third, although it constantly presents high spiritual goals and ideals, it does so in a moderate and flexible manner. St. Benedict continually shows a deep understanding and compassion for the human situation and human weaknesses, and the Rule is marked by a spirit of moderation and discretion. The emphasis is on living a simple life in community in a spirit of obedience, humility, and charity, rather than on individual ascetic practices and penances.

The content of the RB is divided into two main parts. The spiritual doctrine is given in the first part (prologue and cc. 1-7), and the regulations for the monastery follow in the second section (cc. 8-73). By way of summary, certain key aspects of the Rule can be briefly mentioned. Chief among them is the concept of stability. St. Benedict was very wary of the wandering type of monk that had sprung up amidst the social flux and disorder that was so prevalent in his times. He wanted his monks to bind themselves to a lifelong commitment to the house of their profession. Thus, they would

---

[20] For the relationship between the RB and the RM and the reasons for assigning precedence to the RM, see *RB 1980, op. cit.*, pp. 79-83.

[21] *Ibid.*, p. 90.

promise stability in the community, *conversatio morum* (ongoing conversion to the monastic way of life), and obedience to the abbot.

The position of abbot is central to the well being of the monastic community. His position is one of great responsibility, for he is Christ's representative in the monastery and he will be accountable for the good of his monks on Judgment Day. He is to be the spiritual father of the community, a person filled with the Holy Spirit, who seeks to lead the monks to holiness and union with God. He must be a person experienced in monastic life and teaching, who leads more by his deeds than his words. Since the monastery is a family, the abbot must seek to develop a family spirit and to assist the monks to live together in harmony and mutual love. The abbot is also a public person who has definite jurisdiction and authority to rule over the monastery in temporal as well as spiritual matters.

The monk in turn owes obedience to the abbot, an obedience that should be rendered with a cheerful spirit to the one who speaks as God's representative. This obedience is intimately connected with the virtue of humility, the virtue Benedict recognizes as central for growth and progress in holiness. In the seventh chapter of the Rule, he develops his teaching on the twelve steps of humility. This growth in humility leads to the flowering of true love, the perfect love of God.

The overall thrust of the monk's life is the service of God. God must be the central focus of the monk's life, and one's prayer and work is undertaken for the praise and glory of God. In order to accomplish this, the RB calls for an order of the day that includes a rhythmic balance of three things: liturgical prayer, *lectio divina*, and manual labor. Several hours of the day were devoted to the divine office. For Benedict, this was the *Opus Dei*, the "Work of God," and he carefully draws up the rubrics for the traditional night office and the seven periods of prayer during the day. About four more hours were given over to *lectio*, the quiet, prayerful, and meditative reading of Scripture and its interpretation by the Fathers and monastic writers. A good part of the day was also devoted to various forms of manual labor that served many purposes: it provided for the support and sustenance of the members of the monastery; it was a form of asceticism that blended in well with the rest of the life; and it could produce a surplus that could be shared with the poor.[22]

The RB shows great concern for those in need, and for travelers and guests who were to be received as Christ coming to them. But nothing is said of apostolic activity or pastoral work. Most of the monks were lay persons like Benedict himself. Also, the RB does not express any academic or cultural goals or programs. The goal is personal sanctification and the seeking of God by living the Christian life as fully as possible in a community, separated from the outside world. There were other monastic rules written in the West after Benedict, but none would surpass it. In time, it would supplant all the others and provide the dominant thrust for monastic developments in the West. The passage of time attested to the wisdom and flexibility of this living and dynamic organism that would long outlive the monastic legislator himself. Outside of the books of Scripture, no other early text was copied in the Middle Ages as much as the Rule of St. Benedict, the Father of Western monasticism.

For Further Reading

Bouyer, Louis, *The Spirituality of the New Testament and the Fathers.* New York: Desclee Company, 1963, pp. 455-530.

Quasten, Johannes, *Patrology*, Vol. IV. Edited by Angelo Di Beradino. Westminster, MD: Christian Classics, 1986.

Kelly, J.N.D., *Jerome, His Life, Writings, and Controversies.* New York: Harper and Row, 1970.

Augustine of Hippo, Selected Writings. Translation and Introduction by Mary T. Clark. New York: Paulist Press, 1984.

Brown, Peter, *Augustine of Hippo: A Biography.* Berkeley: University of California Press, 1969.

---

[22] *Ibid.*, p. 96.

The Confessions of St. Augustine. Trans. with an Introduction by John K. Ryan. New York: Doubleday Image Books, 1960.

John Cassian, *Conferences.* Translation and Preface by Colm Luibheid. Introduction by Owen Chadwick. New York: Paulist Press, 1985.

Chadwick, Owen, *John Cassian.* Cambridge: Cambridge University Press, 1968.

RB 1980. The Rule of St. Benedict in Latin and English with Notes. Timothy Fry, O.S.B., Editor. Collegeville: The Liturgical Press, 1981.

Western Monasticism. Selected Translations with Introduction and Notes by Owen Chadwick. Philadelphia: Westminster, 1958. (Contains the *Sayings of the Fathers*, the *Conferences* of Cassian, and the *Rule* of St. Benedict).

4   *Early Middle Ages*

1. St. Gregory the Great

The period that was to be known as the Middle Ages had already
begun when Gregory the Great was pope. He himself is a patristic
figure, esteemed by later generations as one of the four great Western Fathers, along with Augustine, Ambrose, and Jerome. However, his influence on the later Middle Ages has been so great that
he has been looked upon as the Father of Western spirituality in the
Middle Ages. Although he belongs primarily to the ancient world,
he is a bridge to the new. As Jean Leclercq points out, "St. Gregory
bridges the gap between the patristic age and the monastic culture
of the Middle Ages."[1]

St. Gregory was born around 540 from a patrician family in
Rome. Destined to follow his father in a career of public service, he
received an excellent education and then became prefect of Rome
around 570. In this capacity he presided over the Roman senate and
assumed responsibility for the defense, safety, and overall administration of the city of Rome. His father died not long after he had
become prefect, and this led to his decision to abandon his political
career and embrace the monastic life. He withdrew to the monas-

---

[1] Jean Leclercq, "St. Gregory, Doctor of Desire," in *The Love of Learning and the Desire
for God* (New York: Mentor Omega Books, 1962), p. 33.

tery he established and dedicated to St. Andrew at his family estate on the Coelian Hill in Rome. There he devoted himself to the ascetic life and a profound study of Scripture and the Latin Fathers.

This period would not last long, for Pope Pelagius II, recognizing his many talents, asked him to leave the monastery and assist him as a regional deacon and advisor. In 579, he was sent to Constantinople as the *apocrisarius* or papal representative at the Byzantine capital. He returned to Rome around 586 and served as a counselor to Pope Pelagius II before succeeding him in the year 590. As pope in a very difficult period of change and social upheaval, Gregory proved to be an outstanding leader. He provided leadership for the city of Rome during the plague that gripped the city after the Tiber had overflowed its banks. Through diplomacy and the payment of tribute he was able to defend Rome from the invading Lombards in 594. From his monastery of St. Andrew he sent St. Augustine of Canterbury and forty other monks to begin the evangelization of Britain. In whatever he set out to do, Gregory had a strong pastoral and practical orientation. Throughout his pontificate, he sought to restore and renew the religious life of the people that had been nearly destroyed by the ongoing social upheavals of the times.

It was through his writings especially that Gregory would have a great and lasting influence. The Bible was the basic source for his varied works; many of his writings are homilies that he gave in a liturgical setting or conferences and commentaries on Scripture. His forty *Gospel Homilies* flowed from the sermons he gave at the liturgical celebrations on Sundays and feast days during the years 590 and 591. They are pastoral talks, popular in tone and directed to the ordinary Christian, in which Gregory makes use of stories and examples to clarify the teaching. There is a strong emphasis on the eschatological themes of the end of the world, death, heaven and hell, traceable in no small part to the grim historical conditions the people were living through. Gregory's twenty-two *Homilies on Ezekiel* are much more profound in their content and deal with Christ, the Church, prayer and contemplation, and other important themes of his spiritual thought. The longest of Gregory's writings is his

Moralia, an exposition of the Book of Job. This work had its beginning with the conferences he gave to the monks who accompanied him to Constantinople when he was papal nuncio. Although it is not a systematic form of writing, it is truly a summa or storehouse of doctrinal and moral teachings, asceticism, and mysticism.

Two treatises of Gregory that would enjoy great popularity in the Middle Ages were his *Pastoral Rule* and his *Dialogues*. The *Pastoral Rule* (*Pastoral Care*) was written primarily for bishops and priests in order to assist them in their pastoral ministry. It is divided into four books and contains a wealth of wise advice, counsel, and instruction for Church leaders. It was widely known and used during the Middle Ages, and it served to guide and assist bishops and priests in a way somewhat equivalent to the direction the monastic rule provided for monks. Even more popular during the Middle Ages was Gregory's *Dialogues*. While the *Pastoral Rule* was intended for bishops and priests, the *Dialogues* was written for the simple and uneducated and is thus more popular in orientation and style. The four books of the *Dialogues* take the form of conversations between Gregory and Peter the Deacon. Three of the books treat of the lives of holy people of the sixth century with an emphasis on their miracles; the entire second book is devoted to the life of St. Benedict. The fourth book treats of the immortality of the soul and other eschatological themes in a way suited to the popular audience for whom it was directed. Mention should also be made of Gregory's numerous published *Letters* that are a rich source for his teaching and for a knowledge of the troubled times of his pontificate.

Gregory's Spirituality

Gregory's spiritual teaching, particularly his mystical theology, has only recently received the recognition and appreciation that it enjoyed throughout the Middle Ages. Gregory's teaching reflects the influence of Augustine, Cassian, and the monastic tradition to which he was heir. His writings also reflect his own personal experience — the experience of a monk and a cultivated Roman. There is also the influence of his poor health that was so much a part of his life. As Jean Leclercq points out, it gave him "a strong sense of human suffering, of the effects of Original Sin, but also of the value of weakness and temptation for spiritual progress."[2]

Gregory's teaching on prayer and contemplation is intimately connected with his concept of the Christian life. He sees the Christian life in terms of exile and pilgrimage. The human person, created in the image of God, was destined to contemplate the uncreated Light. This state was changed by the Fall, and the Christian life is now marked by a process of detachment and desire: a detachment from worldly desires and sin, and a growing desire for God, heaven, and spiritual realities.

Gregory's emphasis on compunction is also closely linked with this theme of the desire for God. Compunction arises in the context of trial and suffering together with one's awareness of sin, alienation from God, and a lack of peace. Compunction is an action of God that pierces or pricks the complacent and lethargic heart and stirs up tears of repentance and a desire for God. Gregory recognizes two aspects of compunction: a compunction of fear and a compunction of love and desire. Both have great value in moving a person towards God, but it is the second aspect that Gregory emphasizes. He writes in the *Dialogues*:

> There are two main types of compunction. First the soul thirsting for God is pierced by fear and afterwards by love. In the beginning the soul is moved to tears at the remembrance of its evil deed and fears the prospects of eternal punishment. But when, after a long and anxious experience of pain, this fear works itself out, then is born in the soul a calmness coming from the assurance of forgiveness and the soul is inflamed with love for heavenly joys. He who previously wept at the prospect of being led to punishment now begins to weep most bitterly because he is far from the King-

---

[2] *Ibid.*, p. 36.

dom.... When the compunction of fear is complete it draws
the soul into the compunction of love.[3]

Thus, the main purpose of compunction is to bring a person to a
greater desire for God and a longing for Heaven. For Gregory the
intense desire for God is really a union with Him and he writes:
"Whoever desires God with his whole mind already possesses the
object of his love."[4]

The vision of God is a theme that is central to Gregory's spiritual thought. The vision is a gift but one can prepare for it through
prayer and purification, and especially by reading Scripture and
reflecting on the mysteries of Christ. Gregory speaks of this vision
in a twofold way: a vision of desire and a vision of rapture. The desire for God can at times, through God's grace, lead to an experience in which the spiritual senses are so open to God that the soul
"flies towards God on spiritual wings" and from a distance contemplates the beauty of God in the knowledge of love. It is a taste, a
relish, and an understanding of God that comes about through a
loving contemplation of God. It is a vision of God that somehow
restores that vision of the light for which we were created. This experience can only be temporary, for the soul falls back upon itself
and resumes its life of desire in the midst of life's ongoing trials,
much stronger now and with a deeper sense of humility that is born
of the knowledge of God.[5] But the experience leaves a person with
the resolve to give oneself to the service of God and the service of
one's brothers and sisters.

In discussing this theme of the vision of God in Gregory, Jean
Leclercq writes by way of summary:

It is not in seeing then, that the vision of faith consists, but
in looking with love and a great longing to see. It is not

---

[3] *Dialogues* 3:34 cited in Michael Casey's "Spiritual Desire in the Gospel Homilies of St.
Gregory the Great," *Cistercian Studies* (vol. xvi, 1981), pp. 309-310.

[4] *Gospel Homilies* 30:1. *Ibid.*, p. 302.

[5] See Leclercq, *op. cit.*, p. 41.

merely a knowledge of God, an act of the understanding, but an act of love by which we possess the divine truth though as yet only imperfectly and obscurely, whereas in heaven we shall lay hold of it full and clearly. This foretaste only gives us a glimpse of the divine light, but the happiness this feeble glimmer brings is so great that it keeps alive in us a longing for the complete bliss of heaven.[6]

2. Celtic Spirituality

It is important to keep in mind that Ireland was never part of the Roman empire and it was never subject to Rome or Roman law. It had its own unique development and its first real contact with Rome was through the Christian faith. St. Patrick was the great apostle to Ireland and his presence and missionary activity left a lasting influence. There were scattered Christians in Ireland before St. Patrick's arrival, but his amazing evangelization brought about a deep planting of the Christian faith and its widespread acceptance and organization.

St. Patrick (c. 385-461) was most likely born in Roman Britain, the son of a Christian father who was a town official. In one of the many raids made upon Britain by pirates, Patrick was captured as a young man and carried off as a slave to Ireland. His time of servitude was spent in solitude, tending his master's flock on a nearby mountain. After a six year period in which he learned the Gaelic language and underwent a spiritual renewal, Patrick escaped to Gaul and then returned to Britain. A deep desire to return to Ireland as a missionary never left him and it led to years of preparation as a monk. After visiting various monastic centers in Gaul, he settled for three years at Lerins where St. Honoratus was abbot, and then spent ten years at the monastery at Auxerre which was under

---

[6] See Jean Leclercq, François Vandenbroucke, Louis Bouyer, *The Spirituality of the Middle Ages* (New York: The Seabury Press, 1968), pp. 26-27.

the direction of St. Germanus, the greatest bishop in Northern Gaul. They were years of growth in holiness and knowledge for Patrick. The planning of the Irish apostolate was begun by St. Germanus in 429. After the death of St. Palladius, who first set out for Ireland, St. Patrick was chosen to lead the mission. He was ordained bishop by St. Germanus and left for Ireland with a number of missionary companions in the year 432.

St. Patrick's missionary activity in Ireland met with great success. Clerics, monks and nuns accompanied him on his missionary journeys, and the results of this evangelizing were amazing. Tribal kings were converted with their people, and churches, schools and monasteries were founded throughout the country. St. Patrick's legacy would be a great and lasting one for the people of Ireland. As one Irish writer observes: "It is doubtful if any evangelizer left such a lasting imprint on his spiritual children as did Patrick."[7]

In the development of Christianity in Ireland, monasticism played a very important role.[8] Great enthusiasm developed for the monastic life, and large numbers of men and women were drawn to embrace this life. It can be said that monasticism in Ireland "attained a popularity without parallel in any other country or at any other time."[9] The fifth and sixth centuries witnessed the founding of many monasteries throughout the country. Many famous names are connected with these monasteries: Saints Ebda, Finnian, Kevin, Brendan, Columcille, and Comgall. St. Brigid of Kildare (c. 459-523) played a very important role in the foundation and organiza-

---

[7] See Diarmuid O'Laoghaire "Celtic Spirituality" in *The Study of Spirituality*, edited by C. Jones, G. Wainwright, and E. Yarnold (New York: Oxford University Press, 1986), pp. 218-219. St. Patrick left two writings, *The Confessions of St. Patrick* and *Letter to the Soldiers of Coroticus*. They can be found with other background material on St. Patrick in Martin P. Harney, S.J., *The Legacy of Saint Patrick* (Boston: Daughters of St. Paul, 1972). See also *The Works of St. Patrick*, translated and annotated by Ludwig Bieler, Ancient Christian Writers Series (New York: Newman Press, 1953).

[8] For a very good study of the movement, see John Ryan, S.J., *Irish Monasticism, Origins and Early Development* (New York: Colgate University Press, 1972). First edition, Dublin, 1931.

[9] *Ibid.*, p. 167.

tion of communities for women. One of the most famous and beloved of all Irish saints, she ruled over the double monastery and church at Kildare with Bishop Conlaed.[10]

Prayer, study, and manual labor were the main components of the life in all of these monasteries. The study of Sacred Scripture was held in the highest esteem, and the whole spirituality of the monasteries was strongly scriptural; the Psalms in particular were central to the life of prayer. In many respects, the Irish monasteries resembled the ideals and practices that developed in the monastic circles in the East and in Gaul. This was particularly true with the heavy emphasis on a life of penance. There was a strong penitential and ascetic element in Irish monasticism, and the monastic life was looked upon as a form of penance. The ultimate manifestation of this life of penance would be the voluntary embracing of exile and perpetual pilgrimage for the sake of Christ. St. Columcille (Columba) was the first great exile for the love of Christ. In 563 he left the monastery he had founded at Derry and established a monastery on the island of Iona. Iona in turn would become a center for learning and missionary activity. In many of the poems attributed to him, St. Columba expresses a longing and a nostalgia for his native land that is very moving.

St. Columbanus (or Columban, and not to be confused with St. Columba above) was the greatest of the Irish missionaries to the Continent. He set out around 589 with twelve other monks from the monastery of Bangor in Ulster and began the great missionary journey that would take him across Europe. Arriving in Burgundy, he founded the monasteries of Annegray, Fontaine and Luxeuil; these Celtic monasteries prospered and became centers of culture and learning with their schools and centers for the evangelization of Gaul. After some years of zealous missionary work, Columban himself was expelled from the Frankish kingdom for his spirit of independence and strong criticism of the royal family. He continued his evangelization of Europe, traveling over the Alps into Swit-

---

[10] *Ibid.*, p. 179 ff.

zerland with St. Gall and other Irish monks. This long and heroic missionary journey ended at Bobbio in Italy. He founded a monastery at Bobbio and remained there until his death in 615. Throughout his travels he founded a number of monasteries, which in turn established others.

Other Irish monks and missionaries followed in St. Columban's footsteps and evangelized Scotland, Wales, Western Gaul, and Spain. Thus, there arose a network of Celtic monasteries throughout Europe that became centers of learning and evangelization for areas that were devastated by barbarian invasions.[11] St. Columban wrote a Rule for Monks (*Regula monachorum*) that was followed in these Celtic monasteries. It was a rigorous and demanding rule and it followed the Celtic liturgical practices rather than the Roman. These monasteries gradually abandoned many of the severe aspects of the rule as well as the Celtic liturgical practice and incorporated aspects from the Rule of St. Benedict. During the seventh and eighth centuries, there was an ever growing tendency for these monasteries to follow a mixed rule that combined aspects from the rules of both St. Columban and St. Benedict.[12]

Some other characteristics of Celtic spirituality should be mentioned briefly.[13] The celebration of Mass was the central act of worship and was solemnly celebrated on Sundays and feast days. The frequent reception of Communion was encouraged. The public prayer of the Office was central to the daily life of the monasteries and carried out with great care and devotion. Private prayer was also nourished by Scripture, particularly the Psalms. The writings of Cassian on prayer were well known and esteemed, and the close

---

[11] Jean Leclercq speaks of this vast missionary activity on the Continent as "The Irish Invasion." See *The Spirituality of the Middle Ages, op. cit.*, p. 31 ff. For a recent account of the Irish contribution to the rebuilding of Europe, see Thomas Cahill, *How the Irish Saved Civilization* (New York: Doubleday, 1995).

[12] For the relationship between these two rules cf. *RB 1980* (Collegeville: The Liturgical Press, 1981), p. 116 ff.

[13] For a fuller development with bibliographical data, cf. O'Laoghaire, *op. cit.* and Ryan, *op. cit.*

connection between prayer and purity of heart was recognized. The many prayers that have come down to us reflect a tender devotion to Christ, the Virgin Mary, and the saints. Many of the prayers were litanic or repetitive in form. The *lorica* (breastplate) prayer was a very popular form, and a number have come down to us in both Latin and Gaelic. The prayer known as the *Lorica of St. Patrick* has always enjoyed a widespread popularity. This long and well-known prayer of invocation begins with the moving words: "I arise today through a mighty strength, the invocation of the Trinity, through belief in the Threeness, through confession of the Oneness towards the Creator."[14]

As noted earlier, there was a strong penitential aspect in Celtic spirituality, and practices of corporal austerity were common, particularly in the monasteries. Fasting was observed, not only during Lent (called the Lent of Jesus), but also during the Lent of Elias in winter and the Lent of Moses after Pentecost. Praying with outstretched arms for long periods was very popular, and the literature often speaks of the practice of standing in cold water while reciting the Psalms. The motivation for such bodily austerities was always found in the love of God.

Another important characteristic of Celtic spirituality was the development of private penance and the confession of devotion. To meet the needs of this popular practice, there sprang up a body of writings known as "penitentials."[15] They were a compilation of sins along with appropriate penances and punishments for transgressions. They were widely used in Ireland itself and then popularized on the continent by the Irish missionaries. Often, the penances would be the opposite of the sin, following the principle of Cassian that contraries are cured by their contraries. For example, the glutton would have to fast and the gossiper keep silence for a period.

---

[14] For the full text see Bieler, *The Works of St. Patrick, op. cit.*, pp. 69-72.

[15] For examples of the Irish penitentials, see The *Irish Penitentials*, edited by L. Bieler (Dublin: Institute for Advanced Studies, 1963).

We read in the penitential of Finnian, abbot of Clonard in the sixth century:

> But, by contraries… let us make haste to cure contraries and to cleanse away these faults from our hearts and introduce heavenly virtues in their place; patience must arise for wrathfulness; kindliness, or the love of God and of one's neighbor, for envy; for detraction, restraint of heart and tongue; for dejection, spiritual joy; for greed, liberality.[16]

Closely connected with private penance and the confession of devotion was the practice of soul-friendship (*anamchardeas*), found both among monks and the laity. It was a form of spiritual direction in which the soul-friend (*anamchara*) assisted another in the growth of a fervent Christian life and that purity of heart that was emphasized in the penitentials. This practice was greatly valued, as attested by the well known maxim, "a person without a soul-friend is a body without a head."

Although the Christian faith was planted in Ireland without martyrdom, the ideal of martyrdom was greatly esteemed in monastic circles; ancient Irish texts expressed it in terms of red, white and green (or blue) martyrdom. "Red" martyrdom, of course, would refer to the actual shedding of one's blood for love of Christ. "White" would represent the first step in renouncing the world, and "green" would entail the practice of exceptional austerity within the monastic life itself. According to one old Irish text, "white martyrdom consists in a man's abandoning everything he loves for God's sake, though he suffer fasting or labor thereat. Green martyrdom consists in this, that by means of fasting and labor he frees himself from his evil desires; or suffers toil in penance and repentance."[17]

---

[16] *Ibid.*, p. 85 (quoted also in O'Laoghaire).

[17] See Ryan *op. cit.*, pp. 197-198.

3. Benedictine Developments

It was not St. Benedict's explicit intention to have his Rule followed by a number of monasteries or to found a particular and separate religious order. However, over the course of many years and due to a number of historical developments as well as a growing recognition of the importance of the rule, the Rule of Benedict (RB) gradually supplanted other monastic rules in the West and became almost the sole norm of Western monasticism.[18] The monks who followed Benedict's ideals and inspiration would have much to do with the rebuilding of Europe and the new Christendom that emerged.

The monastery at Monte Cassino was destroyed during the Lombard invasion somewhere around the year 580. This famous place remained deserted until it was restored about 717. St. Gregory the Great reports in his *Dialogues* that the monks escaped safely, and a later tradition tells us that they took refuge in Rome, bringing the Rule of Benedict with them. St. Gregory knew of the Rule and speaks highly of it in the *Dialogues*, but it is not clear how much of the RB was followed at his monastery of St. Andrew on the Coelian Hill. At any rate, it was from this monastery that Pope Gregory sent St. Augustine of Canterbury and some forty other monks to evangelize England in 596. This mission among the Anglo-Saxons, as well as the other missions that came later, met with great success, leading to the conversion of the Anglo-Saxon kings and their subjects.

The Roman missionary monks were not the first to evangelize England. Monks had come from Gaul in the fifth century, and Irish monks from the monasteries at Iona and Lindisfarne had spread Christianity in Scotland and northern England, establishing monasteries and schools. In time, conflicts developed between the monasteries that followed the Celtic liturgical practices and

---

[18] See *RB 1980, The Rule of St. Benedict*, op. cit., p. 113 ff. See also Edward Cuthbert Butler, *Benedictine Monachism*, 2nd edition (London: Longmans, 1924).

those that followed the Roman practices. Tensions were finally resolved at the Synod of Whitby in 664 when King Oswiu decided in favor of the Roman liturgical usage. Gradually, England became firmly allied to the Roman tradition, and the RB became more and more widely known and observed in monastic circles.[19]

St. Hilda of Whitby (614-680) attests to the important role women played in the early English Church. After embracing the monastic life under St. Aidan's guidance at the age of thirty-three, she became abbess of the monastery at Hartlepool and later founded the double monastery at Whitby in 657, where she was the superior until her death. She was responsible for the training of young scholars, and it was she who recognized and encouraged the ability of Caedmon, the first English Christian poet.

By the end of the seventh century, Anglo-Saxon monks were setting out from England for missionary work in the Low Countries on the Continent. The greatest of these was St. Boniface (680-755), who did so much to evangelize Germany. Like the Irish monks who came before him, the strong desire for the *peregrinatio*, the pilgrimage for the love of Christ, played a strong role in his missionary journeys. From 718 until his martyrdom in 754, he labored heroically, founding churches, monasteries, and schools in Germany, and then working in Gaul for the reform of the Frankish Church. He was greatly assisted in his work by the monks, nuns, and clerics who came from England to share his labors. In organizing the church in Germany, St. Boniface worked closely with the popes in Rome, seeking their authorization, protection and guidance. The monasteries he established became centers of education, learning, and evangelization. St. Lioba and many other nuns were invaluable assistants, particularly through their prayers and the copying of the books for which he had constant need. A number of the Benedictine nuns were active in the monastic schools that were established.

---

[19] For the monastic developments in England and the role played by the Benedictines, see David Knowles, *The Monastic Order in England*, second edition (Cambridge: Cambridge University Press, 1963).

The letters of St. Boniface are a rich source for information about the methods used in the evangelization of Europe and the relations between the missionaries and those who assisted them.

In addition to this missionary work, the Benedictine monasteries contributed greatly to scholarship and learning.[20] The love of learning that developed among the monks led to a cultural renaissance. One of the earliest contributions to the love of scholarship and learning that developed in the monasteries was made by Cassiodorus (c. 485-c. 580). A learned and cultured lay person who had served four Gothic kings, he established a monastery around 540 on his estate at Vivarium in Calabria that was to be a center of prayer and study. Here he built up a library, set up a scriptorium for copying manuscripts, and wrote his *Introduction to Divine and Human Readings (Institutiones)*.

Saint Bede (673-735), traditionally known as the Venerable, is an outstanding example of the monk-scholar. He spent his entire life as a monk at the monastery at Jarrow in England. There is a serenity, joy, and a spirit of deep faith and simplicity that seems to radiate from Bede and his writings. His spirituality was an admirable blending of prayer and study, and the love of God and the love of learning. His written works include scriptural commentaries and various monastic and spiritual treatises very much in the tradition of St. Augustine and St. Gregory the Great. The most famous of his writings is his *Ecclesiastical History of the English People*, a work that is both a rich source for historical information and one that is deeply spiritual.[21]

---

[20] See Jean Leclercq, *The Love of Learning and the Desire for God, op. cit.*

[21] See Bede, *Ecclesiastical History of the English Nation* (London: Dent, 1910). See also the study by M.T.A. Carroll, *The Venerable Bede, His Spiritual Teaching* (Washington: 1946).

4. The Carolingian Renewal[22]

The Carolingian era roughly comprised the hundred year period between the middle of the eighth to the middle of the ninth century. The long reign of Charlemagne (768-814) was central to this time of peace and unity, but the period also included the ruling eras of his predecessor, Pepin the Short, and his son and successor, Louis the Pious. It was a time of order, reform, and fervor that stands out in sharp contrast to the periods before and after it. It was Charlemagne's vision to form a united Frankish empire that would be marked by a strong allegiance to the Christian faith and a return to and renewal of the Roman Empire. Charlemagne himself was crowned Holy Roman Emperor by Pope Leo III in the year 800.

The reforms Charlemagne undertook to revitalize the liturgy and the monastic life led to a literary renaissance and the renewal of classical studies. The monasteries with their schools would play a very important role in this process. A key figure in these educational and literary developments was Alcuin (735-804). He was educated at the monastery of York in England and came in 782 to direct the court school that Charlemagne had set up, assuming responsibility for the curriculum and the teaching. Many of the pupils who studied there brought the fruit of their learning and study to other monastic centers throughout Europe, where they in turn founded schools at their own monasteries. An example of such a pupil was Rabanus Maurus, the future abbot of the monastery at Fulda in Germany.

Since the monasteries were to play such an important role in Charlemagne's plan for the unity and order of his kingdom, he realized that the monasteries themselves had to be centers of genuine spirituality and learning. He himself began this work of monastic reform, but it became a reality only after his death with the work of

---

[22] For an overall treatment of the spirituality of this period, see Jean Leclercq's chapter "The Carolingian Renewal" in *The Spirituality of the Middle Ages, op. cit.,* pp. 68-94.

St. Benedict of Aniane (c. 750-821).[23] Benedict would play a central role in the unification and renewal of the monastic life, and he is often referred to as "the second founder of Benedictinism." He began his work of reform first at his own monastery at Aniane and then, with the support of the new emperor, Louis the Pious, at the monastery called Inde, built near the royal palace. The monastic observance followed at Inde became the model for the reform and unification of the many monasteries throughout the empire, and Benedict was authorized to enforce this standard observance in all the monasteries in France and Germany.

The monastic reforms of St. Benedict of Aniane met with great success. This uniform observance put an end to the "mixed rules" that had developed over the years, and the Rule of Benedict now became the sole monastic rule that was followed in the monasteries in the West. It was not, however, simply a case of returning to the primitive RB. St. Benedict of Aniane recognized the layers of tradition that had become part of monastic observance over the years. His uniform observance incorporated many of them, and we find, for example, the addition of extra liturgical practices and a greater emphasis on the practice of *lectio divina*. To assist him in his work of monastic reform, Benedict drew up the *Codex Regularum*, a collection of the existing Latin rules, and the *Concordia Regularum*, a commentary on the RB. These monastic reforms were codified at the councils held at Aachen under Louis the Pious in 816 and 817. Clear distinctions were drawn up between monks and canons and their religious practices; the *Rule of St. Augustine* was to be followed by the canons and the *Rule of St. Benedict* by the monks.

Although Benedict of Aniane's reforms met with great success, they were not able to withstand the breakdown of the Carolingian empire and the new wave of invasions. When it was possible to rebuild again, however, it was on Benedict of Aniane's foundation that this took place. His place in Benedictine history is an esteemed and valued one.

---

[23] See *RB 1980, The Rule of St. Benedict, op. cit.*, p. 121 ff.

In time, the monks of the great abbeys in Gaul and Germany would become an educated class, and the monasteries would be important centers of culture and learning.[24] Their schools did much to revive a profound knowledge of the Latin language and the patristic and classical literature. The important work of the monks in copying Latin manuscripts did much to preserve the writings of antiquity for future ages. Many of the monks also developed the capacity to write elegant Latin prose and verse. The creative and artistic gifts of many were directed in a special way to calligraphy and the illumination of the texts, particularly the scriptural texts. A number of these large and beautiful Carolingian Bibles have come down to us, and they are recognized as masterpieces of an art that drew its inspiration from a love of the Word of God.

As Jean Leclercq points out, Carolingian piety was marked by two things that were intimately connected: a love of the Bible and a love of the Liturgy. Charlemagne wrote in an encyclical of his in 789: "Many desire to pray well, but because of faulty books they pray badly."[25] In order to remedy this, he set in motion a revision of the Bible in which Alcuin played an important role. The authentic text of St. Jerome was sought in this revision, and once it was completed, this Vulgate text was widely copied and used in the monasteries and churches.

Various commentaries were also written for all classes of people in order to help them to understand Scripture. The writers of these commentaries drew extensively from such earlier Latin writers as St. Jerome, St. Augustine, St. Gregory the Great, St. Isidore, and the Venerable Bede. Origen's scriptural commentaries, as known through the translations of St. Jerome and Rufinus, were an important early source. It was Origen's capacity to draw out the spiritual meaning of Scripture that endeared him to these writers.[26]

---

[24] Cf. Jean Leclercq's chapter "Cult and Culture" in *The Love of Learning and the Desire for God, op. cit.*, pp. 44-56.

[25] See Jean Leclercq, *History, op. cit.*, p. 84.

[26] *Ibid.*, pp. 85-86.

In order to enhance the liturgical celebrations and to bring about a desired uniformity, the Gelasian sacramentaries from Rome were used. Again in this area Alcuin played an important role, for under the direction of Charlemagne, he undertook a revision of the Gelasian sacramentary, missal, and lectionary. With these improved liturgical texts, the public worship was carried out with great beauty and solemnity. New compositions, particularly hymns, were often added to the public worship. Solemn feasts became more numerous with the introduction of the Roman calendar. The life of the clergy to a great extent centered around the Mass and the Divine Office, and they were expected to take part in the daily celebration of the various hours in their churches.[27]

Some other aspects of the spirituality in this Carolingian period can be briefly mentioned. An ascetic spirit was still very much alive, but it tended to be more moderate than it was in earlier, more chaotic times. There was less emphasis on bodily austerities and heroic penances both among the monks and the laity, and more of an interior asceticism and the practice of virtue and good works. All this is reflected in the lives of the saints of the times. The Mass and Holy Communion were at the center of worship and prayer. Collections of prayers, hymns, and verses from the Psalms, all flowing from public prayer, were drawn up for private prayer. In all the devotional literature, the theme of Christ's victory in His redemptive activity was stressed. Devotion to the Blessed Virgin was widespread, and the custom of offering a votive Mass in honor of Our Lady on Saturdays goes back to this time. A doctrine of contemplation developed in monastic circles and, following Cassian and Gregory the Great, it emphasized the theme of purity of heart. For example, in a treatise on prayer by Rabanus Maurus, the abbot of Fulda, the first two books are entitled *De Videndo Deum* (*On Seeing God*) and *De puritate cordis* (*On Purity of Heart*).

Before leaving this period, some mention should be made of John Scotus Eriugena (c. 810-877). He was an Irishman, perhaps a

---

[27] *Ibid.*, p. 87 ff.

monk or cleric, who directed the palace school at the court of the Frankish king, Charles the Bald, in the middle of the ninth century. He was an exception to the main writers and thinkers of this time and more original in his approach, finding his inspiration in the Greek Fathers and Neo-Platonic thought. He translated into Latin some works of Pseudo-Dionysius, St. Maximus the Confessor, and St. Gregory of Nyssa, and wrote commentaries on Pseudo-Dionysius. Thus, he was instrumental in introducing Neo-Platonism to the Christian West; in the development of his own thought, he is very speculative and apophatic. His important work of synthesis is called *Periphyseon,* or *De divisione naturae* in Latin *(The Division of Nature).* The knowledge of God was a key aspect of his thought, and he developed the various degrees of this knowledge — sense, discernment of hidden realities, and an intellectual knowledge that leads to the return to God. Eriugena's subtle and speculative doctrine easily led to misunderstanding, and in the thirteenth century his writings were suspected of pantheism and condemned by the Church. His writings did have an influence on William of St. Thierry in the twelfth century, who modified his intellectualism and integrated it into traditional spirituality.[28]

5. Anarchy and Reform

The renaissance that marked the Carolingian era was not to last. The centralized power that had maintained unity and order collapsed with the strife and division that developed among the sons of Louis the Pious. There were also the renewed wave of invasions, particularly on the part of the Danes and Vikings from the north. As a result, the empire fell into disintegration and chaos, and all sorts of abuses arose. Churches and monasteries fell under secular

---

[28] For a fuller treatment of Eriugena's dialectical mysticism, see Bernard McGinn, *The Growth of Mysticism.* Vol. II of *The Presence of God: A History of Western Christian Mysticism* (New York: Crossroad, 1994), pp. 80-118. See also Leclercq, *History, op. cit.,* pp. 90-94.

control. The Papacy itself was wracked with divisions and scandals. The monasteries that were able to survive were seized by the grasping lords who sought the lands and riches that had accumulated, and monastic life fell into a sorry state. The lives of the clergy were marked by such abuses and vices as simony and widespread failures in celibacy. The light from the Carolingian era was indeed extinguished, and the period between 950 and 1050 was very dark indeed. And yet, elements of reform were never absent throughout these difficult times. With the passage of time, the reforms grew stronger and stronger, reaching their culmination with the so-called "Gregorian reforms" that marked the important papacy of Gregory VII (1073-1085).

As was true in the past, the monasteries manifested their capacity to reform themselves from within. The new revival in monasticism first began with the development of clusters of monasteries that were organized for mutual help and support. They were linked together by their connection to one central reformed monastery, whose observance and spirit they all followed. In this reforming movement of federated monasteries in Europe, there were three great names: Cluny, founded in Burgundy in 910; Gorze, founded in Lorraine in 933; and the older and venerated Monte Cassino in Italy.

The influence of Cluny as a reforming monastery was monumental. This famous abbey was founded in 910 by Duke William of Acquitaine, who wisely set it up with an exemption from all external authority except that of the Holy See. This gave it a freedom to develop and prosper apart from any other secular or ecclesiastical interference or control. The abbey began as a fervent monastery that followed the Rule of Benedict as adapted by the legislation of Benedict of Aniane. Customaries and collections of statutes were drawn up to make particular applications of the RB. The religious observance at Cluny placed a strong emphasis on liturgical prayer. It was regulated carefully and carried out with lengthy and splendid ceremonies. A refined monastic culture emerged from this life of prayer and work, and the ongoing, prayerful study of Scripture and the patristic literature. In the course of its long development,

Cluny had the good fortune to be ruled by a succession of very holy and capable abbots, who often had long terms as the head of the monastery. Abbots such as Odo, Majolus, Odile, Hugh the Great, and Peter the Venerable contributed much to the success of Cluny and Church reform.

The growth in the number of other monasteries that became affiliated with Cluny was rapid and far reaching. These monasteries sprang up in other parts of France, as well as in England, Germany, Italy, and Spain. At the peak of this development, there were over eleven hundred such monasteries. The priors of these dependent monasteries were appointed by the Abbot of Cluny and they remained under his jurisdiction. The customaries of Cluny were sent to all of these houses, uniting them by a common observance and discipline. Thus, there came into existence a Cluniac "order" of monasteries. The positive effects of the so-called Cluniac reform spread beyond the monasteries themselves and contributed to reforms among the clergy and the laity. There would also come from the ranks of the Cluniac monks a number who served the wider Church as legates, cardinals, bishops and popes.

In the latter part of the tenth century, another form of monastic revival and reform came into existence in Italy. This current was Benedictine in its orientation, but it sought greater simplicity and solitude and thus was much more eremitical and austere. St. Romuald (c. 950-1022) was the key figure in this movement. His distinctive contribution to monasticism was to bring an order and regularity into the lives of those who were drawn to a love of solitude and austerity. He drew up a rule for them, adapting the Benedictine rule as much as it could be to the eremitical life. He merits the title of "the father of spiritual hermits, of those who live according to a rule."[29] The wise teaching of St. Romuald provided a solid guide for the many disciples who gathered around him.

It was a teaching that lived on in two congregations of eremitical Benedictine monks. St. Peter Damian (988-1072), a disciple of

---

[29] See Leclercq, *History, op. cit.,* p. 111.

St. Romuald, entered the monastery that St. Romuald founded at
Fonte Avellana in Italy and became the dominant figure there.
When he became superior in 1044, he wrote a rule that helped to
organize the eremitical life in common. He later became a cardinal
and worked zealously for Church reform, especially for the reform
of the diocesan clergy. A very learned and gifted man, he is the author of many works on monastic spirituality and Church reform.
The second eremitical monastic center in Italy, Camaldoli, would
become the motherhouse of the Camaldolese. Although St.
Romuald founded this monastery, it was Blessed Rudolph who at
a later date brought together the traditions inherited from St.
Romuald and wrote the *Constitutions* for the community. It lays
down a program for a contemplative life in solitude that is marked
by prayer, reading, and penitential practices. St. John Gualbert
(990-1073) also lived at Camaldoli before founding a similar monastic group of hermits at Vallambrosa near Florence.

6. The New Orders

The eleventh century saw the emergence of a number of new
religious communities that were very much a part of the reforming
spirit. They sought to meet both the needs of the times and the
hopes and aspirations of many men and women in a way that the
established monasteries could not. As a result of the reforms that
had taken place, the traditional monasteries were again flourishing
in both number and quality. The growth in numbers and land hold-
ings, however, brought with it an inevitable movement towards
greater institutionalism and structures. For increasingly large numbers of fervent and generous people, the traditional monasteries
were not able to satisfy their ascetic desires. These ascetic aspirations were marked by two strong tendencies: a desire for greater
solitude and an attraction for a life of greater poverty and simplicity. It should be kept in mind that towns had frequently grown up
around the traditional monasteries, and even though the individual
monks owned nothing, many of the monasteries themselves had

grown wealthy with the acquisition of large areas of land and other material resources.

This movement towards greater solitude and poverty gave rise to a widespread "eremitical movement" in the latter part of the eleventh century.[30] It was eremitical in the sense that greater solitude was sought. It was a movement in which a large number of women played an extensive role, and this period saw much growth in the monasteries of nuns. In its early stages, it was often marked by laypersons living as hermits, but gradually individuals came together and formed groups and communities. Some of the hermits left their hermitages and became wandering preachers in the countryside and towns. They did not hesitate to speak out against abuses, particularly on the part of the clergy.

Blessed Robert of Arbrissel (c. 1055-1117) was one of the many who combined the austere life of a hermit and itinerant preaching among the people in the towns. His preaching met with great success and attracted many followers, of both men and women. He established for some of them at Fontevrault in 1099 a double monastery of monks and nuns, all under the jurisdiction of the prioress. This must have met a real need of many people, for eventually over a hundred other houses were part of the congregation of Fontevrault. St. Gilbert of Sempringham founded a similar order in England that followed the Benedictine rule.[31]

The second half of the eleventh century and the beginning of the twelfth also saw the rise and growth of the Canons Regular. This movement was one of the results of the Gregorian reform of the clergy, and it incorporated and stabilized many of the best aspects of the "eremitical movement."[32] It developed from various sources and took shape with a variety of forms. Some communities were

---

[30] For a fuller description of this movement, see Leclercq, *History, op. cit.*, p. 129.

[31] For the growth of women religious in England see Sharon K. Elkins, *Holy Women of Twelfth-Century England* (Chapel Hill: University of North Carolina Press, 1988).

[32] *Ibid.*, p. 137. The term "canon" was first given to priests who were appointed members of a cathedral chapter. They were known as secular canons. Among their responsibilities was the singing of the office in the cathedral.

formed by canons attached to a cathedral. Others emerged from the coming together of hermit clerics. Some of the communities of canons were joined by lay men and women, leading in time to the formation of autonomous monasteries for women or double monasteries of canons and nuns.

Although these new communities differed greatly from one another, there were certain characteristics that were shared by all. The basic rule that was followed was the Rule of St. Augustine. There was a strong emphasis on the *vita apostolica* (apostolic life), referring not so much to apostolic activity, but to the renouncing of all property and living in community in a spirit of unity and love. It was a life that was to be modeled on the life of the apostles and the early Christians in Jerusalem as described in the Acts of the Apostles. It was to be a life of prayer, simplicity and humility, lived in common under the superior. Gradually, the various monasteries of the Canons Regular united and formed various congregations such as the Victorines and the Norbertines.

Among the various communities that emerged as part of this canonical movement, the Norbertines or Premonstratensians have an important place. The founder, St. Norbert Gennep (c. 1080-1134), was at first a secular canon in the diocese of Cologne in Germany. After undergoing a conversion experience in 1115, he sought a life of prayer and penance in solitude. As a priest hermit, he later became a very effective itinerant preacher, speaking out against the abuses that were found among the clergy and laity. Later, the bishop of Laon in France asked him to found a monastery in his diocese at Premontré. This monastery grew and flourished under his leadership. After Norbert was made archbishop of Magdeburg in Germany in 1126, he called upon his religious for assistance in the work of reform in his diocese and for missionary work in other parts of Germany.

Like many of the other communities of Canons Regular, the spirituality of the Norbertines reflected the strong desire for solitude and poverty that was so much a part of the reforming spirit of these times. The life was lived in common but away from the towns where there could be greater solitude. There was a strong emphasis on simplicity of life, recollection and interior silence. The practice of poverty was held in high regard and pastoral work would always play a part, even growing more explicit as time went by. The balance that was achieved between the life of the cloister and reaching out in pastoral activity was an original feature of Norbertine spirituality.

Among the new orders, the purest form of the eremitical movement and the quest for solitude would be reached with St. Bruno (c. 1030-1101) and the Carthusians. It would be an order of hermits in which the common life would play only a small part. Bruno had been a teacher at Rheims and then chancellor of the cathedral there before embracing the life of a hermit. After living as a hermit in France for a period, Bruno went with several companions and established a hermitage at Chartreuse in the diocese of Grenoble, more than a thousand feet high in a remote area of the Alps. Living in separate cells they sought God alone in prayer and solitude. Bruno and his companions subsequently left the Chartreuse when Pope Urban II, a former pupil of Bruno at Rheims, called him to Rome to assist him as an advisor. After a few months, all of the monks except Bruno were able to return to Chartreuse. Later in his life, Bruno was able to live the solitary life in Calabria where he died in 1101.

Bruno's example and teaching were followed at the Chartreuse and his spirit continued to inspire others to embrace this lofty but rare vocation to the solitary life in which God alone was sought. The monastic observances that were adopted by St. Bruno and his early companions continued to be followed. They were later written down and codified by Guigo, one of Bruno's successors as prior. Guigo drew up the *Customs* between 1121 and 1128, seeking as he tells us "to lay down wise laws, full of mercy." An avalanche in 1132 that took the lives of seven of the monks forced the survivors to move lower down in the valley where the famous monastery of the Grande Chartreuse remains to the present day.

The most successful of the monastic reforms in the cenobitic tradition was that of the Cistercians. In the year 1098, St. Robert, the abbot of the Benedictine monastery of Molemnes, led a group of his monks into the wilderness area of Citeaux in France. Sharing also in that strong desire for a life of greater solitude and poverty, they were seeking to live the Benedictine rule more simply and perfectly. They sought in the uncultivated area of Citeaux a separation from the world and society that they were not able to achieve at Molemnes. Robert had to return to Molemnes at the direction of the Pope, but the others were able to remain at Citeaux. There they lived the monastic life in a simple and austere manner, first under Robert's successor, St. Alberic, and then under St. Stephen Harding. The foundation flourished, particularly after the great St. Bernard entered in 1112 along with thirty companions. Europe soon was dotted with Cistercian abbeys, and the twelfth century was indeed the golden age of Cistercian monasticism. At the time of Bernard's death there were 343 Cistercian monasteries; at the end of the twelfth century, there were 525.[33]

The organizational structure of the Cistercians contributed to the order's growth and development. During the time St. Stephen Harding was abbot of Citeaux, a document known as the *Carta caritatis* was drawn up to regulate their monastic life. A common observance was carefully carried out in all the autonomous monasteries, but each separate house was subject to some control by the general chapters that met annually and by the visitations of the abbot from the mother house. Simplicity and poverty marked every aspect of the life. This simplicity was found in food, dress, and living quarters, as well as in the celebration of the Liturgy. There was a strong emphasis, too, on manual labor, and in this they were returning to the original vision of St. Benedict. This stress on simplicity and austere living was carried out with a view to a greater spirit of prayer and union with God. A life of contemplative union with

---

[33] For studies on the Cistercians, see Louis J. Lekai, *The Cistercians: Ideals and Reality* (Kent State, Ohio: Kent State University Press, 1977), and Louis Bouyer, *The Cistercian Heritage* (Westminster, MD: Newman Press, 1958). See also Leclercq, *History, op. cit.*, pp. 187-220.

God was highly valued, as the writings of St. Bernard of Clairvaux and the other Cistercian writers of the twelfth century clearly manifest. To safeguard this spirit of contemplative recollection, the Cistercians did not involve themselves in apostolic undertakings or priestly work. With the emphasis on separation from the world and a focusing on the monastic ideal of *God alone*, the eschatological dimension of the Christian life had a prominent place in Cistercian spirituality.

Two other original features of Cistercian life should be briefly mentioned. First, they introduced a class of monks who became known as *conversi* or lay monks. This opened up the monastic life to a different social group, for the *conversi* came mainly from the lower and uneducated classes. They did not spend the hours reciting the Divine Office as the choir monks did. Instead they were more engaged in the tilling of the fields and the other manual work that kept the monasteries functioning. Secondly, the Cistercians also did away with the traditional oblate system, that is the acceptance of children into the monasteries, many of whom later became monks. The Cistericans only accepted those of an adult age into their monasteries.

Before concluding this treatment of the new orders of this time, brief mention should be made of the military orders that sprang up in connection with the Crusades. The Knights Templar and the Hospitallers or Johannites (later known as the Knights of Malta) are the most well known of these groups. The Knights Templar were founded in Jerusalem around 1118. They were attached to the Canons Regular of the Church of the Holy Sepulchre and their purpose was to provide for the safety and protection of the Christians in Jerusalem. St. Bernard wrote a treatise in defense of this new type of religious order, for the Knights Templar were monk-soldiers following a rule of life that was adapted from the established monastic and canonical rules. The Hospitallers were also founded in Jerusalem with the purpose of looking after the hospital of St. John the Baptist. From Jerusalem, the Knights Templar and Knights Hospitallers spread throughout Europe.

7. Spiritual Writers of the Eleventh and Twelfth Centuries

The various reform movements and the new orders that emerged at this time clearly indicate the religious vitality and fervor that was present. This climate fostered a number of important spiritual writers, particularly among the older Benedictine communities and the newly established Cistercians. All of these writers reflect the richness of the monastic tradition and culture that reached its peak in the twelfth century. With the exception of John of Fécamp and St. Anselm who lived in the eleventh century, all of the following writers flourished in the twelfth century.

a. Benedictine Spiritual Writers

John of Fécamp (c. 990-1078) was born in Ravenna in Italy. As a young man he joined the Benedictine abbey at Fruttuaria where his uncle, the great reformer St. William of Volpiano, was abbot. Later, he went with his uncle to the new foundation of St. Benignus at Dijon. In 1017 he became prior of the monastery at Fécamp, not far from the abbey of Bec in Normandy, and then from 1028 until his death he served as abbot of this monastery. In the midst of his many duties as abbot of his own monastery and head of a congregation of abbeys, he brought forth a number of writings on prayer that were very popular during the Middle Ages.

His writings have had a curious history. They were included in the collections that were published in the sixteenth and seventeenth centuries, but under the names of such writers as St. Ambrose, Cassian, Alcuin, St. Anselm and St. Bernard. Recent scholarship has restored John's name to his manuscripts, and he is now recognized as a very important spiritual writer of the early Middle Ages.[34] He is the author of a number of poems, letters, and

---

[34] Dom André Wilmart is responsible for restoring the proper authorship to John of Fécamp. See his *Auteurs Spirituels et textes devots* (Paris, 1952); see also J. Leclercq and J.P. Bonnes, *Un maitre de la vie spirituelle au XIe siecle* (Paris: Vrin, 1946); and Gerard Sitwell, O.S.B., *Spiritual Writers of the Middle Ages* (New York: Hawthorn, 1961), pp. 25-32.

prayers, and the longer works known as the *Confessio theologica*, the *Confessio fidei*, and the *Letter to a Nun*.

John of Fécamp clearly reflects the whole tradition of medieval spirituality that preceded him. Much of it blossoms forth in his writings on contemplative prayer where he illustrates so well the spirituality that grew out of the *lectio divina*. In his most important work, the *Confessio theologica*, John uses the word *confessio* as St. Augustine did, that is addressing God directly in a confession of praise, gratitude and love. He brings together many passages from Scripture, the liturgy, and writers such as Augustine, Gregory the Great and Alcuin to lead the reader to union with God in contemplative prayer. The various texts center around certain themes and are brought together in the form of a continuous prayer. In the following passage from the end of the *Confessio theologica*, John simply but clearly describes the contemplative prayer he has in mind.

> There are many kinds of contemplation in which the soul devoted to Thee, O Christ, takes its delight, but in none of these do I so rejoice as in that which, ignoring all things, directs a simple glance of the untroubled spirit to Thee alone, O God. What peace and rest and joy does the soul find in Thee then. For while my mind yearns for divine contemplation, and meditates, and expresses Thy glory to the best of its ability, the burden of the flesh weighs less heavily upon it; the tumult of thoughts dies down; the weight of mortality and misery no longer exerts its accustomed pressure; all is silent and tranquil. The heart burns within, the spirit rejoices, the memory grows fresh, the intellect clear, and the whole spirit, on fire with longing for the vision of Thy beauty, sees itself carried away to the love of those things which are invisible. And so it is not from any presumptuous boldness, but from a great longing to feel a desire for Thee that I have made this little posy, so that I might always be able to carry about with me a short manual of the word of God, from the reading of which I might rekindle the flame of my love.[35]

---

[35] See Sitwell, *op. cit.*, pp. 27-28.

The method is simple but effective. "Quiet, meditative reading occupies the mind with thoughts about God, the thoughts give rise to acts, to affective prayer, and this may become simplified till it merges into a prayer which is contemplative."[36]

St. Anselm

St. Anselm (1033-1109) is the greatest figure among the Benedictines of the eleventh century. He entered the reform abbey of Notre Dame at Bec in Normandy in 1060, later becoming prior and then abbot. He was the abbot of Bec from 1078 until 1093 and then became the archbishop of Canterbury in England. St. Anselm is known principally for his work as a speculative theologian and philosopher and he was a forerunner of the later scholastic theologians. His theological work on Christ's redemptive activity, *Cur Deus Homo*, was of great significance and influence. He is famous, too, for his "ontological" argument for the existence of God which he developed in his work the *Proslogion*. Yet, he has also made a distinct contribution to the development of medieval spirituality, particularly through his work, *Prayers and Meditations.*[37]

The *Prayers and Meditations*[38] of Anselm was written to help people to pray; many friends had written to him requesting his assistance. He writes in the preface that the purpose of these prayers and meditations is to arouse the reader to a love and fear of God or to self-examination. They should be read slowly and in peace, a little at a time. "The reader should not trouble about reading the whole of any of them, but only as much as by God's help, he finds useful in stirring up his spirit to pray."[39] These prayers, which are very

---

[36] *Ibid.*, p. 28.

[37] For Anselm's spirituality, see Benedicta Ward, "Anselm of Canterbury and His Influence," in *Christian Spirituality: Origins to the Twelfth Century* (New York: Crossroad, 1986), pp. 196-205. See also Leclercq, *History, op. cit.*, pp. 162-166.

[38] For an English translation see *The Prayers and Meditations of St. Anselm with the Proslogion*, translated with an introduction by Benedicta Ward (New York: Penguin Books, 1973).

[39] *Ibid.*, p. 89.

affective in tone, suggest to the readers meditations on Christ, the Mass and Holy Communion, the Virgin Mary, and many of the saints. Anselm's spirituality comes through very clearly in these prayers and meditations, but in all his other writings theology and devotion are closely linked. The speculative work *Proslogion* was written in the form of an extended meditation, and it is introduced by one of Anselm's most beautiful prayers. At the end of this prayer he writes: "I do not seek to understand so that I may believe, but I believe so that I may understand; and what is more, I believe that unless I do believe I shall not understand."[40] And in the "Meditation on Human Redemption," which is a counterpart to the speculative *Cur Deus Homo,* he writes: "I pray you, Lord, make me taste by love what I taste by knowledge; let me know by love what I know by understanding."[41]

St. Hildegard and St. Elisabeth of Schönau

Hildegard of Bingen (1098-1179) attained great fame as a visionary and prophet during her lifetime.[42] Born into a noble family in Germany, she was brought up and educated from the age of eight by the anchorite, Jutta, in a hermitage that was attached to the monastery of St. Disibod. In the course of time, the hermitage became a Benedictine convent of nuns, and it was there that Hildegard as a young woman professed her virginity and received the Benedictine habit. She succeeded Jutta as superior in 1136.

From the age of three, Hildegard was favored with visions that continued all her life. Uneasy and uncertain about these visions, she remained silent about them for many years. In 1141, when

---

[40] *Ibid.* p. 244

[41] *Ibid.*, p. 237.

[42] For background on Hildegard's life and writings, see Sabina Flanagan, *Hildegard of Bingen: A Visionary Life* (London and New York: Routledge, 1989); *Hildegard of Bingen, Mystical Writings,* edited and introduced by Fiona Bowie and Oliver Davies with new translations by Robert Carver (New York: Crossroad, 1992); and Barbara Newman, *Sister of Wisdom, St. Hildegard's Theology of the Feminine* (Berkeley: University of California Press, 1987).

Hildegard was forty-three, an interior voice commanded her to make the visions known. With the support of St. Bernard of Clairvaux (whom she had consulted about the visions), and Archbishop Henry of Mainz, Hildegard received papal support and endorsement from Pope Eugenius. With the help of the monk, Volmar, who acted as her secretary, she began recording her visions and their significance in her most famous work, *Scivias* (*Know the Ways*). From this time, her fame spread far and wide and people from all walks of life sought her prayers and counsel.

Around 1149, Hildegard moved her monastery from St. Disibod to a new foundation at Rupertsberg near Bingen on the Rhine River. At a later date she founded a second monastery at Eibingen across the river, and under her wise leadership both monasteries flourished. In spite of the chronic poor health that was so much a part of her entire life, Hildegard continued her remarkable and varied apostolic work until her death in 1179 at the age of eighty-one. At the age of sixty, she began the first of four missionary tours that furthered the Gregorian reform movement in the Church, preaching publicly at various monasteries and towns in Germany. There was a strong apocalyptic thrust to the preaching of the woman who became known as the "Sibyl of the Rhine."

Among all of Hildegard's remarkable accomplishments, her visionary writings brought her the greatest fame. With the help of her secretary, Volmar, the *Scivias* was composed over the ten year period that followed the mandate she received to made the visions known.[43] It is divided into three books, treating creation, redemption and sanctification. Each book follows the same pattern; Hildegard first records one of the visions in detail and then presents a theological explanation. The work can be looked upon as both a book of allegorical visions and a compendium or summa of Christian doctrine. Thus, it can be truly said of her that she is the first

---

[43] For an English translation of the *Scivias* and some very good introductory material, see *Hildegard of Bingen, Scivias*, translated by Mother Columba Hart and Jane Bishop, introduction by Barbara J. Newman (New York: Paulist Press, 1990).

great woman theologian in Christian history. It should be noted that one of the earliest manuscripts of the *Scivias* from the Rupertsburg monastery was illuminated with thirty-five remarkable illustrations. Two other visionary writings of Hildegard that followed the *Scivias* were *Liber divinorum operum* (*The Book of Divine Works*) and the *Liber vitae meritorum* (*The Book of Life's Merits*).

Hildegard's writings are far from being limited to her visionary works. She authored a scientific study, *The Natural History*, and a medical compendium, *Causes and Cures*, that reflect her creative and inquisitive spirit. She also composed a number of hymns, antiphons, and responsories for the liturgical year that were later collected and published as her *Symphonia*. There is also her musical composition known as the *Ordo virtutum* (*Play of the Virtues*), a morality play that is set to music. This work may well have been performed by the nuns at Rupertsberg at the dedication of their new church in 1152. This musical play has been performed and recorded in recent times. Finally, there are the many *Letters* of Hildegard that show her to be a very wise spiritual director in guiding not only the members of her own religious communities, but also the many people who sought her advice and counsel.

St. Elisabeth of Schönau (1129-1164) has often been linked with Hildegard. A younger contemporary of Hildegard, she also was a German Benedictine visionary.[44] She visited Hildegard, corresponded with her, and knowing her writings, held her in great respect as a spiritual mother. Directed and assisted by her brother Eckbert, a Benedictine monk, Elisabeth recorded her visions in three books. Another work, *Liber viarum Dei*, seems to have been influenced in its format by Hildegard's *Scivias*. Like Hildegard, Elisabeth believed her mission was to work for Church reform, to write letters of spiritual advice and counsel, and to issue apocalyptic warnings. Her life, like that of Hildegard, was also marked by continual attacks of illness.

---

[44] For a recent study see Anne L. Clark, *Elisabeth of Schönau: A Twelfth Century Visionary* (Philadelphia: University of Pennsylvania Press, 1992).

But there were also differences between the two visionaries, particularly in the nature of the visions. Those of Elisabeth took place while she was in ecstasy and were accompanied by extraordinary manifestations. Hildegard's visions took place while she was conscious and not in any dream-like or ecstatic state. The visions of Elisabeth also took place more publicly since they occurred during the celebration of the liturgy. The writings of Elisabeth were more popular than Hildegard's in the later Middle Ages, perhaps because they were less theological in content and more similar to the accounts of the later medieval visionaries.

b. Cistercian Spiritual Writers

Medieval monasticism reached its fullest development in the spirituality of the twelfth-century Cistercians. A number of spiritual writers came forth from this new monastic order and brought to a full flowering the monastic tradition of mysticism that had been developing since the time of St. Augustine and St. Gregory the Great. Among all the Cistercian writers of the twelfth century, St. Bernard, "the last of the Fathers, and not inferior to the earliest," holds the central position. Although there are certainly differences among them, the Cistercian spiritual writers of this period share so many common themes and values that they have often been said to have formed a particular school of spirituality.[45] Here we will focus on three of the greatest Cistercian writers of the twelfth century, St. Bernard of Clairvaux, William of St. Thierry, and Aelred of Rievaulx.

St. Bernard of Clairvaux

Bernard (1090-1153) entered the relatively new Cistercian monastery at Citeaux, along with a number of relatives and friends,

---

[45] Leclercq's chapter on these writers in his history is entitled "The School of Citeaux" (pp. 187-220).

in 1112. Three years later he was sent to establish a new foundation at Clairvaux where he remained as abbot until his death. Over
the course of thirty-five years he made sixty-eight other monastic
foundations from Clairvaux, and so he was very instrumental in the
great growth among the Cistercians at this time. Gradually Bernard
became more and more involved in broader Church issues and affairs, and his fame spread far beyond the monastery of Clairvaux.
As advisor to popes and kings, he worked for years to heal the
schism that took place in the papacy; he participated at various
councils and synods; he preached the second crusade; he became
involved in various theological and ecclesiastical disputes. A man
of great energy and zeal, he emerged as the dominant ecclesiastical
figure for much of the first half of the twelfth century.

Bernard was also a gifted writer. Among all the Latin writers
of the Middle Ages, few could equal him for his elegant style and
capacity to move the reader deeply. In the history of Christian
thought, he is a major spiritual and mystical writer and an important theologian.[46] Most of his writing was done while he was engaged in his various other activities, often as the result of a particular request. His first treatise *The Steps of Humility and Pride* (c.
1124) was written for the monks of his community. This was followed by the other monastic treatises, *On Loving God* and the *Apology to William of St. Thierry* (a defense of the Cistercian against the
Cluniacs). There were also the treatises *On the Conduct and Duties
of Bishops, On Grace and Free Will, To the Knights Templar in Praise
of the New Militia* and *Sermons on the Liturgical Year*. In 1135 Bernard began the *Sermons on the Song of Songs*, his masterpiece that
contains so much of his teaching on mystical prayer. He continued
working on these sermons throughout the rest of his life and they
numbered eighty-six at the time of his death. Later works included

---

[46] For an overall look at Bernard, see the introduction by Jean Leclercq in *Bernard of
Clairvaux, Selected Works*, translation and foreword by G.R. Evans, introduction by Jean
Leclercq, O.S.B. (New York: Paulist Press, 1987), pp. 13-57. For fuller treatments see
Etienne Gilson, *The Mystical Theology of St. Bernard* (London: Sheed and Ward, 1940);
and Bernard McGinn, *The Growth of Mysticism, op. cit.*, 158-224.

the lengthy *Consideration*, which was written for Pope Eugenius III, and the *Life of St. Malachy*, an Irish bishop who died at Clairvaux. Finally, there are the collection of his letters and other sermons that shed so much light on the man himself.[47]

Two points should be kept in mind when considering Bernard's theology and spirituality: the central place that Sacred Scripture has in all his writings; and the important role of experience — both his own and that of the reader. At times in his writings Bernard appeals to his own experience and he frequently urges readers to reflect on their own experiences so that they will be able to grasp his message. He often refers to the "book of experience"; for example, we find him introducing his third *Sermon on the Song of Songs:* "Today we read the book of experience. Let us turn to ourselves and let each of us search his own conscience about what is said."

All of Bernard's teaching flows from Scripture. He sought to explain the book of Sacred Scripture so that it could come alive and resonate in the hearts of his listeners. Following in the footsteps of such earlier writers as Origen and Gregory the Great, he wanted to draw out the hidden meaning from the text that reveals God's love. Tradition has bestowed on him the title "Doctor Mellifluous" because of his deep love for Scripture. As honey is made to flow from the honeycomb, so he sought to draw the deeper meaning from the pages of God's word. If one is to experience the truths of Scripture in one's life, he or she must read the biblical text carefully under God's grace and meditate on it with love.

St. Bernard looked upon the spiritual life as an ongoing return to God. It is a journey that begins with self knowledge and humility and one that can lead to a loving, ecstatic union with God.[48] It is love that moves a person at every stage of the interior journey.

---

[47] Most of Bernard's writings are available in English translation in the Cistercian Fathers Series. See also *Bernard of Clairvaux, Selected Writings, op. cit.*

[48] See Leclercq, *History, op. cit.*, p. 194 ff. and his introduction to *Selected Writings, op. cit.*, p. 35 ff.

Growth in the love of God brings about the restoration of God's image in the human person, the image that has been deformed and darkened by sin. It is a movement from "the land of unlikeness" to the likeness of God.

In *The Steps of Humility and Pride*, Bernard developed the various stages in the growth of humility, a virtue that is so dear to St. Benedict. This must be the foundation for any growth in the love of God. Humility is a knowledge of one's self and one's state of misery apart from God. It is a gift of God that enables a person to recognize the forms of pride and self love that raise a barrier against God. It leads to compunction and a hope and trust in God's mercy; it leads to charity and a compassion for others who share the same human condition; it enables a person to grow in the love of God.

The movement towards greater freedom is intimately connected with growth in the love of God; one must be free to love God. Bernard carefully delineates degrees of this freedom, for greater freedom will lead to a greater capacity to love God. In his treatise *On Loving God*, Bernard also speaks of four degrees of love that describe the soul's progress in the love of God. The first degree is the love of self for the sake of self; the second is the love of God for sake of self; the third degree is the love of God for God's sake; and the final degree is the love of self for God's sake.

In the midst of all his activity, Bernard remained a great contemplative and mystical writer. It is in his masterpiece, the *Sermons on the Song of Songs*, that he eloquently develops his teaching on the mystical union with God. Only a few ideas from his rich thought can be given here. First Bernard emphasizes the role of God's grace and the action of the Holy Spirit. He writes in the first sermon: "Only the touch of the Spirit can inspire a song like this, and only personal experience can unfold its meaning. Let those who are versed in the mystery revel in it; let all others burn with desire rather to attain to this experience than merely to learn about it."[49] In com-

---

[49] *Bernard of Clairvaux — On the Song of Songs I*, trans. by Kilian Walsh, O.C.S.O. (Kalamazoo, MI: Cistercian Publications, 1976), Sermon 1, no. 1.

menting on the opening words of the Song of Songs, "Let him kiss me with the kisses of his mouth," Bernard speaks of a threefold kiss of Christ, of his feet, of his hand, and of his mouth. Although he doesn't use the terms explicitly, Bernard's stages parallel the traditional purgative, illuminative, and unitive ways. The kiss of the feet symbolizes the penitential preparation; the kiss of the hand is given to those making progress; and the kiss of the mouth is a rare experience, given only to the perfect.

Bernard describes this rare stage of union as an interior "visit" of Christ the Bridegroom to the soul, the Bride. There is a very moving description of this mystical visit in the seventy-fourth sermon, where Bernard speaks eloquently from his own experience:

> Now bear with my foolishness a little. I want to tell you of my own experience, as I promised. Not that it is of any importance .... I admit that the Word has also come to me — I speak as a fool — and has come many times. But although he has come to me, I have never been conscious of the moment of his coming. I perceived his presence, I remembered afterwards that he had been with me; sometimes I had a presentiment that he would come, but I was never conscious of his coming or his going. And where he comes from when he visits my soul, and where he goes, and by what means he enters and goes out, I admit that I do not know even now.[50]

Still, these moments of contemplation should lead outwards at times to the service of the Church and others. As Bernard writes: "It is characteristic of true and pure contemplation that when the mind is ardently aglow with God's love, it is sometimes so filled with zeal and the desire to gather to God those who will love him with equal abandon that it gladly foregoes contemplative leisure for the endeavor of preaching."[51]

---

[50] *On the Song of Songs IV*, Sermon 74, no. 5.
[51] *On the Song of Songs III*, Sermon 57, no. 9.

Before leaving this great saint and doctor of the Church, some mention should be made of his devotion to the humanity of Christ. This comes through clearly in his *Sermons on the Liturgical Year*. It is through remembrance and imitation that one grows in knowledge and love of Christ. Reading the Bible with care in a spirit of prayer and reflection is a means of nourishing this devotion. Finally, like all the Cistercian writers that followed him, Bernard had a tender and filial devotion to Mary, the mother of the Lord, a devotion that is reflected in his many Marian sermons.

William of St. Thierry

William of St. Thierry (c. 1095-1148) was born in Liege and entered the Benedictine abbey of St. Nicasius in Rheims. Around 1119 he was elected abbot of the monastery of St. Thierry. Shortly before he became abbot of St. Thierry, he met St. Bernard of Clairvaux and came to admire him greatly. On more than one occasion, beginning in 1124, he sought Bernard's permission to join the Cistercians at Clairvaux, but he was never able to gain his consent. In 1135 he was able to resign as abbot of St. Thierry and he became a monk at the Cistercian abbey of Signy near Rheims, remaining there until his death in 1148.

In was only in the twentieth century that William's importance as a medieval theologian and spiritual writer was rediscovered. Some of his writings were widely read during the later Middle Ages but they were ascribed to St. Bernard. After the Middle Ages, his writings received little attention. Recent scholarship has changed that, and today William is recognized as a theologian and mystical writer of great originality and depth of thought.[52] In his writings, he reflects a broad knowledge of the patristic writers; the influence of St. Augustine and St. Gregory the Great is strong, but he was also

---

[52] Among the important studies on William see J.M. Dechanet, *William of St. Thierry: The Man and His Work*, translated by R. Strachan (Kalamazoo, MI: Cistercian Publications, 1972). See also McGinn, *op. cit.*, 225-274.

influenced by some of the early Eastern writers, particularly Origen and Gregory of Nyssa. His knowledge of the Greek Fathers may account for his interest in the more theoretical aspects of contemplation.

His earliest treatises, *On Contemplating God* and *The Nature and Dignity of Love*, were written during his years as abbot at St. Thierry. His move to the Cistercian abbey at Signy gave him more time for writing and his most important works flow from this period. There he completed his *Meditations* and worked on his important *Exposition on the Song of Songs*. During his early years at Signy he also wrote *The Nature of the Body and Soul, The Making of Man*, and the *Exposition on the Epistle to the Romans*. His two treatises on faith, *Mirror of Faith* and *Enigma of Faith* were written after 1140 and were most likely occasioned by William's involvement in the controversy over the writings of the scholastic theologian, Abelard. A visit to the Carthusian charterhouse at Mont Dieu near Rheims led to the writing of his most popular work, *A Letter to the Brethren at Mont Dieu* (the *Golden Epistle*, as it was later called).[53] At the time of his death, William left unfinished a biography of his esteemed friend, St. Bernard of Clairvaux.

William of St. Thierry's Trinitarian mysticism requires careful study, given its richness and complexity. Only a few aspects can be highlighted here. Like so many of the patristic and monastic authors, William looked upon the spiritual life as a journey and ascent from the region of unlikeness to a greater and greater restoration of the image and likeness of God in the human person. For William, resemblance to God constitutes the whole of the human person's perfection. As Bernard McGinn summarizes, "The way in which we come to regain the *similitudo* or resemblance to God in gradual and imperfect fashion during this life and perfectly in heaven is the whole content of William's mystical theology."[54]

---

[53] Many of William of St. Thierry's writings are available in English translation by Cistercian Publications.

[54] McGinn, *op. cit.*, p. 231.

In the *Golden Epistle*, William speaks of three stages of growth in the soul's ascent to God: the "animal," the "rational," and the "spiritual," corresponding to the beginner, the progressive, and the perfect in the spiritual life. In the same treatise he discusses a three-fold likeness or resemblance to God in the human soul. The first likeness to God is found in the very nature of the human person, and this image of God can be lost only with life itself. The second likeness is one that is freely willed; it is the embracing of a life of virtue by which one becomes more like the Supreme Good. Higher than this is the likeness William calls the "unity of spirit," the unity with God that comes from the indwelling of the Holy Spirit. This likeness to God brings about a mystical experience of the Trinity by which a person shares and experiences the life of the Trinity it-self. It is a loving knowledge of the Triune God that is a foretaste of the beatific vision. In describing the unity of the spirit, William writes: "It makes a person one with God, one spirit, not only with the unity which comes of willing the same thing but with a greater fullness of virtue, as has been said: the inability to will anything else."[55]

Aelred of Rievaulx

Aelred of Rievaulx, an English Cistercian, was born at Hexham in Northumbria around 1109. He spent much of his youth at the Scottish court of King David I. At the age of twenty-four, he entered the newly founded Cistercian abbey at Rievaulx in York-shire, a daughter house of Clairvaux. He was novice master there for a short period and then was elected abbot of Revesby, a foun-dation of Rievaulx. In 1147 he returned to Rievaulx as abbot and wisely and successfully directed this monastery until his death in 1167. He suffered much from poor health and during his last years

---

[55] *William of St. Thierry — The Golden Epistle*, translated by Theodore Berkeley, O.C.S.O. (Kalamazoo, MI: Cistercian Publications, 1971), p. 95.

he was forced to direct the monastery from his infirmary living quarters.

From the biography written by one of his disciples and from his own writings, Aelred emerges as a very warm, compassionate, and beloved person with a great gift for friendship. He has often been referred to as the "Bernard of the North." Although he never matched the breadth of Bernard's accomplishments, there is the same warmth of sentiment in his writings and a wonderful ability to administer and organize. Under his leadership, the monastery at Rievaulx grew rapidly in numbers. Walter Daniel in his *Life of Aelred* writes of Rievaulx under Aelred:

> Was there ever anyone weak in body or character expelled from that house unless his evil ways gave offense to the whole community or ruined his own hope of salvation? Hence there came to Rievaulx from foreign nations and distant lands a stream of monks who needed brotherly mercy and true compassion, and there they found the peace and sanctity without which no man can see God. Yea, those who were restless in the world and to whom no religious house gave entry, coming to Rievaulx the mother of mercy and finding the gates wide open, freely entered therein.[56]

Aelred himself writes in his *Spiritual Friendship* about his walking around his monastery and reflecting: "In that multitude of brethren I found no one whom I did not love, and no one by whom, I felt sure, I was not loved. I was filled with such joy that it surpassed all the delights of this world."[57]

Although Aelred wrote various sermons, prayers and treatises

---

[56] See the edition by F.M. Powicke, *The Life of Aelred of Rievaulx* by Walter Daniel (London: Thomas Nelson, 1963). The above quote is from David Knowles' chapter on Aelred in *Saints and Scholars* (Cambridge: Cambridge University Press, 1962), p. 41.

[57] Aelred of Rievaulx, *Spiritual Friendship*, translated by Mary Eugenia Laker, S.S.N.D. and introduction by Douglass Roby (Kalamazoo, MI: Cistercian Publications, 1977), p. 112.

such as *Jesus at the Age of Twelve* and *A Rule of Life for a Recluse,*
his two major writings are the *Mirror of Charity* and *Spiritual
Friendship.*[58] The *Mirror of Charity* was written at the insistence of
St. Bernard and flowed from the conferences he gave to his novices.
Aelred writes about the spiritual life as a response to God's love,
freely choosing the love of God over the love of self. He also develops the theme so dear to all of the Cistercians of the restoration of
God's image and likeness in the human person, made possible
through Christ's coming. It is with his emphasis on friendship as a
way to God, however, that Aelred has made a distinct and unique
contribution among the monastic writers. Aelred had long been
familiar with the Latin writer Cicero's work on friendship, *De
Amicitia.* He uses that format of dialogue to develop his teaching
on spiritual friendship, a friendship rooted in the love of Christ. He
sees friendship as a gift from God that is realized in Christ. For
Aelred, God is friendship and "he that abides in friendship abides
in God and God in him."[59]

Finally, there is found in the writings of Aelred the same devotion to the humanity of Christ that was so much a part of St.
Bernard's spiritual writings. This is apparent in his treatise *On Jesus
as a Boy of Twelve,* and the treatise he wrote for his sister who was
living as a recluse, *Rule of Life for a Recluse,* has a series of meditations on the life of Christ.

Before leaving these monastic spiritual writings of the twelfth
century, mention should be made of a representative from the
Carthusians, Guigo II. He was the ninth prior of their motherhouse,
the Grande Chartreuse, from 1174-80, and his little treatise, *The
Ladder of Monks,* was one of the most popular of medieval spiritual writings. He brings together a great deal of traditional mate-

---

[58] English translations of both are available in the Cistercian Publications' series. For a recent study on Aelred's thought, see Aelred Squire, *Aelred of Rievaulx: A Study*
(Kalamazoo, MI: Cistercian Publications, 1969). See also McGinn, *op. cit.,* pp. 309-323.

[59] See *Spiritual Friendship, op. cit.,* pp. 65-66.

rial and organizes it in a very readable and creative way. He speaks about four stages in the process of contemplative prayer: reading, meditation, prayer, and contemplation. Each one is a rung on the ladder by which monks are lifted up from earth to heaven. He writes:

> Reading is the careful study of the Scriptures, concentrating all one's powers on it. Meditation is the busy application of the mind to seek with the help of one's own reason for knowledge of hidden truth. Prayer is the heart's devoted turning to God to drive away evil and obtain what is good. Contemplation is when the mind is in some sort lifted up to God and held above itself, so that it tastes the joys of everlasting sweetness.[60]

Developing the metaphor of eating, Guigo likens reading to putting food in the mouth, meditation to chewing it and breaking it up, prayer to extracting the flavor, and contemplation to the sweetness itself which gladdens and refreshes. He illustrates this process by taking the well-known words from Scripture: "Blessed are the pure in heart, for they shall see God."

Conclusion

The period from St. Gregory the Great to St. Bernard of Clairvaux comprises a long period of history. It was a time that was marked by a gradual development of the monastic culture that reached its high point in the writings of St. Bernard in the twelfth century. But the twelfth century was also a time of change and transition that saw the emergence of new developments and trends. It has often been described as a century of renaissance and reawak-

---

[60] See Guigo II, *The Ladder of Monks and Twelve Meditations*, translated with an introduction by Edmund Colledge, O.S.A. and James Walsh, S.J. (Kalamazoo, MI: Cistercian Publications, 1981), p. 68.

ening. On one hand, it brought to a full flowering the earlier traditional forms of Western spirituality, and on the other hand, it ushered in the new developments that built upon the earlier tradition.
In the next chapter we can turn to these new trends and challenges
that began in the twelfth century but look more to the future and
the higher Middle Ages.[61]

For Further Reading

Jean Leclercq, François Vandenbroucke, and Louis Bouyer, *The Spirituality of the Middle Ages*. New York: The Seabury Press, 1968,
pp. 1-220.

Butler, Dom Cuthbert, *Western Mysticism*. 3rd edition. London, 1967.

Dudden, Frederick H., *Gregory the Great: His Place in History and
Thought*. 2 vols. New York: Russell and Russell, 1967.

Leclercq, Jean, O.S.B., *The Love of Learning and the Desire for God*. New
York: Fordham University Press, 1961.

McGinn, Bernard, *The Growth of Mysticism*. Vol. II of *The Presence of
God: A History of Western Christian Mysticism*. New York:
Crossroad, 1994.

Ryan, John, *Irish Monasticism, Origins and Early Development*. New
York: Colgate University Press, 1972.

Sitwell, Gerard, O.S.B., *Spiritual Writers of the Middle Ages*. New York:
Hawthorn Books, 1961.

Bouyer, Louis, *The Cistercian Heritage*. Westminster, MD: Newman,
1958.

Gilson, Etienne, *The Mystical Theology of St. Bernard*. London: Sheed
and Ward, 1940.

Hildegard of Bingen, Scivias. Trans. by Mother Columba Hart and Jane
Bishop. Introduction by Barbara J. Newman. New York: Paulist
Press, 1990.

---

[61] Part Two of *The Spirituality of the Middle Ages* (Leclercq, Vandenbroucke, Bouyer) is
entitled "New Milieux, New Problems."

Bernard of Clairvaux, Selected Works. Translation and Foreword by
G.R. Evans. Introduction by Jean Leclercq, O.S.B. New York:
Paulist Press, 1987.

5 High Middle Ages — New Trends and Currents

1. New Developments

The twelfth century was a time of transition in many respects. A number of new developments took place that came to a flowering in the thirteenth century. The Crusades brought about greater communication between the East and the West. There was the decline of feudal structures and the rise of towns and cities in importance. Gothic cathedrals began to be built in the towns as a symbol of the faith of the people. It was a period that witnessed the emergence of new classes of people with greater possibilities and opportunities available to them. Greek philosophy and literature were rediscovered through Arab contacts. Schools and universities sprang up in the towns and cities and in time replaced the monasteries as centers of learning and scholarship. This century also saw the beginnings of a literature that was written in the vernacular languages of the people. National identities emerged more clearly, and struggles and conflicts intensified between Church and State over rights and jurisdiction. England, for example, witnessed the conflict between Henry II and St. Thomas Becket, Archbishop of Canterbury.

All of these developments contributed to making the twelfth century a period of reawakening. Many writers have referred to it as a time of intellectual renaissance and a growth in humanism. It did not constitute a break with the immediate past in the way that the renaissance of the fifteenth century in Europe did. It was more of a return to the sources of Christianity — the Bible, the Fathers, and the monastic heritage. It is important to note that this spiritual awakening was much more open to the laity than was the case in the earlier Middle Ages that saw spirituality more as the domain of monks and clergy.

The emerging cathedral schools and universities in the cities throughout Europe played a very significant role in this intellectual reawakening. Among the many universities in France, Paris became a major center, and students from all of Europe came there to hear the lectures of Peter Abelard, Peter Lombard, Alan of Lille and others. Universities sprang up in Italy, and Bologna became famous as a center for studies in civil and canon law. In time universities emerged throughout Spain, and Oxford and Cambridge became centers of learning in England. By the thirteenth century these medieval universities were firmly established as the centers for the intellectual life in Europe.

New methods of teaching and study came to the fore, for there was a need to systematize the vast amount of new knowledge that was available. Greek, Arabic, and Jewish writings were now found in Latin translation, thus opening up new sources for study and commentary. These developments led to a new form of theology that was more scientific in approach and method. The theology of the schools, or scholasticism as it came to be called, was greatly influenced by the logic and philosophy of Aristotle. It was more speculative and deductive in character with a strong emphasis on reason and dialectic. It sought to systematize Church doctrine by arranging the "sentences" of the Fathers and theologians around particular questions. Peter Lombard was the forerunner of this method and his famous work, *The Four Books of Sentences*, became the basic textbook for theological teaching in the universities.

This newer theology came to enjoy great success in the twelfth century and would go on to reach a development and flowering in the thirteenth century with the writings of St. Thomas Aquinas and other great medieval theologians. This more scientific and speculative method and approach, however, did bring about a lessening of the close connection that had existed previously between theology and devotion in monastic circles.[1]

2. The Victorine School

The twelfth century witnessed different conceptions and approaches regarding the pursuit of knowledge and theological inquiry.[2] There was first of all the viewpoint favored by the monastic writers and theologians as exemplified by St. Bernard of Clairvaux. It was practical and direct in its approach, more affective in tone and appealing more to the heart. Knowledge was primarily sought in so far as it brought a person closer to God and helped one to live a fuller Christian life. Thus, it was closely connected with the pursuit of eternal salvation. In this approach, theology and spirituality were closely connected.

The second approach was that of the scholastic theologians like Peter Abelard, Peter Lombard, and many of the teachers at the medieval universities. This approach to knowledge was more theoretical and speculative with a strong emphasis on theology as a scientific and intellectual discipline. The pursuit of knowledge in itself claimed more attention than its practical application to the Christian life. This method appealed more to the intellect than to the heart and will.

But there was also an approach which sought to combine both the speculative and affective, and the theoretical and the practical. This was the approach of the theologians of the school of St. Victor and its most famous teachers, Hugh and Richard. This school was more open to the scientific methodology of the new theology than

---

[1]   On this point see Vandenbroucke, p. 225 and 229 in *The Spirituality of the Middle Ages* (Leclercq, Vandenbroucke, Bouyer), vol. II of *A History of Christian Spirituality* (New York: The Seabury Press, 1968).

[2]   For a development of these theological approaches see P. Pourrat, *Christian Spirituality* (Westminster, MD: The Newman Press, 1953), vol. II, pp. 100-104.

were the monastic theologians, but it also shared the goals and aspirations of the earlier spiritual writers. Since the spiritual synthesis achieved by the Victorines had much influence on later spiritual writers, their main contributions should be treated at this point.

The founder of the school of St. Victor was William of Champeaux, a renowned teacher and a friend of St. Bernard. After teaching for many years at the school of Notre Dame in Paris, he retired in 1108 to the hermitage of St. Victor near Paris with some companions. Later the group adopted the Rule of St. Augustine and became established as a congregation of canons regular that rapidly grew in numbers. William resumed his teaching and became the director of a school that was soon famous as a theological and spiritual center. The fame that came to St. Victor's was due primarily to two of its outstanding theologians, Hugh of St. Victor and Richard of St. Victor.

There were certain characteristics that were very much a part of that school's approach to study and the pursuit of knowledge. Following Platonic thought, there was first of all a strong emphasis on the symbolic conception of the world. The Victorines believed that the sensible world hides invisible realities. The whole of creation is like a book that contains the teachings of God. Because of Christ's Incarnation and His redemptive activity, human beings can perceive the invisible reality that is hidden in sensible things. This is particularly true of Sacred Scripture, and the deeper meaning of the text can be found through spiritual interpretation. As Pourrat writes: "Since the material world as a whole is looked upon as a discourse of the Word, each being of which is a word, the task of the mystic then is to discover the eternal truths which God has willed each thing to express."[3]

For the Victorines, one discovers the mind of God in created beings through intuitive meditation and contemplation. It is through contemplation that we arrive at truth; it is mystical theol-

---

[3] *Ibid.*, p. 113.

ogy, far more than speculative or abstract theology, that brings us to the knowledge of God. In all of their writings on contemplation, the Victorines reflect the strong influence of St. Augustine. They also did much to bring the writings of Pseudo-Dionysius into the mainstream of Western theological and mystical thought.

Hugh of St. Victor

Very little is known about Hugh's life before he entered the community at St. Victor's somewhere around 1120. He succeeded William of Champeaux as the director of the school and flourished as its renowned teacher until his death in 1141. He was a man of vast learning and a prolific author who excelled as a synthesizer. His interests and writings included works of philosophy, biblical exegesis, theology, and contemplation. He was very much in the tradition of the Fathers and the monastic writers, and he became known in history as "the second Augustine." In keeping with this tradition, his theological thought is clearly Christocentric, ecclesial, and sacramental. His major writings include the *Didascalicon*, a work of biblical interpretation in which he relates the three senses of Scripture (literal, allegorical, and tropological or moral) to the study of history, theology, and contemplation; his theological summa, *De sacramentis christianae fidei* (*The Mysteries of the Christian Faith*); and his two writings on contemplation that highlight the use of Noah's ark as a symbol, *Noah's Moral Ark* and *Noah's Mystical Ark*. For Hugh there were no divisions between learning, study, and contemplation.

Hugh's writings on contemplation comprise a vast and somewhat complex synthesis; here only a few points will be mentioned.[4] He sees the spiritual life as a return to God that is made possible through Christ's work of redemption and restoration. It is an ascent to God through knowledge and virtue that reaches its climax

---

[4] For a fuller treatment see Bernard McGinn, *The Growth of Mysticism* (New York: Crossroad, 1994), pp. 375-395.

in the experience of contemplation. For Hugh, Noah's ark is a structural symbol of the stages of this return to God and the unfolding of sacred history. He also speaks of five steps or stages of this ascent to perfection (God): reading, meditation, prayer, growth in charity and virtue, and the final step of loving contemplation. Since all created things are the means through which God makes his thoughts known, we must read them carefully and examine them attentively. The second step, meditation, enables the seeker to discover the divine thought in the written word of Scripture or that which is veiled beneath the sensible images. Since God's grace is constantly needed in this ascent, prayer must follow this meditation. But the seeking of truth requires moral purification as well as intellectual activity and so there must be the ongoing practice of love and growth in virtue. The goal is loving contemplation in which the soul is enkindled with the flames of divine love. As he writes in the *Didascalicon*: "First, reading gives understanding; second, meditation provides counsel; third, prayer makes petition; fourth, performance seeks; fifth, contemplation finds."[5]

To illustrate the various steps of this ascent, Hugh makes use of the metaphor of green wood burning in a fire. He writes in the first homily on Ecclesiastes:

> Our carnal heart is like green wood; it is still soaked with the moisture of concupiscence. If it receive some spark of the fear of God or of divine love the smoke of evil desires and rebellious passions first of all arises. Then the soul becomes strengthened, the flame of love becomes more ardent and more bright, and soon the smoke of passion disappears, and the mind, thus purified, is lifted up to the contemplation of truth. Finally, when by constant contemplation the heart has become penetrated with truth, when it has attained to the very source of the sovereign truth in all its ardor, when it has been kindled by it, and when it has become transformed into the fire of divine love it feels neither distress nor

---

[5] *Didascalicon* 5.9; quoted in McGinn, p. 374.

agitation any more. It has found tranquillity and peace.

Thus, at the beginning, when, in the midst of danger-
ous temptations, the soul seeks enlightenment in meditation, there is the smoke and flame. Afterwards, when it is
purified and begins to contemplate the truth, there is flame
without smoke. Then, when it has fully found the truth and
charity is perfected within it, it has no longer anything to
seek; it rests sweetly in the tranquillity and in the fire of divine love.[6]

Although Hugh carefully laid the framework for this mystical ascent, he did not write at any great length on the nature of contemplation. This was done by his disciple, Richard, who focused
much of his attention on contemplation itself.

Richard of St. Victor

Richard seems to have been born in Scotland but very little is
known of his early life. He entered the abbey of St. Victor in the early
1150's and followed in the footsteps of Hugh whom he referred to
as "the best theologian of our time." He held positions of responsibility at the abbey, serving first as subprior and then as prior until
his death in 1173. Through his teaching, preaching, and writing,
Richard made a very significant contribution to the Victorine tradition of contemplation (mystical theology).

Although Richard was the author of the creative theological
treatise *De Trinitate* (*On the Trinity*), it was as a mystical writer that
he received his greatest acclaim by subsequent generations, for he
was one of the first to develop a systematic treatment of the mystical ascent to God.[7] His two major works on contemplation are *The*

---

[6] Quoted in Pourrat, *op. cit.*, p. 119.

[7] For fuller developments of Richard's thought, see the introduction by Grover A. Zinn
in *Richard of St. Victor, The Twelve Patriarchs, The Mystical Ark, Book Three of the
Trinity,* translation and introduction by Grover A. Zinn (New York: Paulist Press, 1979),
pp. 1-49; and McGinn, *op. cit.*, pp. 398-421.

Twelve Patriarchs (also known as *Benjamin Minor*) and *The Mystical Ark* (also known as *Benjamin Major*). These mystical writings are fed by the texts of Sacred Scripture. Richard made extensive use of biblical persons and events to express the various states and stages of the contemplative experience. He presented them as symbolic expressions of his teaching, interpreting Scripture in a spiritual and tropological (moral) sense.

In *The Twelve Patriarchs*, Richard concentrates on the preparation for contemplation. He realized that the mystical ascent required a growth in moderation and virtue, and an interior quiet that can only take place after the mind and body have been disciplined and brought into harmony. The patriarch, Jacob, his wives and twelve sons became symbols for his teaching of this preparation. For example, Jacob symbolizes the rational soul and his wives, Rachel and Leah, represent the principal powers of the soul — reason and affection. The sons that are born symbolize the various virtues and the different stages of the preparation for contemplation. The son, Joseph, symbolizes discretion or full self-knowledge, and Richard provides careful and perceptive instruction about its importance, for it involves a person in the art of guiding oneself wisely. The youngest son, Benjamin, symbolizes ecstatic contemplation itself. Actually Richard begins *The Twelve Patriarchs* with the words: "Benjamin, a young man in ecstasy of mind" (Ps 67:28, Vulgate). After the birth of the last son, Benjamin, Richard introduces the symbol of the transfiguration of Jesus.

In *The Mystical Ark*, Richard focuses on the nature of contemplation itself. For Richard, "contemplation is the free, more penetrating gaze of a mind, suspended with wonder concerning manifestations of wisdom" (1,4). He also defines it as "a penetrating and free gaze of a soul extended everywhere in perceiving things" (1,4).[8] For his teaching here he makes use of the Ark of the Covenant and the two accompanying seraphim (Exodus, chapter 25) as symbolic representations of the different degrees of contem-

---

[8]   Richard of St. Victor, *op. cit.*, p. 157.

plation. Richard carefully analyzes six degrees of contemplation that are ordered according to the way in which the object of contemplation is known. After developing these six degrees or kinds of contemplation, Richard goes on to develop three different *modes* by which the quality of contemplation may vary. They are: (1) enlarging of the mind; (2) raising of the mind; and (3) alienation of the mind or ecstasy. Again biblical figures such as Abraham, Elijah, the Queen of Sheba, Moses and St. Peter are given as personifications and examples of the different modes of the contemplative experience.

Richard of St. Victor was not only a major spiritual writer of the twelfth century but also a person whose influence was significant on many subsequent mystical writers. For example, Dante in his *Paradiso* 11:32 speaks of him as being "in contemplation more than human." St. Bonaventure in the thirteenth century held Richard in high regard. Richard's influence can be found in Bonaventure's *Itinerarium mentis in Deum* (*The Journey of the Mind into God*), on the anonymous fourteenth century author of *The Cloud of Unknowing*, and such later works as the *Ascent of Mount Sion* by the sixteenth century Spanish writer, Bernadino de Laredo.

Before leaving the Victorines, some mention should be made of a later Victorine, Thomas Gallus (d. 1246). Thomas was a member of the community at the abbey of St. Victor early in the thirteenth century. He left in 1219 to assist in the founding of the Victorine monastery of St. Andrew at Vercelli in Italy and later became its first abbot. He wrote a number of scriptural commentaries that expounded his mystical theology including one on the Canticle of Canticles. Following Hugh of St. Victor, he was greatly attracted to the writings of Pseudo-Dionysius and he wrote a number of commentaries explaining and developing his mystical thought. In his commentaries Thomas emphasized the Areopagite's theme of "the divine darkness" and his apophatic theology. The writings of Thomas Gallus did much to make the mystical theology of Pseudo-Dionysius known to later mystical writers, especially the Rhineland mystics of the fourteenth century.

3. Lay Spirituality in the Twelfth Century[9]

Popular piety in the twelfth century was deeply influenced by the Bible. For many of the laity there was a strong attraction to the reading of the Scriptures, particularly the Gospels. This interest was focused to a great extent on the literal and historical meaning of the biblical text. This trend, along with the awakened consciousness of the Holy Land that the Crusades brought, led to a strong and tender devotion to the sacred humanity of Christ. There was present both in the monasteries and among the laity a strong interest in the various aspects of Christ's historical life, especially the suffering he endured in his passion and death. This was reflected in the religious art of the time as well as the popular mystery plays and liturgical dramas that began to emerge and develop. This period also witnessed a growing devotion to the name of Jesus. The well-known hymn *Jesu dulcis memoria*, written by an English Cistercian of the twelfth century, did much to further a tender love of Christ and the veneration of his holy name.

This devotion to Christ led to a stronger veneration of the Blessed Sacrament. Confraternities of the Blessed Sacrament sprang up among the laity to further this Eucharistic devotion. The practice of the elevation of the sacred host during Mass was introduced at this time, and there was present a strong desire to gaze upon the elevated host with an ardent love and desire. Often certain prayers were said at the time of the elevation of the host. It seems that the act of looking replaced that of eating because the receiving of Holy Communion became infrequent. Other factors played a part such as a sense of unworthiness and a consciousness of sin, but the practice of infrequent communion became so widespread that the Fourth Lateran Council of 1215 made it a matter of obligation to receive Holy Communion during the Easter season. The practice

---

[9] In this section I am following the treatment found in Vandenbroucke, *op. cit.*, pp. 243-282.

of devotional confession, however, became more and more general at this time.

The popularity of devotion to the humanity of Christ also led to a renewed devotion to Mary, a practice that was based on her unique role in Christ's life and his redemptive activity. This increasing devotion to Mary can be seen in the artistic works of the time and the great cathedrals and countless smaller churches and chapels dedicated to her. These witnessed to the strong desire to seek her assistance and protection. Popular prayers to Mary also became widespread in the twelfth century. This was especially true of the *Ave Maria* (the first half) and its themes were developed in a number of popular hymns. The *Salve Regina, Ave, Maris Stella,* and *Alma Redemptoris,* hymns that are still used in the Breviary today, were very well known at this time.

Popular piety at this time was also characterized by a strong devotional attraction to the saints and angels. Towns, labor guilds, and various other groups and places had patron saints, and their intercession and assistance were constantly sought by the people. The popularity of such saints as St. Martin of Tours, St. John the Baptist, and St. Michael the Archangel was widespread while that of others was more localized. Biographies of the saints continued to be written. Paintings, stained-glass windows, and other artistic works also depicted various scenes from the lives of saints and the miracles attributed to them. Relics of the saints were eagerly sought and the tombs of such saints as St. James at Compostela in Spain and St. Thomas Becket at Canterbury in England became very popular places for pilgrimages. The process for the canonization of saints became more carefully regulated in the twelfth century, and the popes began to reserve the official process to themselves. It should be noted that there was also a strong element of superstition present in the popular devotion to the saints. Along with the many healthy and legitimate elements of the veneration of the saints, there were also mingled a number of superstitious concerns and practices.

This period was also characterized by the strong desire expressed by many to live the gospel in a purer and simpler way. This desire was nourished by an ardent devotion to Christ and the attraction to imitate the simplicity and poverty of his life more closely. This led to popular reactions against the clerics and religious who were not living up to these ideals. Many writers of this period denounced the vices of the clergy and vehemently criticized Church leaders for being too closely connected with the ruling and wealthy classes. In this climate of reaction and unrest, a number of small groups sprang up that sought to live a more evangelical way of life. The desire for a life of greater poverty was a common strand among the various groups. These groups, generally speaking, moved in two directions: first, there were those who would be instruments of renewal and reform while remaining orthodox and united with the institutional Church, such as the Mendicants of the thirteenth century; secondly, there were other groups who joined a political and social unrest to their religious unrest and gradually drifted into schism and heresy. Included in this latter group were the Arnoldi, the followers of Arnold of Brescia, and those who were led by Hugo Speroni. There were also such evangelical groups as the "Poor Men of Lyons" or the Waldensians founded by Peter Waldo, and the Lombards in Italy. Another formidable group was the Cathari, who revived the Eastern dualistic heresy of Manichaeanism in the West. They were particularly strong in the diocese of Albi in southern France and thus were also known as the Albigensians. They were suppressed only after many years of violence and bloody warfare.[10]

Joachim of Fiore (c. 1130-1202) did much to popularize an apocalyptic and spiritual vision of history within a Trinitarian framework, thus looking to the future rather than the past. He entered the Cistercian abbey at Corazzo in Calabria and later became its abbot. He left the Cistercians with papal approval around 1192 and founded the monastery of San Giovanni in Fiore also in Calabria. This new monastic Order soon had many daughter houses. Joachim was a seer who looked to the future with apocalyptic expectations. The main thrust of his spirituality was a "Trinitar-

---

[10] For further information on these groups see Vandenbroucke, *op. cit.*, pp. 261-264.

ian conception" of the world. He spoke of a new age to come, the age of the Holy Spirit. This would succeed the age of the Son (post New Testament) which had previously succeeded the age of the Father (the Old Testament). He described this final age of the Spirit in apocalyptic terms, for he found in the biblical book of the Apocalypse the promise of the new age of the Spirit. A spiritual Church under the leadership of "spiritual men" would take the place of the visible Church then present. The active life would be absorbed by the contemplative life, wars would cease, and universal love would reign.

In his lifetime, Joachim was greatly esteemed and regarded as a holy and devout monk by his contemporaries. Before his death he publicly submitted his writings for papal judgment but died before any decision was made. After his death, his teaching spread in many directions, often on a popular level, and his followers became known as Joachimites. Some of these subsequent currents went beyond his own thought, adding various other apocalyptic ideas of a more extreme and bizarre nature.

The twelfth century also saw a renewed interest on the part of many to seek a life of holiness in solitude. There was nothing new of course in this way of life, for the eremitic life had been lived by individuals since ancient times. What was new was some of the forms it began to take at this time as well as its popularity among lay persons. Some first lived the cenobitic life in an established monastery and then lived as hermits near that particular monastery. Others had no monastic connection and took up an independent form of solitude from the beginning and lived in greater isolation. Many women lived the solitary life as anchoresses or recluses. They lived in reclusion in cells which were attached to churches. A number of rules or directives were gradually drawn up to regulate the life of the recluses. The most famous one was written in England and is now known as the *Ancrene Riwle* or the *Ancrene Wisse*.[11] This

---

[11] For a modern translation of this text and a good introduction to the anchoritic life, see *Anchoritic Spirituality, Ancrene Wisse and Associated Works,* translated and introduced by Anne Savage and Nicholas Watson (New York: Paulist Press, 1991).

is a guide for anchoresses that contains many observations concerning the anchoritic life as well as rules and observances for daily living and words of advice and encouragement for this demanding vocation. After an introduction in which the gospels are stressed, the eight sections deal with devotional practices, custody of the outer and inner senses, temptations, confession, penance, love, and the external rules. In general, the ascetic side of the anchoress' life is stressed rather than the pursuit of contemplative prayer. The love of God is expressed primarily through a life of penance in imitation of the suffering Christ.

The practice of chivalry also came to have its own religious character in the twelfth century. The knight's vocation came to be regarded as a sacred one. Before taking up arms, he was blessed during a religious ceremony. Confession, communion, and sometimes a vigil of prayer preceded the knight's "dubbing," that is the blessing of his weapons and his investiture. With these arms he was to defend himself and the weak and protect the Church against its enemies. The rise of "courtly love" at this time was connected with chivalry. A new attitude towards women was marked by a code of politeness, purity, fidelity, and "courtesy." A body of literature that focused on the romances of chivalry came into existence such as the *Quest of the Holy Grail* and the *Romance of the Rose*. This, too, was the age of the troubadours, the lyric poets and musicians, and they flourished particularly in southern France.[12]

4. The Rise of the Mendicants

With all this change, turmoil and unrest of the twelfth century, the Church faced huge problems and challenges. Both the clergy and the monks were in need of much reform, and the lives of ordinary Christians were marked more by ignorance and superstition than any vibrant knowledge of the faith. There was a particu-

---

[12] See Vandenbroucke, *op. cit.*, pp. 277-282.

lar need for orthodox preachers to go among the people in the towns and bring to them the good news of the gospel message. But if these heralds of the gospel were to be effective in any lasting way, they would have to give clear witness to the poverty and simplicity of Christ in their own lives. As a providential answer to these great needs, the thirteenth century witnessed the birth of the two influential mendicant orders, the Franciscans and the Dominicans. Their religious thrust would be marked by service to the Church and the evangelical practice of poverty.[13]

a. The Franciscans — Franciscan Spirituality

The life and story of St. Francis of Assisi (c. 1182-1226) is one that easily touches the minds and hearts of all Christians. His appeal has been great for both Catholics and Protestants alike, for he has the capacity to bring people to Christ and the gospel message in a special way. It is a story that has been told many times, and many biographies of the "Poverello" have come down to us. A number of legends and traditions have also become attached to his life, so it is not always easy to draw a completely accurate account of his inspiring life.[14] But it is his life that is the source and inspiration for Franciscan life and spirituality and one that bears repeating. The writings of Francis are not extensive but what is available is significant. Among his writings are the *First Rule*, the *Later Rule*, his final *Testament*, and various letters, prayers and words of encouragement.[15]

---

[13] Here we will focus on the Franciscans and the Dominicans. For a treatment of two other mendicant orders see the essays in *Christian Spirituality, High Middle Ages and Reformation*, edited by Jill Raitt (New York: Crossroad, 1989) by Keith Egan, "The Spirituality of the Carmelites," pp. 50-62, and Adolara Zumkeller, "The Spirituality of the Augustinians," pp. 63-74.

[14] For a recent and significant biography of Francis, see Raoul Manselli, *St. Francis of Assisi*, trans. by Paul Duggan (Chicago: Franciscan Herald Pess, 1988). For some of the challenges for the biographer, see Vandenbroucke, *op. cit.*, pp. 285-287.

[15] See Francis of Assisi and Clare of Assisi, *Francis and Clare: The Complete Works*, translated by Regis Armstrong and Ignatius Brady (New York: Paulist Press, 1982).

Francis' father was a prosperous merchant in Assisi and his mother was from a distinguished French family. As a young man Francis took part in a drawn out war between the towns of Assisi and neighboring Perugia and in one of the battles he was taken prisoner. When peace was restored, he returned as a sick man to Assisi, and his recuperation became the occasion for the beginning of his conversion experience. After his return from a pilgrimage to Rome, he embraced a poor and penitential life and was drawn to work among the lepers. He writes of this early experience in his *Testament*, which he composed shortly before his death:

> The Lord granted me, Brother Francis, to begin to do penance in this way: While I was in sin, it seemed very bitter to me to see lepers. And the Lord himself led me among them and I had mercy upon them. And when I left them that which seemed bitter to me was changed into sweetness of soul and body; and afterward I lingered a little and left the world.[16]

He also began the practice of rebuilding churches in the vicinity that were in need of repair. He was led in this direction after hearing the words spoken to him from the Byzantine crucifix at the little chapel of San Damiano: "Francis, see to the repair of my house, which is falling into ruin."

These events led to both a public break with his father, who was concerned about his son's seemingly eccentric behavior, and the renunciation on Francis' part of all his possessions. For the next two or three years he continued the work of restoring churches, begging for the material he used and for his other basic needs. While attending Mass one day at the little chapel of St. Mary of the Angels (the Portiuncula), he heard the words from Matthew's Gospel (10:9-11) that spoke of Christ's instructions to his disciples as he sent them on their missionary journey. These words spoke to his heart and he came to realize that his mission was not to rebuild churches but to

---

[16] *Ibid.*, p. 154.

rebuild the Church itself through the proclamation of the gospel and the witness of a poor and simple life.

Francis' preaching attracted other "brothers" to join him in his simple and penitential way of life. When the number reached twelve, he drew up the first rule (no longer extant) that was approved orally by Pope Innocent III. The twelve received the tonsure and were given permission to preach. In spite of this papal approval and encouragement, the brothers encountered initial suspicion because in their poverty and apostolic endeavors they resembled many of the heretical penitential groups that had sprung up all over Italy. But in his rule Francis makes it very clear that he expected his followers to be faithful members of the Church and to observe humble obedience to those having legitimate authority. This love and devotion to the Church soon became evident in their daily lives.

The numbers expanded rapidly. Clare, a member of a patrician family in Assisi, was deeply moved by the vision and preaching of Francis. At the age of eighteen, St. Clare (c. 1193-1253) received the religious habit in 1212 at the Portiuncula, which had now become the center of Franciscan life. Francis provided Clare with a preliminary rule for her way of life and she took up residence at San Damiano where she lived a life of prayer, poverty and penance for the next forty-two years. Many disciples came to join her and the "Poor Ladies" of Assisi thus came into existence. Throughout her long and holy life, Clare did much to preserve the Franciscan ideal of poverty. The preaching of Francis and the other friars also led to a penitential movement among the laity that later developed into the Franciscan third order.

Francis had a strong desire to spread his preaching of the gospel to the Moslem world, and he made three unsuccessful attempts during the course of his life. During his third absence in the East in 1219, those left in charge of the growing numbers introduced changes that were foreign to the primitive spirit. These included such innovations as the provision for study, various practices of discipline, and the building of churches and convents. These changes seemed to be demanded by the new organizational structures that the larger numbers now required. What was appropriate at first for a small band now appeared problematic for the larger numbers. Upon his return from the East, Francis asked Pope Honorius III to appoint a Cardinal protector for the Order. Shortly afterwards Francis turned much of the actual leadership over to other friars, although he continued to work on a revision of the rule. General chapters met regularly to provide direction and stability for the growing Order. For example, the chapter held in 1219, known as the "chapter of mats," was attended by three thousand friars. The chapter that met in 1221 approved and promulgated a revision of the first rule of 1209 or 1210. The definitive rule was drawn up in 1223 and approved by Pope Honorius III on November 29, 1223.

With his health rapidly declining, Francis continued to give himself to the spiritual growth of the Order through circular letters and other writings of encouragement, while also devoting himself to prayer, preaching, and penance. On September 14, 1224 he received the stigmata while in solitary prayer on the mountain of Alvernia (La Verna), the first documented case of a person receiving the imprints of the wounds of the Crucified Christ. In 1226, at a time of increasing sickness and blindness, Francis composed at San Damiano his beautiful poem of praise of God's creation, the *Canticle of the Sun*. Death came to the Poverello on October 3, 1226 at his beloved Portiuncula, the Church of St. Mary of the Angels. Scarcely two years after his death, Pope Gregory IX enrolled him among the saints, confirming what had been recognized by the *vox populi* during Francis' lifetime.

The gospel vision of Francis would have a lasting influence. His own life was marked by an openness to God and a spirit of freedom that allowed God's word to take deep root in his heart and flourish in a dramatic and inspiring way. His eyes were always focused on Christ, the Incarnate Word, and His mission of salvation. Francis in turn led his followers to the Cross and altar to see the Victim of love, or to nature to see the many traces of God's goodness, majesty, and love. He always emphasized the joy and dignity of their vocations as children of God and brothers and sisters in

Christ to one another. Above all he sought to bring them to a simple, childlike acceptance and fulfillment of the Gospel in their lives and a sincere imitation of the poor, humble and suffering Christ. A life of poverty was the means to free a person for a life of greater love and service of the Lord.[17]

In spite of the tensions that developed after Francis' death between the observance of the primitive spirit and the need for adaptation and evolution as the order expanded, and the divisions that took place over the interpretation of poverty, Francis' spirit and legacy remained very much alive.[18] The prayer long associated with St. Francis' name sums up this spirit so well:

> Lord, make me an instrument of your peace.
> Where there is hatred, let me sow love;
> Where there is injury, pardon;
> Where there is doubt, faith;
> Where there is despair, hope;
> Where there is darkness, light;
> and where there is sadness, joy.
> O Divine Master, grant that I may not so much seek
> to be consoled as to console;
> to be understood as to understand;
> to be loved as to love;
> For it is in giving that we receive;
> It is in pardoning that we are pardoned;
> And it is in dying that we are born to eternal life.

---

[17] See Thomas M. Gannon, S.J. and George W. Traub, S.J., *The Desert and the City* (New York: The Macmillan Company, 1969), p. 89.

[18] For these historical developments, see Cajetan Esser, *Origins of the Franciscan Order*, trans., by Aedan Daly and Trini Lynch (Chicago: Franciscan Herald Press, 1970); and John R.H. Moorman, *A History of the Franciscan Order: From its Origins to the Year 1517* (London: Oxford University Press, 1968).

Franciscan Theologians and Mystics

With the constant growth of the Order, the Franciscans soon branched out into the area of study and scholarship, and there emerged in time such notable theologians as Alexander of Hales, St. Anthony of Padua, Roger Bacon, and John Duns Scotus. Among all the medieval Franciscan theologians, St. Bonaventure holds a special place.

St. Bonaventure (c. 1217-1274) was born in the small town of Bagnoregio in central Italy, about sixty miles north of Rome. At the age of seventeen he went to study at the University of Paris where he came in contact with the Franciscans who were already established there. He entered the Franciscans in 1243, and after further studies under such teachers as the renowned Alexander of Hales, he began lecturing. He continued teaching at the Franciscan school in Paris until he was elected the Minister General of the Order in 1257. For the next seventeen years he led the Order in a critical time of growth, succeeding in the difficult task of remaining faithful to the ideals of Francis while at the same time allowing for the adaptations that the growing and evolving Order required. For example, he did not find any radical conflict between learning and study and Franciscan simplicity. Bonaventure was named cardinal bishop of Albano in 1273 and began assisting Pope Gregory X in the preparations for the Second Council of Lyons. In the midst of his active participation at the council itself, he died on July 15, 1274.

In spite of his many administrative duties, Bonaventure's writings are extensive, assuring him a place among the outstanding theologians of the Middle Ages. He follows in the tradition of Pseudo-Dionysius, Augustine, Bernard, and the Victorines, but he also clearly reflects his Franciscan heritage. In his writings he emerges as an outstanding synthesizer of the spiritual life. It can be said that he accomplished in his synthesis of spirituality what St. Thomas Aquinas accomplished for theology. Bonaventure's major works include his systematic account of the contemplative ascent to God, the *Itinerarium mentis ad Deum (The Soul's Journey into*

God); *De triplici via* (*The Triple Way*), his study of the three stages of spiritual growth — purgation, illumination, and perfection (union); *The Tree of Life*, a devotional meditation on the life of Christ that closely follows the gospel accounts; and two biographies of St. Francis of Assisi. There are other mystical works such *The Fire of the Love, The Six Wings of the Seraph,* and *The Mystical Vine.*[19]

In the prologue to his masterpiece, *The Soul's Journey into God,* Bonaventure narrates the source of the book's format. He retired one day in prayer to La Verna, the place where Francis received the stigmata. While meditating on Francis' vision of the six-winged Seraph in the form of the Crucified, he "saw at once that this vision represented our father's rapture in contemplation and the road by which this rapture is reached."[20] For Bonaventure, the six wings of the Seraph symbolized the six steps or stages that begin with creatures and lead up to God. It is only through the love of the Crucified Jesus that one can take this journey. He devotes a chapter to each one of the six stages of the journey and the seventh and final chapter focuses on the final stage of ecstasy. The soul progressively ascends and contemplates God through His vestiges in the universe, in His vestiges in the sense world, in His image in the natural faculties of the soul and then those faculties reformed by grace. The soul then contemplates God as Being and the Good before passing over into the final stage of mystical ecstasy.[21]

Jacopone da Todi (c. 1230-1306) was one of the many Franciscan friars who were inspired by the writings of Bonaventure to compose their own mystical works. After the tragic death of his wife and a conversion experience, he became first a Third Order Franciscan and then entered the Friars Minor in 1278. As a Franciscan

---

[19] For a good representation of St. Bonaventure's writings, see *Bonaventure, The Soul's Journey Into God, The Tree of Life, The Life of St. Francis,* translation and introduction by Ewert Cousins (New York: Paulist Press, 1978).

[20] *Ibid.,* p. 54.

[21] For a development of these points and other aspects of Bonaventure's thought see the introduction by Ewert Cousin, *ibid.,* pp. 1-48.

he was associated with the Spirituals, the Franciscans who favored a strict interpretation of the observance of poverty, and he was also imprisoned for a number of years for his part in the rebellion against the election of Pope Boniface VIII. His mystical poetry is marked by an intense and moving love of Christ and a strong desire to be united with his suffering and humiliation. There is also a paradoxical combination of fierceness and austerity and gentle sweetness. "Love, Love Jesus" is a constant refrain in his ardent religious poetry. He is particularly known for his work of mystical poetry, *The Lauds*.[22] The *Stabat Mater* is the best known hymn from this work and it is still found today in the Roman missal.

Among the Franciscan mystics, Blessed Angela of Foligno (c. 1248-1309) has a distinctive place. As a widow she became a Franciscan tertiary, that is a layperson affiliated with the Order who sought to follow the Franciscan spirit in a penitential way of life inspired by the poor and suffering Christ. She lived as an anchoress near the Franciscan church at Foligno. Her mystical experiences flowed from her intense meditations on the passion of Christ. She dictated her mystical visions to her Franciscan confessor, and they have been preserved as the *Memorial* and the *Instructions*.[23]

Blessed Raymond Lull (1232-1316) was also a Franciscan tertiary. Born in Majorca, his early life was that of a worldly troubadour, but after a conversion experience that was marked by a vision of the crucified Christ, he became Christ's troubadour and the "Fool of Love." Much of his life was devoted to Christian-Moslem dialogue and an attempt to find a synthesis of Christian and Islamic theological thought. A strong desire to convert Moslems led to his preaching among them and ultimately to martyrdom at the hands of North African Moors late in his life. He wrote a number of books on mystical prayer, following Bonaventure's format of the ascent of the soul to God. In his *Art of Contemplation*, he writes about a

[22] For a recent English edition see *Jacopone da Todi, The Lauds*, translated by Serge and Elizabeth Hughes (New York: Paulist Press, 1982).

[23] See *Angela of Foligno, Complete Works*, trans. with intro. by Paul Lachance, O.F.M. (New York: Paulist Press, 1993).

method of contemplation that involves the methodical application of the three powers of the soul — memory, understanding, and will, a method that perhaps influenced St. Ignatius of Loyola two centuries later. His most famous work, the tender and devotional *Book of the Lover and the Beloved*, attained great popularity in the Middle Ages. He writes in no. 97:

> They asked the Lover… "Where do you come from?" "From Love." "Where are you going?" "To love." "Where do you live?" "In love." "Have you anything except love?" "Yes," he answered, "I have faults, and I have sins against my Beloved." "Is there pardon in your Beloved?" "Yes," answered the Lover, "in my Beloved there is mercy and justice, and therefore I am lodged between fear and hope."[24]

b. The Dominicans — Dominican Spirituality[25]

St. Dominic Guzman (c. 1173-1221) was the founder of the Dominicans (Order of Preachers). Like the Franciscans they adopted a poor and simple lifestyle and placed an even stronger emphasis on the ministry of preaching. Dominic was born in Castile in Spain and after receiving a solid education and preparing himself for the clerical life, he entered the cathedral chapter at Osma as an Augustinian canon. He later became subprior. Between the years 1203 and 1206, he made two journeys to Denmark with Bishop Diego of Osma on missions for the king. During the course of these journeys, both men became acutely aware of the inroads of heresy in the southern part of France and the great needs of the Church there.

---

[24] Ramon Lull, *The Book of the Lover and Beloved*, ed. by Kenneth Leech, trans. by W. Allison Peers (London: Sheldon Press, 1978), p. 37.

[25] See *Early Dominicans, Selected Writings*, edited with an introduction by Simon Tugwell, O.P. (New York: Paulist Press, 1982); and William A. Hinnebusch, O.P., *The History of the Dominican Order*, 2 volumes (New York: Alba House, 1973).

While returning from the second mission to Denmark in June of 1206, Dominic and Bishop Diego had a decisive meeting with the three Cistercians who led the papal delegation for the preaching mission among the Albigensians (Catharists). The legates were discouraged at their lack of success in their missionary endeavors. Bishop Diego suggested that they change their approach entirely and go about their work of preaching to the heretics as poor men begging for their bread, thus imitating the original preaching mission of the apostles. This was put into effect and with it the seed for the future Order of Friar Preachers was planted.

Dominic continued preaching in this manner in southern France while Bishop Diego returned to his diocese to recruit more missionary preachers. His death shortly after his return to Spain left Dominic to carry on this dynamic movement that had come into being. This he did for the next few years in spite of the obstacles created after 1209 by the Albigensian Crusade. In 1215 Dominic took up residence in Toulouse with a small band of companions at the invitation of its bishop. Bishop Fulk had sought out their help in fulfilling his responsibilities of teaching and preaching in his diocese. In that same year Dominic accompanied Bishop Fulk to Rome and sought papal approval for his band as a religious community of preachers. After adopting the Rule of St. Augustine, in accordance with the recent stipulation of the Fourth Lateran Council (1215) that new religious orders must adopt an existing rule, the new community was definitively approved by Pope Honorius III on December 22, 1216. To supplement the Rule of St. Augustine, Dominic had drawn up a *Book of Customs* that were based on the *Institutiones* of the Premonstratensians.

Even though the numbers at Toulouse were still relatively small, Dominic broadened his vision and in 1217 took the decisive step of disbanding the group and sending the friars on missions to various places. Thus the Order spread and expanded, first to such centers as Paris, Bologna, Madrid, and Rome, and then to all parts of Europe. Dominic had only four more years to live, but it was a period filled with many journeys and labors, all the while encouraging and inspiring the apostolic work of the friars. He directed the growth and expansion of the Order and set it on a firm structural basis. General chapters were held to assist him in the organizing of the Order and the formation of houses and provinces. Houses were also established for women, and Dominic continued to devote himself with great apostolic zeal to the ministry of preaching. Worn out by his many labors, Dominic died in Bologna on August 6, 1221, greatly loved and esteemed by the family he had left behind to carry out his vision. He was canonized in 1234 by Pope Gregory IX.

Right from the beginning, the apostolic thrust of the Dominicans was clear. They were an Order founded for the sake of preaching and the salvation of souls. Dominic's vision was inspired, as was that of Francis of Assisi, by the same missionary text found in Matthew 10 and Luke 10. Dominic was responding to the great needs of the Church at the time, and thus preaching was to be at the very heart of the Dominican vocation and mission. Poverty was an essential element in this ministry of preaching, for the follower of Dominic was to be a poor preacher. However, since it was understood from the beginning that the practice of poverty was always subject to the primacy of apostolic preaching, subsequent Dominican history did not have the conflicts and divisions over the practice of poverty that took place among the Franciscans. The unity of the Order in the apostolic work of preaching was also built on the vow of obedience that each preacher made to Dominic or his successors.

A life of ongoing study was also at the heart of Dominican spirituality, for the preaching of the friar was to be nourished by a firm grasp of doctrinal teaching. Each Dominican house was to be a house of study with a resident lecturer in theology. Ongoing study for the Dominican preacher took the place of the traditional manual labor of the monks, and for the sake of study, dispensations were possible from canonical prayer. And yet there was to be a contemplative dimension to the life of the Dominican. The friar was to bring forth and communicate, through his preaching and teaching, the fruit of his own contemplative study and prayer. It should be noted that from this stress on prayer and study there developed the Dominican tradition of the ministry of spiritual direction.

As early as 1217 Dominic sent some of his disciples from Toulouse to study at the University of Paris. A year later a house was opened at Bologna, the other great university center. Soon Dominicans were very much a part of university life as students and professors. Two of the most outstanding examples were the scholar-saints, St. Albert the Great (c. 1206-1280) and St. Thomas Aquinas.[26]

St. Thomas Aquinas (1225-1274) was born in Rocca Secca, near Monte Cassino in Italy. His early education was at the famous Benedictine Abbey of Monte Cassino where his family hoped he would ultimately enter and possibly become its abbot. In spite of family objections, he joined the Dominicans in Naples around 1244 after studying philosophy at the university there. His early years as a friar were spent at Paris and Cologne studying under Albert the Great, and then after further studies at Paris, he began his own teaching career. He was involved in study, teaching and writing for the rest of his life, either at Paris or Naples where he had set up a *studium generale* for the Dominican Order. He fell sick on his way to assist at the Council of Lyons and died at the Cistercian monastery of Fossanova between Naples and Rome on March 7, 1274. His life was so productive that it can be truly said that few men in history have been able to look back on so fruitful and holy a life.

Thomas' written legacy is a vast one, comparable to that of his teacher, Albert the Great. He has left works in such areas as philosophy, systematic theology, moral theology, and scriptural exegesis. In works like his *Summa Theologica*, he reveals himself as a creative, powerful, and original thinker. He did much to develop the scholastic method, incorporating and applying much of the thought of the Greek philosopher, Aristotle, to his work of synthesizing the Christian faith. His teaching on the relationship between faith and reason has had much influence on subsequent thinkers. He had great confidence in the power of the human intellect, and his

---

[26] For helpful introductions to both Albert and Thomas and a good selection of their writings (particularly Thomas) see *Albert and Thomas, Selected Writings*, translated, edited, and introduced by Simon Tugwell, O.P. (New York: Paulist Press, 1988).

thought is definitely marked by an approach that acknowledges the primacy of the intellect over the will. Thomas' teaching in such areas as Christian perfection, grace, the role of charity, contemplation and its relation to action, the theological virtues and the gifts of the Holy Spirit have been carefully and thoroughly studied.

Before leaving this treatment of these two main orders, the Dominicans and Franciscans, one difference in approach should be noted. The Franciscans did not follow St. Thomas and the Dominicans in emphasizing the primacy of the intellect. Following St. Augustine and St. Bernard, they favored the approach that highlighted the primacy of love in contemplation. Union with God was expressed more in terms of loving possession and enjoyment than in terms of understanding. It is a question more of emphasis than opposition but as time went on, the difference came more and more to the fore.[27]

The diverging approaches over the above question did not prevent the Franciscans and Dominicans from uniting to defend themselves against the objections raised by the secular masters at the University of Paris. A sharp controversy took place between 1252 and 1270 over questions of religious observances and states of perfection. In 1252 William of St. Armour, a secular priest and professor at the University of Paris, vehemently attacked the relatively new orders over their practice of poverty and their religious observances that departed from some traditional monastic forms. Both St. Bonaventure and St. Thomas Aquinas wrote treatises in defense of mendicant practices. Later the disputes focused on the question of states of perfection with particular reference to the lives of bishops, parish priests, and vowed religious. St. Thomas Aquinas played an important role in these discussions and he made a number of careful distinctions in his writings.[28]

---

[27] See Vandenbroucke, *op. cit.*, pp. 334-336. There is an interesting passage in Thomas Merton's autobiography where he reflects on the comment of his teacher and friend, Dan Walsh, that his bent of mind was more Augustinian than Thomistic. See *The Seven Storey Mountain* (New York: Signet Books, 1952), pp. 216-217.

[28] See Vandenbroucke, pp. 336-343.

5. The Beguine Movement

The thirteenth century witnessed the continuation of the desire that was expressed so strongly in the twelfth century on the part of many people to live the life of the gospel as fully as possible, but not as part of the traditional monastic life. The reforms that came forth from the Fourth Lateran Council of 1215 greatly helped to nourish and enhance the religious and moral lives of the people. A number of religious writings in both Latin and the vernacular languages became available. Didactic in intent, they did much to lessen the widespread ignorance of Christian doctrine and to bring about in both the clergy and laity a more vibrant knowledge of the faith. They contained instructions on such areas as the creed, the commandments, the virtues, prayer, and devotional practices.[29]

Devotion to the humanity of Christ and to Mary continued to be a strong part of popular piety. This was also true for devotion to the saints, and the lives of the saints and the miracle stories connected with them became the material for popular religious dramas and plays. Pilgrimages to the sanctuaries of many well-known saints also took on an added importance. Popular piety was also nourished in many ways by the Bible. This was particularly true of the various artistic forms. The churches and cathedrals with their paintings, works of sculpture, and the stained glass windows that depicted so much from the Bible, contributed a great deal to the nourishing of the faith in the lives of the people. In this regard they have often been referred to as "pictorial Bibles" or "the Bibles of the poor."

The heretical and anti-clerical groups that came to life in the twelfth century continued to exist in the thirteenth century, but in general this period did not see any newer groups emerging. The new mendicant orders helped to bring about more stability and more of a spiritual equilibrium. The friars were able to mix with the laity much more than the monks and so their influence on popular piety

---

[29] For a fuller development of this popular piety in the thirteenth century see *ibid.*, p. 344 ff.

was much greater. The growth of the Franciscan and Dominican third orders among the laity also were positive influences. The tendency to form spiritual groups that shared a common life and engaged in some charitable work continued to be very popular among the clergy and laity. Among these groups the Beguines (women) and Begherds (men) were the most prominent. Since the Beguines were the much larger group and comprised a much more significant movement, the focus here will be on this women's group.

The origins of the Beguines are somewhat complex.[30] There was no particular founder nor any particular rule that they all followed. It is not even clear how they came to be called Beguines; it may have come from the color of the habits that they wore. The Beguines emerged as a spiritual movement of women at the end of the twelfth century in the Low Countries of northern Europe and the neighboring areas of the Rhineland and northern France. They sought to live a devout and evangelical life in a newer and different form than the traditional life of women religious up to this time. The movement seemed to meet the needs of both those who were unable to enter the existing communities of religious women for various reasons, and those who wanted to live a religious life in a less institutionalized and regulated form.

The Beguines usually lived around a church in one of the towns that was serviced by the mendicants. In general, their way of life took two forms: those who lived individually and those who lived a more communal life in a house that came to be referred to as a beguinage. Their lives were marked by a simple and poor lifestyle and a tender and strong devotion to the humanity of Christ. The motive for their penitential lifestyle was the desire to imitate Christ. They met at the church for prayers and devotions at fixed times. They did not take any perpetual vows but they made a promise of chastity for as long as they stayed at the beguinage. A promise of

---

[30] The classic study in English is that of Ernest McDonnell, *The Beguines and Begherds in Medieval Culture: With Special Emphasis on the Belgian Scene* (New Brunswick, NJ: Rutgers University Press, 1954). See also the essay by Philip Sheldrake, "Context and Conflicts: The Beguines" in his *Spirituality and History* (New York: Crossroad, 1992), pp. 133-159.

obedience was made to follow the statutes of the house and to the mistress of the house. A poor life was held in great esteem and each Beguine normally supported herself by some manual work, usually the work of sewing, spinning, and weaving that was part of the growing textile industry of the day. Some cared for the sick and elderly or taught young children. Mutual support was a central element in their lives. The Beguines were free at any time to depart from the beguinage either to return to their former way of life or to marry. Thus, there was a certain flexibility and mobility to the Beguine vocation. As time went on, however, the beguinages in some places grew quite large and even formed independent parishes in enclosed quarters of the town, thus taking on a more formalized and institutionalized existence.

Gradually the Beguines came under increasing criticism and suspicion in many quarters. On one hand they did not quite fit in with the normal structures for religious women. They could be looked upon as a group of lay women seeking a serious living out of the gospel or as a semi-religious Order of women. Often Church authorities were uncomfortable with their more informal status, for the Beguines looked and lived like religious women but were not canonically established as such and thus did not fall under the usual ecclesiastical control. Suspicions of heresy among some of them also arose. Things came to a head with the condemnation of the Beguines and Begherds at the Council of Vienne in 1311-12. It appears that some of them were identified with the heretical group known as the Brethren of the Free Spirit. The Council of Vienne did add a clause that stated that the censure only applied to the Beguines who were actually guilty of the errors condemned. There was also the well-known case of Marguerite Porete, a Beguine who was burned at the stake as a heretic in Paris in 1310. She was the author of *The Mirror of Simple Souls*, a work that continued to survive anonymously after her death in monasteries and convents.[31]

---

[31] See *Marguerite Porete, The Mirror of Simple Souls*, translated and introduced by Ellen L. Babinsky (New York: Paulist Press, 1993).

Beguine Mystics

Beguine life and spirituality gave birth to a number of mystics and mystical writings.[32] This mystical trend was inspired by a tender devotion to Christ and the Eucharist. It was expressed in the language of spiritual marriage and has been called bridal or love mysticism (*brautmystik* or *minnemystik*). Among the finest representatives from the Beguines were Mary of Oignies, Beatrice of Nazareth, Hadewijch of Antwerp, and Mechthild of Magdeburg.

The life of Mary of Oignies (d. 1213) was written by Jacques de Vitry, an Augustinian canon and later cardinal who was greatly impressed by the holiness of her life. Mary was one of the originators of the Beguine movement and the account of her life provides us with important information about its beginnings and spirituality.

Beatrice of Nazareth (1200-1268) was taught by the Beguines before becoming a Cistercian nun. She died as prioress of the monastery of Our Lady of Nazareth at Lierre, near Antwerp. The connection between the Beguines and the Cistercian nuns was always a very close one. Although Beatrice composed a number of works during her lifetime, the only one that has come down to us is her treatise, the *Seven Degrees of Love*, one of the first writings on mysticism that was written in a vernacular language. [33] She traces the steps or degrees that move from purification and the lower forms of love to the union of eternal Love.

Mechthild of Magdeburg (c 1212-c.1297) lived as a Beguine for some forty years before becoming a Cistercian nun at the famous monastery at Helfta around the year 1270. It was at the age of twelve that she began to experience the visions that played such an impor-

---

[32] On this subject see Emilie Zum Brunn and Georgette Epiney-Burgard, *Women Mystics in Medieval Europe* (New York: Paragon House, 1989), and *Beguine Spirituality, Mystical Writings of Mechthild of Magdeburg, Beatrice of Nazareth, and Hadewijch of Brabant*, edited and introduced by Fiona Bowie, translated by Oliver Davies (New York: Crossroad, 1990).

[33] A complete English translation of this work can be found in E. Colledge, *Medieval Netherlands Religious Literature* (New York: 1965).

tant role in her life. Her main work, *The Flowing Light of the God-head* gives an account of these visions. This work is very much in the tradition of the bridal mysticism and often expresses imagery from the courtly love tradition.[34] She was very outspoken in her criticism of the failures and abuses in the lives of the clergy and religious, and this resulted in opposition against her on the part of Church authorities. This most likely precipitated her move to the Cistercian monastery at Helfta in her later years.

Very little is known about Hadewijch who lived in the thirteenth century and was very much in the tradition of love or bridal mysticism in her written works of visions, letters and poems.[35] The return to God is described in the language of love and spiritual marriage. The desire for God and the love of God is expressed in poetic language of great joy and anguish. She probably was a Flemish Beguine and is thought to have been mistress of a Beguine convent. Her writings were lost for a number of years and only rediscovered in the nineteenth century. They were well known by John Ruusbroec in the fourteenth century who found much inspiration in them.

Although Hadewijch is clearly in the tradition of bridal or love mysticism, there are some traces in her writings of what is referred to as "essence mysticism." As we shall see a little later, this is a theme that will be greatly developed by the Rhineland mystics of the fourteenth century. This tradition speaks of the return to God in terms of the restoring of God's image in the human person by an essential union in which the soul recovers its lost likeness. The union with God is described in intellectual and speculative language that emphasizes a spiritual emptying and nakedness. This theme is more explicit in the poetry of a later writer of the fourteenth century who

---

[34] For a complete English translation see L. Menzies, *The Revelations of Mechthild of Magdeburg* or *The Flowing Light of the Godhead* (London: Longman, Green and Co., 1953).

[35] For an English translation of her writings see *Hadewijch, The Complete Works*, translation and introduction by Mother Columba Hart, O.S.B. (New York: Paulist Press, 1980).

was also known as Hadewijch. This second Hadewijch probably was a Flemish Beguine who may have been influenced by the writings of Meister Eckhart.[36]

6. The Mystics of Helfta

The convent at Helfta in Saxony, Germany had among its members a number of saintly women whose writings had a great influence on Christian life during the high Middle Ages.[37] The convent was first founded at Mansfeld in 1228, moved to Rossbach in 1234, and then to Helfta in 1258. Under the leadership of Abbess Gertrude of Hackeborn (1251-1292), Helfta became a very prayerful and observant convent and an important center for study, learning, and mysticism. The community followed the Cistercian constitutions although it was not officially attached to the Order. The Dominicans from Halle provided spiritual direction for the nuns. In their writings the Helfta mystics were very much in the tradition of bridal mysticism. Nourished by an ongoing liturgical life centered around the Eucharist, the mystics expressed in the accounts of their visions and revelations their bridal relationship and their mystical union with Christ. The spirituality of Helfta was also characterized by a strong devotion to the Sacred Heart.

As noted earlier, Mechthild of Magdeburg, the author of *The Flowing Light of the Godhead*, entered Helfta in 1270 after living many years as a Beguine. There she joined the two younger mystics, Mechthild of Hackeborn and Gertrude the Great. Mechthild of Hackeborn (c. 1241-1299) was the younger sister of the abbess, Gertrude of Hackeborn. She has left us an account of her revela-

---

[36] For an example of her poetry with its stress on the theme of spiritual emptiness and nakedness, see Vandenbroucke, *op. cit.*, pp. 362-363.

[37] For a study of the Helfta mystics see Caroline Walker Bynum's "Women Mystics in the Thirteenth Century: The Case of the Nuns of Helfta" in *Jesus as Mother, Studies in the Spirituality of the High Middle Ages* (Berkeley: University of California Press, 1982), pp. 170-262.

tions in the work, *The Book of Special Grace*, and did much to further devotion to the Sacred Heart. The most famous of the Helfta mystics was Gertrude the Great (1256-1301 or 1302). Her first mystical experience when she was twenty-five was a profound moment of conversion. It was for her a vibrant encounter with Christ and a deep realization of the love that bound them. Her two main writings are the seven meditations known as *Spiritual Exercises* and the account of her revelations, *The Herald of Divine Love*.[38] Gertrude was a very gifted and intelligent woman and her writings reflect the Scriptures that she knew so well and the liturgy that was so much a part of her life. As was true of her contemporary, Mechthild of Hackeborn, her strong Christocentric perspective found expression in devotion to the Sacred Heart.

7. Dante: A Mystical Poet

Some mention of Dante Alighieri (1265-1321) should be made before leaving this particular period.[39] His place as one of the greatest poets of all times is assured with his masterpiece, the *Divine Comedy*. He brought together in this great work so much of the best in medieval Christian life and thought. He was one of the most learned laymen of his day and someone who played a very active role in the political, social, and ecclesiastical affairs of his time. His last years were spent in exile from his beloved city of Florence, and it was during these years of wandering and hardship that he completed the *Divine Comedy*. It is a creative synthesis of Christian thought and a work through the medium of poetry that is comparable to the theological and spiritual *summas* of St. Thomas Aquinas and St. Bonaventure.

---

[38] See *Gertrude of Helfta, The Herald of Divine Love*, translated and edited by Margaret Winkworth and introduced by Sister Maximilian Marnau (New York: Paulist Press, 1993).

[39] See Vandenbroucke, *op. cit.*, pp. 364-372.

The *Divine Comedy* is above all a mystical work. The influence of St. Augustine, St. Bernard, and Richard of St. Victor are apparent. As Vandenbroucke writes: "The important thing to note is the doctrine that emerges from this great work. It is impregnated with mysticism; it is impossible to understand the *Divine Comedy*, and especially the *Paradiso*, if that is not realized at once."[40] It is the coherent narrative of the ascent of the human person from darkness to God. Basing his journey on a vision that came to him, the Poet passes through three stages to the vision of the Holy Trinity. In his ascent through the stages of hell, purgatory, and heaven, he is led successively by the famous Latin poet, Virgil, the inspired love of his early life, Beatrice, and the great contemplative, St. Bernard of Clairvaux.

Conclusion

With all the new developments in the universities and the towns, the unique contributions of the Victorines, the lively spiritual currents among the laity, the rise of the mendicants, and the flourishing movements of women mystics, the twelfth and thirteenth centuries were indeed vibrant and productive periods in the history of Christian spirituality. This would not continue, however, into the fourteenth century. This century would witness such a gradual decline and even a stagnation in so many areas that the vibrancy and excitement of the high Middle Ages would soon give way to a mood of somberness and pessimism. But this would also be a period that saw the birth of a very significant mystical movement, particularly in the Rhineland. It is to this strong mystical current and to the other spiritual movements of the late Middle Ages that we will turn next.

[*Ibid.*, p. 365.

For Further Reading

Jean Leclercq, François Vandenbroucke, and Louis Bouyer, *The Spirituality of the Middle Ages*. New York: The Seabury Press, 1968, pp. 221-372.

Christian Spirituality, High Middle Ages and Reformation. Edited by Jill Raitt. New York: Crossroad, 1989.

P. Pourrat, *Christian Spirituality*. Westminster, MD: The Newman Press, 1953. Vol. II, pp. 79-195.

Richard of St. Victor, *The Twelve Patriarchs, The Mystical Ark, Book Three of the Trinity*. Translation and Introduction by Grover A. Zinn. New York: Paulist Press, 1979.

Francis and Clare, *The Complete Works*. Translation and Introduction by Regis J. Armstong, O.F.M. Cap. and Ignatius Brady, O.F.M. New York: Paulist Press, 1982.

Bonaventure, *The Soul's Journey Into God, The Tree of Life, The Life of St. Francis*. Translation and Introduction by Ewert Cousins. New York: Paulist Press, 1978.

Early Dominicans, Selected Writings. Edited with an Introduction by Simon Tugwell, O.P. New York: Paulist Press, 1982.

Ernest McDonnell, *The Beguines and Begherds in Medieval Culture: With Special Emphasis on the Belgian Scene*. New Brunswick, NJ: Rutgers University Press, 1954.

Emilie Zum Brunn and Georgette Epiney-Burgard, *Women Mystics in Medieval Europe*. New York: Paragon House, 1989.

Hadewijch, *The Complete Works*. Translation and Introduction by Mother Columba Hart, O.S.B. New York: Paulist Press, 1980.

6   *Late Middle Ages*

1. Darkening Times

A number of factors contributed to the somber and even pessimistic climate of the fourteenth century. The Great Plague that swept through Europe at this time certainly looms large. This terrible plague reached its high point in the years 1348 and 1349 and it caused havoc at all levels of society. It is estimated that one third of the population living between India and Iceland perished before this disaster finally subsided and left a devastated Europe that was slow to recover. It was also a period of drawn out warfare. England and France were locked in that long and bitter struggle that is known historically as the Hundred Years' War.[1]

Burdened with its own conflicts and divisions, the Church was in no position at this time to be an effective agency of reform and renewal. Kings and popes fought bitterly over questions of jurisdiction and temporal power. Ludwig of Bavaria had himself crowned Holy Roman Emperor without papal consent. Pope Boniface VIII's long struggle with the French King, Philip the Fair, culminated in the pope's shocking arrest and imprisonment that led

---

[1] For an interesting account of this century, see Barbara W. Tuchman, *A Distant Mirror: The Calamitous 14th Century* (New York: Alfred A. Knopf, 1978).

shortly to his death. The move of the seat of the papacy from Rome to Avignon in France in 1305 (and thus under greater French influence) ushered in the period often referred to as the "Babylonian Captivity." The return of the papacy to Rome in 1377 soon led, however, to the disaster of the Great Western Schism which so greatly undermined Church unity. This schism, caused by rival claimants to the papacy, continued to divide the Church until it was finally resolved at the Council of Constance early in the fifteenth century.

The overall spiritual condition of the times was also marked by a number of extremes and divisions that added to the general unrest and turmoil. Among the Franciscans, the bitter controversies over the observance of poverty caused deep divisions. The proponents of strict poverty, the Spirituals, reacted strongly to any modifications in the practice of poverty, and some seriously challenged Church authority. Heretical movements also emerged in various parts of the continent. In northern Europe there sprang up those who were called the Brethren of the Free Spirit.[2] They were accused of pantheistic tendencies and of claiming to have reached such a special relationship and union with God that they were not subject to a moral code. Some of the Beguine communities in Germany and the Low Countries seem to have been adversely influenced by their teaching. Finally, the state of theological study and learning was in sharp decline, and the division between theology and spirituality grew wider and wider, often leaving popular piety open to various excesses.

In the midst of this time of turmoil and upheaval, there emerged a flowering of the mystical tradition. This took place particularly in the German-speaking areas of northern Europe. There may have been a connection and relationship between this revival of interest in mysticism and the conditions of the times, but this is difficult to determine with any certainty. The type of mystical

---

[2] For a study of the heresy of the "free spirit" see Robert Lerner, *The Heresy of the Free Spirit in the Later Middle Ages* (Berkeley: University of California Press, 1972).

prayer that arose in the Rhineland and surrounding areas took a different direction from that of the earlier Middle Ages. The previous writings in the West on contemplation and mysticism tended to be affective in tone and kataphatic in approach. They spoke more to the heart than to the intellect and they described the union with God through various images and metaphors. One has only to recall the writings of St. Bernard of Clairvaux and the other Cistercians, as well as the writers in the tradition of the *Brautmystik* (bridal mysticism).

In sharp contrast, the Rhineland mystics were speculative in their approach and apophatic in their method. They advocated a way of darkness and a method of emptying and bypassing all images as one sought God through detachment and spiritual poverty. With this approach, they were much more in accord with the predominant method that developed in the Greek mystical tradition that reached its culmination in the writings of Pseudo-Dionysius.

Pseudo-Dionysius came to enjoy great popularity in the later Middle Ages. As noted earlier, he was probably a Syrian monk who lived around 500 and identified himself as an author with Dionysius the Areopagite who is mentioned in the Acts of the Apostles. (This identification was accepted in the Middle Ages but was abandoned after the sixteenth century.) John Scotus Eriugena provided a Latin translation of some of his writings in the ninth century, but then Pseudo-Dionysius fell into oblivion until the twelfth century. The Victorines, particularly Thomas Gallus, did much to make him known again in the West, and by the fourteenth century his apophatic writings were very influential in Western circles.

2. The Rhineland Mystics

The three main figures among the so-called Rhineland mystics were Meister Eckhart, John Tauler, and Henry Suso. Meister Eckhart was the dominant figure and an important speculative thinker, but his posthumous condemnation led to the waning of his influence until recent times. All three were Dominican friars and heirs to their Order's illustrious intellectual tradition. They were also popular preachers and renowned spiritual directors, particularly for the many religious women in the German-speaking countries who were drawn to the higher forms of contemplative prayer. In the fourteenth century there were a number of convents of cloistered Dominican nuns in southern Germany and northern Switzerland that were centers of fervent prayer and a highly developed mystical spirituality.

The mystical teaching of the Rhineland mystics will emerge more clearly as we consider them individually, but it might be well to look briefly at some of the main aspects of their thought at this point. First of all they were steeped in traditional religious practices and always upheld the necessity of this foundation. They realized that the cultivation of higher forms of prayer presupposes the practice of a virtuous and righteous way of life. But assuming and building on this, they focused their attention on the soul's union with God. They spoke about this union, not in terms of a loving union and a mysticism of love as most of the earlier Western writers did, but in terms of an *essential union* and a *mysticism of being.* It is a union of what is most essential within the human person and what is most essential within God. The soul seeks to return to God by recovering the likeness of God that has been lost.

Thus, the Rhineland mystics spoke in terms that are clearly intellectual and speculative. They described the union between God and the soul as the birth of the Word in the *ground* or *spark* of the soul. For these mystical writers, the spark or ground of the soul was the image or reflection of God, and the birth of the Word was the actualization of this image. They spoke of this union as a knowing that takes place beyond any images and beyond the reaches of the intellect. It can only be reached by renouncing all created things and through the practice of detachment and spiritual poverty.[3]

---

[3] See Gerard Sitwell, O.S.B., *Spiritual Writers of the Middle Ages* (New York: Hawthorn Books, 1961), p. 75 ff.

It is clear from this brief description that the mysticism of the Rhineland writers is in the tradition of the Greek mystical writers, particularly Pseudo-Dionysius. This has commonly been referred to as the apophatic way or the via negativa or the 'negative way.' Since they developed their theory also in such speculative terms, their writings present a particular challenge to the reader of their texts.

Meister Eckhart

Meister Eckhart (c. 1260-1327) was born at Hochheim in the province of Thuringia in the eastern part of Germany. As a young man he entered the Dominican priory at Erfurt where he did his early studies. He later went for further studies to the Dominicans' *studium generale* at Cologne, the center for advanced studies that had become famous under the leadership of St. Albert the Great. It is possible that these studies were also supplemented by an early stay at Paris. He was soon elected to positions of leadership in the Dominican Order, serving as vicar of the province of Thuringia and prior of the community at Erfurt. He was sent to Paris around 1300 for advanced studies and in 1302 the title of Master of Theology was conferred upon him.

From 1304 until 1311 Eckhart was provincial of the Dominican province of Saxony, also serving for part of this time as Vicar General of the province of Bohemia. In 1311 the General Chapter of the Dominicans that met at Naples chose him to assume the Dominican chair of teaching at the University of Paris. He remained in Paris until 1314 and then moved to Strasbourg where he taught theology and perhaps directed the Dominican house of studies. During these years he was also very active in pastoral work, preaching and providing spiritual direction for the many convents of women religious. His final move was to Cologne in 1324 where he continued his teaching, writing, and pastoral work.

Over the course of these many years, Meister Eckhart achieved great success as a scholar and a popular preacher. His biblical commentaries and other scholarly works were written for the most part in Latin, while his popular sermons were composed in German. It was in his sermons that he developed many of the themes connected with his mysticism, such as the divine spark in the soul through which union with God is attained, the "birth of the word" in the soul, and the state of detachment and poverty of spirit that is necessary for this union with God. Evidently Meister Eckhart was a dynamic and forceful preacher. He was one of the first preachers who sought to express many profound and complex truths in the German language, and so there were bound to be imperfections in his use of the language. His style in preaching was somewhat poetical and even bold. He seemed to have a tendency to push language to its limits and to make use of bold paradoxes to heighten the effect of his words upon his listeners. The combination of a profound message and an unusual manner of expressing it easily led to some misunderstandings. It has been often said that Eckhart's profound message and unusual style make him a difficult writer to grasp.[4]

Still it came as a great surprise to Eckhart himself and to his many admirers when his teaching fell under suspicion in 1326. At this time he was an elderly and revered figure in his Dominican Order and in the Church at large. Inquisitional proceedings were set in motion by Henry of Virneburg, the Franciscan archbishop of Cologne, who throughout the investigations seemed to have little sympathy for the writings of Eckhart. Besides the nature of the writings themselves, others factors played some part in the long and drawn out investigation and trial. Church authorities were uneasy over the activities in the area of the adherents of the sect of the Free Spirit and some heterodox Begherds and Beguines. There were also the rivalries that emerged at times between the Franciscans and

---

[4] For a good study of Eckhart, see Richard Woods, O.P., *Eckhart's Way* (Wilmington, DE: Michael Glazier, 1986). See also *Meister Eckhart, The Essential Sermons, Commentaries, Treatises, and Defense*, translation and introduction by Edmund Colledge, O.S.A. and Bernard McGinn (New York: Paulist Press, 1981); and *Meister Eckhart, Teacher and Preacher*, edited by Bernard McGinn (New York: Paulist Press, 1986).

Dominicans, as well as those between the supporters and enemies of the Avignon pope, John XXII.

Eckhart defended himself against the articles that were drawn up against him by the Cologne inquisitors. He affirmed his fidelity to the Church and to its teaching and sought to explain the true meaning of the propositions that were taken from his writings, particularly from his sermons. Meeting with little success in Cologne, Eckhart later appealed directly to the Holy See for a hearing, submitting in advance to its decision. He subsequently set out for Avignon to defend himself in person before the papal commission that was drawn up. The final decision against Eckhart was handed down in March of 1329, and it condemned 28 propositions that were taken from his writings. Eckhart himself died, presumably at Avignon, before the decision was promulgated.

As a result of the condemnation, Eckhart and his writings faded for the most part from sight, although there was still a distinct influence upon the Rhineland mystics that followed him. A renewed interest in Eckhart took place in the nineteenth century and this has continued until the present day. He still remains a controversial and enigmatic figure, although a number of scholars today argue for a more orthodox interpretation of the condemned propositions when they are studied in the light of his complete thought and not taken out of context.[5]

John Tauler

Exact details are sparse about the life of this disciple of Eckhart, who achieved such great fame through his preaching and sermons.[6] John Tauler was born in Strasbourg of a prosperous fam-

---

[5] For details of Eckhart's condemnation and evaluations see Woods, *op. cit.*, p. 151 ff. and Colledge and McGinn, *op. cit.*, p. 12 ff.

[6] For background information on Tauler see the introductions in John Tauler, *Spiritual Conferences*, translated and edited by Eric Colledge and Sister M. Jane, O.P. (St. Louis: Herder, 1961), pp. 1-32; and Johannes Tauler, *Sermons*, translation by Maria Shrady, Introduction by Josef Schmidt (New York: Paulist Press, 1985), pp. 1-34. Both of these works have a good selection of Tauler's sermons in English. See also Oliver Davies, *God Within, The Mystical Tradition of Northern Europe* (New York: Paulist Press, 1988), pp. 73-98.

ily and entered the Dominican friary in that city around the age of fifteen. As a young Dominican, he may have studied under Meister Eckhart either at Strasbourg or later at the Dominican *studium generale* in Cologne. He was ordained a priest around 1325 and later began his pastoral work as a preacher and spiritual director at Strasbourg. The Dominican friars had assumed responsibility for providing preachers and spiritual directors for the large number of Dominican nuns in the vicinity, and Tauler was one of the well trained friars who undertook this work. The growth in the number of these convents had been rapid. When the new Dominican province of Teutonia was formed in 1303, there were approximately seventy convents of Dominican nuns in that area. Strasbourg itself had seven large Dominican convents and a number of smaller communities of Beguines, and it was to these convents that Tauler directed much of his pastoral activity.

The Dominican friars were forced to leave Strasbourg in 1339 because of their support of the pope during the bitter struggle between the emperor, Ludwig of Bavaria, and the pope, John XXII. Tauler continued his pastoral work of preaching and spiritual direction at Basel. His influence spread through his extensive contact at Basel with a group of people known as the "Friends of God." This designation was given to the large number of men and women from all ranks of society, who were strongly drawn to a life of intense prayer and interior devotion. They found much inspiration in the writings of Eckhart, Tauler, and Ruusbroec. This mystical movement flourished in all the German-speaking territories and in the Low Countries and attested to the strong spirit of prayer and piety that was present in northern Europe in these times of social upheaval and unrest. Tauler's leadership and influence among the Friends of God did much to prevent the movement from falling into the excesses and extremes of heretical groups such as the Brethren of the Free Spirit.

Tauler's pastoral work involved him in quite a bit of traveling. His preaching in churches and convents and the spiritual direction he undertook in many convents of religious women, as well as his many contacts with the Friends of God, took him to many areas of the Rhineland. His last years were spent at Strasbourg, where he died on June 16, 1361.

Strictly speaking, Tauler did not publish anything in his own lifetime. His sermons, however, were taken down by his listeners and later published; they quickly achieved great popularity. Tauler was not a theologian by profession as Eckhart was, but a pastor who was constantly engaged with people through his preaching and spiritual direction. Thus, his sermons are much more practical and pastorally oriented than the speculative writings of Eckhart. All of his sermons were written in German and they reflected the basic themes of Eckhart's doctrine. However, since Tauler was preaching after Eckhart's condemnation, he was careful to avoid any of the controversial points that marked Eckhart's writings. Given his pastoral and practical orientation, Tauler was much more cautious and circumspect than Eckhart. It is not hard to see why his sermons achieved such popularity. They are very readable, gentle and calm in style, and very sensitive to the practical needs of his listeners. He draws many of his examples and images from the daily lives of farmers and artisans and avoids theological speculation and subtleties. His main focus is to encourage his listeners to a profound and intense interior life.

The widespread popularity Tauler's sermons enjoyed in his lifetime continued after his death. Various editions of his sermons were published at different times with works of other authors also attached to his name. An edition was published at Leipzig in 1498 and another at Cologne in 1543; the later was the work of the German Jesuit, St. Peter Canisius. The Latin edition of the Carthusian monk, Laurentius Surius, appeared in Cologne in 1548. This version had wide circulation and was the basis for many vernacular translations. It is only in recent times that critical editions have sought to establish the authentic Tauler sermons from the pseudo additions. Finally, it should be noted that the young Martin Luther was drawn to Tauler's sermons, an interest that was widely shared by other Protestants.

Henry Suso

More information about the life of Henry Suso (c. 1295-1366) is available than is the case for Meister Eckhart and John Tauler. This is due primarily to the existence of the account of his life, the *Life of the Servant.*[7] Born in the province of Swabia, he entered the Dominican friary at Constance at the age of thirteen. The *Life of the Servant* speaks of a conversion experience he had at the age of eighteen that led to his adoption of a very penitential and austere way of life. After his studies at Constance, Strasbourg, and the *studium generale* at Cologne (where he probably studied for a time under Meister Eckhart), he began teaching at the Dominican priory at Constance. Around 1330, he was removed from this teaching position by a Dominican provincial chapter. This was most likely due to his defense of Meister Eckhart in his first book, *The Little Book of Truth.* From this point on Suso devoted himself, as did his contemporary, Tauler, to the work of preaching and spiritual direction, ministering especially to the many convents of Dominican nuns in the Rhineland and to the Friends of God. During these years he also served as prior for a period at the Dominican friary in Constance.

Suso had to leave Constance in 1338 with all the other Dominicans because of their support of the papal interdict against the emperor, Ludwig of Bavaria. It is not clear where Suso moved during this time of exile from Constance, but we do know that his last years were spent at the Dominican house in Ulm. Before his death in this city in 1366, Suso brought forth an edition of his German writings under the title of *The Exemplar.*[8] He was greatly assisted in this undertaking by the Dominican prioress of Toss, Elsbeth

---

[7] This seems to be the joint work of Suso and his disciple, Elsbeth Stagel, the prioress of the convent at Toss in Switzerland. She most likely brought the material together that he provided for her.

[8] The *Exemplar* includes Suso's *Life of the Servant*, the *Little Book of Eternal Wisdom*, the *Little Book of Truth*, the *Little Book of Letters*, and two of his sermons. For a good introduction to these works and English translations see *Henry Suso, The Exemplar, With Two German Sermons*, translated, edited, and introduced by Frank Tobin (New York: Paulist Press, 1989).

Stagel, who collected many of his letters and contributed much to the writing of his autobiography, the *Life of the Servant*. Although Suso suffered many trials and tribulations over the course of the years, he lived to see his life and writings fully exonerated. Venerated for his holiness during his lifetime, he was beatified in 1831 by Pope Gregory XVI.

Suso was of a different temperament than Eckhart and Tauler, and this is reflected in his writings. More sensitive and intense, he is much more personal and devotional. He is the poet and lyricist of the German mystics, more the "knight of divine wisdom" than the theologian and speculative thinker. He was in the tradition of the German minnesingers, those who followed in the tradition of the French troubadours with its courtly love, chivalry, music and poetry.

His first book, the *Little Book of Truth*, is his most speculative and theological work. This was written while Suso was finishing his own studies and preparing to teach, so it understandably reflects much of the theology and philosophy of the schools. It is written in the form of a dialogue between the disciple and Eternal Truth. The influence of Meister Eckhart is evident, and Suso writes about many of Eckhart's themes, particularly the true detachment that leads to mystical union. He seeks to defend Eckhart against the heretical interpretations of the Brethren of the Free Spirit, and he attacks their pantheistic teaching and assertions that the truly spiritual person cannot sin.

Suso's second book, the *Little Book of Eternal Wisdom*, is a much different work — simpler and more practical in design, more devotional and affective in tone. Again in this work, much of the teaching is cast in the form of a dialogue. Suso stresses a tender, affective and personal love of Christ. Jesus must be at the center of one's life. Suso presents meditations on Christ's passion in order to renew the interior life of the reader and to stir up an ardent love for Christ. This approach corresponded with Suso's personal experience, for his own journey was marked by an evolving identification with the cross of Christ. This for him was the way to mystical union.

Later in his life, Suso wrote what can be considered a Latin version of this work, *Horologium Sapientiae* (The Clock of Wisdom). Both of these versions achieved great popularity as devotional works after Suso's death.

The *Life of the Servant* was completed by Suso when he was editing his *Exemplar* towards the end of his life.[9] Like the *Confessions* of St. Augustine, it takes the form of a spiritual journey. Suso is much more concerned about the inner life than he is about external events and occurrences. It is also very much in the medieval tradition with its emphasis on visions, dreams, miracles, and corporal austerities. Suso presents his own mystical experiences as God's servant as a model or "exemplar" for the path that leads to union with God. Thus, it should be seen not only as an autobiographical work but one of hagiography as well.[10]

Theologia Germanica

A later work very much in the tradition of the Rhineland mystics that was widely copied and circulated was the *Theologia Germanica* (*Theologia Deutsch*). The name of the author is unknown, but he is believed to have been a member of the Knights of the Teutonic Order who lived near Frankfurt and had close connections with the Friends of God. It is a work of practical piety that focuses on the interior life and a life of virtue. It is traditional in its format, following the classical division of the three ways: purgative, illuminative, and unitive. There is a strong emphasis on the role of Christ in the pursuit of a holy life. This treatise was greatly esteemed by Martin Luther. He discovered a shortened version of the text around 1515 and published it in 1516. He later discovered a fuller text and published this version in 1518.[11]

---

[9] For reflections on the genre of this particular work and the parts written by Suso and those by his disciple Elsbeth Stagel see *ibid.*, p. 38 ff.

[10] *Ibid.*, p. 40 ff.

[11] For an English translation of Luther's 1518 version, see *The Theologia Germanica of Martin Luther*, translation, introduction, and commentary by Bengt Hoffman (New York: Paulist Press, 1980).

Another anonymous work that achieved much popularity, although not to the extent of the *Theologia Germanica*, was the spiritual treatise, the *Book of Spiritual Poverty*. It was long attributed to John Tauler, but it is now believed to be the work of one of his disciples. As the title indicates, it focuses on one of the central themes of the Rhineland mystics, spiritual poverty. It emphasizes that the poverty of spirit of the gospel beatitude is the way "one attains to the imitation of Christ, to the perfection of the virtues, to peace of heart, to spiritual death, and finally to contemplation and union with God."[12]

The contributions of the Dominican women mystics of the Rhineland should also be noted. Mention has already been made of Elsbeth Stagel and her part in the writing of the life of Henry Suso. She also wrote biographies of some of her companions in religious life. Christina Ebner (1277-1356), the prioress of Engeltal, has left an account of her revelations. Through her spiritual director, the diocesan priest Henry of Nordlingen, she came to know the writings of John Tauler and others in the circles of the Friends of God. Blessed Margaret Ebner (1291-1351) of the monastery of Dominican nuns at Maria Medingen near Dillingen on the Danube also wrote her *Revelations* with the encouragement of her director Henry of Nordlingen. The letters from Henry to Margaret Ebner provide much information about her life and writings.[13]

3. John Ruusbroec

John Ruusbroec (1293-1381), the greatest of the Flemish mystics, is often grouped with the Rhineland mystical writers, for he shares many common themes with them. And yet he also has his

---

[12] See Vandenbroucke, pp. 397-398 in *The Spirituality of the Middle Ages* (Leclercq, Vandenbroucke, Bouyer), vol. II of *A History of Christian Spirituality* (New York: The Seabury Press, 1968).

[13] For background on Margaret Ebner's life and her writings, see *Margaret Ebner, Major Works,* translated and edited by Leonard P. Hindsley, introduced by Margot Schmidt and Leonard P. Hindsley (New York: Paulist Press, 1993).

own distinctiveness that sets him apart from them.[14] First, he lived
in the neighboring Low Countries and he wrote in Dutch rather
than German. Secondly, his writings clearly reflect the currents of
spirituality that were particularly prominent in this area. These
would include the influence of the Beguine mystical writers and
those in the Cistercian school of spirituality, especially William of
St. Thierry. Thus, although the speculative dimension is clearly
present in Ruusbroec's writings, there is also found a much greater
emphasis on a Trinitarian mysticism expressed in terms of love.

John Ruusbroec (also spelled Ruysbroeck in English) took his
name from his native village in Brabant that was situated about five
miles south of Brussels. At the age of eleven, he went to Brussels
for his studies and lived with a relative who was a canon at the col-
legiate church of St. Gudula. He was ordained to the priesthood at
the age of twenty-four and for the next twenty-six years ministered
as a diocesan priest at the church of St. Gudula. As priest and chaplain at the church, Ruusbroec also served as a spiritual advisor for
many of the Beguines who lived in the area. He also began the writing of his treatises which would number eleven at the time of his
death. These early writings include *The Kingdom of Lovers, The
Spiritual Espousals* and *The Sparkling Stone*. In these writings,
Ruusbroec spoke out forcefully against the false mystical teachings
of such groups as the Brethren of the Free Spirit.

Seeking a life of greater solitude and prayer, Ruusbroec left
Brussels in 1343 with two other priests and formed a community
at Groenendaal ("The Green Valley") in the forest of Soignes just
outside Brussels. Others came to join them, and after a few years
the community formally adopted the Rule of St. Augustine and
became a monastery of canons regular. Ruusbroec became the prior
and remained in that position until his death in the year 1381. His
mystical writings during this period include *A Mirror of Eternal*

---

[14] For background on Ruusbroec, see Paul Verdeyen, S.J., *Ruusbroec and His Mysticism*
(Collegeville: The Liturgical Press, 1994); and the introduction to *John Ruusbroec, The
Spiritual Espousals and Other Works*, introduction and translation by James A. Wiseman,
O.S.B. (New York: Paulist Press, 1985).

Blessedness, The Seven Rungs in the Ladder of Spiritual Love and
The Little Book of Clarification.

Ruusbroec lived a quiet and prayerful life at Groenendaal for
thirty-eight years. He was revered by the members of his community for the holiness of his life and for the depth of his spiritual writings. Many others made pilgrimages to Groenendaal in order to
consult with this spiritual master. Gerard Groote, the founder of
the *Devotio Moderna*, visited him in 1377, after reading and greatly
appreciating many of his mystical writings. It is also very likely that
John Tauler came to consult with him. After his death in 1381, at
the advanced age of eighty-eight, Ruusbroec was buried in the
monastery chapel. After the suppression of the monastery in the late
eighteenth century, his remains were moved to the church of St.
Gudula in Brussels, where he had spent so many years as a diocesan priest. Ruusbroec was beatified in 1909, and his feast day is
celebrated on December 2, the anniversary of his death.

The Spiritual Espousals is generally considered to be
Ruusbroec's masterpiece and a work that provides a good summary
of many of his important themes.[15] It is a treatise that is carefully
constructed and remarkably organized. The treatise is divided into
three "books": the first focuses on the active life, the second on the
interior life (or the God-desiring life), and the third on the contemplative life. Ruusbroec develops his thoughts in each one of these
books by using as a leitmotif the sentence from Matthew's gospel,
"Look, the Bridegroom is coming, go out to meet him" (Mt. 25:6).
The movement towards unity with God is at the heart of
Ruusbroec's thought, and he seeks to develop this theme from various perspectives. For example, he speaks about a union with God
"through an intermediary," a union with God "without intermediary," and a union "without difference."

Trinitarian exemplarism is also central to Ruusbroec's mys-

---

[15] For a helpful treatment of *The Spiritual Espousals*, see the introduction by James
Wiseman to *John Ruusbroec, The Spiritual Espousals and Other Works, op. cit.* In addi-
tion to *The Spiritual Espousals* this volume has English translations of *The Sparkling
Stone, A Mirror of Eternal Blessedness* and *The Little Book of Clarification.*

tical thought. The Trinitarian principle of three in one runs through all of his mystical writings. As a living mirror which reflects the image of the Trinity, the human person is associated with the life of the three divine persons. This is a life that is marked by the simultaneous interplay between repose and activity, rest and work. This movement also "characterizes the lives of all those who have been created in the divine image and who live in accordance with that image."[16]

Ruusbroec's works were widely circulated after his death, particularly in Carthusian circles and among those connected with the *Devotio Moderna*. The Dutch Franciscan, Henry Hemp (often known by his Latin name of Harphius), did much to popularize his thought and even earned the title "the herald of Ruusbroec." Later writers in the community at Groenendaal, such as John van Leeuwen, clearly reflected the influence of Ruusbroec in their writings, although they were much less speculative than the master. Finally, it should be noted that the English writer on mysticism, Evelyn Underhill, gives a very prominent place to Ruusbroec in her twentieth century classic, *Mysticism*. She considered him one of the greatest mystics of the Church.

The tradition of speculative mysticism in the Rhineland and the Low Countries went into a decline after the death of Ruusbroec.[17] This is reflected in the writings of St. Catherine of Siena, St. Bridget of Sweden, the proponents of the *Devotio Moderna*, and the works of the English mystics. In these writings to which we will now turn, there is found a greater attraction to visions and revelations as well as a desire to restore love to the central place in contemplation.

---

[16] *Ibid.*, p. 11.

[17] Vandenbroucke in the second volume of *A History of Spirituality* speaks of this decline in a chapter entitled "Disrepute," p. 407 ff.

4. St. Catherine of Siena

Catherine of Siena (c. 1347-1380) was a remarkable woman who played a major role in ecclesial and political affairs in a turbulent and troubled period of medieval history. As a laywoman who lived only thirty-three years, she combined mystical gifts of prayer with constant activity and involvement in the great issues of her day. Endowed with a strong and charismatic personality, she had great influence on people from every walk of life. Although she had no formal education, her writings were widely circulated after her death. Today she is honored as a saint and doctor of the Roman Catholic Church and as the patroness of Italy.

Caterina di Giacomo di Benincasa (known to subsequent history as Catherine of Siena) was born in Siena, the twenty-fourth of twenty-five children.[18] Her father was a wool dyer of comfortable means. From an early age, Catherine was drawn to a life of prayer and devotion. Firmly resisting family pressures to marry, she was finally left in peace to pursue her strong religious inclinations. Around the age of eighteen, Catherine joined the *Mantellate,* a group of third order Dominican laywomen living in Siena. At this time, too, she began to live a life of silence and solitude in her room, leaving the house only to attend Mass at the nearby Dominican church. It was a period in which she devoted herself to prayer, fasting, and other austerities.

This three year period of solitude came to end when Catherine was twenty-one. She experienced a mystical espousal to Christ and felt called to leave her total seclusion in order to serve others. She began to assist the *Mantellate* in their works of mercy in Siena,

---

[18] The main sources for Catherine's life are the *Leggenda Maiora,* a biography written by her confessor and great friend, Raymond of Capua, and her own authentic writings. For a recent English translation of the *Leggenda Maiora,* see Raymond of Capua, *The Life of Catherine of Siena,* translated, introduced and annotated by Conleth Kearns, O.P. (Wilmington: Michael Glazier, 1980). In his helpful introduction, the translator discusses the issues involved in assessing the historical data about Catherine. The many later biographies of Catherine attest to her great popularity.

attending to the poor, the sick, and the dying. During this renewed activity, she continued her austere practices and long periods of prayer and contemplation. Her holiness of life and heroic charity drew many disciples to her, creating an extended family with Catherine assuming the role of mother and leader. The formation of this family, together with her desire to reach out to the needs of others, led Catherine to begin her extensive apostolate of letter-writing.

In 1374, Catherine made her first journey to Florence while the General Chapter of the Dominicans was in session. The distinguished Dominican, Blessed Raymond of Capua, became her confessor and spiritual director at this time. He was a source of great support to her for the rest of her life, and she would refer to him in one of her last letters as "the father and son given to me by that gentle mother Mary."

At this point in her life, Catherine's apostolate began to extend far beyond Siena. Her many letters from this period attest to this growing involvement. She became active in the preaching of a new Crusade, and she was asked to assume the role of peacemaker in the growing conflict between the city-states of Florence and Pisa and the papacy. In 1376 she traveled to Florence and then to Avignon to act as a mediator for peace. This led to her work for the reform of the clergy and for the return of the papacy to Rome. Pope Gregory XI returned to Rome on January 13, 1377, but with his death in 1378 and the election of Urban VI, the Church was plunged into the Great Schism in the West that was to cause such havoc to the Church.

Catherine's last years were spent in Rome at the request of Pope Urban VI. Living there with a number of her disciples, she continued working for Church unity and reform. Her health declined rapidly in 1380, and she died in Rome on April 29th of that year. She had accomplished much in the relatively short life span of her thirty-three years. Catherine was canonized in 1461 and declared a doctor of the Church by Pope Paul VI in 1970.

The authentic writings of Catherine of Siena include her *Letters*, her *Prayers*, and her major work, the *Dialogue*. There are three hundred and eighty-two extant letters of Catherine, and they are a rich source of information about Catherine herself and the events that surrounded her.[19] The majority of her letters were written during the last years of her life, the period between 1374 and her death in 1380. They are addressed to people from all walks of life: to popes, cardinals, bishops, monks, family members, relatives, politicians, soldiers, prisoners, queens, etc. Dictated to members of her family who assisted her, they are spontaneous in tone and they serve as a window for our knowledge of her strong convictions and view of things.[20] The *Prayers* of Catherine were preserved through members of her family of disciples, who wrote down her spoken words while she was rapt in prayer. Her prayers reflect the teachings found in her other writings, the scriptural readings of the daily liturgy, and her day to day concerns.[21]

Catherine's teaching finds its loftiest expression in her major work, the *Dialogue*.[22] It was composed late in her life and entrusted to Raymond of Capua before her death as a final summary and testament of her teaching. In her pursuit of truth, Catherine addresses four petitions to God at the beginning of the *Dialogue*: (1) for herself; (2) for the reform of the Church; (3) for the whole world in general, and in particular for the peace of Christians who are rebelling against holy Church; and (4) for divine providence in all things, but specifically in regard to "a certain case that had arisen." God responds to these petitions and Catherine reacts with thanksgiving to each response. Various topics and themes are developed such as

---

[19] The first of a projected four volumes of Catherine's complete letters in English translation is now available. See *The Letters of St. Catherine of Siena*, Volume I, translated with introduction and notes by Suzanne Noffke, O.P. (Binghamton, NY: 1988).

[20] *Ibid.*, p. 3.

[21] For an English translation of twenty-six of these prayers, see *The Prayers of Catherine of Siena*, edited by Suzanne Noffke, O.P. (New York: Paulist Press, 1983).

[22] See *Catherine of Siena, The Dialogue*, translation and introduction by Suzanne Noffke, O.P. (New York: Paulist Press, 1980).

Christ as bridge, tears, truth, the mystical body of holy Church, divine providence, and obedience.

In Catherine's spirituality, the relationship between knowledge and love plays a very prominent role. She is fond of speaking of God as Gentle First Truth; the way to God is through knowledge and love, and truth is nourished by love. As she writes in the opening words of the prologue:

> A soul rises up, restless with tremendous desire for God's honor and the salvation of souls. She has for some time exercised herself in virtue and has become accustomed to dwelling in the cell of self-knowledge in order to know better God's goodness toward her, since upon knowledge follows love. And loving, she seeks to pursue truth and clothes herself in it.[23]

For Catherine, Christ crucified is the Way of Truth, the Bridge that leads to the supreme truth of God's love for humanity. In her writings she is very fond of expressing God's creative and redemptive love through the symbol of the Precious Blood of Christ.

Finally, it is important to note how well Catherine integrated a life of contemplation and a life of action. There was no distinct separation between her mystical prayer and her activity; they both nourished one another. It was what she experienced in mystical prayer that led her to her many apostolic endeavors. And the many issues she faced and dealt with in her life were always present in her prayer. This integration is a characteristic mark of her mysticism.[24]

A contemporary of St. Catherine of Siena who also played an active role in the events of the day was St. Bridget (Birgitta) of Swe-

---

[23] *Ibid.*, p.25.

[24] On this point see *ibid.*, pp. 7-9. For some recent studies of Catherine's spirituality, see Suzanne Noffke, O.P., *Catherine of Siena, Vision Through a Distant Eye* (Collegeville: The Liturgical Press, 1996) (This work contains a very helpful annotated bibliography of works on Catherine of Siena in English, pp. 233-267); Mary Ann Fatula, O.P., *Catherine of Siena's Way* (Wilmington: Michael Glazier, 1987); and Catherine M. Meade, *My Nature is Fire: Saint Catherine of Siena* (New York: Alba House, 1991).

den (c. 1303-1373). Born into a noble family, she married and raised a family of eight children, one of which was St. Catherine of Sweden. After the death of her husband Ulf in 1344, she lived as a penitent at the Cistercian monastery at Alvastra in Sweden. In 1349 Bridget went to Rome and remained there until her death in 1373. The visions and revelations that she experienced throughout her life became more frequent during these years and she began to write them down. She was active in the cause of Church reform, especially in seeking the return of the Avignon popes to Rome. After her death the Order she founded at Vadstena in Sweden flourished in northern Europe.[25]

5. The English Mystics

There are four important English mystics of the fourteenth century: Richard Rolle, Walter Hilton, Julian of Norwich, and the author of the *Cloud of Unknowing*.[26] They belong to the ancient, patristic tradition, which was brought to Britain by the early monks and has always remained an integral part of English spirituality. In recent times, all of these writers have enjoyed a renewed and widespread interest. This has been particularly true in the case of Julian of Norwich. These English mystics are not a homogeneous group and they do not form any particular school, as was the case with the Rhineland mystics. There are certain characteristics, however, that all of these writers share.

---

[25] For further background on St. Bridget, see *Birgitta of Sweden, Life and Selected Revelations*, edited with a preface by Marguerite Tjader Harris, translation and notes by Albert Rylekezel, and introduction by Tore Nyberg (New York: Paulist Press, 1990); P. Pourrat, *Christian Spirituality* (Westminster, MD: The Newman Press, 1953), Vol. 2, pp. 92-98; and J. Jorgensen, *Saint Bridget of Sweden*, trans. by Ingeborg Lund, 2 vols. (London: Longmans, 1954).

[26] See David Knowles, *The English Mystical Tradition* (New York: 1961), first published in 1927 as *The English Mystics*; Clifton Wolters, "The English Mystics" in *The Study of Spirituality* (New York: Oxford University Press, 1986), pp. 328-337; and Vandenbroucke, *op. cit.*, pp. 416-428.

First of all, the individual element is prominent in all four of these writers. They wrote in their own native English, and there is a distinctiveness and particularity to each of them. It can be said that they were individuals writing for other individuals. As we shall see, all of them were somehow connected with the solitary life. In their writings they also express little attraction for abstract speculation. They are practical and direct in their outlook, and they seek to be helpful guides and directors to others in a clear, concrete, and realistic manner. As Thomas Merton writes of them: "The English mystics have a charm and simplicity that are unequaled by any other school. And they are also, it may be said, generally quite clear, down-to-earth, and practical, even when they are concerned with the loftiest of matters."[27] Finally, it should be noted, that even though these writers lived in turbulent times, there is very little of this background reflected in their writings.

Richard Rolle

Richard Rolle (c. 1300-1349) was born in Thornton-le-dale in Yorkshire at the beginning of the fourteenth century.[28] He studied at Oxford for a period (there is some speculation that he also studied theology at the Sorbonne), but he abandoned his studies at the age of nineteen and began living as a hermit. He pursued the hermit's vocation at various places, ending his days at Hampole. He was a prolific writer as a hermit, and judging from the many manuscripts still in existence, he was also a very popular writer. He wrote treatises, commentaries, and poetry on many different topics in both Latin and English. Important works written in Latin include

---

[27] Thomas Merton, "The English Mystics," *Mystics and Zen Masters* (New York: Delta Books, 1967), pp. 128-153.

[28] The main source for information about Rolle's life is the liturgical *Office* of nine lessons that was drawn up after his death by the Cistercian sisters at Hampole in the hope of his canonization. For a thorough study of Richard Rolle, see Hope Emily Allen, *Writings Ascribed to Richard Rolle, Hermit of Hampole and Materials for his Biography* (New York: Heath and Co., 1927).

Incendium Amoris (*Fire of Love*), *Emendatio Vitae* (*Mending of Life*), and *Contra Amatores Mundi* (*Against the Lovers of the World*). Among his English writings are *Ego Dormio, The Commandment, The Form of Living,* and *Meditations on the Passion.*[29] A colorful and somewhat complex personality emerges from the pages of these writings. Rolle shows himself to be a sincere, enthusiastic, and devout person for whom the love of God was central to his life. His preference is clearly for the solitary life, and he distances himself from contact with the established monastic and religious communities. He has strong opinions about many things and is quick at times to make them known. Elements of anti-intellectualism and misogynism can be found in his writings. In his earlier works, there are instances of sharp criticism of those he felt were not measuring up to his standards, criticisms which did not endear him to many people. On the other hand, he could reach out with tenderness and concern to the weak and the poor. It can be said that the later mystic was a much more mellow and balanced person than the youthful enthusiast.

Rolle's major work, *The Fire of Love,* summarizes much of his teaching. Strongly affective in tone, it is a spirited defense of the solitary life and the contemplative experience of the love of God. It is the love of God that must take the central place in one's life and nothing else should interfere with it. He never tires of emphasizing the need to love God and to desire him continually. For example, he writes simply at the beginning of chapter four: "There must be a serious intention... to long continually for the love of God." For Rolle, the contemplative experience is a gift of God; one can only prepare for it by a wholehearted and total love of God. In speaking about his own contemplative prayer in chapter fifteen, Rolle de-

---

[29] For modern English translations of some of Rolle's writings with helpful introductions, see *Richard Rolle, The English Writings,* translated, edited, and introduced by Rosamund S. Allen (New York: Paulist Press, 1988); *The Fire of Love and The Mending of Life by Richard Rolle,* translated with an introduction by M.L. del Mastro (New York: Doubleday, 1981); and Richard Rolle, *The Fire of Love,* translated into modern English with an introduction by Clifton Wolters (New York: Penguin Books, 1972).

scribes it in terms of bodily warmth, sweetness, and heavenly melody. Some of his contemporaries and some later commentators have not been sympathetic to these psychosomatic effects of prayer, finding them too emotionally charged or merely being the marks of a beginner in prayer. But others have hastened to point out Rolle's affinity in this regard with writers in the Eastern Christian tradition, who emphasize that prayer can affect the whole person.[30] It should be noted, too, that in speaking about rapture in prayer (chapter 37), Rolle makes a clear distinction between a rapture or love that holds the senses bound, and a love that leaves the senses intact.

There is also found in Rolle's writings an affective and tender devotion to Christ (especially in his passion) and to Mary that is very Franciscan in spirit. Rolle is a strong advocate of a devotion to the Holy Name of Jesus, and he encourages the loving repetition of the name of Jesus in a way that has a strong affinity to the Jesus Prayer in Eastern spirituality. He writes in the letter known as "The Commandment": "I'll give you one piece of advice: don't neglect his name, 'Jesus.' Meditate on it in your heart night and day as your personal and precious treasure. Love it more than life. Root it in your mind."[31]

The Cloud of Unknowing

This little gem of fourteenth century English spirituality rightly enjoys a widespread popularity today.[32] As the title indicates,

---

[30] For example, see Merton's remarks in the essay previously mentioned, p. 148; and Wolters in his introduction to *The Fire of Love*, p. 126.

[31] See *The English Writings, op. cit.*, p. 150. See also c. 9 of "The Form of Living," *ibid.*, 173.

[32] The contemporary practice of "centering prayer" is traceable to a method found in this work. For translations into modern English with introductory material see, *The Cloud of Unknowing*, translated with an introduction by Clifton Wolters (Harmondsworth: Penguin Books, 1961); *The Cloud of Unknowing and The Book of Privy Counseling*, edited with an introduction by William Johnston (New York: Doubleday Image Books, 1973); and *The Cloud of Unknowing*, edited with an introduction by James Walsh, S.J. (New York: Paulist Press, 1981). For a study of the text itself, see William Johnston, *The Mysticism of the Cloud of Unknowing* (St. Meinrad: Abbey Press, 1975).

it is the only writing of the English mystics that is definitely in the apophatic tradition, that is the way of negation and darkness. The unknown author clearly acknowledges his debt to Pseudo-Dionysius. But unlike Pseudo-Dionysius and the Rhineland mystics, *The Cloud of Unknowing* is affective rather than speculative in its thrust. It is a mysticism of love that clearly characterizes this work. It is only "the sharp dart of longing love" that pierces the "cloud of unknowing." This particular work is intended for those advanced in the spiritual life and presupposes a firm foundation in Christian life and practice.

There has been much speculation as to the identity of the author. The text seems to indicate that he was a priest, but it provides us with little additional information about his life. Various conjectures have identified him as a Carthusian, a hermit, a cloistered monk, and a country parson. His identification as a Carthusian seems to be the most persistent one. Whoever he was, he emerges as a learned, devout, and competent guide. The author writes in a serene and balanced way, with a ring of sincerity, discretion, and even humor. Although *The Cloud of Unknowing* is his major work, there are six other treatises attributed to the anonymous author that apply the teaching of *The Cloud* to various situations. These include *The Epistle of Privy Counsel, The Epistle of Prayer, The Epistle of Discretion in the Stirrings of the Soul* and the *Treatise of Discerning of Spirits*. There is also the *Hid Divinite*, a commentary on the *Mystical Theology* of Pseudo-Dionysius, and a free translation of the *Benjamin Minor* of Richard of St. Victor.[33]

Pseudo-Dionysius (St. Denis as he is called by our author) is the only source that the author mentions explicitly in the text of *The Cloud*. Toward the end of the work (chapter 70), the author of *The Cloud* acknowledges his debt by stating that whoever reads the works of Denis will find there a confirmation of all he has said from the beginning to the end. There are also other unnamed influences.

---

[33] For these writings, see *The Pursuit of Wisdom and Other Works by the Author of The Cloud of Unknowing*, translated, edited, and annotated by James A. Walsh, S.J. (New York: Paulist Press, 1988).

Among them are Richard of St. Victor, St. Augustine, *The Ladder of Monks* of Guigo II, and the works of the Victorine abbot, Thomas Gallus. The influence of the *De Adhaerendo Deo*, popularly attributed to St. Albert the Great, has also been noted.

What then is the basic teaching of *The Cloud of Unknowing*? The author proposes to his disciple a way of life that is marked by a love and a longing for God. For it is only love, not knowledge, that can comprehend God. Therefore God must be the chief aim of one's heart and sought humbly and simply in love. The author writes early in the work: "Lift your heart up to the Lord, with a gentle stirring of love desiring him for his own sake and not for his gifts. Center all your attention and desire on him and let this be the sole concern of your mind and heart."[34]

Between God and the soul that seeks him there is a darkness, a Cloud of Unknowing, in which one can only pray in "naked love." It is a cloud that can only be pierced by a longing love. Only a love that is emptied of all knowledge can comprehend God, for "by love God can be caught and held, but by thinking never" (chapter 6). Thus those seeking God must empty themselves of all other thoughts, images, and concepts, even if they are good and devout. They must be buried in the "cloud of forgetting" that lies between the contemplative and created reality. The author does suggest that one use a single word such as "God" or "love" as a help to turn away from other thoughts and to avoid distractions.

Since this is a way of life and not merely a method of prayer, the author of *The Cloud* emphasizes that it is a rare gift and a life to which one can only be called by God. It calls for a fidelity and maturity in the Christian life that is demanding and total. It presupposes that a person has a firm foundation in all aspects of the Christian life and has been called to this "work" of contemplation by discernible signs. Two signs are mentioned explicitly by the author: the first is a growing desire for contemplation that constantly intrudes itself in a person's daily devotion; and the second is a joyful

---

[34] C. 3. See Johnston, *op. cit.*, p. 48.

enthusiasm that persistently arises when one hears or reads about contemplation.

These brief remarks certainly do not do justice to the richness of the sound teaching and advice contained in this spiritual classic. There is a statement in the author's little treatise, the *Discernment of Stirrings*, that summarizes well the basic teaching of *The Cloud of Unknowing*. He writes:

> God cannot be known by reason, he cannot be thought, caught, or sought by understanding. But he can be loved and chosen by the true, loving will of your heart.... If God is your love and your purpose, the chief aim of your heart, it is all you need in this life, although you never see more of him with the eye of reason your whole life long. Such a blind shot with the sharp dart of longing love will never miss its mark, which is God.[35]

Walter Hilton

The little information we have about Walter Hilton (c. 1330-c. 1395) comes from some scattered references in the manuscript copies of his writings. It is generally accepted that he spent the last years of his life as a Canon of Saint Augustine at the Thurgarton priory in Nottinghamshire. The manuscripts also suggest that he was a doctor of theology who had probably studied at Cambridge, and that he also lived as a hermit for a period before becoming an Augustinian canon. His most famous work is *The Scale (Ladder) of Perfection*, but he is also the author of some other spiritual treatises that were written both in Latin and English.[36]

---

[35] See *The Study of Spirituality, op. cit.*, p. 334.

[36] For modern translations of Hilton's main work with background material, see *The Scale of Perfection*, translated into modern English with an introduction and notes by Dom Gerard Sitwell, O.S.B. (London: Burns Oates, 1953); *The Stairway of Perfection*, translated with an introduction by M.L. Del Mastro (New York: Doubleday Image Books, 1979); and *The Scale of Perfection*, translated with an introduction and notes by John P.H. Clark and Rosemary Dorward (New York: Paulist Press, 1991).

More than any of the other English mystics, Hilton is the spiritual director, a knowledgeable and balanced teacher for those who wish to grow in the interior life. He is much more the practical guide of others than an exponent of speculative thought. He is simple and straightforward in his teaching, and there is a charity, moderation and balance to his outlook that many have found appealing. He seems to be able to combine the teaching of high spiritual ideals with an understanding and sympathy for human weakness. Although *The Scale of Perfection* was written for an anchoress who had requested guidance in living out her particular vocation, Hilton writes in such a way that his teaching can be adaptable and helpful for those living the active life. In a sense, he writes for anyone who possesses a strong desire to love and serve God.

In the early chapters of *The Scale*, Hilton distinguishes between the active life and the contemplative life, and then goes on to speak about three stages or degrees of contemplation. The first stage consists of the knowledge of God and spiritual things that comes about though reason, human teaching, and the study of Sacred Scripture. The second consists principally in the love of God and spiritual things. In this stage, there is the fervor of love and spiritual sweetness that comes from God's grace, but the intellect receives no special light. The third and highest degree consists of both knowledge and love; it involves a person in the knowledge of God and the perfect love of Him. Through God's grace the intellect is illumined to see Truth itself, and the will is inflamed "with a soft, sweet, burning love." Through this love one is for a time united with God and conformed to the image of the Trinity. For Hilton, this experience is a foretaste of the bliss of heaven.

In seeking to lead his disciple to a growth in the contemplative life, Hilton develops the traditional theological theme of the restoration through Christ of the divine image in the human person. He uses the term "reformation" for the restoration of God's image. Full reformation can take place only in heaven, but a partial reformation can take place here on earth. This partial reformation on earth is of two types: a reformation in faith, and a reformation in feeling or experience. Reformation in faith occurs when a person is in God's grace through baptism and the sacrament of penance. Reformation in feeling or experience involves one in a much higher state of union with God. A person at this stage has some direct awareness of God's grace working in one's life through an illumination of the Holy Spirit. Reformation in faith can come easily and in a short time, but reformation in feeling can only come about through much spiritual labor and over a long period of time.[37]

Hilton makes use of a number of images as he seeks to provide guidance for this arduous interior journey. For example, one must pass through a dark night before the reformation in feeling is possible. A person's only recourse at this time is to hold fast to a naked awareness of Jesus who is hidden entirely within this darkness, and to desire to have nothing but the Lord.[38] There is also the image of the pilgrim on the road to Jerusalem, which Hilton develops so vividly in one of his chapters. Just as the true pilgrim to Jerusalem must keep his or her eyes fixed on the goal and be willing to suffer the hardships along the way, so the true contemplative must manifest a perseverance and determination in pursuit of the contemplative goal in spite of the difficulties and hardships. One's heart must be wholly intent on having nothing but the love of Jesus and the spiritual vision of Himself that He will give.[39]

Julian of Norwich

We know very little about Julian (1343-c. 1423) outside of the fact that she lived as an anchoress in a cell attached to the church of St. Julian at Norwich in England. The only writing of hers that has come down to us is the *Revelations (Showings) of Divine Love.* Her significance as a mystic and theologian, however, is widely recognized at the present time. Thomas Merton writes of her: "Of all the

---

[37] See Book II, chapter 5. For a development of this see Sitwell, *op. cit.*, p. xi ff.

[38] See for example, Book I, chapter 54.

[39] See Book II, c. 21.

English mystics, Julian of Norwich is perhaps the best known and the most charming. She is the English equivalent of Siena's Catherine and Sweden's Bridget, except that, unlike her great contemporaries, she did not concern herself with the problems of kingdoms and of the Church, but lived as a recluse in her quiet corner.... There can be no doubt that Lady Julian is the greatest of the English mystics."[40]

The writing of the *Revelations* emerged from unique circumstances. Julian tells us that on May 8, 1373, during an illness that was thought to be fatal, she was favored with sixteen revelations (or showings as she called them). She was thirty years old at the time, and she took these revelations to be a response to three prayerful petitions that she had made earlier in her life. Sometime after these revelations took place, she composed a short account of them. Then, many years later, after much prayer and reflection, she wrote a longer account of them. Thus, we have a short version and a long version of the revelations.

In the written account of her revelations, Julian discusses a number of theological themes and Church doctrines. In fact, with Julian we have someone who provides an excellent synthesis of mystical experience and theological reflection. Her theological insights flow from her mystical experiences, and she presents a prayerful commentary on many basic doctrines of the Christian faith. For this reason, the text of the *Revelations* can be a challenging one that requires careful reading. Her writings also indicate that she is a woman of learning who is well read in the Western spiritual tradition. This leads some commentators to believe that Julian was a member of a monastic community before taking up the life of an anchoress.

---

[40] Merton, *op cit.*, 140. For studies of Julian's thought see Paul Molinari, S.J., *Julian of Norwich, The Teaching of a 14th Century Mystic* (London: Longmans, Green and Co., 1958); Grace M. Jantzen, *Julian of Norwich, Mystic and Theologian* (New York: Paulist Press, 1988); and Brant Pelphrey, *Julian of Norwich* (Wilmington, DE: Michael Glazier, 1989). For a translation of the *Revelations* in modern English with a very good introduction, see *Julian of Norwich, Showings*, translated from the critical text with an introduction by Edmund Colledge, O.S.A. and James Walsh, S.J. (New York: Paulist Press, 1978).

Of all the theological themes and issues that she discusses, it is the love of God for all creation and for all human beings that is clearly emphasized. The divine love is shown in many ways, but especially in the passion and death of Christ on the Cross. Julian speaks of God's all embracing love with warmth and tenderness. For example, she is fond of using the word "homely" in describing God's love, a term equivalent in modern usage to such words as "friendly" or "intimate." She also describes God's love as being "courteous" to bring out God's loving condescension, kindness and loyalty. For Julian, it is God's love that protects us. "He is our clothing, who wraps and enfolds us for love, embraces us and shelters us, surrounds us for his love, which is so tender that he may never desert us."[41]

Two other important points should be mentioned briefly. First, there is Julian's use of the term "mother" in speaking about God and Jesus. This she does with great simplicity, tenderness and insight. Secondly, there is her ongoing struggle to reconcile the reality of sin and evil with God's mercy and the mystery of redemption. Julian's ultimate optimism is based on the reassurance she receives from the words of Christ to her: "I shall make all things well."[42]

There is a passage at the end of the *Revelations of Divine Love* that has often been quoted, since it sums up so much of her thought. Julian writes:

> And from the time that it was revealed, I desired many times to know in what was our Lord's meaning. And fifteen years after and more, I was answered in spiritual understanding, and it was said: What, do you wish to know your Lord's meaning in this thing? Know it well, love was his meaning. Who reveals it to you? Love. What did he reveal to you? Love. Why does he reveal it to you? For love. Remain in

---

[41] *Showings*, Colledge and Walsh, *op. cit.*, p. 183.
[42] *Ibid.*, p. 229.

this, and you will know more of the same. But you will never
know different, without end.[43]

Margery Kempe (c. 1373-c. 1440) was a contemporary of
Julian who at one time visited her in her cell at Norwich. She had
heard of Julian's reputation as a wise spiritual guide and went there
seeking spiritual counsel. A wife and mother of many children, she
later took a vow of chastity and devoted herself with much enthusiasm to religious practices, while remaining a laywoman. Toward
the end of her life, she dictated an account of her life, but it was soon
lost from sight. The manuscript in its entirety was rediscovered in
1934, and published as *The Book of Marjory Kempe*.[44] It is a work
of much historical value that colorfully narrates her struggles, visions, pilgrimages, and adventures. She emerges as a sincere, deeply
religious, and very emotional person, whose behavior at times appeared strange to many of her contemporaries. She lived in an age
that was often marked by a spirit of enthusiasm and exaggeration,
and this is reflected in the interesting life of this spirited and independent woman.

6. The *"Devotio Moderna"*

Toward the end of the fourteenth century, a movement began in the Netherlands that came to be known as the *Devotio
Moderna* (the *New Devotion*).[45] It was a renewal movement that
brought about some much needed new blood and religious vitality

---

[43] *Ibid.*, p. 342.

[44] For modern translations, see *The Book of Margery Kempe*, a modern version by W. But-
ler-Bowdon, with an introduction by R.W. Chambers (New York: The Devin-Adair
Company, 1944); and *The Book of Margery Kempe, The Autobiography of the Madwoman
of God*, a new translation by Tony D. Triggs (Liguori, Missouri: Triumph Books, 1995).

[45] See Pourrat, *op. cit.*, Vol. II, pp. 252-264; Vandenbroucke *op. cit.*, pp. 428-439. For a
helpful introduction and for some of the early writings of the movement, see *Devotio
Moderna, Basic Writings*, translated and introduced by John Van Engen (New York:
Paulist Press, 1988).

into an historical period that was spiritually impoverished. It was marked by an affective piety and a strong devotion to Christ, with its roots definitely in the earlier classical and monastic tradition. Its newer thrust, however, lay in the largely popular character of its piety and the small part given to intellectual considerations in its overall spirituality. *The Imitation of Christ* of Thomas à Kempis is the best known book that emerged from the spirituality of the *New Devotion.*

The beginnings of the movement are clearly traceable to Gerard Groote (1340-1384). Born of a prosperous family in Deventer in present day Holland, his early life was devoted to study, travel, and clerical ambition. In 1374, however, at the age of thirty-four, he underwent a religious conversion that brought profound changes to his life. He renounced his ecclesiastical benefices and adopted a penitential and prayerful way of life. He spent a lengthy period of retreat at a Carthusian monastery, visited the Flemish mystic, John Ruusbroec, at his priory at Groenendaal, but felt no inclination to join any established religious or monastic community. He declined ordination to the priesthood out of humility, but was ordained a deacon and received permission to preach throughout the diocese of Utrecht. He preached in Latin to the clergy and in Dutch to the people. His somewhat strident criticisms of clerical abuses led to opposition from the hierarchy, and his permission to preach in the diocese of Utrecht was revoked in 1383. He died a year later at the age of forty-four.

Gerard Groote was a reformer. He saw all around him the poor state of the spiritual life of the clergy, religious and laity, and he sought to do what he could in a very practical way. His basic message was one of repentance and renewal. He emphasized conversion of heart, perseverance in the life of devotion and in following the suffering Christ, growth in the virtues, and the importance of eternal salvation. As a spiritual legacy to his disciples, he also left a number of writings that include autobiographical works, sermons, letters and various treatises on the spiritual life.

Before his early death, Groote had attracted a number of fervent disciples. One of the first was Florent Radewijns (1350-1400), who did much to organize and direct the houses of the "Brothers and Sisters of the Common Life" that had begun to form and spread. They were separate communities of pious men and women who came together voluntarily to live a life "in common." They supported themselves from their work, the brothers primarily as copyists of spiritual and liturgical books, and the sisters as seamstresses. They were not religious in the strict sense, for they did not take vows, but they did seek to live an ordered life of prayer and work. They sought to live together in humility and love, to grow in the virtues, and to practice the life of devotion inspired by the vision of Gerard Groote. Later, the brothers also founded and directed schools that came to be very successful and well known.[46]

A further development took place with some of the brothers going from Deventer to Windesheim to found a monastery. This group became religious in the strict sense, adopting the Rule of the Canons Regular of Saint Augustine. The monastery at Windesheim, which was approved by Pope Boniface IX in 1395, flourished and expanded. A Windesheim congregation was formed, and eventually it grew to a point where there were in the Netherlands and in the surrounding areas eighty-four monasteries for men and thirteen for women. These monasteries of the Windesheim congregation became centers for the spread of devotional writings, and greatly influenced reform and renewal among many of the older monastic and religious communities.

A significant number of spiritual writings emerged from the entire movement, clearly attesting to its vitality and influence. These writings developed many of the basic themes of the spirituality that characterized the *Devotio Moderna*. There was first of all the strong devotion to the person of Christ, an emphasis that was very much in harmony with the earlier Cistercian and Franciscan tradition. The focus on the life and passion of Christ was to be nourished by the ongoing prayerful reading of spiritual writings, espe-

---

[46] For some of this early history, see *ibid.*, p. 12 ff.

cially Sacred Scripture. Progress in the virtues, especially charity and humility, was also a theme that was returned to over and over. All of this was intended to lead to a deepened spirit of "inwardness" or "interiority" in one's life of prayer and work. Many of the writings of the *Devotio Moderna* also provided methods of meditation and other systematic exercises as practical aids for prayer and devotion. An important devotional work that summarizes well all the main elements of the movement is *The Spiritual Ascents* of Gerard Zerbolt of Zutphern (1367-1398).[47] The best known, however, of all the writings of the *Devotio Moderna* is undoubtedly, *The Imitation of Christ*.

The Imitation of Christ holds a special place in the history of Christian spirituality. Since its first appearance in Latin in the early fifteenth century, this classic of devotional literature has gone through countless editions and translations.[48] It has had the distinction of being the best known and most popular religious writing outside of the Bible in the Western world, and over the centuries it has nourished the interior lives of people in all walks of life.

The Imitation of Christ is generally attributed to Thomas à Kempis (c. 1379-1471), although this has not always met with universal agreement. After completing his schooling at Deventer in 1398, he was admitted by Florent Radewijns into the community of copyists. A year later, he entered one of the monasteries connected with Windesheim, where his brother was prior, and it was here at the monastery of Mount Saint Agnes near Zwolle that he lived out his long life in calm and peace. He copied books but he also composed ascetic and historical treatises of his own.

---

[47] For an English translation of this work, see *ibid.*, pp. 245-315.

[48] Among the many English editions are *The Imitation of Christ*, edited with an introduction by Harold Gardiner, S.J. (New York: Image Books, 1955); *My Imitation of Christ*, trans. by Msgr. John J. Gorman (Brooklyn, NY: Confraternity of the Precious Blood, 1982); *The Imitation of Christ, A New Translation*, trans. by Joseph Tylenda, S.J. (Wilmington: Michael Glazier, 1984); *The Imitation of Christ, A New Reading*, translated by William Creasy (Macon: Mercer University Press, 1989); *The Imitation of Christ with Reflections from the Documents of Vatican II for Each Chapter* (New York: Alba House, 1995); and *The Imitation of Christ Paraphrased* by Donald Demaray (New York: Alba House, 1997).

The title usually given to *The Imitation of Christ* comes from the heading of the first chapter: "Of the Imitation or Following of Christ and the Despising of All Vanities of the World." The text of the book as we know it has been traditionally divided into four books. Book I contains admonitions useful to the spiritual life; Book II speaks of admonitions concerning interior things; Book III treats of interior consolation and the inward speaking of Christ to a faithful soul; and Book IV is devoted to a treatise on the Blessed Sacrament.

There is no logical sequence between any of the books or chapters and, as a result, it can be picked up at any place and read at random. The various chapters contain unconnected spiritual maxims and other sayings, which seek to arouse the reader to a greater knowledge and love of God and a knowledge of oneself. There are many allusions and references to Scripture. There are also frequent colloquies directed to God in touching terms, and often, particularly in the third book, there are moving dialogues between Christ and the individual.

The spirituality of *The Imitation of Christ* is predominantly inward looking. The relationship between the individual and God assumes the prominent position. Recognizing the importance of the knowledge of God and the knowledge of self for the growth and development of the interior life, it stresses St. Augustine's prayer: "Grant, Lord, that I may know myself and that I may know thee." To attain this, there should be the continual examination of one's conscience and the consideration of one's position before God. Acknowledging our weakness and misery, we turn to God from whom comes all our strength.

Closely connected with this stress on the knowledge of God and the knowledge of self, is the theme of renunciation of self or *resignatio*. This involves a complete sacrifice of oneself and at the same time a trustful abandonment to God. It is a going out of oneself and embracing the divine will with all one's heart and strength; it is focusing one's eyes firmly on God in love and valuing him above all things.

There is also the theme of the following of Christ. Christ the

Master is the way, the truth and the life, who invites us to follow him. He teaches us through his doctrine, but more through his example of renunciation of self and resignation to the will of the Father. If we wish to follow Jesus seriously, we must enter courageously upon the royal road of the Cross, "for we shall seek him elsewhere in vain." It is only through obedience, humility, poverty, freedom from earthly goods, and especially patience in adversity that we will find him.

Perhaps the secret of *The Imitation of Christ* and its great strength lies in its ability to move the heart and inspire the reader to turn to God with renewed hope, dedication, love and trust. It has a unique power to awaken in the reader a profound awareness of God and his reality. And yet, it is not without its limitations, and this has often been pointed out. There is, first of all, the charge that *The Imitation* tends to be anti-intellectual in its approach and attitude, and that its piety is not related sufficiently to doctrine. Secondly, the "withdrawal from the world" aspect is very pronounced, and along with this is a certain negativism towards oneself and other created persons and things. Thirdly, some have found the "vertical dimension" too strong with the emphasis on God and the individual. These objections, which are certainly valid, should be seen in light of the book's history and the particular context in which it was written. The *Devotio Moderna* school was reacting against the excesses of an overly speculative spirituality, and the book itself came out of a monastic setting. Still, in spite of its limitations, it remains an important spiritual classic and a work that has been very helpful to countless people.

The movement known as the *Devotio Moderna* was a very significant means of reform and renewal in the fourteenth and fifteenth centuries. With its practical, direct approach, and its emphasis on the primacy of love and the fervent following of Christ, it provided a healthy reaction to some of the excesses of speculation. However, it played a part in adding to the division that was growing between theology and spirituality. This was a tendency in Western spirituality that would become more pronounced in the following years.

John Gerson

John Gerson (1363-1429) was an attractive person in many ways. As a priest, theologian, and chancellor of the University of Paris, he was called upon to take an active role in many of the ecclesiastical and political issues of the turbulent age in which he lived. He worked for Church unity and reform and was active at the Council of Constance (1414-1418), which finally brought the tragic schism in the Church to an end. But he was also a very significant spiritual writer of the late Middle Ages. Like the proponents of the *Devotio Moderna,* he reacted against the excessive spirit of speculation in both theology and spirituality. With his theological and academic background, however, he was more inclined to seek an integration and synthesis of theology and piety. In a very practical way, he sought to use his learning for the good of the Church and the individual Christian.[49]

In his writings, Gerson shows that he belongs more to the tradition of the earlier Middle Ages, that of St. Bernard, the Victorines, and St. Bonaventure, and that he has somewhat of a distrust for the Rhineland mystics and John Ruusbroec. In one of his major works, *On Mystical Theology, Speculative and Practical,* he develops his thoughts on the distinction and connection between speculative theology and mysticism. As a spiritual director and guide, he also sought to distinguish true mystics from false ones, and in two of his treatises he carefully and prudently focuses on guidelines for the discernment of spirits. He was also an effective preacher and many of his sermons have been preserved in both Latin and the vernacular.

John Gerson was forced to leave Paris after the Council of Constance because of the political opposition of the Burgundians, and he was never able to return. His last years were spent in Lyons,

---

[49] For further background on Gerson, see James L. Connolly, *Jean Gerson: Reformer and Mystic* (Dubuque, Iowa: Brown, 1962); and Pourrat, *op. cit.,* vol. II, pp. 268-284. Gerson's *Opera Omnia* were published at Antwerp in 1703.

where he continued his writing, while also humbly teaching and instructing young children.

Another important mystical theologian of the fifteenth century was Denis of Rijckel, also known as Denis the Carthusian (1402-1471). He spent most of his life at the Carthusian charterhouse of Roermond near Liege and was a prolific author. He was able to remain independent of many of the negative currents of his own time, and his own vast learning was nourished by the Bible, the Fathers, and the theologians who wrote before the fourteenth century. Among his many writings are biblical commentaries, studies on the writings of Pseudo-Dionysius, and various treatises on mystical theology. Although he was not an original thinker, he had a great gift of summarizing, synthesizing, and evaluating the valuable earlier tradition, and unlike most of his own contemporaries, he did not divorce theology and mysticism. He also sought to assist others to lead a more fervent Christian life by writing a number of practical treatises addressed to individual classes of people. These included treatises for such diverse groups as bishops, novices in religious communities, princes, nobles, soldiers, merchants, married people, widows, etc. Denis was a significant writer in his own right, but he was also part of the great medieval Carthusian tradition, of those gentle and humble solitaries who contributed so much to the spirituality of the Middle Ages.

7. Popular Piety[50]

Some general characteristics should be kept in mind when speaking about popular piety in the late Middle Ages. First of all, the overall spirit of pessimism that permeated the age was a reality that could not be ignored. The ongoing wars, the plagues, the schism in the Church, the greed and vices of many church leaders — these and many other factors led to this deep-seated pessimism.

---

[50] See Vandenbroucke's chapter nine, "Lay Spirituality from the fourteenth to the sixteenth century," pp. 481-505.

The old Christendom was crumbling away, and the divisions and breakdowns continued to increase at every level of society. These included the constant deteriorating relations between Church and civil societies, the breakdown of loyalty and the spirit of chivalry, the sense of separation and growing disillusionment that the ordinary Christian felt toward Church leaders, the growing division between theology and spirituality, and the overall sense of sin, tragedy, and mortality that permeated the age. It is not surprising that a great concern with death and dying was very present in the minds of many people. This was reflected in the numerous spiritual treatises on the "art of dying," as well as in the secular literature of the *Danses macabre* (Dances of Death).

A disturbing element that emerged from this somber climate was an obsessive, superstitious fear of Satan and his powers. This "Satanic fever" appeared early in the fifteenth century and grew in intensity as the century wore on. The Inquisition soon was charged with the task of rooting out the various perceived forms of witchcraft and worship of the devil. The fear reached such a point that in December of 1484, Innocent VII issued a papal bull that gave broad powers of procedure to the inquisitors. This was followed by the publication of the *Malleus maleficarum* ("The Hammer of Witches"), a treatise written by two Dominicans, Henry Kramer and James Sprenger. This influential document set down the rules and procedures for witchcraft trials. As an official guide for investigations and interrogations, some of its methods, such as the use of torture for extracting confessions, were far from humane. Although it reached a high point in the fifteenth century, this irrational fear of Satan and witchcraft continued to be present in both Catholic and Protestant circles until the seventeenth century.

There was more, however, to popular piety than this spirit of pessimism and excessive fear of Satanism. Even in these difficult times, faith remained vibrant. The Bible and the Eucharist continued to nourish that faith, as it had in the earlier years of the Middle Ages. Devotion to Christ, Mary, and the saints continued to be very much a part of popular piety. But there were other characteristics of this period that were more problematic. There was a tendency on the part of many towards a formalism in religious practices that smacked of superstition. This was evident in such areas as relics, prayers for indulgences, pilgrimages, and large alms to monasteries. There was an excessive belief on the part of many that these would be effective protections from misfortunes in this world and from damnation in the next.[51]

There was also a growing movement toward a greater spirit of individualism, along with a progressive weakening of the traditional bonds that united those in the Christian community. Private prayers and devotions played a much stronger role than the common worship and prayer. The emphasis was on one's personal relation with God, and this relationship was primarily expressed in an affective and devotional form of piety. The mediating role of the Church, with its liturgy and sacramental system, was not valued as highly as it had been in the past. In a very real sense, this new trend in popular piety was sowing the seed for elements of the piety of the Reformation in the sixteenth century.

Saints and mystics were still present among the laity, even in these difficult and challenging times. It is interesting to note that the particular vocation of many of them tended to be of a more special and individualized type. Two laywomen stand out: St. Frances of Rome (1383-1440) and St. Catherine of Genoa (1447-1510). Frances, a wife and mother, combined a life of contemplative graces with service of the poor and the sick in the Trastevere section of Rome. Similar work was carried on by St. Catherine of Genoa. Catherine was born into an aristocratic, Genovese family, and at an early age she was forced into a marriage of family and political convenience. After many years of much unhappiness, Catherine underwent a religious conversion that left her with a profound conviction of the pure love of God and brought great and lasting changes to her life. She gave herself to a life of prayer and penance, and began her work of service to the poor and sick in Genoa that

---

[51] *Ibid.*, p. 497.

would last for the rest of her life. Later, her husband abandoned his wayward lifestyle, and together they devoted themselves full time to the service of the sick and the poor at the Pammatone Hospital in Genoa. Catherine continued this work after his death, even serving for a number of years as the director of the hospital.

St. Catherine did not leave any writings herself. After her death, however, her confessor and spiritual director, Cattaneo Marabotto, and some of her other disciples, gathered together what she had told them of her mystical experiences and sufferings. These writings include the *Life*, the *Purgation and Purgatory*, and *The Spiritual Dialogue*. These writings comprise her spiritual legacy and her teaching on the Pure Love of God. One of her closest disciples, Ettore Vernazza, carried on her spirit in a very influential way with his founding of the Oratory of Divine Love in Genoa in 1497. Catherine's life and teaching continued to have great influence in both Catholic and Protestant circles in the centuries after her death.[52]

The most extraordinary saint of the fifteenth century was St. Joan of Arc (1412-1431), the Maid of Orleans. Her story is well known and has often been told in many literary and dramatic forms. As a young girl of thirteen in her native village of Domremy in France, she was impelled by heavenly "voices," those of St. Michael the Archangel, St. Catherine and St. Margaret, to go to the aid of France at a dire moment in its long struggle with England. Her military leadership led to the raising of the English siege at Orleans, the liberation of other parts of France, and the coronation of the Dauphin as King at Rheims in 1429. Ultimately, she was wounded in battle, captured and imprisoned. Her infamous trial ended with her condemnation for witchcraft and relapsed heresy. She was

---

[52] For background on Saint Catherine and her writings, see *Catherine of Genoa: Purgation and Purgatory, The Spiritual Dialogue*, translation and notes by Serge Hughes, introduction by Benedict J. Groeschel, O.F.M., Cap. (New York: Paulist Press, 1979). Friedrich von Hügel is the author of a very influential study of Catherine. See his *The Mystical Element of Religion as Studied in Saint Catherine of Genoa and Her Friends* (London: J.M. Dent, 1908).

burned at the stake at Rouen on May 30, 1431. Twenty-five years later her trial was reopened, and Joan was found innocent of all charges. She was canonized on May 16, 1920 for her heroic charity and purity of life.

8. The Humanist Renaissance

The Humanist Renaissance arose in Italy in the fourteenth century, flowered in the fifteenth century, and gradually spread across the European continent. In Italy, Florence led the way, and under the intellectual leadership of Francesco Petrarch (1304-1374) and Boccaccio (d. 1375), it became a center for literature and the arts. This movement found its inspiration, not in the learning and culture of the Middle Ages, but in a return to classical antiquity. The proponents of this primarily literary movement believed that the study of the style and content of the writings of such ancient Latin authors as Cicero and Virgil would positively influence people's lives and morals. This classical literature had for the Humanists a strong didactic, formative, and ethical component. Rhetoric, the art of eloquent and persuasive discourse, was especially valued since it was so helpful in leading others to a life of virtue. The Humanists considered this new approach much more effective than the more abstract, dialectical and logical emphasis of the Scholastic method of learning.[53]

There were other significant shifts and emphases that were part of the new approach of the Renaissance Humanists to learning and culture. In general, it can be said that the Humanists were more optimistic about human nature and the human person. They definitely moved away from the pessimistic approach that charac-

---

[53] For Renaissance spirituality, see Pourrat, *op. cit.*, Vol. III, pp. 49-62; and William J. Bouwsma, "The Spirituality of Renaissance Humanism" in *Christian Spirituality, High Middle Ages and Reformation*, edited by Jill Raitt (New York: Crossroad, 1989), pp. 236-251.

terized so much of the late Middle Ages. With their greater focus on the human person, one can also speak of the more "anthropomorphic" approach of the Humanists, as contrasted with the "theocentric" or God-centered approach that characterized the Middle Ages. This approach is reflected in the art work of the Renaissance.

It is true that some of the Renaissance Humanists, in their return to classical antiquity, abandoned Christianity entirely. The majority, however, definitely intended to remain faithful to the Christian faith and practice, while also seeking to bring literature and art into the service of the Christian religion and piety. These were the Christian Humanists and they included such people as Nicholas of Cusa in Germany, Giovanni Pico della Mirandola in Italy, St. Thomas More and John Colet in England, Christine of Pisano and Jacques Lefèvre d'Etaples in France, and the great Renaissance figure, Erasmus of Rotterdam.

Desiderius Erasmus (c. 1467-1536) studied at the schools of the Brothers of the Common Life as a young boy. He entered the priory of the Canons Regular at Steyn in 1487 and later studied at Paris. His scholarly life was devoted primarily to the study of the ancient classical authors, the Fathers of the Church, and Sacred Scripture. Through the fame of his extensive writings, his many travels, and his widespread contacts, he became one of the most celebrated figures of the Renaissance era. He also made an important contribution as a spiritual writer through such works as the *Enchiridion Militis Christiani* (*The Handbook of the Christian Knight*).

Erasmus wrote the *Enchiridion Militis Christiani* around 1503 as an early summary of his conception of the Christian life, intended mainly for the educated Christian. He never abandoned this framework, and his later writings only developed and expanded his basic points. In general, he had little regard for the popular religious piety that placed such an emphasis on the formalistic observance of external religious practices without making any effort to reform one's life and to become closely united with Christ. True piety, he argued, must be found in the developing and nourishing of the interior life. For Erasmus, the Christian was involved in an ongoing battle against the world. The Christian must be constantly alert in the struggle against vice and armed with the weapons of prayer and knowledge. For Erasmus, prayer directs us to heaven and provides us with a citadel that is inaccessible to the enemy. Knowledge fortifies the mind and keeps virtue ever before us. The prayerful study of Scripture is very important and Christians must keep their eyes steadily on Christ. It is through prayer and knowledge that the Christian grows in the interior life.[54]

Conclusion

With the writings of the Rhineland mystics, John Ruusbroec, Catherine of Siena, the English mystics, and the *Devotio Moderna*, the late Middle Ages left its own impressive legacy, even though the times were troubled. After the *Devotio Moderna*, there were no new or vibrant movements. The long period of the Middle Ages was drawing to an end, with little energy or resources left to deal with the new challenges that lay ahead. The sixteenth century, the beginning of the modern era, would bring profound changes to Church and society. From the Reformation would come the divisions that have remained in the Western Church to the present day. It is to the spirituality that emerged from this movement that we will now turn. First, however, we must look once again to the East and to the developments that took place in the spirituality of the Byzantine world.

---

[54] For an English translation of the *Enchiridion*, as well as his *In Praise of Folly* and some other spiritual writings, see *The Essential Erasmus*, translated with an introduction and commentary by John P. Dolan (New York: New American Library, 1964).

For Further Reading

Christian Spirituality II, High Middle Ages and Reformation. Edited by Jill Raitt. New York: Crossroad, 1989.

Davies, Oliver, *God Within, The Mystical Tradition of Northern Europe.* New York: Paulist Press, 1988.

David Knowles, *The English Mystical Tradition.* New York: 1961.

Thomas Merton, "The English Mystics," in *Mystics and Zen Masters.* New York: Delta Books, 1967, pp. 138-153.

Sitwell, Gerard, O.S.B., *Spiritual Writers of the Middle Ages.* New York: Hawthorn Books, 1961.

Jean Leclercq, François Vandenbroucke, and Louis Bouyer, *The Spirituality of the Middle Ages.* New York: The Seabury Press, 1968, pp. 373-543.

For individual writers, see the suggestions in the appropriate footnotes.

7 Byzantine and Early Protestant Spirituality

A. BYZANTINE SPIRITUALITY[1]

The term "Byzantium" usually refers to the Eastern, Greek-speaking empire that was in existence from the death of the emperor Justinian in 565 until the fall of Constantinople to the forces of Islam in 1453. This extended period witnessed a number of conflicts and tensions between the Eastern and Western Churches that led inexorably to a final and lasting rupture. There was no one, clear-cut event that caused the schism, but there were a number of religious and political factors that played a significant role over the centuries. Among them was the iconoclast conflict that lasted over a century (726-843) and caused such bitter strife in the East. The coronation of Charlemagne as the Holy Roman Emperor in the West in 800 brought about consternation in the East. The disputed election of Photius as patriarch of Constantinople in the ninth century caused further divisions. The final rupture occurred in the eleventh century, when the dispute between the patriarch, Michael Cerularius, and the papal legates ended with mutual excommunications. The sack of Constantinople during the Fourth Crusade in 1204, and the

---

[1] See the appendix on Byzantine Spirituality by Louis Bouyer, in *The Spirituality of the Middle Ages* (New York: The Seabury Press, 1968), pp. 545-590.

establishment of a Latin Empire that lasted about fifty years, led to further bitterness and a deep and perduring mistrust of the West on the part of the East. Promising attempts at reunion, such as those at the time of the Council of Lyons (1274) and the Council of Florence (1439), ended in failure.

1. Byzantine Monasticism

As Louis Bouyer emphasizes, monasticism always had a central role in Byzantine spirituality and culture.[2] Two important and fruitful tendencies developed within this monasticism, and each was associated with two main centers. They are usually referred to as the Sinaitic and Studite traditions.

The Sinaitic tradition takes its name and spirit from the famous monastery of Mt. Sinai in Egypt. As early as the fourth century, Mt. Sinai and the surrounding areas were populated by a number of monks living as solitaries. Adequate security against desert nomads was always a problem for the scattered monks, and so in the sixth century a large, fortress-like monastery was built under the emperor, Justinian. Most of the hermits came together to form a community at this place. As a result of these early beginnings, the monastery of Mt. Sinai preserved an eremitical spirit, even in this cenobitic setting. It should be recalled that during the seventh century St. John Climacus lived as a hermit for forty years in the Sinai desert not far from the famous monastery, and then became its abbot. It was there that he wrote his influential book, the *Ladder of Divine Ascent*.

In addition to the eremitic thrust and the corresponding emphasis on separation from the world, the Sinaitic tradition of Byzantine monasticism was also characterized by a significant mystical dimension and spirit. Also associated with it was a charismatic and spontaneous element, as well as such traditional aspects of Byz-

---

[2] *Ibid.*, p. 555 ff.

antine spirituality as the Jesus Prayer, breathing exercises, and various other practices connected with the method of prayer known as hesychasm.

Constantinople was the center for Studite monasticism. In the fifth century, the consul, Studios, established a monastery in the city. Soon this foundation, whose monks were known as Studites, became an important monastic center and one that was involved in many social and charitable activities. In the ninth century, the abbot, St. Theodore, gave them a rule that was based on that of St. Basil the Great. The influence of this Studite rule at Constantinople was extensive, for it became the model rule for the other great cenobitic monasteries of the East during the following centuries. The Studite tradition, then, had a strong cenobitic thrust and a corresponding emphasis on a hierarchical and organizational structure. Byzantine liturgy and iconography were highly developed in the Studite monasteries, and a strong social and apostolic dimension was also present.

These two traditions, Sinaitic and Studite, were not in opposition to one another. They provided a healthy tension that gave birth to creative and different elements in Byzantine spirituality. Symeon the New Theologian, for example, was someone who lived in the midst of Studite monasticism, but brought there a charismatic and mystical spirituality.

2. Symeon the New Theologian

The designation of St. Symeon (949-1022) as "the New Theologian" has come down to us through the centuries. It is usually interpreted as implying a comparison with St. John the Evangelist (the Divine), and St. Gregory Nazianzen, who was known in antiquity as "the Theologian." Symeon was a theologian, not in the modern academic sense, but in the earlier meaning of Eastern Christianity, namely a person of prayer and experience of God, who writes about God on the basis of what has been seen and tasted. The knowledge and wisdom comes through the infusion of the Holy Spirit after a person has been purified through ascetic practices and a spirit of repentance. St. Symeon as the "New Theologian" renewed in the eleventh century the tradition of mystical prayer that St. John gave witness to in the first century and St. Gregory of Nazianzus in the fourth.[3]

There is a close affinity between Symeon the New Theologian and the tradition of Pseudo-Macarius. This is apparent in the emphasis Symeon has in his teaching and writings on such themes as the symbol of light, the conscious experience of the Holy Spirit in one's life, the centrality of Christ, and his insistence that the direct experience of the Spirit is a normal part of the authentic Christian life. Symeon often referred to himself as the "enthusiastic zealot." He is an attractive and charismatic figure in Eastern spirituality, whose influence has been significant.

Born in Galatia in Asia Minor, Symeon came at an early age to study at Constantinople. As a student he met Symeon the Studite, a holy monk of the monastery of Studios, who became the young Symeon's spiritual director. At the age of twenty, Symeon experienced the first in a series of visions of divine light. A few years later, he gave up his plans for a political career and became a monk at the monastery of St. Mamas at Constantinople. Ordained a priest there, he soon was elected abbot of the monastery and served in that position for over twenty years.

The monastery became a fervent one under his leadership as abbot, but these years were not without their difficulties. Some of the monks in his own community resented his charismatic and reforming ways, particularly his teaching that his own mystical experiences were normative for all true Christians. There were also his conflicts with Archbishop Stephen of Nicomedia, a leading theologian at Constantinople. As a more speculatively oriented theologian, Stephen had very little sympathy with Symeon's charismatic

---

[3] See the article by Kallistos Ware, "Symeon the New Theologian" in *The Study of Spirituality* (New York: Oxford University Press, 1986), p. 237.

and mystical approach and his teaching on the necessity of the consciousness of grace. Also, Symeon's teaching on the primacy of personal experience of God was seen as a threat to legitimate ecclesiastical authority by Stephen and other members of the hierarchy. These conflicts led to an ecclesiastical trial and Symeon's banishment in 1109 to the small town of Paloukiton on the Asiatic side of the Bosphorus. The exile was soon lifted by the Patriarch Sergios and Symeon was offered an archbishopric. He declined and spent his last years in relative solitude in the little monastery he established at Paloukiton with a few of his disciples, devoting himself to prayer and writing. At a later date, Symeon was canonized by the Orthodox Church and given the title of "the New Theologian."

Symeon's principal writings are *The Discourses* and *The Hymns of Divine Love*. *The Discourses* were originally given as conferences to his monks during the years he was abbot.[4] *The Hymns of Divine Love*, composed during his last years, are in a sense a poetic version of *The Discourses*.[5] In all of Symeon's writings, there is a strong personal and autobiographical dimension. More than any other Eastern spiritual writer, Symeon often shares his own mystical experiences with the reader.

Symeon's writings are very much in the tradition of such earlier writers as Evagrius Ponticus, John Climacus, Pseudo-Macarius, and Diadochus. He develops all the traditional themes of the ascetic practices that lead to true contemplation. These include repentance, renunciation, remembrance of death, sorrow for sins, purity of heart, growth in the virtues, works of mercy, faith, contemplation, and divinization. Symeon's first conference to his monks was on charity, and it continued to be a constant theme, for he was convinced that true holiness manifests itself in love of one's neighbor.

---

[4] For an English translation of *The Discourses* with some very good background material, see *Symeon the New Theologian, The Discourses*, translation by C.J. de Catanazaro, introduction by George A. Maloney, S.J. (New York: Paulist Press, 1980).

[5] See *Hymns of Divine Love* by St. Symeon the New Theologian, introduction and translation by George A. Maloney, S.J. (Denville, New Jersey: Dimension Books, 1976).

There is a strong emphasis on Jesus as light, and the visions of light are highlighted. The light of Christ is only given to those who seek him in repentance and purification. Also, with the exception of Isaac the Syrian, there is no one who stresses more the importance of receiving the gift of tears from the Holy Spirit. The abiding sorrow for sin (*penthos*) reaches its highest point when, through the gift of the Holy Spirit, one pours out tears in abundance.

What is particularly unique about Symeon is his emphasis on the role of the Holy Spirit. Seven of his thirty-four discourses are devoted to the operations of the Holy Spirit in the process of leading a person to mystical union. For Symeon, it is the Holy Spirit who stirs the Christian to a spirit of true repentance; it is the Holy Spirit who comes as a sudden transforming experience; it is the Holy Spirit who brings a person to a mystical union with the indwelling Trinity; it is only the Holy Spirit who makes it possible for someone to teach or guide another effectively.

Although Symeon the New Theologian develops many different themes and aspects of the spiritual life, the overall goal is constantly before his mind. That goal is to be more and more divinized through God's grace. As Fr. George Maloney aptly summarizes: "The ascetic practices that he develops and the constant stress on purification and repentance have meaning only in the light of the goal, the divinization of the individual Christian into a loving child of God, more and more consciously aware of the transforming love of the indwelling Trinity that makes him 'a god by adoption and grace,' a phrase repeated continually by Symeon."[6]

3. Byzantine Liturgy and Iconography

The more ecclesiastical and institutional Studite tradition was responsible for the heights that the liturgy and iconography reached

---

[6] See his introduction to *The Discourses*, p. 35.

in Byzantine spirituality.[7] Many elements of the liturgy were traceable to Syrian sources. The earliest Byzantine hymns came from Syria. The monks at the great Studios monastery in Constantinople brought to the capital city the liturgical books that were in use at the monastery of St. Sabbas in Syria. These monks then developed and perfected the books and texts of the Byzantine liturgy. This liturgical usage spread throughout the empire. It took place, however, only after the defeat of the Iconoclasts.

The Iconoclast controversy brought great turmoil to the Byzantine empire during the long period that extended from 726 until the middle of the ninth century. The Iconoclasts attacked the use of icons (the artistic and pictorial representations of Christ, Mary, the saints and angels) in liturgical worship and devotional practice. The long period of controversy finally came to an end with the restoration of the icons to the churches in the spring of 843, an event that came to be known later as the "Triumph of Orthodoxy." Among the important defenders of the icons were St. Germanus of Constantinople, St. John Damascene, and St. Theodore the Studite, the abbot of the Studios monastery at Constantinople. They developed in their writings a rich theology and spirituality of the role of the icons in liturgical worship.

Basic to a theology and spirituality of icons is the understanding of the visible creation as a symbol of the invisible, and material and human reality as a vehicle and channel of the spiritual and divine.[8] Thus, the liturgy is seen as veiling under visible symbols the reality of heavenly worship. In a sense, the church building as a whole is an icon. The church is the heaven on earth in which God dwells and moves. The icons that cover the cupola and the walls of the church are doors or windows that make it possible for the worshippers here on earth to participate in the heavenly choir. In the context of prayer and worship, the icons become a means of com-

---

[7] See Bouyer, *op. cit.*, pp. 572-576.

[8] See *ibid.*, p. 573 ff. See also Kallistos Ware, "The Spirituality of the Icon," in *The Study of Spirituality*, pp. 195-197.

munion that bring about a vibrant contact and encounter with the person or mystery that is depicted. "Present through their icons, the Mother of God, the angels and the saints become fellow-worshippers with the living, concelebrants in the same liturgical act."[9]

4. St. Gregory Palamas and Athonite Hesychasm

The liturgy and iconography certainly nourished Byzantine piety, but there was also another important and significant spiritual tradition that enriched Eastern spirituality. This was the interior and prayerful movement known as hesychasm. The Greek word *hesychia* denotes a state of "quietude" or "tranquillity." In monastic literature going back to the fourth century, the term was used to designate the way of life chosen by hermits who devoted themselves to a life of constant prayer. The monks themselves were referred to as *hesychasts*. Later, the term was used in a more restrictive sense to describe those whose spirituality centered on a systematic repetition of the Jesus Prayer ("Lord, Jesus Christ, Son of God, have mercy on me"),[10] accompanied by rhythmic breathing and certain bodily positions. This form of prayer reached a high development at Mt. Athos in Greece. It was there that St. Gregory Palamas defended this tradition of prayer during the famous Hesychast controversy that took place in the fourteenth century.

Mount Athos in Greece had a number of hermits living in its solitary regions as early as the ninth century. In the tenth century the first cenobitic monastery was built, and soon the mountainous peninsula was populated by a growing number of monasteries whose members came from different countries. In time Mount

---

[9] *Ibid.*, p. 197.

[10] For background on the Jesus Prayer, see I. Hausherr, *The Name of Jesus*, Cistercian Studies Series 44 (Kalamazoo, MI: 1978); and Kallistos Ware, "The Origins of the Jesus Prayer: Diadochus, Gaza, Sinai" in *The Study of Spirituality*, pp. 175-184.

Athos became the most important center of Byzantine spirituality.[11] It was here on the "Holy Mountain," as it came to be called, that the Jesus Prayer and the practice of hesychasm took on a more developed and systematic form.

Among the early witnesses of this tradition on Mount Athos were Nicephorus the Hesychast, and St. Gregory of Sinai (d. 1346). There is also a treatise attributed to Symeon the New Theologian, but this is most likely the work of Nicephorus also. The basic principles of the Hesychastic technique are developed in their writings. One is to sit with the head bowed and the eye directed to the navel of the body. While seeking to establish a basic calm in oneself, the rhythm of the breathing is to be slowed down and controlled by deliberately holding the breath. The goal is to find the place of the heart by making the intellect (*nous*) descend into the heart. The heart is seen as the deepest center of the person, and so the prayer of the heart is the prayer of the whole person. The continual repetition of the Jesus Prayer should come from the heart. This prayer helps to keep the intellect free from images and is a source of nourishment. The Jesus Prayer can lead to feelings of compunction and a warmth in the heart that brings a person to the contemplation of the divine light.[12] In the fourteenth century, this tradition of Hesychasm was called into question, reexamined, and then reaffirmed by the Byzantine Church. The attack came from a learned Greek from Calabria in Italy by the name of Barlaam (c. 1290-1348). The successful defense was led by St. Gregory Palamas (1296-1359). The controversy was a complex one, involving a number of philosophical and theological issues. Basic to the dispute was the question of the possibility of a direct knowledge and experience of God in this life. Barlaam argued that our knowledge of God could

---

[11] For an informative account of the monasteries of Mount Athos today, see Basil Pennington, O.C.S.O., *O Holy Mountain: Journal of a Retreat at Mount Athos* (New York: Doubleday, 1978).

[12] See Kallistos Ware, "The Hesychasts: Gregory of Sinai, Gregory Palamas, Nicolas Cabasilas" in *The Study of Spirituality*, pp. 242-255.

only be indirect, and so he disavowed the claim of the Hesychasts of seeing the uncreated light of the Godhead with their bodily eyes. He also criticized the physical practices and techniques of the Hesychasts as materialistic and superstitious. He used the term *omphalopsychoi* ("those who locate the soul in the navel") to describe the Hesychasts.

St. Gregory Palamas was well qualified to defend the Hesychast tradition against the charges of Barlaam. He had followed this way of life both as a monk at Mount Athos and at Thessalonica where he was forced to take refuge for some years following Turkish raids on Mount Athos. He was able to return to the Holy Mountain in 1331 and continued to live as a Hesychast at the hermitage of St. Sabbas. Between 1338-1341 he composed the nine treatises, *For the Defense of Those Who Practice Sacred Quietude*, in response to the charges of Barlaam. These treatises were published in three groups of three books and so are also called *The Triads*.[13]

In response to Barlaam, Gregory emphasizes his key distinction between God's essence and God's energies.[14] God remains unknowable in his essence because God is Creator and we are creatures. But God can be known by creatures in his energies; human beings can directly participate in God's energies even in this life. God acts in this world through the divine energies. These uncreated energies are divine graces. The light which the Hesychasts behold in prayer is a manifestation of the divine energies. Kallistos Ware writes: "The vision of the light is the vision of God himself; of God, however, in his energies and not in his essence. What the saints see is the same uncreated light that shone from Christ at the Transfigu-

---

[13] For selections in English of this work, see Gregory Palamas, *The Triads*, edited with an introduction by John Meyendorff, translation by Nicholas Gendle (New York: Paulist Press, 1983).

[14] This distinction of Gregory Palamas has generated much dispute and controversy among scholars over the years. For a helpful study of the issues see John Meyendorff, *A Study of Gregory Palamas*, translated by George Lawrence (London: The Faith Press, 1964); and John Meyendorff, *St. Gregory Palamas and Orthodox Spirituality* (Crestwood, NY: St. Vladimir's Seminary Press, 1974).

ration on Mount Tabor, and that will shine from him equally at his Second Coming."[15]

The experience of uncreated light for Palamas, then, has a strong eschatological thrust. The divinization or deification that takes place here on earth is a foretaste of the Parousia and of eternal life. It should also be noted that for Gregory Palamas, there is a close interaction between body and soul in the whole process of experiencing the vision of God. The physical techniques of Hesychasm cannot be dismissed as materialistic (as Barlaam does), because the body is intimately connected with the soul in the movement towards God.

The teaching of Gregory Palamas was upheld by synods that met at Constantinople in 1341 and confirmed by the later synods of 1347 and 1351. Gregory was elected archbishop of Thessalonica in 1347 and served as archbishop until his death in 1359. He was canonized in 1368 by the patriarch, Philotheus, at the Synod of Constantinople.

B. Early Protestant Spirituality

The sixteenth century in Europe was a period of great change and upheaval. The Middle Ages gave way to the beginnings of the modern period and a seemingly new world. National powers arose. In 1492 Columbus discovered the Americas. His voyages were followed by those of the Spanish and Portuguese, and then by the French, Spanish, and Dutch. Further discoveries and widespread colonization rapidly took place. The invention of the printing press also brought profound changes in learning and educational practices.

In 1517 Martin Luther nailed his theses on indulgences to the church door at Wittenburg in Germany and ushered in the Protes-

---

[15] See Ware, "The Hesychasts," *op. cit.*, p. 252.

tant Reformation. Bitter and protracted religious wars broke out in Germany and continued until religious divisions between Lutherans and Catholics were established according to the Latin dictum "Cujus regio, ejus religio": the religion of the area followed that of the ruler. The Lutheran tradition spread north to Scandinavia and the Baltic countries. In Germany itself, Martin Luther had to contend with the more radical Anabaptist sect which did not think that he went far enough in his reforms.

Switzerland became another center of reform. The Reformed movement took shape in Zurich under the leadership of Zwingli, but his influence was supplanted by John Calvin. Geneva became the center for Calvinism, which spread into France, the Netherlands, Scotland, and England. France was the scene of much unrest and bloody warfare between the French Huguenots (Calvinists) and Catholics. Peace finally came to the ravaged country in 1598 with the Huguenots having made only a limited impact in France. The Reformation had little lasting influence in Spain and Italy.

England initially remained untouched by the Protestant reform. King Henry VIII early received the title "Defender of the Faith" for his writings. But subsequent difficulties, arising from his divorce of Catherine of Aragon, led to schism and the formation of the Church of England with the king having supreme authority. Anglicanism became the established religion, although separatist groups like the Puritans soon came into existence in England.

These events gave rise to different Protestant traditions and churches that continued as independent Christian bodies. Foremost among these traditions were the Lutheran, Reformed, Anabaptist, Anglican, and Puritan. It is to an examination of the spirituality of these early Protestant traditions that we now turn.

1. Martin Luther

Martin Luther (1483-1546) entered the novitiate of the Hermits of St. Augustine at Erfurt in Germany in 1505. As an Augustinian monk, he completed his studies for the doctorate in theology at Wittenberg in 1512 and then remained in that city as a professor of Scripture. His active role in the controversy over the granting of indulgences in 1517 brought him very much to the public eye. His writings and his strong criticism of Church structures and practices led to sharp conflicts with Rome and eventually to his excommunication in 1520.

Luther occupied a pivotal position in Germany and northern Europe in the first half of the sixteenth century. On the one hand, he was a man who had deep roots in the life and spirituality of Germany's medieval Church. On the other hand, through his life and extensive writings, he opened up many new areas of thought and inaugurated profound changes in the way the Christian life was viewed and practiced. His was a life that was marked in a unique way by continuity and change.

Luther's continuity with the Middle Ages is evident in his familiarity with the German mystical tradition. He had great praise for the sermons of John Tauler, and the anonymous work known as the *Theologica Germanica* was a great favorite of his. In the preface to the second of the two editions that he published of this work, he stated that, with the exception of the Bible and St. Augustine, no other book had taught him more about God, Christ, and the human condition. As Luther's thought developed, he distanced himself more and more from the mystical writers, but it is clear that they were a significant influence on his spiritual thinking.[16]

---

[16] For Luther's spiritual thought, see Jared Wicks, *Luther and His Spiritual Legacy* (Wilmington, DE: Michael Glazier, 1983); Frank C. Senn, "Lutheran Spirituality" in *Protestant Spiritual Traditions*, edited by Frank C. Senn (New York: Paulist Press, 1986), pp. 9-54; and Marc Lienhard, "Luther and the Beginnings of the Reformation" in *Christian Spirituality, High Middle Ages and Reformation*, edited by Jill Raitt (New York: Crossroad, 1989), pp. 268-299.

The most significant component in the formation of Luther's spirituality was his own personal struggles and experience. For much of his life, he was greatly tormented by a condition that he referred to as *anfectung*. It left him distressed by his sinfulness and seemingly alienated from God. He found no peace or reconciliation in confessing his sins or in seeking to please God through the faithful observance of religious practices. Relief from this condition came ultimately through the insights he gained from his study of Scripture and the conviction that justification or righteousness came only from faith in God. For Luther, the righteousness of God is revealed by the gospel. It is a gratuitous gift of God that is revealed to us in the cross of Christ. A person becomes righteous, not through his or her good works, but only through faith in Christ. This basic insight had profound implications for the way Luther subsequently viewed the relationship between God and the human person. It particularly limited the role of good works and many of the religious practices that had been so much a part of medieval spirituality.

The Word of God became central to Luther's spirituality. It is through the Word that God communicates Himself to the believer. The Word is God's personal intervention in the life of the person of faith, and the personal response in faith to the Word is vital to one's relationship with God. Luther made Scripture more available to the German people with his translation of the entire Bible into the vernacular.

Luther's liturgical reforms were aimed at the revitalization of popular piety, particularly with the emphasis on preaching and the frequent reception of communion. Preaching was central to the liturgical celebration, for its purpose was to bring the Scriptures alive in the hearts of the listeners. Luther himself was a popular preacher, and his numerous extant sermons provide clear testimony of his effectiveness as a preacher.

Two other areas that figure prominently in Luther's spirituality are those of hymnody and catechetical writings. Luther encouraged the writing of hymns for both liturgical use and catechetical purposes. Various sources, such as earlier liturgical chants, German sacred *lieder*, and German folk songs were utilized in the composition of hymns. New texts and melodies were also composed by the reformers. One of the most popular was Luther's own composition, "A mighty fortress is our God."

Luther's catechetical writings grew out of his concern over the poor knowledge of the faith among the clergy and the laity. In 1529 he published the *Large Catechism*, a work intended mainly for the clergy. It was based on his earlier catechetical sermons that treated such areas as the Ten Commandments, the Apostles' Creed, and the Our Father. Around the same time, Luther also published the *Small Catechism*. This work was addressed to the ordinary believer for use in the family setting and has none of the polemical overtones that can be found in the *Large Catechism*. The emphasis is on a personal relationship with God and a loving response to the God who has created and redeemed us. Luther's ability to communicate in a simple and direct manner is very much in evidence in this influential *Small Catechism*. His gift as a communicator on a popular level is also evident in his little work, *A Simple Way to Pray*, in which he gives a number of suggestions for prayer. For example, he suggests a method of using each of the Ten Commandments for prayer that comprises four steps: (1) recalling the teaching; (2) giving thanks to God; (3) making confession; and (4) offering petitionary prayer.

Finally, mention should also be made of the importance Luther gave to the doctrine of the priesthood of the faithful, the share in Christ's priesthood imparted to all through the reception of baptism. This provided a theological base for his development of a lay spirituality. Louis Bouyer states: "Luther was the first, at least since patristic times, to proclaim the priesthood of the faithful so clearly and to propose so concretely a genuinely lay spirituality such as would sanctify life in the world with all its domestic or professional responsibilities."[17]

---

[17] Bouyer, *op. cit.*, p. 76.

Johann Arndt and his True Christianity

The century after Luther's death was marked by attempts on the part of his followers to synthesize and defend his teaching. Lutheran theology had evolved into an orthodox or confessional stage in which a scholasticism that had its basis in Aristotelian thought came to the fore. The emphasis in theological writings and sermons was on "pure doctrine" and on the defense of orthodox Lutheranism against Catholics and those Lutherans who wished to incorporate elements from Reformed theology. There were other Lutheran theologians, however, whose main interest was to promote a genuine spiritual renewal. Foremost among them was Johann Arndt (1555-1621).

Arndt's *True Christianity* met with great success and became in time the most popular devotional book in the history of Lutheranism.[18] In this influential work, Arndt sought to lead theological students away from a predominantly polemical and scholastic theology and more to a doctrine of the spiritual life. For Arndt, this would enable them to foster a living faith in themselves and in the faithful.[19] He developed Luther's thought by incorporating the ideas of many of his sources. These included Stauptiz, Luther's spiritual director when he was an Augustinian, St. Bernard of Clairvaux, John Tauler, and writers of the *Devotio Moderna*. Thus, through the writings of Arndt, much of the earlier mystical tradition found its way back into Lutheran piety. With Arndt there was an attempt to fuse justification and sanctification. The basis of his teaching was the deep union with Christ that would penetrate the whole life of the believer. As he writes in the foreword of his classic: "True Christianity consists, namely, in the exhibition of a true, living faith, active in genuine godliness and the fruits of righteousness... we bear the name of Christ, not only because we ought to

---

[18] For an English translation, see Johann Arndt, *True Christianity*, translation and introduction by Peter Erb (New York: Paulist Press, 1979).

[19] See Bouyer, *op. cit.*, p. 100.

believe in Christ, but also because we are to live in Christ and he in us."[20]

Jacob Boehme

A later writer in the German Lutheran tradition who came to be widely read after his death was Jacob Boehme (1575-1624). The mystical writings of this shoemaker from Gorlitz provoked constant opposition in orthodox Lutheran circles during his lifetime, but also gained him a wide and significant following. He was a self-taught man, who, in his home town of Gorlitz, came into contact with such varied currents of thought as the Jewish mystical tradition of the Kabala, the neo-Platonism of the Renaissance, and the work of the alchemist, Paracelsus. Since Boehme made use of all of these sources of knowledge in his writings, in addition to his extensive knowledge of the Bible, many have found his attempts to expound his experiences of God somewhat obscure and esoteric. He was a visionary who experienced a prophetic call to explain his vision of the universe and to grapple with the problem of evil in the world.

Boehme's first book, *Aurora* or *Day-Dawning*, was published in 1612 and was denounced as heretical soon afterwards by his Lutheran pastor. This led to a ban of further writings on the part of the municipal authorities. Boehme observed this for a number of years until he felt called once more to resume his prophetic calling. A number of published works followed, including *Forty Questions on the Soul*, *Three Principles*, *Mysterium Magnum* and the *Clavis* or *Key* to his main teachings. During the last five years of his life, he wrote *The Way to Christ*, a series of devotional treatises on such themes as repentance, prayer, resignation, the new birth, and divine contemplation.[21] The theme of divine wisdom is central to

---

[20] *True Christianity, op. cit.*, p. 21.

[21] For an English translation of this work with background information, see *Jacob Boehme, The Way to Christ*, translation and introduction by Peter Erb (New York: Paulist Press, 1978). See also Jacob Boehme, *Essential Readings*, edited and introduced by Robin Waterfield (Wellingborough, England: Crucible, 1989).

Boehme's religious thought. The way to Christ for him is the way back to Paradise and union with the Virgin Sophia.

The enthusiastic reception of his writings by his disciples caused further problems for Boehme. During his last years he was banished to Dresden. He was later able to return to Gorlitz and died there in communion with the Lutheran Church in 1624. His writings were widely read after his death and were very influential on many later thinkers. Louis Bouyer recognizes Boehme's great ability to arouse a genuinely Christian search, but he concludes that this search will only be substantially fruitful when Boehme's system is left behind.[22] Be that as it may, Boehme's writings have influenced not only such subsequent religious thinkers as Angelus Silesius, William Law, Philip Spener and other later Pietists, but also such German romantic philosophers as Hegel and Schelling.

2. Reformed Spirituality — John Calvin

It would be quite inaccurate to equate reformed spirituality and Calvinism. The historical roots and developments of reformed spirituality are varied and somewhat complex. When Calvin began his reform at Geneva, there was already a reformed tradition and spirituality in existence. Although his theology and spirituality came to have great influence, it never completely replaced what had developed earlier.

The early leader of the reformed movement was Ulrich Zwingli (1484-1531), a contemporary of Martin Luther.[23] He was a parish priest in Zurich, Switzerland, who was greatly influenced by the humanist movement and its strong emphasis on biblical studies. Zwinglian Protestantism was very biblical. For Zwingli, the

---

[22] Bouyer, *op. cit.*, p. 167.

[23] For Zwingli's spirituality, see Bouyer, *op. cit.*, pp. 77-84; Howard G. Hagerman, "Reformed Spirituality" in *Protestant Spiritual Traditions*, pp. 55-59; and Fritz Busser, "The Spirituality of Zwingli and Bullinger in the Reformation of Zurich" in *Christian Spirituality, High Middle Ages and Reformation, op. cit.*, pp. 300-317.

preaching of the Word was to occupy the central position, and he was quick to do away with anything that detracted from the centrality of the Word. Thus, he moved much farther away from Catholic tradition and practices than Luther did.

Two tendencies followed from this emphasis on the Bible in Zwingli's spirituality. First, it brought forth a piety that had a strong inward focus. Secondly, there was an emphasis on a right knowledge that was necessary for overcoming ignorance. For Zwingli, this knowledge could only be derived from a study of Scripture. It has frequently been pointed out that these tendencies towards inwardness and knowledge led at times in later Zwinglian piety to a distorted inner subjectivity and over-rational approach to Scripture.[24]

As a second generation reformer, John Calvin (1509-1564) did not have the same roots in the medieval Church that Martin Luther did. His spirituality had its origins more in the tradition of the Humanist Renaissance. He was well acquainted with the biblical scholarship of Erasmus. As a young lawyer of twenty-seven, he came to Geneva in 1536 and found Zwinglian Protestantism firmly established there. Gradually, his theology and his practical sense of organization came to have great influence. The spirituality of John Calvin has never received the attention that his theology has, particularly his theological teaching on predestination and God's sovereignty. His spirituality, however, constitutes a rich part of his legacy to the Reformed Church.[25]

In his spirituality, Calvin begins with the believer's union with Christ. From this union come all Christ's gifts and blessings. This living relationship with Christ begins with baptism and continues to grow and develop during the course of one's life. Calvin is much less hesitant to speak about growth than Luther. With his strong

---

[24] On this point, see Bouyer, pp. 82-83 and Hageman, pp. 58-59.

[25] For Calvin's spirituality see Lucien Joseph Richard, *The Spirituality of John Calvin* (Atlanta, GA: John Knox Press, 1974); William J. Bouwsma, "The Spirituality of John Calvin" in *Christian Spirituality, High Middle Ages and Reformation, op. cit.*, pp. 318-333; Hageman, *op. cit.*, pp. 60-72; and Bouyer, *op. cit.*, pp. 84-94.

emphasis on justification by faith alone and his insistence that good works play no part in the process of justification, Luther was reluctant to speak about growth and development in the spiritual life. Calvin agreed with Luther's teaching that justification was by grace alone, but he was able to integrate human activity a little more with his teaching on sanctification. As Louis Bouyer points out: "Calvin, on the other hand, while also maintaining that justification precedes, and is hence independent of, any possible works that man may do, added that a faith that did not produce both external works and the progressive sanctification of our whole being was but an appearance of faith and therefore would not have justified us."[26] For Calvin, justification and sanctification are both gifts that come from our union with Christ.

The role of the Church in this growth and development is vital in Calvin's thought. The Church is the mother of all the faithful. It is in the Church, Christ's body, that union with him is nourished and sustained and that growth in the Christian life takes place. It takes place in the Church as a gift of grace and primarily through the preaching of the Word. The preaching of the Word provides a living contact with Christ through the guidance of the Holy Spirit. But in Calvin's spirituality, the liturgy is not reduced essentially to the preaching of the Word, as it was for Zwingli. It also includes prayer, worship and especially the celebration of the Eucharist. There was for Calvin a real presence of Christ in both the Word and the Eucharist.

A final emphasis of Calvin's spirituality was placed on obedient ethical activity in the world. Union with Christ should lead a person to live a life in keeping with that relationship. One gives glory to God not only in liturgical worship but also in righteous and ethical living. An assurance of belonging to Christ is found in obedience to God's law and service of one's neighbor.

We can end this treatment of Calvin's spirituality with the

---

[26] Bouyer, p. 86.

succinct summary given by Howard Hageman in his essay. He writes:

> What was the spirituality of John Calvin? Once we have
> been received into God's new people by baptism, we are
> given everything that Jesus Christ is and has and are enabled
> to appropriate it in increasing measure by sharing Christ in
> the preaching of his Word, in the receiving of his supper,
> in the liturgical life of his body, the Church. From the power
> and the strength which we receive in these ways, we are
> enabled and expected for obedient service in the world
> which is under his promise.[27]

3. Anabaptist Spirituality

Those who were part of the so-called "Radical Reformation" found themselves on the margins of the mainline Protestant Churches of the sixteenth century. These varied and minority sects have often been grouped together and referred to as "the left wing of the Reformation." Luther had little sympathy for them and used the German word *schwärmer* in speaking about them. In his influential study of this reformation movement, George H. Williams used the term "the Radical Reformation" to designate the various groups of religious innovators who belonged neither to the Roman Catholic nor to mainline Protestant Churches.[28] He divided them into three major sections that were both distinct and interrelated: Anabaptists, Spiritualists, and Evangelical Rationalists. Each of these groups had further divisions. For example, Williams speaks of three streams of Anabaptism: evangelical (Swiss Brethren, Men-

---

[27] Hageman, *op. cit.*, pp. 71-72.

[28] George H. Williams, *The Radical Reformation* (Philadelphia: Westminster Press, 1963); published also in a 3rd revised edition (Kirksville: Sixteenth Century Journal Publishers, 1992).

nonites, Hutterites); revolutionary (Münsterites); and contemplative (Hans Denck). The revolutionary branch lasted only a short time, dying out not long after their brief takeover of the city of Münster in 1535. Peaceful Anabaptists continued to flourish, particularly in Switzerland, southern Germany, Austria, and in Dutch speaking areas of the Lowlands.

In spite of the great variety and diversity that marked these groups, there were a number of common characteristics attributable to all of them. They were all radical in the sense that they wanted to cut through the traditions that had built up in the established Churches and return to the authentic root of the Christian faith as they envisaged it. Adult baptism was the mark of their new birth and thus they were strongly opposed to infant baptism. ("Anabaptist" means "rebaptizer.") They comprised a lay movement for the most part, and they neither received nor wanted any political support or protection. They advocated a complete separation from the world and gave witness to a very distinct and uncompromising lifestyle. They had a strong desire to fulfill God's will completely and to live a simple and holy life.

A distinct spirituality was part of this life, a spirituality that has only recently been carefully studied.[29] The sources for this piety are found for the most part, not in any learned treatises or theological works, but in devotional writings, court records, letters of encouragement (often originating from prison), sermons, hymns, prayers, and stories of the martyrs.

A basic and recurring theme is that of the immediate experience of God. Anabaptist thirst for God was accompanied by an insistence that this experience of the divine should be a direct and unmediated one. Each person can and should approach God di-

---

[29] For Anabaptist spirituality, see Timothy George, "The Spirituality of the Radical Reformation" in *Christian Spirituality, High Middle Ages and Reformation, op. cit.*, pp. 334-371; Peter C. Erb, "Anabaptist Spirituality" in *Protestant Spiritual Traditions, op. cit.*, pp. 80-123. For some early Anabaptist writings, see *Early Anabaptist Spirituality, Selected Writings*, translated and edited with an introduction by Daniel Liechty (New York: Paulist Press, 1994).

rectly, apart from any reliance on external religious practices or means. The experience of the Spirit within a person was extremely important and should be sought wholeheartedly. This emphasis led in turn to a minimizing of external means of grace. It also led to a strong and vehement anticlericalism. In one's relationship with God, it is the personal, experiential, individual, and subjective aspect that really counts and the one that should be nourished. In fact, an experience of a new birth or a new awakening was the prerequisite for baptism. The reception of baptism was often the climax of a process of conversion and the direct experiencing of God's grace. This emphasis on the direct experience of God led at times to excessive claims on the part of some, but in general, the Anabaptists led quiet, moderate, and simple lives.

Another important aspect of Anabaptist spirituality was that of discipleship (*nachfolge*). The generous and loyal following of Christ was at the heart of their way of life. Differing from Luther, they were optimistic about human potential and its ability to respond to the divine will and follow faithfully the example and teaching of Christ. It was their concept of loyal discipleship that brought them quickly into conflict with secular leaders. The refusal on the part of the Anabaptists to take part in military service, to take civil oaths, or give to the magistrates any authority in religious matters was rooted in their understanding of the demands of discipleship and the complete following of Christ. A theology of suffering was also intimately connected with this discipleship. The cross of Christ was an inevitable part of the daily life of the true disciple, for the members of the Body are called to share in the suffering of the Head. They must share in this suffering with that same spirit of surrender and resignation that marked Christ's acceptance of the cross.

The Anabaptists who suffered martyrdom gave concrete witness to this theme of suffering. Right from the beginning, the Anabaptists were looked upon as heretical and seditious because of their teaching and their way of life. This led to bitter persecution and imprisonment and in many instances to a bloody death at the hands of governmental and ecclesiastical authorities. These martyrs were remembered with great admiration, and their lives and deaths were immortalized in song and story. These various writings about the martyrs became an important form of Anabaptist spirituality. A popular and influential example of this type of literature, written in Dutch in 1660, was the book known as *The Bloody Theater* or *Martyrs' Mirror of the Defenseless Christians Who Baptized Only Upon Confession of Faith, and Who Suffered And Died for the Testimony of Jesus their Savior.*[30]

Finally, Anabaptist spirituality was characterized by the strong emphasis placed on the corporate nature of the Christian life.[31] The gathered assembly of the believers constituted the body of Christ, and it was within this gathering that one was united with Christ. It was within a community of love and support that the process of discipleship took place. Adult baptism marked the entrance into the community and served as the public pledge of separation from the world and a commitment to the community on the part of the repentant believer. In many respects, this act was reminiscent of the monastic vow that signified the monk's radical break with a previous life and a commitment to a new way of life. The celebration of the Eucharist was greatly simplified and understood primarily as a commemoration of Christ's death on the Cross and a meal of fellowship. Many Anabaptists lived together in conventicles and shared things in common. Here, too, their lives had an affinity with that of the early Franciscans and the Brothers and Sisters of the Common Life. Note should also be made of the strong apocalyptic tone that was associated with much of Anabaptist piety and the strong eschatological interest in the Second Coming of Christ.

Because of the ongoing persecutions, many Anabaptists sought refuge in Holland as did Separatist groups from England. Later, some migrated to rural areas of the United States. The Men-

---

[30] See Thieleman J. Van Braght, *The Bloody Theater* or *Martyrs' Mirror* (Scottdale, PA: Mennonite Publishing House, 1951). For the text of a poignant last testament to a baby born in prison to a mother awaiting execution, see George, *op. cit.*, pp. 344-345.

[31] See *Early Anabaptist Spirituality, op. cit.*, p. 11 ff.

nonite and Amish Churches are descendants of the Anabaptists and follow the basic teaching of Menno Simons (1496-1561), an important leader of the Dutch Anabaptists.

Conclusion

Our treatment of Protestant spiritualities of the sixteenth century has been limited here to Lutheran, Reformed, and Anabaptist. Since the Reformation in England came a little later than it did on the continent, we will treat Anglicanism in a later chapter. The same will be true for Puritanism. Our focus in the next chapter will be on the spirituality that emerged in the context of the reformation that took place in the Catholic Church in the sixteenth century.

For Further Reading

Jean Leclercq, François Vandenbroucke, and Louis Bouyer, *The Spirituality of the Middle Ages*. Volume II of *A History of Christian Spirituality*. New York: The Seabury Press, 1968. See the appendix, "Byzantine Spirituality" by Louis Bouyer, pp. 545-590.

Louis Bouyer, *Orthodox Spirituality and Protestant and Anglican Spirituality*. Volume III of *A History of Christian Spirituality*. New York: The Seabury Press, 1982.

Christian Spirituality II, High Middle Ages and Reformation. Edited by Jill Raitt. New York: Crossroad, 1989.

The Study of Spirituality. Edited by Cheslyn Jones, Geoffry Wainwright, Edward Yarnold, S.J. New York: Oxford University Press, 1986.

John Meyendorff, *St. Gregory Palamas and Orthodox Spirituality*. St. Vladimir's Seminary Press, 1974.

Protestant Spiritual Traditions. Edited by Frank C. Senn. New York: Paulist Press, 1986.

Jared Wicks, *Luther and His Spiritual Legacy*. Wilmington, DE: Michael Glazier, 1983.

Lucien Joseph Richard, *The Spirituality of John Calvin*. Atlanta, GA: John Knox Press, 1974.

Early Anabaptist Spirituality, Selected Writings. Translated and edited, with an Introduction by Daniel Liechty. New York: Paulist Press, 1994.

8 Post-Reformation Spirituality

1. Sixteenth-Century Spain

Spain emerged in the sixteenth century as the dominant national power in Europe. Toward the end of the fifteenth century, the kingdoms of Castile and Aragon were united by the marriage of Isabella and Ferdinand. With the conquest of the Moorish kingdom of Granada in 1492, a united Spain came into existence. Under the joint leadership of Isabella and Ferdinand, it came to enjoy much stability and prosperity and entered what was to be referred to as Spain's Golden Age. An important figure for Church reform and renewal in the country was Cardinal Ximenes, the archbishop of Toledo from 1495 to 1517. Among his many contributions was the foundation of the University of Alcala. An excellent faculty of theology was established there, and it provided clerical education at many levels. With the exploration and colonization that followed the discoveries of Christopher Columbus, the Spanish empire also expanded widely.

Universities spread and flourished throughout Spain. The spirit and ideas of Humanism were warmly welcomed at these universities, particularly at Alcala. The writings and religious thought of Erasmus were greatly admired and exercised a wide influence among Spanish scholars. His *Handbook of the Christian Knight* was translated into Spanish in 1524, and his emphasis on religious reform and the development of a strong interior life had wide appeal.

Due to a number of various reasons, the Protestant Reformation made few inroads in Spain. There was first of all the geographical barrier of the Pyrenees mountains. The Spanish temperament as well as the nation's struggle to free itself of Moorish influence also played their parts. Above all, there was the pervasive and relentless activity of the Spanish Inquisition. The result was that sixteenth-century Spain was spared most of the religious turmoil, warfare, and profound ruptures that characterized the countries of northern Europe.

Spain in the sixteenth century also witnessed a significant mystical flowering. The mysticism that flourished at this time was very much in continuity with the mysticism of the Middle Ages. The three great mystics associated with this period are St. Ignatius of Loyola, St. Teresa of Avila, and St. John of the Cross. But there were many other mystical writers and currents of mystical thought that marked this vibrant period of Christian spirituality. Here too, as we shall see, the Spanish Inquisition was quick to root out false and heretical movements and tendencies. This was done, however, at the price of hindering or preventing many legitimate developments.

2. St. Ignatius of Loyola and Jesuit Spirituality

Ignatius of Loyola (c. 1491-1556), saint, mystic, founder of a religious order, was an important figure in the history of the Catholic Counter-Reformation.[1] The religious order he founded in 1540, the

---

[1] For a biography of St. Ignatius, see Candido de Dalmases, S.J., *Ignatius of Loyola, Founder of the Jesuits*, translated by Jerome Aixala, S.J. (St. Louis: Institute of Jesuit Sources, 1985); and Paul Dudon, S.J., *St. Ignatius of Loyola*, translated by W.J. Young, S.J. (Milwaukee: Bruce, 1949). For a general introduction and selected writings, see *Ignatius of Loyola, Spiritual Exercises and Selected Works*, edited by George E. Ganss, S.J. (New York: Paulist Press, 1991). For Ignatius' mysticism, see Harvey D. Egan, S.J., *Ignatius Loyola the Mystic* (Wilmington: Michael Glazier, 1987); and also his *The Spiritual Exercises and the Ignatian Mystical Horizon* (St. Louis: Institute of Jesuit Sources, 1976).

Society of Jesus (Jesuits), was apostolic in its main thrust, and its members played an active role in the life of the Church at this critical period. He was the author of the *Spiritual Exercises*, a handbook on prayer that continues to make a profound contribution to the spiritual growth of many. The *Constitutions* that he carefully drew up had an important influence on a number of subsequent apostolic communities of religious men and women. In our treatment here, we will look first at Ignatius' own spiritual journey, for if one is to understand Ignatian spirituality, one must begin with the graced experiences of the founder. A valuable source for his conversion and early spiritual journey is the little autobiography he drew up late in his life.[2]

Born around 1491 at the castle of Loyola in the Basque province of Guipuzco in Spain, Inigo (as he was called in his early years) was attracted at an early age to a military life. At the household of the chief treasurer of Queen Isabella, the young Ignatius received the basic formation of a Spanish gentleman and courtier. It was a life marked, as he tells us in his autobiography "with a great and vain desire to win honor," and he delighted in the military exercises. In 1521 Ignatius was seriously wounded while defending the citadel at Pamplona against French soldiers. The French treated the gallant soldier with respect and courtesy and had him transported by stretcher to his ancestral castle at Loyola. Further operations on his shattered leg led to an extended period of convalescence at Loyola.

This period of convalescence was to be the turning point of his life, for he would rise from the sick bed a profoundly changed person, seeking a totally new direction in his life. During his days of enforced idleness, he sought books to read. He would have preferred the romances he was accustomed to read, but the only books available were the *Life of Christ* by the Carthusian, Ludolph of Saxony, and the popular medieval lives of the saints known as *The*

---

[2] See *St. Ignatius' Own Story as Told to Luis Gonzalez da Camara*, translated by Walter J. Young, S.J. (Chicago: Loyola University Press, 1968); and *Selected Writings, op. cit.*, pp. 67-111.

Golden Legend by a thirteenth century Dominican, Jacopo de Voragine. Under God's grace, these books were to affect him deeply and to stir up many holy thoughts and desires. He pictured Christ as a King who calls his followers to engage in a warfare, and the saints as knights in his special service, and he dreamed of emulating the deeds of St. Francis of Assisi and St. Dominic. But these reflections alternated in his mind with his dreams of romantic and military conquests. He imagined the honors he would win at the royal court and what he would do in the service of a certain lady, the words he would say to her, and the armed exploits he would perform in her service. These latter thoughts gave him pleasure while he dwelt upon them but they later left him feeling dry and dissatisfied. He slowly recognized, on the other hand, that the holy thoughts and desires brought him a peace and consolation that remained with him long after his reading and reflection. Gradually he came to an awareness of the sources of these interior movements, and he began to discern and distinguish which were from a divine source and which were not. He came to look upon the human person as a battleground between the forces of good and the forces of evil, and he clearly saw that a choice and a commitment had to be made. Moved by God's grace, Ignatius committed himself generously to God's service with that energy and devotion with which he had previously pursued his courtly and military career.

Ten months after he fell in battle, Ignatius set out from the castle at Loyola with the firm resolution in his mind to journey to the Holy Land as a pilgrim. His first stop was at the famous Benedictine monastery of Montserrat in Spain. After some days of prayer, he made a general confession of his life and then symbolically left his sword and dagger with his confessor to be placed in the church on the altar of Our Lady. He spent the night in prayer before the altar, an act that was reminiscent of the knightly vigil of prayer before battle. No longer would it be military battle for Ignatius, but spiritual warfare in which he would engage himself totally and heroically.

Dressed as a pilgrim, Ignatius set out for the nearby town of

Manresa where he planned to spend a few days copying some notes in a spiritual journal he was keeping. As so often happens in the lives of great leaders before their periods of intense creativity and activity, he needed an extended period of withdrawal and solitude, and so the few days lengthened to almost a year. During these days, he begged for his daily bread, helped the sick in the hospital, attended daily Mass and Vespers at the Cathedral, spent long hours in prayer, and practiced severe penances. It was a time of many mystical graces and consolations, but it was also a time of purgation, trials, and temptations. "God was leading him like a child," he tells us in his autobiography. The novice in the spiritual life was slowly, and at times painfully, being transformed into a master of the spiritual life. God's grace was abundant and the pilgrim cooperated generously. The *Spiritual Exercises* of St. Ignatius stem from these days at Manresa, although they would undergo much development and revision before their final publication many years later. The core of the work goes back to the notes he kept at Manresa, the notes that flowed basically from his own prayerful experience of God's grace working within him.

Toward the end of February, 1523, Ignatius left Manresa and traveled by way of Rome to Venice, the port of embarkation for pilgrims to the Holy Land. After two months of waiting for a ship, he finally secured passage and arrived safely at Joppa. Days of great consolation followed. Ignatius felt called to remain in the Holy Land and work for the conversion of the Moslems, but given the precarious situation between the Christians and the Turks, the Franciscan superior who had ecclesiastical authority kindly but firmly vetoed this plan.

With the collapse of these hopes, Ignatius was forced to reassess his plans for the future and especially for his apostolic activity. He decided to pursue a formal education, since he recognized its necessity for any effective apostolate. He was thirty-three years old at the time and his course of studies would involve him for the next eleven years, taking him first to the Spanish universities at Barcelona, Alcala, and Salamanca, and then to the University of Paris.

At the University of Paris, a small band formed around Ignatius: Francis Xavier, Simon Rodrigues, Diego Laynez, Alonso Salmeron, and Nicholas Bobadilla. At first it was a loosely formed group, bound only by ties of friendship and a common vision and set of ideals. Through his own personal influence and also by directing them in the *Spiritual Exercises*, Ignatius inspired them with his strong apostolic thrust, love of God above all things, and a strong desire to serve Christ the King. Gradually, and after long discussion and prayer, they decided that after completing their studies they would remain together as a group and labor in the Holy Land for the conversion of the Moslems. In order to strengthen their determination and their bond of unity, they decided to take three vows: poverty, chastity, and a resolve to go to the Holy Land. If this third vow proved impossible to fulfill, they would go to Rome and offer their services to the Pope. These plans were ratified when the seven men pronounced their vows on August 15, 1534, the Feast of the Assumption of Mary, at the chapel dedicated to St. Denis on the slope of Montmartre in Paris. The decision to form a religious order with Ignatius at its head still lay in the future, but an important foundation stone had been laid at Montmartre, and it has always been a revered moment in Jesuit history.

In early 1537 the founding fathers, now numbering ten, were reunited in Venice after the completion of their studies in Paris. Ignatius was ordained to the priesthood at Venice with some of the others. The ongoing war between Venice and the Turks made any sea passage to the Holy Land impossible, and so they decided to travel to Rome. On the journey to Rome, Ignatius stopped to pray at the little chapel at La Storta just outside of Rome. There in prayer Ignatius was graced with a vision of God the Father placing him with His Son. He was also greatly strengthened and confirmed in his plans and desires by the words of the Father: "I will be propitious to you in Rome."

The pilgrim priests were warmly received at Rome by the Pope and they made a deep impression in the city through their holy lives and their learning, as they continued to preach and minister to the sick. It was clear by early 1539 that they would not be able to go to the Holy Land. They offered their services to the Pope and expressed their willingness to go to the Indies or any other part of the world where there was an apostolic need. After a month of prayer and deliberation in seeking God's will, the ten made the historic decision to form a religious order and to take a vow of obedience to one of their members. Ignatius drew up the document which summed up their purpose and aim, and it was approved by the others. The opening words of this document, known as the *Formula of the Institute*, form a strong link with Ignatius' particular vision and the spirit of the *Spiritual Exercises* : "Whoever desires to serve as a soldier of God beneath the banner of the cross in our Society, which we desire to be designated by the name of Jesus, and to serve the Lord alone and the Church...." The fundamental points which would be developed later in the *Constitutions* of the Society of Jesus were contained in this document in seed form, namely the strong apostolic dimension, loyalty to the Holy See, a readiness to go anywhere in the world, a prompt and persevering obedience to the General they would elect from the group, and the sacrifice of the traditional chant in common for the interest of the apostolate.[3] In general, it was a new and pioneering type of religious order and one well suited to the needs of the Church at the time, with its stress on mobility and flexibility. Pope Paul III gave formal approbation on September 27, 1540 in the papal document, *Regimini militantis ecclesiae*, and during Lent of 1541, Ignatius was elected the first General.

For the last sixteen years of his life, Ignatius remained in Rome, fulfilling the demanding duties of General of the new Order. The founding fathers were soon engaged in such varied apostolic activities as preaching and giving the *Spiritual Exercises*, acting as theologians at the Council of Trent, serving as papal legates,

---

[3] For an English translation of the Constitutions, see *The Constitutions of the Society of Jesus*, translated, with an introduction and commentary, by George E. Ganss, S.J. (St. Louis: Institute of Jesuit Sources, 1979); and *The Constitutions of the Society of Jesus and Their Complementary Norms* (St. Louis: Institute of Jesuit Sources, 1996).

teaching, and laboring in foreign missions. Francis Xavier left Europe almost immediately after the formal formation of the group to begin his great missionary activity. The work that took him to the Indies and Japan came to an end with his death on a lonely island while he was awaiting passage to the mainland of China.

During the sixteen years of Ignatius' generalate, the original ten companions would grow in number to a thousand, and the direction of the Jesuits laboring on four continents would absorb his time and energy. There are six thousand letters of Ignatius dating from this period.[4] Given the needs of the times, it would not be long before the work of the foreign missions and education would assume primary importance.

In addition to this work of organization and administration, Ignatius gave himself to the important task of drawing up the *Constitutions* of the Society. Organizational genius that he was, he clearly saw that if his vision and spirit were to remain after his death and be imparted to others, it would have to be carefully and painstakingly spelled out in writing. What he accomplished in his own lifetime through personal contact and influence could only continue if there were a written legacy. Ignatius' legacy to his followers is contained in the *Spiritual Exercises* and the *Constitutions*. Ignatius died in Rome in 1556 and was succeeded as General by one of his original companions, Diego Laynez. In 1622, he was solemnly canonized together with St. Francis Xavier.[5]

---

[4] For some of his letters, see *Letters of St. Ignatius of Loyola*, selected and translated by William J. Young, S.J. (Chicago: Loyola University Press, 1959); and Hugo Rahner, S.J., *St. Ignatius Loyola, Letters to Women*, trans. by Kathleen Pond and S.A.H. Weetman (New York: Herder and Herder, 1960).

[5] For historical studies of the Jesuits, see John W. O'Malley, S.J., *The First Jesuits* (Cambridge: Harvard University Press, 1993); James Broderick, S.J., *The Origins of the Jesuits* (London: Longmans, Green, 1940); James Broderick, S.J., *The Progress of the Jesuits* (London: Longmans, Green, 1947); and William V. Bangert, S.J., *A History of the Society of Jesus* (St. Louis: Institute of Jesuit Sources, 1962).

Jesuit Spirituality[6]

It should be emphasized once again that Jesuit spirituality flows from Ignatian spirituality, from the uniquely graced experience of the founder. In Jesuit spirituality, a strong emphasis is placed on apostolic work and a generosity in the service of Christ. It is a service that is marked by a strong and abiding love of Jesus Christ and one that strives to be open and responsive to the call of Christ the King. "To seek to know Christ more intimately, so as to love him more ardently and follow him more closely" is the way Ignatius expresses it in his *Spiritual Exercises*. All of this requires a spirit of freedom and detachment and self-sacrifice.

Ignatius' ideal also calls for a readiness to go anywhere in the world where the service of Christ requires, and where there is possibility that the greater good, the *magis*, can be accomplished. Thus, a spirit of flexibility and mobility in the apostolate take on added importance in Jesuit spirituality. It should also be noted that the apostolic work is not an individual affair. It is carried out by those who are bonded together in a union of minds and hearts. We have seen how the original companions that gathered around Ignatius formed a supportive band of "Friends in the Lord" as members of the Company of Jesus.

Finally, it must be kept in mind that Ignatius' vision calls not for just an active person and one totally committed to his apostolic work, but for a person who brings a strong and abiding contemplative dimension to that work. A faith-filled perspective should permeate and be at the heart of all the activity. "Finding God in all things" and being "a contemplative in action" are the traditional expressions that bring out this essential orientation. This is based on the conviction that God's plan unfolds in human activity. Through this faith-filled perspective, a Jesuit sees his work as part

---

[6] For a classical study of Jesuit spirituality, see Joseph de Guibert, S.J., *The Jesuits: Their Spiritual Doctrine and Practice. A Historical Study*, translated by W.J. Young, S.J., (St. Louis: Institute of Jesuit Sources, 1972).

of the unfolding of God's plan and as contributing to the spread of God's Kingdom here on earth. One seeks to begin and continue this work, whatever it might be, "for the greater glory of God." The familiar prayer of St. Ignatius sums up so much of this spirit:

> Dearest Lord, teach me to be generous. Teach me to serve You as You deserve; to give and not to count the cost; to fight and not to heed the wounds, to toil and not to seek for rest; to labor and not ask for reward save that of knowing that I am doing Your will.

3. Methods of Prayer — Spiritual Exercises

Methods of prayer and various forms of spiritual exercises began to take on greater importance at the end of the Middle Ages and the beginning of the Renaissance period. The emergence of these methodical forms of prayer corresponded with the general decline and breakdown of a spiritual fervor among the clergy and members of the religious orders. Conditions at the end of the Middle Ages had led to a sharp decline in religious fervor, and some of the pagan elements that were revived in the Humanist Renaissance further weakened Christian life and practice. Thus, the chief aim of methodical forms of prayer was the renewal and reform of the Christian life, especially among the clergy and religious. The *Spiritual Exercises* of St. Ignatius of Loyola were destined to have the greatest impact and influence, but it is important to realize that they were the culmination of earlier historical developments.[7]

Methods of prayer were widely used in the circles of the New Devotion in the Low Countries in the fourteenth and fifteenth centuries. The practice of meditation was highly esteemed among the Brothers and Sisters of the Common Life and the religious at the monasteries connected with Windesheim. To assist in the practice

---

[7] For this historical development, see the chapter in Pierre Pourrat, *Christian Spirituality*, vol. III, translated by W.H. Mitchell (Westminster, MD: The Newman Press, 1953), pp. 1-22.

of meditation, a number of collections centering on Christ's life were drawn up at the Windesheim monasteries. They were arranged according to specific days of the week with various steps suggested as aids for prayer. The Windesheim reforms spread from the Lowlands to France, particularly through one of its monks, John Mauburnus. He left a large collection of exercises and meditations in a work known as the *Rosetum* (*Spiritual Rosary*). Many Benedictine monasteries in Italy and Spain also were renewed through the practice of methodical meditation.

A significant contribution to these developments was made in Spain by Garcia Ximenes de Cisneros (1455-1510). He was the reforming abbot of the Benedictine monastery at Montserrat in Spain. As a means to spiritual renewal, he had all his monks make the *Spiritual Exercises* that he had drawn up and composed. These exercises were divided into three weeks, with each week corresponding to the purgative, illuminative, and unitive ways. Appropriate material was assigned for each day of the week, and detailed explanations and directions were given in order to help the person making them. After developing the series of meditations, Cisneros turns to the subject of contemplation in the last part of his *Exercises*. In his treatment of contemplation, he follows the Benedictine tradition of the early Middle Ages, seeing contemplation arising out of meditation.

The development of methods of prayer culminated with the *Spiritual Exercises* of St. Ignatius, a work that would go on to enjoy a special place among the spiritual classics.[8] As indicated earlier, the core of the *Exercises* goes back to the notes Ignatius kept at Manresa, notes that flowed basically from his own prayerful experience of God's grace working within him. Briefly stated, the purpose of the *Spiritual Exercises* is to bring about a very active and generous conformity to the will of God. They are simply a series of spiritual ex-

---

[8] For English translations see *The Spiritual Exercises of St. Ignatius*, translated by Louis J. Puhl, S.J. (Chicago: Loyola University Press, 1968); *The Spiritual Exercises of St. Ignatius*, translated by Anthony Mottola, with an introduction by Robert W. Gleason, S.J. (New York: Doubleday, 1964); and David L. Fleming, S.J., *The Spiritual Exercises of St. Ignatius, A Literal Translation and A Contemporary Reading* (St. Louis: The Institute of Jesuit Sources, 1978).

ercises — meditations, considerations, and contemplations — that the individual makes in a context of prayer under the guidance of a director. They seek to free persons from inordinate attachments and disorders so that they might be free to surrender to the call of grace in seeking, finding, and accomplishing God's will in their lives.

The *Exercises* begin with a number of annotations or introductory observations that seek to provide a proper understanding for the director and for the one making the exercises. For example, the first annotation states:

> By the term "Spiritual Exercises" is meant every method of examination of conscience, of meditation, of contemplation, of vocal and mental prayer, and of other spiritual activities that will be mentioned later. For just as taking a walk, journeying on foot, and running are bodily exercises, so we call Spiritual Exercises every way of preparing and disposing the soul to rid itself of all inordinate attachments, and, after their removal, of seeking and finding the will of God in the disposition of our life for the salvation of our soul.

The *Exercises* are divided into four periods or "weeks." The first week is devoted to a consideration of sin and its consequences, and it seeks to bring the retreatant to a conviction of being a sinner who has experienced God's mercy and compassion. Various prayers, petitions, colloquies, and other suggestions accompany the main meditations. The second week focuses on the following of Christ and seeks to bring the exercitant to a generous and magnanimous response to Christ's personal call. The retreatant is led to contemplate the mysteries of Christ's life so as to know him more intimately, to love him more ardently, and to follow him more closely. A key element in the second week is the election or choice of a state or way of life. The exercises of the third week are given to a contemplation of Christ's passion and death and the great love manifested in these mysteries. The fourth week centers on Christ's glorious resurrection. A key exercise in this final week is the *Contemplation to Attain the Love of God*. In addition to the material for prayer pertinent to each week, the *Spiritual Exercises* include various methods of prayer, as well as a number of guidelines such as rules for the discernment of spirits, rules for thinking with the Church, and rules for eating.

Such in bare outline is a summary of the *Spiritual Exercises* of St. Ignatius. They are meant to be flexible and adaptable to the particular needs of the individual retreatant. Although there is much material that is presented objectively, the retreatant is encouraged to be sensitive to the unique way God reveals himself, to be attentive to the interior movements of grace, and to follow the light and guidance of the Holy Spirit in prayer. The *Exercises* have been a powerful source of spiritual growth for countless men and women over the years, for they are Ignatius' rich legacy not only to the Order he founded but to the entire Church.

4. Early Spanish Mysticism

Sixteenth-century Spain witnessed a flowering of mysticism that had many different currents and trends.[9] The renewal and reforms that had taken place in Spain in the religious communities led many to seek a fervent life of prayer and a rich interior life. A school of mysticism that was very visible in the early sixteenth century was a way called "recollection" (*recogimiento*). This "way of recollection" was particularly characteristic of many Franciscan houses of prayer. It was a spirituality that was nourished by Scripture and such earlier spiritual authors as Augustine, Gregory the Great, Bernard, the Victorines, and Bonaventure. It emphasized self-knowledge, the imitation of Christ, and union or transformation with God through love. In keeping with earlier Franciscan piety, there was a strong attraction to a loving meditation on the passion and death of Christ.

---

[9] See E. Allison Peers, *Studies of the Spanish Mystics*, 3 vols. (London: Sheldon Press, 1927-30, vols. 1-2; London: SPCK, 1960, vol. 3); and Kieran Kavanaugh, O.C.D., "Spanish Sixteenth Century: Carmel and Surrounding Movements" in *Christian Spirituality III: Post-Reformation and Modern*, edited by Louis Dupre and Don E. Saliers (New York: Crossroad, 1989), pp. 69-92.

But the prayer of recollection also sought to attain an absorption in God by a process of emptying and "thinking of nothing" (*no pensar nada*). Some Franciscans associated with this way of recollection were Francisco de Osuna, Bernardino de Laredo, and St. Peter Alcantara.

Francisco de Osuna (c.1492-c.1540) published his most important work, *The Third Spiritual Alphabet*, in 1527.[10] It was a book that had a great impact on St. Teresa of Avila when it was given to her by her uncle at a critical time in her spiritual development. She tells us in her autobiography that she followed the path of recollection recommended by Osuna and derived great profit from it. In this mystical study, Osuna carefully develops the theory and practice of recollection that he considers open to all. At the beginning of the first of the twenty-three treatises, he writes that friendship and communion with God are possible in this life of exile. This communion is to be sought by fixing the heart only on God.

Another Franciscan, Bernardino de Laredo (1482-1545), wrote *The Ascent of Mount Sion*.[11] This work, published in 1535, has three parts: the first focuses on the purgative way and seeks to bring about self-knowledge through discursive meditation; the second part has meditations on the life, death, and resurrection of Christ; and the final part treats mystical prayer and the prayer of quiet. The third part was particularly helpful to St. Teresa of Avila at a time that she was unable to meditate on the passion. Mention should also be made of St. Peter Alcantara (1499-1562). He played an important role in the reform of the Franciscans in Spain, and he was a friend and adviser to St. Teresa. He is the author of the *Treatise on Prayer and Meditation*, a work that is generally believed to be an adaptation and summary of a work by Louis of Granada.

In addition to the "way of recollection" (*recogimiento*), there also sprang up in Spain at the same time adherents of what has been

---

[10] For an English translation and background material, see *Francisco de Osuna, The Third Spiritual Alphabet*, translation and introduction by Mary E. Giles (New York: Paulist Press, 1981).

[11] See Bernardino of Laredo, *The Ascent of Mount Sion*, translated by E. Allison Peers ((London: Faber and Faber, 1952).

called the "way of abandonment" (*dejamiento*). These were proponents of a recollection that fell under increasing suspicion. They built their spirituality on the idea of abandonment to the love of God and greatly emphasized interior illumination and passivity. They sought to reach a state of quietude and passivity in which they were perfectly abandoned to God. This preoccupation with abandonment led them to belittle and even reject human efforts, the sacramental life, and other external observances and practices. Some seemed to claim that this abandonment rendered them exempt from moral restrictions, a claim that led easily to various excesses and aberrations. In time the proponents of abandonment became known as the false mystics or Illuminists, and later were grouped under the name of the *Alumbrados*.

It was not long before the Spanish Inquisition took direct action against the *Alumbrados*. An edict was published in 1525, along with a condemnation of forty-eight Illuminist propositions. The *Alumbrados* were also accused of Lutheran tendencies with their emphasis on interior religion and their antipathy towards external religious practices. This was the beginning of many actions taken by the Inquisition against those suspected of false mysticism. The relentless and often ruthless procedures did stamp out the false sects, but it also gave rise to an anti-mystical climate in which healthy and orthodox movements were checked. Many innocent people also suffered in the over-suspicious atmosphere. Even St. Ignatius fell under the suspicion of the Inquisition while he was studying at the University of Alcala. He was imprisoned and interrogated and then instructed not to teach others until he was ordained.

Although they were fewer in number, there were still important spiritual writers in Spain during the years immediately following the intervention of the Inquisition in 1525. Louis of Granada (1505-1588) was the foremost spiritual writer among the Spanish Dominicans of the sixteenth century. Writing in a practical and direct way, his books met the needs of those seeking to deepen their life of prayer and they enjoyed great popularity. This was particularly true of his *Book of Prayer and Meditation* and *The Sinner's*

Guide. Given the anti-mystical climate, he generally avoided writing on mystical prayer, but this did not prevent two of his books from being placed on the Index that was published in Spain in 1559. He later submitted the books to the Council of Trent and he received official approbation for them.

St. John of Avila (1500-1569), a diocesan priest in Andalusia, was another whose great potential for writing on mystical prayer was unfortunately curtailed by the Spanish Inquisition. Early in his life he was denounced to the Inquisition and spent a year in prison before being exonerated. This understandably led him to exercise great caution and discretion in writing about mystical prayer. His principal work, *Audi filia et vide,* was first published without his consent. It is a commentary on the words of Psalm 44, "Hearken, O daughter, and see, and incline thy ear." His priestly life was marked by personal mystical graces, a gift for discernment, and a great capacity to lead others to God. St. Teresa sent to him a copy of her *Life,* seeking his advice and reassurance.

Luis de Leon (1527-1591), an Augustinian and a professor at the University of Salamanca, was not as discreet as John of Avila and suffered for it. He was arrested by the Inquisition after publishing a translation and commentary on the Canticle of Canticles and spent almost five years in prison. Later, his great masterpiece, *The Names of Christ,* met with great success and won him much acclaim.[12] He is also known for his poems. Later in his life, he was chosen to edit the first edition of St. Teresa of Avila's writings.

The Jesuits were not spared their struggles over the place of mysticism in their ranks. The *Spiritual Exercises* were fiercely attacked in Spain by the Dominican theologian, Melchior Cano, but since they had papal approval, his opposition was not effective. But the question of the delicate balance between prayer and apostolic work continued to be an issue in the newly formed religious order.

---

[12] For an English translation of this work, see *Luis Ponce de Leon, The Names of Christ,* translation and introduction by Manuel Duran and William Klubach (New York: Paulist Press, 1984). For an English edition of his poetry, see *The Unknown Light: The Poems of Fray Luis de Leon* (Albany: State University of New York Press, 1979).

Also, in a climate in which charges of illuminism were easily made, Jesuit superiors were more inclined to favor an ascetic interpretation of the *Exercises* rather than a mystical one. The issue became a key one in the case of the revered Jesuit, Balthazar Alvarez (1533-1580). As a young priest, he served as St. Teresa's confessor for six years. Later, he himself experienced mystical graces and the prayer of quiet and union. His advocacy of this prayer of quiet and the simple presence of God led to an ongoing concern on the part of his superiors and resulted in a decision on the part of the Jesuit general, Edward Mercurian, that he should not depart from the more ascetic and practical way of interpreting the *Exercises*.

This more ascetic thrust in Jesuit spirituality was reflected in a very famous book published in 1609 by the Spanish Jesuit, Alonso Rodriguez (1531-1617). The three volumes of his *Practice of Christian Perfection* were translated into many languages and enjoyed great popularity well into the twentieth century. The ascetic, practical, and moral focus of this work may be explained to some extent by the anti-mystical atmosphere of the times.

A later period and one a little more favorable to the mystical dimension, however, saw the mystical element in Jesuit spirituality come more to the fore. Blessed Luis de la Puente (1554-1624), in addition to his other writings on mystical prayer, published a biography of Balthazar Alvarez in which he summarized the mystical thought of his teacher. In this way Alvarez's thought was preserved and exercised a wide influence on subsequent spiritual writers. Mention should also be made of the Jesuit, Alvarez de Paz (1560-1620), who published an extensive synthesis of ascetic and mystical theology. His fourfold division of mental prayer into discursive meditation, affective prayer, initial contemplation, and perfect contemplation was followed by many subsequent writers.[13]

Spanish mysticism in the sixteenth century would come to a full flowering with St. Teresa of Avila and St. John of the Cross.

---

[13] For these developments in Jesuit spirituality, see John O'Malley, "Early Jesuit Spirituality: Spain and Italy" in *Christian Spirituality III: Post-Reformation and Modern, op. cit.*, pp. 3-27.

They had inherited a rich and varied legacy and would bring it to a lofty summit. It is to the lives and writings of these two great Carmelite saints, mystics, and doctors of the Church that we now turn.

5. St. Teresa of Avila

St. Teresa of Avila (1515-1582) was one of the most remarkable women in the history of Christian spirituality. She holds a place among the greatest mystics of the Church. She was the reformer of the Carmelites in Spain in the sixteenth century, and her writings on prayer and mysticism have become spiritual classics. When Pope Paul VI solemnly declared her a Doctor of the Church in 1970, he spoke of her as a teacher of "marvelous profundity."[14]

Teresa de Ahumada was born at Avila in central Spain and grew up in a large, religiously oriented family. Her mother died when she was twelve, and a little later she went to a school for girls run by the Augustinian nuns. At the age of twenty-one, she entered the Carmelite monastery of the Incarnation at Avila. Not long after her profession in 1537, Teresa became seriously ill and came very close to death. Recovery was very slow and for the next three years she was unable to walk. During this period of convalescence, she read *The Third Spiritual Alphabet* of Francisco de Osuna and seriously began the practice of recollection recommended by him. This led in time to a prayer of quiet and union with God, her first experiences of mystical prayer. This was not to last, however, and she soon entered a period of dryness and struggles in prayer that was to last for many years.

As she tells us in the autobiography she wrote in later years, a new life began for her when she was thirty-nine. God's graces were plentiful and they led her to a deepening conversion and commitment to Christ. Her prayer of passive quiet and union with God took

---

[14] St. Teresa's autobiography is a rich source of her life. For an English translation, see St. Teresa, *The Life*, translated by E. Allison Peers (New York: Sheed and Ward, 1946). For a biography, see W.T. Walsh, *Saint Teresa of Avila* (Milwaukee: Bruce, 1954).

on added depth, and she was favored with many accompanying mystical experiences such as raptures, locutions (the hearing of words spoken by Christ), and intellectual and imaginative visions. These gifts, coming at a time when there was a widespread suspicion of mystical prayer and its manifestations, led her humbly to seek guidance and direction from various spiritual directors and confessors. Some greatly helped her and others misunderstood and hindered her. She was often instructed to give an account of her mystical experiences, and these occasions provided the impetus for much of her spiritual teaching. The last stages of her spiritual journey were marked by Trinitarian mystical experiences. In 1572 she was graced with a unitive experience that she referred to as a "spiritual marriage." This was given to her through an intellectual and imaginative vision of Christ in his sacred humanity.

Her new way of life also led her to an increasing involvement with the renewal and development of the Carmelites in Spain. In 1562 she established the first of the reformed houses, the Carmel of St. Joseph at Avila, where a new manner of living the contemplative life was begun. With the encouragement of the General of the Carmelite Order, she then began her important work of founding other reformed houses for Carmelite nuns throughout Spain. Later, the reform spread to the Carmelite friars, and for these developments she enlisted the help of St. John of the Cross. The establishment of the foundations did not take place without a great deal of effort, patience, strength, and humility on her part, and they attest to her many human gifts for leadership, organization, and a capacity to work with many types of people. Her work as a reformer took her to all parts of Spain and brought her into contact with people from all walks of life. Her many letters that have been preserved attest to her great involvement in the many issues of the times.

Death came to Teresa of Avila in the midst of a wearying journey in 1582. Although none of her writings were published during her lifetime, they were edited shortly after her death by the Augustinian, Luis de Leon, and published at Salamanca in 1588. She was beatified in 1614 and canonized in 1622. She was declared a Doctor of the Church by Pope Paul VI in 1970, the first woman to be honored with this title.

Saint Teresa's major writings are *The Book of Her Life, The Way of Perfection, The Interior Castle,* and *The Book of Foundations.*[15] Her *Life* was first composed in 1562 and then revised around 1565. She discusses in this great work both the events of her external life and her interior spiritual journey. She speaks of her struggles and growth, the mystical graces she received, while at the same time presenting some wonderful teaching on prayer. *The Way of Perfection* was written a little later and was composed for the Sisters who were with her at the first Carmel foundation. The least mystical of her books, it was written to provide some practical advice and guidance for her Sisters in their prayer. There are helpful suggestions for vocal prayer and the prayer of recollection, and it also contains a very beautiful commentary on the *Our Father.* The *Book of Foundations,* written in stages during her last years, gives us the history of the other Carmels that she established in her work of reform. Her masterpiece, *The Interior Castle,* was written in 1577. It flows from her own life of prayer and is the best synthesis of her teaching on the stages of mystical prayer. Mention should also be made of the 440 *Letters* that have been preserved, most of which were written during the latter part of her life.[16]

There were certain books that St. Teresa found helpful during the years of her spiritual journey. At various times in her life, she was greatly assisted by such books as the *Letters* of St. Jerome, the *Morals* of Gregory the Great, the *Confessions* of St. Augustine, the *Conferences* of Cassian, *The Imitation of Christ,* and such contemporary Spanish spiritual writers as Francisco de Osuna and Ber-

---

[15] For English editions of St. Teresa's complete works, see *The Collected Works of St. Teresa of Avila,* translated by Kieran Kavanaugh, O.C.D. and Otilio Rodriguez, O.C.D., 3 vols. (Washington, D.C.: Institute of Carmelite Studies, 1976, 1980, 1985); and *The Complete Works of St. Teresa,* translated and edited by E. Allison Peers, 3 vols. (New York: Sheed and Ward, 1946).

[16] See *The Letters of St. Teresa,* translated by E. Allison Peers, 2 vols. (London: 1951).

nardino de Laredo. Yet, it is important to note that her own teaching and writing flowed primarily, not from such sources, but from her own experience. There is a very strong autobiographical dimension in all of her teaching and writing. Teresa relates her own spiritual story, the way God works so powerfully in her life, and then draws lessons that may help others. She often narrates the graces she received, her difficulties, failures and successes, and then draws from them a number of practical applications and counsels. Thus, there is always a very practical thrust to her writings with this close connection between experience and teaching. She also writes in a direct, colorful, and spontaneous manner, with common sense and humor never absent. As a result, she is a very readable author and this is attested to by her continuing popularity over the years.

Teresa's basic teaching is very Christological. It is friendship with Christ that is central to her spiritual thought. Her famous description of prayer brings out this dimension clearly. She writes in chapter 8 of her *Life*: "For mental prayer in my opinion is nothing else than an intimate sharing between friends; it means taking time frequently to be alone with Him who we know loves us."[17] It is through Christ that all blessings come to us. Thus, it is to Him that we must draw near. Through the prayer of recollection we seek to be near and present to Him who is near and present to us. Teresa's way of prayer then is the way of light. Even in the midst of the highest mystical prayer she wants to keep Christ before her eyes. That is why locutions and visions are always so important to her. In this emphasis, she departs from St. John of the Cross, who advocates the apophatic way, the way of darkness and emptying.

In an important section of her autobiography, Teresa provides us with her well-known treatment of the four degrees of prayer.[18] She makes use of the image of a garden that is watered in four different ways. In the first method, one brings water from a well; in the second, the water is brought by turning a water wheel or by

---

[17] See *The Book of Her Life*, vol. I of *The Collected Works of St. Teresa of Avila*, translated by Kavanaugh and Rodriguez, *op. cit.*, p. 67.

[18] See chapter eleven, *ibid.*, p. 80 ff.

aqueducts; in the third, it flows from a river or stream; finally, it can be provided by the falling of much rain. Beginners in prayer are like those who draw the water in buckets from the well. The way of prayer is that of discursive meditation and it involves much work on their part. The prayer of quiet corresponds to the second way of bringing water, a way that requires much less effort than the first. In the deeper prayer of the third degree, it seems as if the Lord Himself becomes the gardener and does all the work. At this stage, Teresa speaks of the sleep of the faculties. The fourth degree is the highest, the prayer of union, in which the soul is lost in God.

Almost fifteen years after writing of these degrees of prayer in *The Book of Her Life*, Teresa composed her masterpiece on the stages of mystical prayer, *The Interior Castle*.[19] In this, her most mature synthesis, she makes use of the image of a castle. The soul is described as a castle made entirely out of a diamond or of very clear crystal that has seven mansions, each having a set of rooms. At the center of the castle dwells the King of Glory. One enters the gate of this castle through prayer and reflection. Passage through the first three of Teresa's seven mansions involves a person in the purgative way, in the ordinary ways of prayer that correspond to the first degree described earlier in her autobiography. In her teaching about these mansions, she is concerned with such topics as the importance of humility, the practice of prayer, meditation, and growth in a life of virtue.

With the fourth mansion, one enters into the stages of mystical prayer. Teresa treats the Prayer of Recollection and the Prayer of Quiet in the fourth mansion. A person begins to experience many spiritual consolations in this passive prayer. The Prayer of Union characterizes the rooms of the fifth mansion, a prayer in which the faculties are suspended as if in sleep. Teresa makes use of the beautiful image of the silkworm that dies in the cocoon and emerges to

---

[19] In addition to the complete editions cited, see *Teresa of Avila, The Interior Castle*, translation by Kieran Kavanaugh, O.C.D. and Otilio Rodriguez, O.C.D., introduction by Kieran Kavanaugh, O.C.D. (New York: Paulist Press, 1979). The introduction is particularly helpful.

the new life of a butterfly to illustrate the soul's experience of death and coming to new life in this union with Christ. In the last two mansions, it is the language of marriage and its preparatory stages that come to the fore. The Spiritual Betrothal takes place in the rooms of the sixth mansion. This experience is often accompanied by raptures, locutions, and intellectual and imaginative visions of Christ. The theme of suffering also plays an important role in her description of the sixth mansion. The seventh mansion is treated in terms of Spiritual Marriage. It is an intellectual vision of the Most Blessed Trinity that marks the entry into the dwelling places of this stage of the spiritual journey. The union of the Spiritual Marriage is also accompanied by visions of Christ's Sacred Humanity.

St. Teresa concludes by emphasizing that all these heavenly favors are meant to fortify our weakness so that we might be able to imitate Christ in His great sufferings. Prayer is to be sought, not for our enjoyment, but to have the strength to serve. Ever practical and realistic, St. Teresa leaves us with the words: "The Lord doesn't look so much at the greatness of our works as at the love with which they are done."[20]

6. St. John of the Cross

St. John of the Cross (1542-1591), like St. Teresa, has a unique and lofty position in the history of Christian spirituality. Their names are often linked together for their paths crossed in so many ways. They both were deeply involved in the Carmelite reform movement in sixteenth-century Spain; they assisted one another in reaching great heights of sanctity; and each has left a rich legacy of mystical writings and teaching that has earned them the title of Doctor of the Church. They are the glory of the Carmelite school of spirituality. Although there are differences in their approach and

---

[20] *Ibid.*, p. 194.

points of emphasis, their works complement one another and they are often studied together.[21]

The personality of John of the Cross does not emerge as clearly from his writings as does that of St. Teresa. He has left us no auto-biography as she has, nor are there the personal reflections that are so much a part of Teresa's literary works. There are also very few of his letters that are extant. John tends to be more objective and systematic as he lays out the spiritual ascent to a profound union with God. Yet the overwhelming and complete love that he has for God comes through very clearly. It should also be recalled that his verse has earned him a place as one of Spain's greatest poets.

John of the Cross (Juan de Yepes y Alvarez) was born into a poor family at Fontiveros in Spain in 1542.[22] His father died when he was a young child and his mother was faced with the difficult task of raising John and his two brothers by herself. As a young man, he was able to attend the newly established Jesuit college at Medina del Campo and shortly afterwards, around the age of twenty-one, he entered the Carmelite monastery of Santa Ana in the same city. After his profession as a Carmelite, he studied for the priesthood at the University of Salamanca. He met St. Teresa of Avila just after his ordination to the priesthood in 1567. At that time she was making plans for the extension of the Primitive Rule to the Carmelite friars. Although John told her of his desires to transfer to the Carthusians in order to live a life of greater solitude and prayer, she was able to persuade him to join her in the work of the Reform. A year later he went to Duruelo and established there the first reformed house of the Carmelite friars. Since the Primitive Rule required them not to wear shoes, they were soon referred to as the *Discalced* (shoeless) Carmelites.

---

[21] See for example E.W. Trueman Dicken, *The Crucible of Love* (New York: Sheed and Ward, 1963); and E. Allison Peers, *Handbook to the Life and Times of St. Teresa and St. John of the Cross* (Westminster, MD: Newman Press, 1954).

[22] For a biography of St. John of the Cross, see Crisogono de Jesus Sacramentado, *The Life of St. John of the Cross*, translated by K. Pond (London: Longmans, Green, 1958).

For the next few years John served as master of novices, rector of the house of studies at Alcala, and confessor for the Carmelite nuns at the monastery of the Incarnation in Avila. He was soon caught up in the turmoil and confusion that accompanied the spread of the Reform, as relations between the two groups of Carmelites grew more and more strained for various ecclesial and political reasons. John himself was kidnapped and imprisoned by the Calced Carmelites at Toledo in December of 1577. For nine months he was kept in a prison cell and treated very harshly for his refusal to renounce the Reform. Some of his celebrated poems were written during this imprisonment. He was eventually able to escape and take refuge at the monastery of El Calvario in the south of Spain. Later he held many responsible administrative positions in the Reform movement and was generous with his time in serving as spiritual director for friars, nuns and lay persons. These years of relative calm, with peace restored between the Discalced and Calced, were also the period of his greatest literary production.

The end of his life, however, was clouded by further conflict, this time within the Reform itself. John fell out of favor with the new Vicar General of the Discalced and with the General Chapter that was called. He was removed from office and sent to the solitude of the La Penuela monastery in Andalusia, arriving there in August of 1591. Efforts were also made by some to have him expelled from the Reform. Two months after he arrived at La Penuela he fell seriously ill. He was sent by his superior to Ubeda for further medical attention, but here there would also be further suffering, for the treatment of the prior of the house towards the sick man left much to be desired. But even in these painful circumstances, John of the Cross remained the gentle, loving, and holy man that he had been throughout his life. Death came to him at the age of forty-nine on December 13, 1591. St. John of the Cross was canonized by Benedict XIII in 1726, and was declared a Doctor of the Church by Pius XI in 1926.

The writings of St. John of the Cross emerged from a life that was actively involved in the work of the Reform of Carmel and the renewal of the religious life. But they also flowed from a heart that was focused entirely on a loving union with God in the midst of these labors. The works of John of the Cross that have come down to us were written during the last fourteen years of his life, that is the years after his imprisonment by the Calced Carmelites at Toledo in 1577. It is quite probable that earlier writings were lost at this time since his papers were seized. The three major extant works of John are *The Ascent of Mount Carmel* and *The Dark Night, The Spiritual Canticle,* and *The Living Flame of Love.* There are also his poems, a few letters, and various maxims and counsels on the spiritual life. None of his works was published during his own lifetime. The earliest publications were in 1618, more than twenty-five years after his death.[23]

The mystical thought of St. John of the Cross is developed on two levels in his writings. First, there are his poems which are considered to be among the finest in the Spanish language. His prose commentaries then seek to explain and expound the rich symbols of the magnificent lyrical poems, often taking them line by line. His prose, however, has not received the same acclaim as his poetry. It is didactic and systematic in form and often tends to be speculative and abstract in tone.

The Ascent of Mount Carmel and *The Dark Night* are usually taken together, for they both constitute a commentary on the first two stanzas of his famous poem *Noche Oscura* (*The Dark Night*). At the beginning of the commentary, John speaks of it as a work which describes the path to be followed to reach perfection, which for him is union with God. The process of purgation and the passage through the dark night of the senses and the dark night of the

---

[23] For English translations of the complete works see *The Collected Works of St. John of the Cross*, translated by Kieran Kavanaugh, O.C.D. and Otilio Rodriguez, O.C.D. with introductions by Kieran Kavanaugh, O.C.D. (Washington, DC: Institute of Carmelite Studies, 1973); and *The Works of St. John of the Cross*, translated by E. Allison Peers, 3 vols. (Westminster, MD: Newman Press, 1954). The translations by E. Allison Peers are also available in the Doubleday Image Book series. See also *John of the Cross, Selected Writings*, edited with an introduction by Kieran Kavanaugh, O.C.D. (New York: Paulist Press, 1987).

spirit receive careful attention. *The Ascent* focuses on the ascetic aspects of the journey, primarily the active purification of the senses and the active purification of the spirit. *The Dark Night* focuses on the passive or infused aspects of the journey. It describes how God brings about the passive purification of the soul and its faculties, and brings its faith and love to perfection.

The Spiritual Canticle takes it name after a poem of the same title. It resumes the account of the journey at the end of the dark night of the spirit and describes the loving search for and union with the Beloved in terms of mystical betrothal and marriage. *The Living Flame of Love* also takes its name after the title of another poem. Although John of the Cross had already spoken in *The Spiritual Canticle* of the highest union with God possible in this life (transformation in God), he tells us in the prologue to *The Living Flame* that he wishes to "treat of a love within this very state of transformation that has a deeper quality and is more perfect."[24] He describes a love of God that can receive an added quality and become more intensified. He writes that "the soul now speaking has reached this enkindled degree, and is so inwardly transformed in the fire of love and has received such quality from it that it is not merely united to this fire but produces within it a living flame."[25]

Few have written so powerfully of the heights of this loving union with God as John of the Cross. But he has also concentrated much of his attention on the *way* that leads to the divine union. His spiritual journey brings a person along the way of darkness, the way of the dark night. It is a very difficult journey to undertake and sustain, for it calls for a willingness to empty and strip oneself of all created reality and to enter into the darkness, armed only with faith and love of God. His mysticism is one of complete renunciation and negation. For John of the Cross, no human knowledge or other aspect of created reality can bring us to the fullness of union with God

---

[24] See *The Living Flame of Love* in *The Collected Works of St. John of the Cross, op. cit.*, p. 578.

[25] *Ibid.*

who is the Absolute One. Thus, it is only after an arduous and complete purification of all the sensory and spiritual faculties that one can be fully illuminated by the light of divine union.

For a number of reasons, the writings of John of the Cross provide a real challenge to the reader. He writes primarily for those who are in the advanced stages of spiritual growth and maturity. His teaching on detachment and purification and his single-mindedness of purpose can appear to be too demanding and austere to many. Others may find his language too subtle and speculative. The careful reader, however, will be amply rewarded, for no one has written more profoundly or eloquently about the heights of divine love than this humble and holy Carmelite friar. No one has surpassed John of the Cross in his attempts to write about the deepest union with God that is possible in this life.

7. The Italian School

Let us leave sixteenth-century Spain and the rich legacy of its Golden Age and turn to some of the other developments of the early Counter-Reformation period. The Council of Trent was by far the most significant. After a number of delays, this extremely important Ecumenical Council of the Catholic Reformation opened at Trent in Italy on December 13, 1545, and closed there on December 4, 1563. Meeting at various times over these eighteen years, the bishops sought to clarify Catholic doctrine and to legislate a thorough reform of the Church. The reform of the clergy, for example, received much needed attention and decrees were issued in this area. Bishops were to reside in their own dioceses and make regular visitations of their parishes, and seminaries were to be established for the education and training of priests. The Council Fathers also called for a General Catechism to be drawn up for pastors, and the *Roman Catechism*, as it came to be called, was published in 1566.

Among the many pastoral programs that flowed gradually from the reforms of the Council of Trent, three were of particular importance: preaching, catechetical works, and home missionary activity. A revival in preaching took place following the lead of the Council of Trent. It soon became evident that good preaching was the most effective means to reach the minds and hearts of the faithful, and popular preachers drew large crowds. St. Peter Canisius' catechism was very popular among German Catholics as early as 1560, and at later periods catechisms for various age groups began to abound in other areas of Europe. Both preaching and catechizing came together in the giving of parish missions. A number of the new orders and congregations that came into existence at this time were very involved in these missions that did much to renew religious life and practice among the faithful.

Italy was the scene of many early reform movements in the sixteenth century. Protestantism never made any great impact in Italy. It seemed to have little appeal to the more expansive Italian temperament. The Humanist Renaissance movement that reached such lofty heights in Italy, particularly in Florence, had many positive results, but there were also lingering elements of paganism that had to be overcome. Great religious figures arose in Italy in the sixteenth century who accomplished much in the renewal of the Christian faith. They did not, however, leave any spiritual writings that were comparable to what took place in Spain.

Italian spirituality of the sixteenth century was primarily practical in orientation and directed to action. The newly established congregations of the Theatines and the Barnabites were good examples of this orientation. The Theatines, founded by St. Cajetan (Gaetano da Thiene) and companions at Rome in 1524, and the Barnabites, founded by St. Anthony Mary Zaccaria and two other priests at Milan in 1530, were orders of Clerics Regular who dedicated themselves to the reform of the clergy. They hoped to do this by the example of a fervent religious life of dedicated priestly ministry. At Brescia in Italy, St. Angela Merici (1474-1540) founded the Ursulines, the first order established for the education of young girls. These groups were soon followed by many other new Orders and Congregations that dedicated themselves primarily to either the renewal of the clergy, the care of the sick, or the education of the young.

St. Philip Neri (1515-1594) has a special place among the many great Italian saints and reformers of this period. A mystic and a saint well known for his joyful spirit and buoyancy, he is the founder of the Congregation of the Oratory. The Oratorians, as they came to be called, were priests who lived in community but did not take religious vows; they dedicated themselves to a life of prayer and preaching. As the "Apostle of Rome," St. Philip Neri was very instrumental in guiding a number of religious leaders to a life of personal holiness.

St. Charles Borromeo (1538-1584), cardinal and archbishop of Milan, was a prominent figure in the Tridentine reform. With his great apostolic zeal and holiness of life, he became a model for the reforming bishop. Even among the mystics of the day, there was an element of the reforming spirit that was reminiscent of St. Catherine of Siena and St. Bridget. The Carmelite mystic and saint, Mary Magdalen dei Pazzi (1566-1607), dictated letters to Church leaders during her ecstasies, encouraging them in the work of Church reform. There is a poetic dimension to her writings that often reflects a sense of wonder and awe over God's creation. A similar desire for reform was manifested in the life of the Dominican mystic, St. Catherine dei Ricci (1522-1590), whose letters urging reform also project an optimistic view of human nature. The Jesuit, St. Robert Bellarmine (1542-1621), is known more for his Counter-Reformation theological writings, but he is also the author of various spiritual writings such as *Ascent of the Soul to God by the Ladder of Creatures* and *The Art of Holy Dying.*[26]

A spiritual treatise from the Italian school that first appeared in 1589 and went on to enjoy great popularity was *The Spiritual Combat*. There has always been some question concerning the authorship of the work, but it has generally been attributed to the Theatine priest, Lorenzo Scupoli (c. 1530-1610). It certainly is reflective of Theatine spirituality, and it is possible that a number of different writers from this school had a hand in its final redac-

---

[26] See *Robert Bellarmine, Spiritual Writings*, translated with an introduction by John Patrick Donnelly and Roland J. Teske (New York: Paulist Press, 1989).

tion. As the title indicates, it is an ascetic work that seeks to provide guidelines and directives for the struggle to conquer self, overcome vice, and grow in a spirit of prayer. Four arms or weapons are recommended to the reader for the combat: (1) distrust of oneself; (2) trust in God; (3) the good use of the faculties of soul and body; and (4) the practice of prayer.[27]

Even though there is a reforming spirit and an ascetic dimension that is clearly present in the spirituality of the Italian school, it avoids falling into any severity or harshness. There is always a certain lightness and spirit of joy that is present, due in no small part to the conviction of Divine Love that permeates Italian spirituality. As Pierre Pourrat writes: "This display of reforming activity, this inward combat, resolute and austere against self, is usually found hidden beneath attractive externals. Italy of the sixteenth century possesses a lovable spirituality which gives the impression of moderation and balance."[28]

Conclusion

From the time of the Renaissance, a strong national spirit came more and more to the fore in the European nations. A greater sense of national identity asserted itself in many countries and had effects in numerous areas. Spirituality was no exception. Unlike the Middle Ages where various spiritualities tended to be grouped around the great religious Orders and families, schools of spirituality now became more identified with the nations themselves. We have seen that this was very much the case in Spain during the period known as its Golden Age, and also in Italy of the sixteenth century. Common goals, currents of thought, historical circumstances,

---

[27] For an English translation of *The Spiritual Combat* along with pertinent background of the Theatines and their spirituality, see *Theatine Spirituality, Selected Writings*, translated, edited with an introduction and notes by William V. Hudon (New York: Paulist Press, 1996).

[28] See Pourrat, *op. cit.*, vol. III, pp. 232-233.

and national temperaments played a part in creating schools of spirituality that were associated with particular countries. France would come into its own politically, nationally, and religiously in the seventeenth century and would be the scene of many rich and important developments in spirituality. It is to the spirituality of seventeenth-century France that we will now turn.

For Further Reading

Christian Spirituality III: Post-Reformation and Modern. Edited by Louis Dupré and Don E. Saliers. New York: Crossroad, 1989.

Cognet, Louis, *Post-Reformation Spirituality.* Translated by P. Hepburne Scott. New York: Hawthorn Books, 1959.

Pourrat, Pierre, *Christian Spirituality.* Translated by W.H. Mitchell. Westminster, MD: The Newman Press, 1953. Vol. III, pp. 1-271.

Egan, Harvey D., S.J., *Christian Mysticism, the Future of a Tradition.* New York: Pueblo Publishing, 1984.

O'Malley, John W., S.J., *The First Jesuits.* Cambridge: Harvard University Press, 1993.

Guibert, Joseph de, S.J., *The Jesuits: Their Spiritual Doctrine and Practice. A Historical Study.* Translated by W.J. Young, S.J. St. Louis: Institute of Jesuit Sources, 1972.

Louis of Granada, *Pathways to Holiness.* Excerpts from the *Summa of the Christian Life* including passages from *The Book of Prayer and Meditation* and *The Sinner's Guide.* Translated and adapted by Jordan Aumann, O.P. New York: Alba House, 1998.

Dicken, E.W. Trueman, *The Crucible of Love: A Study of the Mysticism of St. Teresa of Jesus and St. John of the Cross.* New York: Sheed and Ward, 1963.

Peers, E. Allison, *Studies of the Spanish Mystics.* 3 volumes. Vols. 1-2 London: The Sheldon Press, 1927-30. Vol. 3, London: SPCK, 1960.

9 French Spirituality in the Seventeenth Century

1. Spiritual Revival in France

During the second half of the sixteenth century, France was torn by the violent religious wars between Catholics and Protestants that left the country broken and devastated. Peace finally came to the troubled country with King Henry IV embracing Catholicism and later issuing the Edict of Nantes in 1598 that extended religious tolerance. France gradually began to recover, politically, economically and spiritually.

France had survived the threat of Calvinism, but the overall religious condition of the country called for much needed reform and renewal. The system of Church benefices for the clergy had led to many abuses. Most sought the benefices of bishoprics, monasteries, parishes, and other religious institutions only for material gain with no spiritual motivation or pastoral interest. It was a rare bishop who resided in his diocese, and the lives of the clergy for the most part were marked by ignorance and immoral living. The state of the religious houses was scarcely better, and most of the Christian faithful, lacking any pastoral leadership, were ignorant of the faith and were steeped in superstitious practices.

Although there were earlier traces of reform even in these conditions, the dawn of the seventeenth century witnessed the rapid development of spiritual renewal in France. The decrees of the

Council of Trent were received and put into effect. The Jesuits returned from exile in 1603 and the Teresian Carmelites were introduced into France a year later. The Capuchins continued the reforming activity they had started in the late sixteenth century. Practically all of the established orders of men and women underwent significant renewal and development during this time. A number of saints, leaders, and founders of new religious communities arose, who sought to meet the spiritual needs of both clergy and laity. For example, Cardinal Bérulle and his disciples directed much of their energy and labor to the education and renewal of the clergy. A number of the new religious congregations devoted themselves to the preaching of parish missions, particularly in the rural areas.

Religious books soon came to abound. Pseudo-Dionysius and other writers from northern Europe were known through the Latin translations of the Cologne Charterhouse. The writings of earlier mystics such as Catherine of Siena, Catherine of Genoa, Tauler, Suso, and Ruusbroec were all translated into French. In the latter part of the sixteenth century, spiritual writings from the Spanish school began to be translated. The works of Teresa of Avila became available in French in 1601, and two decades later the writings of John of the Cross appeared in translation. These and other writings did much to nourish the mystical tendencies that were present in many circles. They helped to foster the mystical movement that was to flourish in France in the seventeenth century.

These and other factors led to a spiritual revival in France that would bring forth a rich harvest and have a vast influence. Indeed, the seventeenth century is the golden age of spirituality in France. It is to an investigation of some of the key persons and movements connected with this period that we now turn.[1]

---

[1] The classic resource for this period is the monumental work of Henri Bremond, *Histoire littéraire du sentiment religieux en France*, 11 volumes (Paris: Librairie Armand Colin, 1916-1936). The first three volumes are available in the English translation, *A Literary History of Religious Thought in France*, translated by K.L. Montgomery (New York: Macmillan, 1930). See also Louis Cognet, *La spiritualité moderne* (Paris: Aubier, 1966). Many of the ideas from this book are summarized in his *Post-Reformation Spirituality*, translated by P. Hepburne Scott (New York: Hawthorn Books, 1959). See also Michael

2. The Abstract School of Mysticism

Madame Barbe Acarie (1566-1618) was a central figure in the early stages of the revival of mysticism in France.[2] She was a wife, mother and mystic who had great influence on people from all walks of life. She was instrumental in introducing the Teresian Carmelites into France, and she herself died as a Carmelite under the name of Marie of the Incarnation. It was by this name that she was beatified. Because of her reputation as a mystic and the holiness of her life, she gathered around her a group of influential people. This group of spiritual leaders that met at her home in Paris included the Capuchin Benet of Canfield; the famous Carthusian spiritual director, Dom Beaucousin; the Sorbonne professor, André Duval, who later wrote a biography of Madame Acarie; the Jesuit, Father Pierre Coton, the confessor to the French King; holy secular priests such as Gallemant, Jean de Bretigny, and the young Bérulle; and devout lay persons such as the future Chancellor Michel de Marillac and the Marquise de Maignelay, the sister of the bishop of Paris.[3] Francis de Sales also had contact with the group when he visited Paris.

This group that gathered around Madame Acarie did much to revitalize Catholicism in France. The members played a key role in social and charitable activities, monastic reform, renewal of the diocesan clergy, the introduction of the Spanish Carmelites of St. Teresa to France, and the foundation of new religious congregations. There was also a distinct mystical orientation to the group. They read and discussed the classical mystical works, particularly those in the tradition of Pseudo-Dionysius and the Rhineland mystics, and as a group they gave birth to a synthesis of mysticism that emphasized a way of emptying and negation of created things that

---

J. Buckley, "Seventeenth-Century French Spirituality: Three Figures" in *Christian Spirituality III: Post-Reformation and Modern,* edited by Louis Dupré and Don E. Saliers (New York: Crossroad, 1989), 28-68.

[2] Bremond treats Madame Acarie in vol. II of his *A Literary History of Religious Thought in France, op. cit.,* pp. 145-194.

[3] See Cognet, *Post-Reformation Spirituality, op. cit.,* p. 59.

led to a union with the divine will. Its main theorist was the Capuchin, Benet of Canfield, and it is usually referred to as the abstract school of mysticism.

Benet of Canfield (1562-1610) was born in the village of Canfield in Essex, England under the name of William Fitch. He was converted from Puritanism as a young man, and then crossed over to France where he entered the Capuchins in 1587. As a Capuchin, he served as master of novices in his own religious community and as a spiritual director and guide for many others. As noted earlier, he was very active and influential in Madame Acarie's circle. His main work, the *Rule of Perfection*, was published in French in 1609, although an English version was in existence earlier, and copies of the work were circulated in manuscript form to those he directed.[4] Louis Cognet writes of this work: "Canfield only lacks style to be one of our greatest spiritual writers, but in spite of clumsy and inaccurate language, the *Rule of Perfection* was read all through the seventeenth century, and all the mysticism of the age was nurtured on it."[5]

The *Rule of Perfection* is a highly developed, systematic presentation of the spiritual journey that focuses on the conformity of the human will with the divine will. It seeks to bring about a total and generous abandonment to the will of God through an emptying process. A surrender to the will of God is at the heart of a process that is described in three stages. The first part of the book focuses on the external will of God that is revealed in Revelation and

---

[4] See Benoit de Canfield, *La Règle de Perfection — The Rule of Perfection*, critical edition edited by Jean Orcibal (Paris: Presses Universitaires de France, 1982); and *Renaissance Dialectic and Renaissance Piety, Benet of Canfield's Rule of Perfection*, a translation and study by Kent Emery, Jr. (Binghamton, NY: Medieval & Renaissance Texts and Studies, 1987).

[5] See Cognet, *Post-Reformation Spirituality, op. cit.*, p. 60. Bremond writes of him: "One thing prevents his being a great writer: he is a man of mixed speech, oscillating between English, French and Latin." *A Literary History, op. cit.*, vol. II, p. 117. Bremond also writes of Canfield: "Master of the masters themselves, of Bérulle, Madame Acarie, Marie de Beauvillier and many others, he, in my opinion, more than anyone else gave our religious renaissance this clearly mystical character which we see already stamping it and which was to last for the next fifty years." *Ibid.*, p. 115.

Tradition. This corresponds to the active life, and the goal is to bring about the conformity of the human will to God's external will. The second part treats the interior will of God that manifests itself through interior graces, movements, and illuminations. The goal of this stage, the contemplative life, is the union of the human will with the interior will of God. The third part of the book treats of a mystical stage of union, a conformity with the essential will of God. Since the essential divine will is God Himself, it cannot be apprehended by any human faculty or power. Canfield refers to this as the supereminent life, in which the essential will of God absorbs the human will in a profound union of love. He himself strikes a cautionary note about the third part of his book, advising that no one enter on this part unless he or she has been judged capable of benefiting from it by one's superior, confessor or director.

3. St. Francis de Sales — Salesian Spirituality

St. Francis de Sales (1567-1622) enjoys a well deserved reputation as one of the most attractive saints and spiritual writers in the history of Christian spirituality.[6] As the bishop of Geneva, his spiritual writings exercised great influence during his own lifetime, and they have continued after his death to enjoy a popularity that has rarely been equaled. His two major works are the *Introduction to the Devout Life* and the *Treatise on the Love of God*, but his spiritual legacy also contains numerous sermons, letters, conferences to religious, and some minor works.

Francis de Sales was born in 1567 of a noble Catholic family in Savoy, a region that was then largely Calvinist. He received his early education at the Jesuit College of Clermont in Paris and then studied law and theology at the University of Padua in Italy. Ordained to the priesthood at Annecy in December of 1593, he labored

---

[6] For biographies of Francis de Sales see Michael de la Bedoyere, *François de Sales* (New York: Harper, 1960); and André Ravier, S.J., *St. Francis de Sales, Sage and Saint* (San Francisco: Ignatius Press, 1980).

as a young priest to restore Catholicism in the Calvinist area of Chablais, south of Lake Geneva. He was appointed coadjutor to the bishop of Geneva in 1599 and three years later succeeded him. He remained the bishop of Geneva for the rest of his life, maintaining his residence at the Alpine village of Annecy in the duchy of Savoy. He was canonized by Pope Alexander VII in 1665 and declared a Doctor of the Church by Pius XI in 1923, the tercentenary of the saintly bishop's death.

Certain characteristics emerge clearly in the life, spirituality, and writings of Francis de Sales. By nature he was kind and sensitive of heart, and endowed with many human and social qualities that drew people to him. God's grace built on these natural gifts. The love of God was the foundation of his own life, and he sought to bring that love of God to life in the hearts of the people he encountered from all walks of life. There is a strong spirit of optimism in his entire outlook; he was well aware of human weakness and frailty, but his emphasis was much more on our restoration in Christ. From his studies he derived a strong humanistic bent, and he is always included among the French writers of this period who are known as "the devout humanists."[7] Above all there is that personal quality that is so much a part of his life and writings. This is nicely summed up in a passage from one of his letters where he discusses the practice of preaching. He writes:

> We should speak candidly and trustfully, really be in love with the doctrine we're trying to teach and get people to accept; the great art is to be art-less. The kindling power of our words must not come from outward show but from within, not from oratory but straight from the heart. Try as hard as you like, but in the end only the language of the heart can ever reach another heart while mere words, as they slip from your tongue, don't get past your listener's ear.[8]

---

[7] Bremond's first volume in his *Literary History of Religious Thought in France* is entitled "Devout Humanism." The third chapter treats Francis de Sales.

[8] Quoted in *Study of Spirituality*, edited by C. Jones, G. Wainwright, and E. Yarnold, S.J. (New York: Oxford University Press, 1986), p. 380. For the full text of this work

This personal touch is evident in his writings. He was well acquainted with the important spiritual works of his day. Spanish writers such as John of Avila, Louis of Granada, and especially St. Teresa of Avila nourished his thought, as did members of the Italian school. *The Spiritual Combat* by Scupoli was a favorite of his. His years of study with the Jesuits also left him with a deep knowledge and appreciation of the Ignatian *Spiritual Exercises.* But he made these and other writers his own in a unique way. His originality lay not so much with the teaching itself but with the way he presented it. The selection and arrangement of the material, the synthesis that is made, the examples and images that are used to illustrate the teaching, the tone of balance and moderation — all these are very much in evidence. They explain to a large extent the immediate and lasting popularity of his classic, the *Introduction to the Devout Life.*

Although the *Introduction to the Devout Life* was first written between the years 1607 and 1608, Francis continued to revise it until the definitive edition appeared in 1619.[9] The beginnings of the book go back to the apostolate of spiritual direction that he carried out on behalf of many devout lay women. He would send to them, particularly to Madame de Charmoisy, pages of general advice, suggestions and instructions as a help to lead them "to the Promised Land of true devotion." He was encouraged to bring these pages together in book form for a larger audience, and his efforts gave birth to a spiritual classic. The work itself was a pioneering one, for it had as its goal something that had not been done before. He sought to extend the pursuit of perfection far beyond a monastic context. Through his hands the piety of the cloister was brought into the world, and monastic devotion was transformed into popular devo-

---

see St. Francis de Sales, *On the Preacher and Preaching,* translated, with an introduction and notes by John K. Ryan (Chicago: Henry Regnery Company, 1964).

[9] For an English translation see St. Francis de Sales, *Introduction to the Devout Life,* translated and edited by John K. Ryan (New York: Image Books, 1972).

tion. He sought to lead ordinary Christians to a full and fervent interior life that would manifest itself in all aspects of their lives.

True devotion for Francis is simply the true love of God that has reached such a degree of perfection that "it not only makes us do good but also to do this carefully, frequently, and promptly."[10] This life of devotion is possible for a person in any vocation or profession, but it is exercised in different ways by "the gentleman, the worker, the servant, the prince, the widow, the young girl, and the married woman."[11] It must also be adapted to the strength, responsibilities, and duties of each person.

The *Introduction to the Devout Life*, as we have it today, is divided into five parts. The first part is concerned with the purgative way and corresponds in general to the first week of the Ignatian *Spiritual Exercises*. The second part gives various instructions on the exercises of piety that are recommended. The Salesian method of mental prayer is described with its stages of preparation, considerations, affections, resolutions, and the spiritual bouquet (a devotional thought from the morning prayer that one can call to mind during the day). The last three parts of the book provide guidance and instruction on the practice of the virtues, counsels on overcoming the most frequent temptations, and exercises for renewing and confirming a person in the pursuit of true devotion. Central to all of this is growth in union with Christ. As Francis writes in his prayer at the beginning of the book: "Live, Jesus! Live, Jesus! Yes, Lord Jesus, live and reign in our hearts forever and ever. Amen."

St. Jane Frances de Chantal (1572-1641) was an important friend and collaborator of Francis de Sales.[12] Their paths first crossed when the young Baroness de Chantal heard him preach at Dijon in 1604. She was a thirty-two year old widow at the time with

---

[10] *Ibid.*, p. 40.

[11] *Ibid.*, p. 43.

[12] For a biography of St. Jane de Chantal, see Elisabeth Stopp, *Madame de Chantal, Portrait of a Saint* (Westminster, MD: Newman Bookshop, 1963). Bremond's last chapter in the second volume of his *Literary History* is on Francis de Sales and Jane de Chantal, pp. 394-429. See also Wendy Wright, *Bond of Perfection: Jeanne de Chantal and François de Sales* (New York: Paulist Press, 1985).

four children. Her husband had died three years earlier as a result of a hunting accident. Six months later Francis de Sales became her spiritual director and began guiding her during a critical time in her life when God's grace was working in a powerful way. The spiritual friendship that grew and developed between these two saints remained strong until Francis' death in 1621, and it was the occasion for many of his important letters of direction.[13]

In June of the year 1610, Francis de Sales and Jane de Chantal established a new religious congregation for women at Annecy. It became known as the Visitation of Holy Mary, and Jane de Chantal was the first superior. It incorporated many of the new ideas for a religious community that Francis de Sales had earlier shared with Madame de Chantal. The new congregation was opened to women who were not strong enough physically to cope with the external austerities that were common to such established religious Orders for women as the Carmelites and the Poor Clares. Another innovation allowed the women to leave the enclosure of the convent during the day in order to visit the sick and the poor. This latter element soon gave way to a more strictly contemplative way of life, but the other aspects of Francis' vision took form and the new community began to flourish. He often gave talks about the religious life to the first members of the Visitation. They were later published as his *Spiritual Conferences* and they reflect the spirit and charism of the new congregation.[14]

Francis de Sales' awakened interest in mysticism was due in no small measure to Jane de Chantal. Drawn to a prayer of simplicity and the ideas of the abstract school of mysticism, she had been in touch with the Carmelite Sisters at Dijon since 1606. She sought the counsel of her spiritual director about the suggestions of the Carmelites that she give up the normal imaginative and conceptual

---

[13] See *Francis de Sales and Jane de Chantal, Letters of Spiritual Direction*, translated by Peronne Marie Thibert, V.H.M., selected and introduced by Wendy M. Wright and Joseph F. Power, O.S.F.S. (New York: Paulist Press, 1988).

[14] See *The Spiritual Conferences of St. Francis de Sales*, translated by Abbot Gasquet and Canon Mackey, O.S.B. (Westminster, MD: Newman Bookshop, 1943).

forms of meditative prayer. At first Francis was cautious about her leaving the more ordinary and surer ways of prayer. Gradually, however, he left her more freedom in this area, noting the extraordinary work of God in her. He was also led to adopt this prayer himself, and he began a serious reading of the mystical authors. Drawing on these readings, as well as his own experience in prayer and his experience of directing many of the Visitation sisters, Francis de Sales began working on his own synthesis of mystical prayer. It culminated with the publication of his *Treatise on the Love of God* in 1616.[15]

The *Treatise on the Love of God* is a carefully constructed and written study of divine love. Francis' purpose in the twelve books that compose the treatise is to represent "the history of the birth, progress, decay, operations, properties, advantages and excellences of divine love."[16] Such a lofty and somewhat complex study cannot be summarized easily, and here only a few key points can be mentioned. For Francis, love expresses itself through the will. He teaches that our love of God is mainly expressed in two ways: an affective way and an effective way. The first is the love of willingness and goodwill (the love of compliance), and it unites us with God's goodness. The second (effective love) is the love of obedience and submission and it urges us to serve God and to carry out his will. Since we show our affective love for God primarily through prayer, Francis devotes Book Six and Book Seven of the *Treatise* to an investigation of prayer, its various manifestations, and the union with God that is brought about through prayer. It is interesting to note that Francis describes the deepest union in terms of a union of person with person. The symbol which is central for him is that of a child in its mother's arms.

If affective love is true, it becomes effective love, that is a love

---

[15] For English translations see Francis de Sales, *On the Love of God*, translated by John K. Ryan, 2 vols. (New York: Image Books, 1963); *Treatise on the Love of God*, translated with an introduction by Henry Benedict Mackey, O.S.B. (Westminster, MD: Newman Bookshop, 1942).

[16] See preface to the *Treatise* in Mackey's translation, *op. cit.*, p. 6.

that is in conformity with God's will. Books Eight and Nine of the *Treatise* focus on the love of God that is shown through the conformity of our will with the divine will. It is a love that seeks to be obedient to God. Francis speaks of a loving obedience to two aspects of God's will: the "will that is signified" and the "will of good pleasure" or permissive will. The first is made known by the ten commandments, the evangelical counsels, and the inspirations of grace. In the second, the love of God is shown by submission to the divine good pleasure as manifested in the events of one's life, including the suffering and trials that are difficult. This love is marked by a spirit of resignation and holy indifference in which the will submits to God with a wholly pure and disinterested love.

4. Bérulle and the French School

The influence of St. Francis de Sales was considerable both during his lifetime and after his death in 1622. His influence, however, great as it was, would not be as widespread in France as that of Bérulle and the French School. The term, *French School*, was first used by Henri Bremond in speaking about Bérulle and his many disciples. Perhaps the *Bérulle School* would be a more apt term, since French spirituality in this period is broader than the French School. But there is no doubt that the French School is the dominant influence, for many great saints, founders of religious congregations, and spiritual writers were connected with this school that had its beginnings with Bérulle. It is a school of the interior life and its spirituality is a lofty one.[17]

Cardinal Pierre de Bérulle (1575-1629) is the major figure in

---

[17] For the French School see Bremond's third volume of his *Literary History*; Raymond Deville, *The French School of Spirituality, An Introduction and Reader*, translated by Agnes Cunningham, S.S.C.M. (Pittsburgh: Duquesne University Press, 1994); *Bérulle and the French School, Selected Writings*, edited with an introduction by William M. Thompson, translation by Lowell M. Glendon, S.S. (New York: Paulist Press, 1989); and John Saward, "Bérulle and the French School" in *The Study of Spirituality, op. cit.*, pp. 386-396.

the origin and teaching of the French School. For all his greatness as a Church leader and writer, however, he is not so well known as many others of this golden age of French spirituality.[18] The future diplomat, theologian, mystic, spiritual writer, and founder of the French Oratory was born of an old and distinguished family and brought up in a deeply religious environment. As a young man he studied with the Jesuits at the College of Clermont and later at the Sorbonne in Paris. He was ordained to the priesthood in 1599 and then devoted himself energetically to various religious activities. He worked zealously for the conversion of Protestants, devoted himself to spiritual direction, and was a strong advocate for the reform of religious communities. As a young priest he played a prominent role in the circle that formed around Madame Acarie. He was a key figure in establishing the Teresian Carmelite Sisters in Paris in 1604. The Carmelites flourished in France and by 1660 there were sixty-two Carmelite monasteries in the country. Bérulle, along with André Duval and Jacques Gallemant, was appointed the ecclesiastical superior of the Carmelite nuns in France by Pope Paul V.

Gradually Bérulle came to see that his special vocation was to work for the education and sanctification of the diocesan clergy. In 1611 he founded the French Oratory at Paris, a congregation of priests that was modeled after the Oratory of St. Philip Neri. The Oratorians quickly grew in France and within eighteen years there were forty-four houses of the Oratory, and they were operating a number of colleges.[19] Foremost in the doctrinal mission of the Oratorians was the restoration of the dignity and grandeur of the Catholic priesthood. Bérulle was convinced that the vocation to holiness was one of the noblest legacies of the diocesan clergy, "the Order of Jesus Christ." Unfortunately, this had been forgotten over

---

[18] Bremond writes: "For Bérulle, at first sight, is not impressive; not one of those who capture the imagination, touch the heart, or master us utterly, as do S. François de Sales, Pascal or Fénelon." See *A Literary History, op. cit.*, vol. III, p. 3.

[19] For the early history and particular charism of the Oratorians in France see Bremond, vol. II, pp. 133-192.

the course of history, and it was to this restoration that he devoted himself for the rest of his life.[20]

During the course of his life of prayer and study, Bérulle also developed many of the ideas that led to his synthesis of theology and spirituality. He was indebted to many of the classical theologians and spiritual writers, particularly St. Augustine, but his own writings bear witness to a very remarkable and original integration of doctrine and piety. Central to Bérulle's thought is the greatness and goodness of God. A realization and acknowledgment of this should lead a person to an ongoing spirit of adoration of God that comes from the depths of one's heart. Bérulle's great sense of God's transcendence and grandeur led to his high regard for the virtue of religion. It is to God that we must look, not to ourselves. This emphasis is usually referred to as the *theocentricism* of Bérulle and the French School.

Intimately connected with this *theocentricism* is Bérulle's exalted teaching on the Incarnate Word and the mystery of the Incarnation. This is so fundamental to his thought that Pope Urban VIII is said to have given him the title of "Apostle of the Incarnate Word." It is only in union with Jesus Christ, the Incarnate Word, that we can adore God in a spirit of humility and love. Only Jesus is the true and perfect adorer of God the Father. Thus, the theme of "adherence" to Christ takes on great importance in Bérulle's thought. A Christian adheres to Christ by seeking consciously to conform one's whole life to the interior life of Jesus, to what Bérulle calls the "states" of the Incarnate Word. For Bérulle, each event or mystery in the historical life of the Incarnate Word involves an action that is finished and will not be repeated, and also a "state" which manifests the feelings and inward dispositions of Christ. Speaking of these mysteries of Christ, Bérulle writes: "They are past in execution, but they are present in their virtue: and neither will this virtue ever pass nor the love with which they were fulfilled. Therefore the spirit, the state, the virtue, the merit of the mystery remain

---

[20] *Ibid.*, p. 136 ff.

present always."[21] Thus, one can be united with Christ in a pro-
found way by sharing in these eternal states. And it is through
Christ and in Christ that we are able to praise and adore the Triune
God.

Adherence to Christ, however, cannot take place without a
corresponding spirit of abnegation or annihilation. Bérulle had written on this theme in the first book that he wrote while studying at
the Jesuit College, *A Brief Discourse on Interior Abnegation*. Unlike
Francis de Sales, Bérulle had little attraction towards a spirit of humanism, and this is manifested in his pessimism about human nature. He writes that abnegation leads one to have a very low esti-
mate of all created things and especially of oneself, and a very high
idea of God. This theme continued to have a prominent place as he
developed his teaching on the Incarnate Word. Abnegation involves
a detachment from all that hinders one from adhering to Jesus. It
enables one to be open to God's grace and the working of the Holy
Spirit. It is only through a radical abnegation of one's very self that
a person can adhere fully to Jesus who is our life and our all. The
object of abnegation or annihilation is to live entirely for God in
Christ Jesus. Bérulle found the main motivation for a spirit of abnegation and annihilation of self in the self-humiliation of the Word
Incarnate, particularly in Christ's state of infancy. For Bérulle, the
conviction that the human nature of Jesus was basically in a state
of servitude in relation to the Word Incarnate led him to stress that
we should place ourselves in a state of servitude to the Word Incarnate. Bérulle, ever mindful of Mary's role as the Mother of the
Incarnate Word, stressed her grandeur and never separated her
from Christ. In time he came to lay great stress in his spirituality
on a devotional vow of servitude to Jesus and Mary.

Bérulle's last years, unfortunately, were clouded by frequent
controversies. There were conflicts with Cardinal Richelieu, the
prime minister, over political and ecclesial policies. There were tensions with the Jesuits over educational issues since the Oratorians

---

[21] Quoted in Buckley, "Seventeenth-Century French Spirituality," *op. cit.*, p. 50.

were also running schools. Conflicts even arose with his beloved Carmelites over his insistence that they adopt the practice of the vow of servitude. This caused tensions between him and his longtime associate, André Duval, and even with Madame Acarie, who was now living as a Carmelite nun. Later, the vow of servitude was attacked by the Carmelite friars and some theologians. In response, Bérulle composed his most famous work, the *Discourse on the State and Glories of Jesus*. It was published in 1623 and it brilliantly provides the theological and doctrinal foundation for the vow of servitude.[22]

Pope Urban VIII named Bérulle a cardinal in 1627. Two years later he died at the age of fifty-four while he was celebrating Mass. His *Complete Works* were edited and published with an introduction fifteen years later by one of the early Oratorians, Francis Bourgoing. The writings themselves did not enjoy any widespread influence after his death for a number of reasons. In speaking of Bérulle's legacy, Louis Cognet writes: "No one denies his importance. Nevertheless, reactions to Bérulle and his spirituality have been varied, divided, and long-standing. Bérulle was never uncontested neither during his lifetime nor after his death."[23] However, it was through the writings of his disciples that Bérulle's teaching would have a profound influence on French spirituality. It can be said that the writings of the disciples achieved a greater popularity than those of the master.

5. The French School After Bérulle

Charles de Condren (1588-1641), Bérulle's immediate successor as Superior General of the Oratorians in France, was a renowned spiritual teacher and mystic.[24] Born of a noble family at Vaubuin

---

[22] For some selections in English of this work, see *Bérulle and the French School, Selected Writings, op. cit.*, pp. 109-157.

[23] L. Cognet, *La Spiritualité Moderne* (Paris: Aubier, 1966), pp. 310-11 (cited in *French School of Spirituality, op. cit.*, p. 46).

[24] Bremond treats Charles de Condren in his *Literary History, op. cit.*, vol. III, pp. 243-358.

near Soissons, he studied theology at the Sorbonne and was ordained to the priesthood in 1614. After he received his doctorate from the Sorbonne in 1615, his professor, André Duval, hoped that Condren would succeed him in his chair of theology, but the young priest chose to enter the Oratory. His early years as an Oratorian were devoted to preaching, teaching, and administrative activities for the community. He apparently had great gifts for directing others and he was held in high regard as a spiritual director. He was elected Bérulle's successor in 1629 and served as Superior General of the Oratorians until his own death in 1641. Condren published nothing during his own lifetime, but the year after his death his *Letters and Discourses* were published and enjoyed wide circulation. Some of his teaching on the priesthood and sacrifice were incorporated later in the book, *Idea of Priesthood and the Sacrifice of Christ*, published by Fr. Quesnel in 1677. His teaching is also reflected in the writings of Jean-Jacques Olier and St. John Eudes.

Condren followed Bérulle with his teaching on abnegation and adherence to Christ, the Word Incarnate. Condren, however, placed great emphasis on the aspect of Christ's sacrifice and immolation of Himself. Jesus is the supreme priest and perfect victim who offered to God the only sacrifice worthy of the Creator. While Bérulle speaks of a general adherence to the states of the Word Incarnate, Condren focuses more directly on Christ's victim state. One must adhere to Christ in this state of sacrificial victim through a process of self-annihilation and total abandonment to God. As Pourrat writes of Condren's spiritual doctrine: "The state of victim, the condition of inward annihilation is everything with Fr. Condren; it is also a summing up of everything he taught."[25] Thus, for Condren, adoration of God is expressed primarily through sacrifice. In one of his letters, Condren writes:

> You must seek and find in Jesus Christ the spirit and grace
> that God wills to give you, so that you may carry this out....

---

[25] See P. Pourrat, *Christian Spirituality* (Westminster, MD: The Newman Press, 1953), vol. III, pp. 350-351.

Adore Jesus, give yourself entirely to him.... Hold on to the intention to renounce everything you are; surrender yourself into his hands, so that you no longer live in your own spirit, but in his; no longer according to your own will, intentions and inclinations, but only in his divine and adorable dispositions.[26]

Jean-Jacques Olier (1608-1657) is much better known than Condren because of his extensive writings and the fact that he is the founder of the Sulpicians, the society of priests that have specialized in the preparation and formation of seminarians for the priesthood for over three hundred years. Bremond considers Olier the poet of the French School. He writes that his "special grace and mission was, not exactly to popularize Berullism, but to present it with such limpidity, richness of imagination and fervor that its apparently somewhat difficult metaphysics are placed invitingly in the reach of most readers."[27]

Destined for an ecclesiastical career, Olier was the recipient of a number of benefices when he was still a young man. After a conversion experience, occasioned by a pilgrimage to Loretto in Italy, he returned to Paris and placed himself under the spiritual direction of St. Vincent de Paul. He was ordained to the priesthood in 1631 and attached himself to the missionaries who were being sent by Vincent de Paul to preach parish missions throughout France. Later he came under the spiritual guidance of Fr. Charles de Condren for whom he always had the highest regard. It was through Condren that he came to know and appreciate the spiritual doctrine of Bérulle. After passing through a period of intense spiritual trial, he moved on to a new stage in his life. With a small group of priests he took up residence in 1642 at the parish of Saint-Sulpice in Paris with the intention of founding a seminary for priests. Here

---

[26] Cited in Denville, *French School of Spirituality, op. cit.,* p. 66.

[27] Bremond, *op. cit.,* vol. III, p. 393. Bremond's treatment of Olier is found in pages 359-434. These pages contain a number of helpful citations from Olier's writings. See also Pierre Pourrat, *Father Olier: Founder of Saint-Sulpice,* translated by W.S. Reilly (Baltimore: Voice Publishing Company, 1932).

he devoted himself for the next ten years to the work of parish renewal and the spiritual formation of the seminarians. Here he founded the Society of the Priests of Saint-Sulpice (Sulpicians) in 1642, and from this center he sent his priests to assist bishops in the foundation of seminaries in various parts of France.

It was during his last years that Olier wrote such works as the *Introduction to the Christian Life and Virtues* and *The Christian Day*.[28] Very much in the general tenor of the French School, he reflects the same pessimism about human nature that is found in Bérulle and Condren. From the teaching of Condren he emphasizes the need of self-effacement, sacrifice, and self-annihilation, so that the Holy Spirit might work more directly within a person. He also follows Bérulle and Condren in stressing the need of adhering to the states of the Incarnate Word. Olier, however, places a particular emphasis on Christ's Eucharistic state. Devotion to the Eucharist and the Blessed Sacrament are very important in Olier's spiritual thought. Given the context of his writing and the audience to whom it was directed, one also finds a practical and pastoral dimension to his works. For example, he suggests a simple method of meditation that "consists in having our Lord before our eyes, in our heart and in our hands."[29] This later developed into the influential and well-known Sulpician method of prayer with its threefold division of adoration, communion, and cooperation.

We can end this brief treatment of Olier with his well-known prayer that sums up so much of his spirit. He slightly amplified the version he received from his revered spiritual director, Charles Condren, and it always was a favorite of his.

> O Jesus living in Mary,
> Come and live in thy servants,
> In the spirit of thy sanctity,
> In the fullness of thy strength,

---

[28] For selections from both of these works see, *Bérulle and the French School, Selected Writings, op. cit.,* pp. 215-220.

[29] *Ibid.,* pp. 228-229.

In the reality of thy virtues,
In the perfection of thy ways,
In the communion of thy mysteries,
Be Lord over every opposing power,
In thine own Spirit, to the glory of the Father. Amen.[30]

St. John Eudes (1601-1680) was the fourth great master of the French School. He became an Oratorian in 1623 and was ordained to the priesthood two years later in Paris. Both Bérulle and Condren were his teachers; thus, his spirituality was shaped and formed by Berullism. As a member of the Oratory in Caen, he first worked with the plague stricken, and then in 1632 he began his missionary work in various parts of France with the preaching of the parish missions that did so much for the renewal of the faith. This missionary work and his ministry of spiritual direction led him to write a number of practical spiritual books that furthered his influential preaching. One of his best known, *The Life and Kingdom of Jesus in Christian Souls*,[31] was written during the course of this missionary work in 1637.

The many years of preaching parish missions convinced John Eudes of the importance of priestly preparation and the need of establishing seminaries for this purpose. Since the Oratorians were not moving in this direction at the time, John Eudes left the Oratory in 1643 and became the founder of the Society of Jesus and Mary (the Eudists), established explicitly for the work of seminaries and parish missions. Earlier, in 1641 at Caen, he had established the women's congregation, first known as Our Lady of Refuge and later as Our Lady of Charity (1651). From his missionary work he had also come to recognize the need of assisting young women who were experiencing serious difficulties, and this new congregation sought to meet this need by providing places of refuge. At a much

---

[30] For the traditional Latin version that was handed down in Sulpician seminaries, see *ibid.*, p. 73.

[31] See *The Life and Kingdom of Jesus in Christian Souls: A Treatise on Christian Perfection for Use by Clergy or Laity*, translated by a Trappist of Gethsemani, introduction by Fulton J. Sheen (New York: Kenedy, 1946).

later period, this group evolved into two separate religious communities for women: Our Lady of Charity of Refuge and Our Lady of Charity of the Good Shepherd.

St. John Eudes is also recognized as the apostle for the devotion to the Sacred Hearts of Jesus and Mary. He composed two Offices, one in honor of the Sacred Heart of Mary in 1648, and one in honor of the Sacred Heart of Jesus in 1672. The last book he wrote was entitled *The Admirable Heart of the Most Holy Mother of God.*[32]

In spite of the opposition he suffered from many sides, particularly from the Jansenists, John Eudes continued his many faceted activities until his death on August 19, 1680. He was beatified in 1909 and canonized in 1925. It was only in the twentieth century that St. John Eudes was in a sense rediscovered. Biographies of him appeared and critical editions of his extensive writings were published in twelve volumes.[33]

St. Vincent de Paul (1581-1660) was also a significant and influential figure during this period of religious revival in France. The great Apostle of Charity is known more as an initiator of extensive pastoral undertakings than as a spiritual writer. Ordained a priest in 1600, he later underwent a conversion process in which Bérulle played an important role. He then devoted himself with great generosity to the preaching of parish missions, priestly renewal, spiritual direction, and serving the poor. In 1625 he established the Congregation of the Missions (usually known as Vincentians or Lazarists) for the purpose of preaching missions to those living in rural areas. In 1633, together with St. Louise de Marillac (1591-1660), he founded the Daughters of Charity.

Vincent de Paul was influenced in his own spirituality by Cardinal Bérulle, but there was also the influence of St. Francis de Sales

---

[32] For St. John Eudes and the devotion to the Sacred Heart, see Bremond, *op. cit.,* vol. III, pp. 536-572.

[33] See *Oeuvres completes du venerable Jean Eudes,* 12 vols., introduction and notes by Joseph Dauphin and Charles Lebrun (Vannes or Paris: P. Lethielleux, 1905-11). With this renewed interest in the writings of St. John Eudes, a number of English translations have appeared. See the bibliography in *Bérulle and the French School, Selected Writings,* pp. 342-343.

whom he knew well. Vincent published nothing during his own life-time. After his death, however, the spiritual conferences that he gave to the Daughters of Charity were published as well as his numerous letters of direction.[34] Vincent de Paul was beatified in 1729 and canonized in 1737. One writer succinctly captures the saint and his many contributions with the words:

> Vincent de Paul was neither a profound nor an original thinker; yet few have accomplished as much. His success was a result of natural talent and a tremendous amount of work, but above all of a profound spiritual life. In this he was deeply influenced by Bérulle and Francis de Sales, but he modified their ideas according to his own insights. The piety that he practiced was simple, non mystical, Christocentric and oriented toward action.[35]

Two later religious leaders and canonized saints who had close ties with the French School were St. John Baptist de La Salle (1651-1719) and St. Louis Marie Grignion de Montfort (1673-1716). Both prepared for the priesthood at the seminary of Saint-Sulpice, and both were founders of new apostolic congregations. St. John Baptist de La Salle's apostolic spirit was focused on the ministry of Christian education. He was the founder of the Brothers of the Christian Schools, whose members dedicated themselves to the work of catechizing and educating the poor. He also composed books on prayer and meditation for the members of his community.[36] The life of St. Louis Marie Grignion de Montfort was marked by a strong apostolic and missionary spirit and a fervent devotion to Mary. During the course of his missionary work, he founded the

---

[34] See *Vincent de Paul and Louise de Marillac, Rules, Conferences, and Writings,* edited by Frances Ryan, D.C. and John E. Rybolt, C.M. (New York: Paulist Press, 1996).

[35] See the article on Vincent de Paul by M.A. Roach in the *New Catholic Encyclopedia* (New York: McGraw-Hill, 1967), vol. 14, p. 683.

[36] See Michael Sauvage and Miguel Campos, *St. John Baptist de La Salle: Announcing the Gospel to the Poor: The Spiritual Experience and Spiritual Teaching of St. John Baptist de La Salle,* translated by Matthew J. O'Connell (Romeoville, IL: Christian Brothers Conference, 1981).

Daughters of Wisdom and the Missionaries of the Company of Mary (Montfort Fathers). He did much to further devotion to Mary through his *Treatise on True Devotion to the Blessed Virgin* and the shorter summary of this work, the *Secret of Mary*.[37] These writings were very influential in popularizing his vow of slavery to Jesus through Mary.

Before leaving the French School, mention should be made of the important role women played in the development of its spiritual tradition. Madame Acarie's central role as an initiator and her influence upon Bérulle has already been noted. Jean-Jacques Olier received much support and encouragement from Mother Agnes de Jesus, prioress of a monastery of contemplative Dominicans, and from Marie Rousseau, a widow and mystic. St. John Eudes always valued the advice and counsel of the mystic, Marie des Vallées. With St. Vincent de Paul, St. Louise Marillac played a pioneering role in the formation and apostolates of the Daughters of Charity. Mention will be made later of some religious women who labored as missionaries in the New World. Here we will focus for a moment on the Carmelite, Madeleine de Saint-Joseph.

Venerable Madeleine de Saint-Joseph (1578-1637) was the first French prioress of the great Carmelite monastery in Paris.[38] She entered this Carmel shortly after its historic founding when the first Carmelite Sisters came to Paris from Spain, and she later was active in the growth and expansion of the Carmelites in France. Serving as prioress of the Great Carmel in Paris for the second time during the years 1624-1637, she came to know Bérulle and his spiritual teaching quite well. Bérulle was deeply impressed by her holiness of life and her mystical experiences, and she, on her part, was a positive influence upon the development of his spirituality. After Bérulle's death she remained devoted to his spiritual teaching and

---

[37] See *True Devotion to Mary*, translated by Frederick Faber (Rockford, IL: Tan Books and Publishers, 1985).

[38] For background on Madeleine de Saint-Joseph, see the introduction to *Bérulle and the French School, Selected Writings, op. cit.*, pp. 22-26.

did much to spread Berullism among the Carmelite nuns in France. During her lifetime, she wrote a biography of the Carmelite mystic, Catherine of Jesus. Her numerous *Letters* also provide solid information about her spirituality which integrates the teachings of St. Teresa and Bérulle.[39]

6. Jansenism and Quietism

Much has been written about the Jansenists and Quietists of seventeenth-century France. Historians have carefully studied and analyzed the complex events and controversies that surrounded these two religious movements. Although our remarks here can only be relatively brief, it has always been recognized that both movements cast large shadows over religious developments in France and involved a number of people in ongoing disputes.

Jansenism[40]

The context of what is known historically as Jansenism is found in the theological controversies over predestination and the relationship between God's grace and human liberty that dominated Catholic theology in the sixteenth and seventeenth centuries.[41] The seventeenth century witnessed a reaction against the optimism of the devout humanists towards human nature and against the theological position known as Molinism that gave weight to the exercise of human freedom. There was a greater attraction to

---

[39] For some selected letters, see *ibid.*, pp. 189-214.

[40] For background on Jansenism see Ronald A. Knox, *Enthusiasm* (New York: Oxford University Press, 1950), chapters 9 and 10; N. Abercrombie, *The Origins of Jansenism* (Oxford: Clarendon, 1936); Pourrat, *op. cit.*, vol. IV, pp. 1-37; Elfrieda Dubois, "Jansenism" in *The Study of Spirituality, op. cit.*, pp. 396-405; and Louis Dupré, "Jansenism and Quietism" in *Christian Spirituality III: Post-Reformation and Modern, op. cit.*, pp. 121-141.

[41] For a concise summary of the theological issues involved, see Pourrat, *op. cit.*, vol. IV, pp. 1-8.

the teachings of St. Augustine that emphasized God's grace and a pessimistic view of human nature. This was true of the Bérulle School that interpreted and emphasized Augustine's teaching in a moderate and orthodox way. Jansenism, however, took Augustine's teaching to an extreme and even heretical position.

Jansenism takes its name from Cornelius Jansen (1585-1636), a theology professor at Louvain and bishop of Ypres in Flanders for the last two years of his life. Shortly after his death, the work that occupied much of his scholarly life, *Augustinus*, was published. It met with a strong reaction, and in the midst of much controversy over the ensuing years, the study was the object of several papal condemnations. Among the points condemned were his teaching on the irresistibility of interior grace and his claim that Christ had not died for all people, but only for some. In all probability, his teaching would not have continued to generate so much subsequent controversy if it were not for the support of a number of strong personalities. Foremost among them was Jean Duvergier de Hauranne.

Jean Duvergier de Hauranne (1581-1643) is usually known historically as Saint-Cyran, since he had been named the commendatory abbot of Saint-Cyran in 1620. Thirteen years later he became the spiritual director of Port-Royal just outside of Paris, and it soon became the center for Jansenism. There was a large monastery of Cistercian nuns at Port-Royal at the time, under the leadership of the young, reforming abbess, Angélique Arnauld. She was one of many from the Arnauld family who had close ties with Port-Royal over the years. Later, a number of educated and professional men came to settle around Port-Royal. Withdrawal from the world was central to their spirituality, and they devoted themselves to a life of prayer and manual and intellectual work. They became known as the *Solitaires*, or *Messieurs de Port-Royal*.

Saint-Cyran emerges as an enigmatic person. There always seemed to be an air of mystery about him, and historians in general have not painted him in flattering terms. He must have been an effective spiritual director and leader, however, for he was held in high regard by the members of the community. Under his leadership,

Port-Royal became a center for a rigorous and penitential religious reform and for the strong defense and support of Jansenist teaching. Port-Royal also propagated a rigorous moral system; this brought about many clashes with the Jesuits whose humanistic tendencies they deplored. Saint-Cyran opposed Cardinal Richelieu on many of his policies and this led to Saint-Cyran's imprisonment in 1638. He was released after Richelieu's death but died shortly afterwards in 1643. With Saint-Cyran's death, the leadership at Port-Royal passed to Antoine Arnauld, the younger brother of Abbess Angélique Arnauld.

If Jansen can be considered the theologian of Jansenism and Saint-Cyran its inspirer, Antoine Arnauld is best described as the popularizer of the movement. Disillusioned by the present state of the Church, he looked backwards and sought to reestablish the practices of the past. He continued the spirit of rigorism that Saint-Cyran had set in motion and he likewise courted constant controversy. This was particularly apparent with the publication of his book, *Frequent Communion*, in 1643. He sought to counter what he considered a spirit of laxity by recommending that one refrain from receiving Holy Communion as a penitential practice. The book did much to encourage many to abstain from Holy Communion for long periods of time. Ultimately, his persistent refusal to accept the condemnation of five propositions from the *Augustinus* led to his own fall from favor and a self-imposed exile.

Another important personality connected with Port-Royal was Blaise Pascal (1623-1662). A prominent mathematician and scientist of his day, he was drawn to the spirituality of Port-Royal and became a supporter of the Jansenist cause. During the years 1656 and 1657 he composed the *Provincial Letters*, a defense of the Jansenist teaching on grace and an attack on the Jesuit moral teaching that the Jansenists considered lax. He tended to oversimplify many complex issues and his polemical methods were not always fair, but the witty and satirical style of the *Letters* brought them a widespread popularity. Another book that was published after his death, the *Pensées*, established Pascal's reputation as an important spiritual author.[42] Written in fragmentary form, it is a collection of spiritual thoughts and a defense of Christianity. Although the pessimism of Port-Royal about human nature is very much present, it is a work that springs from a deep faith. It also stresses the primacy of experience over reason with such well-known sayings as, "It is the heart that is conscious of God, and not the reason"; and "The heart has its reasons, which reason knows not, as we see in a thousand instances."[43] Mention should also be made of the moving description of the mystical experience that Pascal underwent during the night of November 23, 1654. He relates in his *Memorial*: "From about half past ten at night, until about half-past twelve. FIRE. God of Abraham, God of Isaac, God of Jacob, not of the philosophers and scientists. Certitude. Certitude. Feeling. Joy. Peace. God of Jesus Christ... Jesus Christ.... May I not be separated from Him for eternity."[44]

Jansenism as a movement and a party came to an end with the suppression of Port-Royal in 1709 at the order of King Louis XIV. As a spirituality, however, it continued to exert a subtle influence, even outside of France, well into the twentieth century. Jansenist piety is marked by a pronounced pessimism concerning human nature, an anti-humanistic spirit and suspicion of the world, and a rigorous moral teaching. Its tendency to stress the fear of God over the love of God can easily lead to a preoccupation with sin and a spirit of legalism. In common usage, the term "Jansenism" is often identified with Puritanism.

Quietism

"Quietism" can be a somewhat elusive term and one that is difficult to define with precision. Here we are referring to the crisis

---

[42] See Blaise Pascal, *Pensées*, translated by A.J. Krailsheimer (New York: Penguin Classics, 1966).

[43] See *The Essential Pascal*, selected and edited by Robert W. Gleason, S.J. and translated by G.F. Pullen (New York: New American Library, 1966), pp. 200-201.

[44] *Ibid.*, pp. 205-6.

in mysticism that occurred in France in the latter part of the seventeenth century and culminated with the public and acrimonious debate between two prominent bishops, Francis Fénelon and Jacques Bossuet.[45] Speaking in general terms, we can describe it as a tendency in prayer that emphasizes the pure (disinterested) love of God, a complete abandonment to the divine will, and a stance of passivity in prayer. It is important to note that Quietism was not a completely new and foreign element that was introduced into the Christian mystical tradition in the seventeenth century. It must be seen rather as the exaggeration of an existing and perfectly orthodox tendency in the development of mysticism. As Ronald Knox writes: "It was the error of a few incautious souls, trying to repeat the lesson they had learned from the saints of the Counter-Reformation, and getting it wrong."[46] As was the case with Jansenism, historians have written at great length on the complex and drawn-out doctrinal controversies surrounding this issue. The modest aim here is to summarize briefly the main points of this crisis that brought about such a negative reaction to mysticism in France.

The famous trial in Rome involving the Spanish priest, Miguel Molinos (1628-1696), brought the issue of Quietism to public attention in a dramatic way. Molinos came to Rome in 1663 to promote the canonization process of a Spanish priest. He remained in Rome and soon became an influential spiritual director and teacher. There was a strong interest on the part of many at the time for contemplative prayer, particularly the prayer of simple regard, and Molinos became a revered guide and teacher in this movement. In 1675 he published his *Spiritual Guide*, a work that became very popular and went through many editions. His teaching moved away from the usual ascetic practices and ordinary forms of prayer and emphasized a passive prayer of quiet and abandonment to God. For reasons that are still not clear, Molinos was arrested in 1685.

---

[45] For background information on Quietism see Ronald Knox, *Enthusiasm, op. cit.*, pp. 230-353; Pourrat, *op. cit.*, vol. IV, pp. 101-260; and Cognet, *Post-Reformation Spirituality, op. cit.*, pp. 126-138.

[46] Knox, p. 259.

After a long and careful investigation of his teaching and his numerous letters of spiritual direction by the Holy Office and a subsequent trial, he was found guilty of immoral conduct and doctrinal errors. Molinos confessed his guilt and was sentenced to life imprisonment in 1687. He still remains an enigmatic figure and somewhat of a puzzle for historians, and they have continued to speculate on the exact reasons for his condemnation and his actual guilt in the whole affair.[47]

In France, an anti-mystical spirit began building up in the latter part of the seventeenth century, rising to its climax with the events of the Quietist controversy.[48] Madame Jeanne-Marie Guyon (1648-1717) played an important role in the early stages of this crisis. Left a widow at a young age, she was drawn to the practice of mystical prayer and later devoted herself to an apostolate of teaching about prayer. Her ministry involved her in a great deal of travel, and she also became a prolific writer. Her two main works on prayer are the *Short and Easy Method for Prayer*, and *The Spiritual Torrents*. In these works she emphasizes the prayer of quiet and "invites the soul to turn and collect itself in its interior, in order to remain in continual adherence to God.... The soul must keep silence in itself, suppressing all its own activity, in order to live in the presence of God, in abandonment and faith."[49]

Francis Fénelon (1651-1715) was a young priest when he first met Madame Guyon in 1688. He was greatly helped by her in his own life of prayer, and he in turn always remained a strong supporter of hers, even at no small cost to his ecclesiastical career.[50] When her views began to be attacked, Madame Guyon, at Fénelon's suggestion, requested that her writings be officially investigated. This was done at the Issy Conference by Bishop Bossuet and two others. They drew up thirty-four articles on various issues

---

[47] On Molinos' trial and condemnation see Knox, *op. cit.*, pp. 295-318; and Pourrat, *op. cit.*, vol. IV, pp. 157-172.

[48] For manifestations of this see Cognet, *op. cit.*, pp. 116-126.

[49] *Ibid.*, 128.

[50] See Michael de la Bedoyere, The *Archbishop and the Lady, The Story of Fénelon and Madame Guyon* (London: Collins, 1956).

of prayer in 1695 and Madame Guyon submitted to them. In all probability, the matter would have rested there had not the controversy moved to another level, that of a direct confrontation between Bossuet, the bishop of Meaux, and Fénelon, now the archbishop of Cambrai. The disagreement centered primarily on pure (disinterested) love and the passive state. Fénelon presented his case with the publication of *Explanations of the Maxims of the Saints on the Interior Life*. In expounding his teaching on pure love, he analyzed five states of love that were distinguished by their degree of disinterestedness. Bossuet countered with his *Instruction on the States of Prayer*. His later document, *Relation on Quietism*, was more polemical in tone and he sought to discredit Fénelon by a more personal attack. In response to Fénelon's appeal to Rome and in a highly charged political atmosphere in which individuals and groups took sides, twenty-three propositions taken from Fénelon's *Maxims of the Saints* were condemned (in terms as mild as possible) in a papal brief of Innocent XII signed on March 12, 1699.[51] Fénelon submitted unreservedly to the decision. Innocent XII's own regard for Fénelon was shown by the fact that he raised him to the cardinalate in October of the same year. Thus, the unfortunate affair came to its conclusion, having played no small part in creating a distrust of mysticism in France and leading to its definite decline in the eighteenth century.

7. French Jesuit School

When Louis Cognet traced the revival of mysticism in France in the early part of the seventeenth century, he divided his investigation into four main divisions: Benet of Canfield and the abstract school; St. Francis de Sales; Cardinal Bérulle; and the Society of Jesus.[52] The Jesuits came to France in 1556, the year their founder,

---

[51] See Cognet, *op. cit.*, p. 136 and Knox, *op. cit.*, pp. 347-350.
[52] See his *Post-Reformation Spirituality, op. cit.*, pp. 56-85.

St. Ignatius of Loyola, died. By 1610 there were more than four-teen hundred French Jesuits working as educators, preachers, spiri-tual directors, confessors to the king, missionaries, and spiritual writers, and their influence would continue to grow. Associated more with the school of the devout humanists, most of the many Jesuit spiritual writers focused on the ordinary forms of prayer and meditation with a strong emphasis on devotion to Christ.[53] There was, however, a mystical current among the French Jesuits, just as there had been with such earlier Spanish Jesuits as Balthazar Alvarez and Luis de la Puente. The most influential mystical writer among the French Jesuits was Louis Lallemant.

Fr. Louis Lallemant (1587-1635) did not publish anything during his own lifetime. The spiritual conferences, however, that he gave as tertian instructor at Rouen to young Jesuit priests dur-ing their final year of spiritual formation were taken down by some of the Jesuits. These notes were preserved and handed on until they were ultimately edited and published in 1694 by Fr. Pierre Cham-pion under the title of *The Life and Spiritual Doctrine of Father Louis Lallemant*.[54] In addition to his own Ignatian tradition, Lallemant was familiar with many traditional mystical sources, since he lived at a time when they were being read widely in France. These would include the Spanish and earlier Rhineland mystics.

Various attempts have been made to summarize the main teaching in Lallemant's *Spiritual Doctrine*.[55] Bremond emphasizes

---

[53] For information about the many Jesuit writers of this period see *ibid.*, pp. 77-85; and Joseph de Guibert, S.J., *The Jesuits, Their Spiritual Doctrine and Practice*, translated by William J. Young, S.J. (Chicago: Loyola University Press, 1964), pp. 349-373. Bremond treats the French Jesuits at length in the fifth volume of his *Histoire littéraire*.

[54] For an English translation from the French see *The Spiritual Doctrine of Father Louis Lallemant of the Society of Jesus preceded by an account of his life by Father Champion*, edited by Alan McDougall (Westminster, MD: Newman Bookshop, 1946).

[55] For a helpful treatment see Buckley, "Seventeenth-Century French Spirituality: Three Figures," *op. cit.*, pp. 53-64; he writes of Lallemant's teaching: "The doctrine charts a journey, one that begins with the experience of human emptiness and terminates with union with God in Christ — and all under the direction of the Holy Spirit" (p. 56). See also De Guibert, *op. cit.*, pp. 353-358.

four points: the second conversion, the critique of action, the guard over the heart, and the guidance of the Holy Spirit. Lallemant himself focuses it even more, highlighting two elements of the spiritual life: purity of heart and docility to the Holy Spirit. He writes:

> The two elements of the spiritual life are the purification of the heart and the direction of the Holy Spirit. These are the two poles of all spirituality. Through these two ways, one comes to perfection: according to the degree of purity which one has acquired and in proportion to the fidelity with which one has cooperated with the movement of the Holy Spirit and has followed his guidance.[56]

For Lallemant, one must be open to the Holy Spirit through purity of heart, and sensitive to the Spirit's guidance through discernment. The gifts of the Holy Spirit also play an important part in his spiritual teaching, as does the importance of contemplative prayer for those involved in apostolic activity.

Jean Joseph Surin (1600-1665) was an important disciple of Lallemant.[57] He was a Jesuit tertian under Lallemant at Rouen during the year 1629-30, and he went on to write a number of spiritual books such as his autobiographical *Spiritual Catechism* and his *Foundations of the Spiritual Life*. He became well-known for the part he played as one of the exorcists at the Ursuline Convent at Loudon during the years 1634-1637, an experience that was ruinous to his own health.[58] In his writings he also emphasized purity of heart and docility to the Holy Spirit, along with a detachment from and complete renunciation of anything that would hinder embracing God's will in all things.

A later Jesuit who was an heir of this mystical tendency among the French Jesuits was Jean Pierre de Caussade (1675-1751). He was the most outstanding representative of the spirituality of abandon-

---

[56] Cited in Buckley, p. 57.

[57] See Pourrat, *op. cit.*, vol. IV, pp. 67-81; and De Guibert, *op. cit.*, pp. 360-363.

[58] See Pourrat, vol. IV, p. 72 ff.

ment to Divine Providence. The little spiritual classic that is associated with his name derives from the time he was spiritual director for the Sisters of the Visitation convent at Nancy. The Sisters preserved the letters of direction that he sent to them and the notes taken down from his spiritual conferences. Many years after his death the material was gathered together and edited by the Jesuit, Henry Ramière, and was published in 1861 under the title, *Abandonment to Divine Providence*.[59] This work has enjoyed great popularity since its first publication and has been translated into several languages. Many have been helped by its message of trusting abandonment to God and its focus on the sacrament and duty of the present moment.

The Jesuit, St. Claude de la Columbiere (1641-1682), was of great assistance to St. Margaret Mary in spreading devotion to the Sacred Heart of Jesus. St. Margaret Mary Alacoque (1647-1690) was a nun at the Visitation convent at Paray-le-Monial when she was favored with visions of Christ that revealed the treasures of love in the Sacred Heart. In these revelations that took place between 1673 and 1675, she was commissioned to spread devotion to the Sacred Heart throughout the world. Claude de la Columbiere was rector of the Jesuit College at Paray-le-Monial when he was chosen to be Margaret Mary's director. He assured her and her superior of the divine origin of the revelations, and when his *Spiritual Retreat* was published two years after his death in 1684, it did much to make known the revelations to the Christian world. Public and private devotion to the Sacred Heart would grow and spread far and wide in the eighteenth and nineteenth centuries.

---

[59] To avoid any charge of Quietism, the editor points out that Caussade looks at abandonment in two ways: "as a *virtue* incumbent on all Christians, and as a particular *state*, in which God puts certain souls for whose special guidance He provides." *Ibid.*, p. 277. Among English translations are *Self-Abandonment to Divine Providence*, translated by Algar Thorld, revised by Father John Joyce, S.J. (London: Collins, 1971), and *The Sacrament of Every Day*, translated by Kitty Muggeridge (San Francisco: Harper & Row, 1984).

8. French Missionaries

The religious needs of the New World in the seventeenth century brought a number of French missionaries to labor in the wilderness of New France in North America. The Recollect Friars, a branch of the Franciscans, arrived in Canada in 1626. The Jesuits came to Quebec in 1632 and the Sulpicians settled in Montreal in 1647. Among the Jesuit missionaries were Jean de Brebeuf, Isaac Jogues, and their companions, who were martyred in North America between the years 1642 and 1649. These eight Jesuit martyrs were canonized by Pius XI on June 29, 1930. The accounts of the missionary work of the French Jesuits in North America have been preserved in the valuable historical document known as the *Jesuit Relations*.[60] They comprise the individual reports of the missionaries that were drawn together each year by the Jesuit superior at Quebec and sent back to France where they were published between the years 1632 and 1673. They did much to arouse a wide interest in the missionary endeavors in New France of North America.

Venerable Marie of the Incarnation (1599-1672) came to Quebec as a pioneering missionary Sister with two other Ursulines in 1639. As a widow and the mother of one son, she had entered the Ursulines at Tours in France eight years earlier. She became the superior of the Ursuline convent at Quebec where the first school for girls in North America was founded. It was established primarily for Indian girls, although later the Ursuline mission was extended to the education of the daughters of the French colonists. In the face of many hardships and challenges, this work of the early Ursulines in Canada flourished. Marie of the Incarnation was also a great mystic and has often been referred to as "the Teresa of her time and of the New World." Her varied writings dealing with her missionary vocation and her mystical experiences have come down

---

[60] For English translations see *Jesuit Relations and Allied Documents*, edited by Reuben Gold Thwaites, 73 volumes (Cleveland: 1896-1903).

to us through the work of her son, Dom Claude Martin, who had become a Benedictine in France.[61]

Another pioneering woman in Canada was St. Marguerite Bourgeoys (1620-1700). She migrated from France to Montreal in 1653, twelve years after this frontier garrison was established in New France. She established the first school in Montreal and this was followed by a school for Indians, an Indian mission, a school for the poor, and a boarding school for the daughters of the French colonists. She was joined in her apostolic undertakings by other women, and the group eventually evolved into a new type of religious congregation. As religious women who were not bound to the cloister, they were able to travel as the needs of the mission required. Their particular charism was "the life of a wayfarer, in dialogue with the neighbor." Their model for this type of life was Mary, the Mother of Jesus, and Mary's Visitation to her cousin Elizabeth was an inspiration for their service to others. The religious community she founded, the Congregation of Notre Dame, received ecclesiastical approval in 1698, two years before her death. Margaret Bourgeoys was beatified by Pius XII in 1950 and canonized by John Paul II in 1982.

Before concluding this chapter, we can return to France itself and briefly mention some significant reforms that took place there in monasticism. The Congregation of St. Maur (Maurists) was a French congregation of Benedictine abbeys that was founded in 1618 as part of a reform movement among the Benedictines. By 1675 there were 178 monasteries in the congregation and the Maurist movement continued to flourish until the time of the French Revolution (1792). The Maurists became famous for their historical scholarship and learned studies, for they had a high re-

---

[61] For selections from her writings and informative background material, see *Marie of the Incarnation, Selected Writings*, edited by Irene Mahoney, O.S.U. (New York: Paulist Press, 1989).

gard for the value of scholarly work for monks. One of their great scholars was John Mabillon (1632-1707).[62]

This same concept of the monastic life was not shared by Armand Jean de Rancé (1626-1700). After a significant conversion experience in 1659, this learned ecclesiastic embraced the monastic life with great generosity and zeal. He later became the abbot of the Cistercian Abbey at La Trappe in Normandy and under his reforming leadership it became a very fervent center. His rigorous and penitential concept of monastic life was somewhat controversial, particularly his insistence that scholarly activity was incompatible with the life of a monk. In place of intellectual and scholarly pursuits, he strongly advocated for the monk a life of demanding manual labor. When the Cistercians of the strict observance became a separate branch in the nineteenth century, it was the spirit of de Rancé that was the dominant influence.

Conclusion

With its saints, reformers, founders of new religious communities, mystics, missionaries, dynamic leaders, and spiritual writers, the seventeenth century was indeed the golden period for French spirituality. France itself benefited greatly from this spiritual revival of such mighty proportions. The rich harvest that was produced, however, had a significance far beyond the confines of France. For the influence of French spirituality was a pervasive one throughout the world in the eighteenth and nineteenth centuries. It is true that it is a spirituality that has its strengths, limitations, and exaggerations. But there is no question that its overall contribution to the history and development of Christian spirituality has been a vast one.

---

[62] For interesting material on the reforms that took place in the Benedictine monasteries for women, see Bremond's chapter "The Reforming Abbesses" in his *Literary History, op. cit.*, vol. II, pp. 292-393.

Significant developments had also taken place in England during the sixteenth and seventeenth centuries, and it is primarily to an investigation of these movements and trends that we will turn in the next chapter.

For Further Reading

Aumann, Jordan, *Christian Spirituality in the Catholic Tradition*. San Francisco: Ignatius Press, 1985.

Bérulle and the French School, Selected Writings. Edited with an introduction by William M. Thompson. Translation by Lowell M. Glendon, S.S. New York: Paulist Press, 1989.

Bremond, Henri, *Histoire litteraire du sentiment religieux en France*. 11 volumes. Paris: Libraire Armand Colin, 1916-1936. The first three volumes are available in English translation, *A Literary History of Religious Thought in France*. Translated by K.L. Montgomery. New York: Macmillan, 1930.

Cognet, Louis, *Post-Reformation Spirituality*. Translated by P. Hepburne Scott. New York: Hawthorn Books, 1959.

Deville, Raymond, *The French School of Spirituality, An Introduction and Reader*. Translation by Agnes Cunningham, S.S.C.M. Pittsburgh: Duquesne University Press, 1994.

Pourrat, Pierre, *Christian Spirituality*. Translated by W.H. Mitchell. Westminster, MD: The Newman Press, 1953. Vol. III, p. 272ff.; and Vol. IV, pp. 1-361.

10   *English Spirituality*

The sixteenth and seventeenth centuries brought forth profound changes in the religious configuration of England. The Reformation came later than it did on the continent, but once it did come it ushered in a period of political and religious turmoil and unrest. After many struggles and fluctuations, Anglicanism emerged as the established state religion and became the dominant spirituality; but there were also present other currents of religious thought and practice such as Puritanism, Quakerism, and much later, Methodism.[1] The rich heritage of England's past was not forgotten and certain aspects were incorporated into the newly established groups. England's monastic tradition was a rich one, and even though the monasteries themselves were suppressed at the time of the Reformation, the influence that remained was a subtle and implicit one.[2] The English mystics of the fourteenth century also continued to have a distinct influence. For example, Walter Hilton's *Scale of*

---

[1] For the history of the Reformation in England, see Philip Hughes, *The Reformation in England*, 3 volumes (New York: 1951-1954).

[2] For background on monasticism in England see David Knowles, *The Monastic Orders in England* (Cambridge: The University Press, 1940) and his *A History of the Religious Orders in England* (Cambridge: The University Press, 1948-59).

Perfection was reprinted five times between 1494 and 1679.[3] It is to an investigation of the various spiritualities and writers that can be grouped under the term of English spirituality that we now turn in the following pages.

1. Post-Reformation Catholic Writers

England's separation from the Roman Catholic Church was initiated during the reign of Henry VIII, with the final break taking place during the early years of the reign of Elizabeth I. The sixteenth century witnessed the era of the Catholic martyrs in England that included such well-known figures as St. Thomas More, St. John Fisher and St. Edmund Campion. Catholicism in England became an underground movement, forced to struggle for its survival. It is not surprising that few Catholic spiritual writers came forth at this time. Two exceptions were Dom Augustine Baker and Richard Challoner.

Dom Augustine Baker (1575-1641) did much to keep alive the earlier English mystical tradition.[4] Born of Protestant parents, he was converted to Catholicism as a young lawyer in England. He entered the Benedictines at Padua in Italy and later became affiliated with the English Benedictine Congregation. After his ordination to the priesthood he was spiritual director for nine years to the English Benedictine Sisters of the newly founded convent at Cambrai in France (now Stanbrook Abbey in England). His last

---

[3] See Martin Thornton, "The Caroline Divines and the Cambridge Platonists," in *The Study of Spirituality*, edited by C. Jones, G. Wainwright, and E. Yarnold (New York: Oxford University Press, 1986). For the rich heritage of English spirituality, see *Pre-Reformation English Spirituality*, edited and introduced by James Walsh, S.J. (London: Burns & Oates); Martin Thornton, *English Spirituality* (London: S.P.C.K., 1963); and *English Spiritual Writers*, edited by Charles Davis (New York: Sheed and Ward, 1961).

[4] For background on Augustine Baker see Renee Haynes "Augustine Baker" in *Pre-Reformation English Spirituality, op. cit.*, pp. 252-264; and David Knowles, "Father Augustine Baker" in *English Spiritual Writers, op. cit.*, pp. 97-111.

years were spent back in England where he narrowly escaped arrest during a revived persecution and where he died in 1641.

Augustine Baker was a man of prayer and spiritual insight who was well read in the mystical tradition. He was especially fond of *The Cloud of Unknowing* and Walter Hilton's *Ladder of Perfection*. A scholar and spiritual director, he was also a prolific writer. The work for which he is famous is *Sancta Sophia*, or *Holy Wisdom*. It was published sixteen years after his death by the Benedictine, Dom Serenus Cressy, who compiled and edited the numerous treatises Baker had written for the nuns at Cambrai. It is a work of both ascetic and mystical theology, containing abundant and valuable instructions for those living a religious life, especially a monastic and contemplative way of life. It is also a full guide for prayer, and the last part of the book is devoted to various instructions for furthering a life of prayer. He emphasized fidelity to the light and inspirations of the Holy Spirit, and he also insisted that directors should be very careful not to impose their own views and preferences on those they direct.

Among Dom Augustine's other writings are a commentary on *The Cloud of Unknowing* and a study of a holy nun of Cambrai, entitled *The Inner Life and Writings of Dame Gertrude More*. Dame Gertrude More, the great-great-granddaughter of St. Thomas More, crossed over from England and joined the English Benedictine convent at Cambrai as a young woman. She was greatly helped by Augustine Baker's wise spiritual direction when she was struggling with methods of prayer as a novice.[5] Her religious life was cut short by her early death at the age of twenty-seven.

Richard Challoner (1691-1781) came at a much later time than Augustine Baker. A convert from Presbyterianism to Catholicism as a youth, he went on to spend twenty-five years at the English College at Douay in France as a student, priest, professor, and administrator. He returned to England as coadjutor bishop and then

---

[5] See the essay by Thomas Merton "Gertrude More and Augustine Baker" in *Mystics and Zen Masters* (New York: Delta Books, 1967), pp. 154-187.

became bishop of the London district in 1758. For the next twenty-three years he was a successful and effective pastoral leader in times that were critical for English Catholics. The challenge for him was clear: it was to save Catholicism in England from extinction. Although the penal laws against Catholics were still in effect, they were not being enforced as strictly as they had been in earlier times. The declining persecution and the pervading influence of the Enlightenment culture gave rise to an increasing indifference. If Catholics as a religious minority were to survive, they would need to have a culture and literature of their own. It was this that Challoner sought to provide.[6]

In seeking to provide English Catholics with an informed faith and a love of prayer, Challoner was inspired and guided by the spirit and method of St. Francis de Sales. Like Francis de Sales, Challoner was writing for a broad spectrum of Catholics and not just for priests and religious. His most popular book was entitled the *Garden of the Soul*, published in 1740. It was a general type of prayer-book and its subtitle, "A Manual of Spiritual Exercises and Instructions for Christians Who, Living in the World, Aspire to Devotion," summarizes its content. This book clearly met the needs of many and it was widely read and used. Among his many other works of history and devotion were *Memoirs of Missionary Priests*, an historical account of the English martyrs, *Britannia Sancta*, a treatment of many of the ancient British, English, Scottish and Irish saints, and a work in two volumes, *Meditations for Every Day*. He also sought to bring about a greater love of Scripture by publishing a revision of the Douay-Rheims Bible. Mention should also be made of his translations into English of such spiritual classics as *The Imitation of Christ*, and the *Introduction to the Devout Life* of Francis de Sales. Although Richard Challoner cannot be considered an original or innovative writer, he had great talent and vision as a compiler, adapter, and abridger, and his voluminous writings clearly met the needs of his age.

---

[6] For background on Richard Challoner see the chapter on him by Joseph Cartmell in *English Spiritual Writers, op. cit.*, pp. 112-122.

2. Anglican Spirituality

Central to the development of Anglican spirituality in the six-teenth and seventeenth centuries was the work of Archbishop Tho-mas Cranmer (1489-1556) and his significant and influential *Book of Common Prayer*.[7] The Prayer Book, as it is usually called by An-glicans, provided the unity and focus for Anglican spirituality. Martin Thornton draws a number of parallels between it and the *Rule* of St. Benedict.[8] Like Benedict's *Rule*, the Prayer Book was meant to be not just a liturgical text or service book but a founda-tional guide for all aspects of Christian living. It was to be a rule of life that would shape and support the Anglican way of being a Christian. One of the most striking aspects of the Prayer Book was Cranmer's reform of the Divine Office. With his formulation of Morning and Evening Prayer (Matins and Evensong), adapted from the traditional monastic hours, he sought to develop a daily liturgy that would correspond to the pastoral needs of the whole Christian community. Louis Bouyer has high praise for his work, stating: "The splendid language of religious majesty and the melodious style in which these formulas were expressed made them a means of edu-cation by worship of which no Church, Catholic or Protestant, has the equivalent today."[9] The influence of the Prayer Book did much to instill Anglican spirituality with a strong corporate and liturgi-cal dimension.

The emergence of Anglican spirituality after the Elizabethan Settlement of 1559 that established Anglicanism was also greatly aided by the contributions of a number of significant writers. Be-tween Richard Hooker's *The Laws of Ecclesiastical Polity* (1593) and

---

[7] For Anglican spirituality see Louis Bouyer, *Orthodox Spirituality and Protestant and Anglican Spirituality* (New York: The Seabury Press, 1982), pp. 104-134; Paul V. Marshall, "Anglican Spirituality" in *Protestant Spiritual Traditions*, edited by Franck C. Senn (New York: Paulist Press, 1986), pp. 125-164; and Martin Thornton, *English Spirituality, op. cit.*

[8] Thornton, *op. cit.*, pp. 257-259.

[9] Bouyer, *op. cit.*, p. 107.

William Law's *A Serious Call to a Devout and Holy Life* (1729), there was a long list of spiritual writers, poets, preachers, and moralists. Many of them were members of the university clergy who were greatly influenced by a Christian humanism in the tradition of Erasmus. Thus, there would also be a marked affinity towards Christian humanism in Anglican spirituality and a basic optimism about creation and human nature.

Richard Hooker (1554-1600), the first apologist for the Elizabethan Settlement and compromise, is often considered the true father of Anglicanism.[10] His massive and integrated work, *The Laws of Ecclesiastical Polity*, has been compared to Thomas Aquinas' *Summa*, although Hooker wrote more as a moralist than a metaphysician. With his great knowledge of the Church Fathers and the thought of St. Thomas, he laid the foundation for much of the spirituality that was to follow.

John Donne (1572-1631) was one of the five Caroline divines who were known as the "metaphysical" or mystical poets. In his Holy Sonnets and in his other religious poetry, he writes with great feeling and passion on the themes of love, sin, and death. Well known are such eloquent words from one of his meditations: "No man is an island, entire of itself; every man is a piece of the continent, a part of the main.... any man's death diminishes me, because I am involved in mankind, and therefore never send to know for whom the bell tolls; it tolls for thee."[11] There are also the words from one of his Holy Sonnets:

> Batter my heart, three person'd God; for, you
> As yet but knocke, breathe, shine, and seeke to mend
> ....
> take mee to you, imprison mee, for I
> Except you'enthrall mee, never shall be free,
> Nor ever chaste, except you ravish mee.[12]

---

[10] *Ibid.*, p. 109.

[11] See *John Donne, Selections From Divine Poems, Sermons, Devotions, and Prayers,* edited and introduced by John Booty (New York: Paulist Press, 1990), p. 272.

[12] *Ibid.*, pp. 81-82.

George Herbert (1593-1633) was another mystical poet.[13] His poetry expresses the personal conflicts he experienced that were resolved only by the acceptance of God's love. Five of his poems were set to music by the twentieth-century English composer Ralph Vaughn-Williams and entitled "Five Mystical Songs." The other three Anglican "metaphysical poets" were Henry Vaughan (1622-1695), Thomas Traherne (c. 1637-1674), and Richard Crashaw (1613-1649).

Both Lancelot Andrews (1555-1626) and Jeremy Taylor (1613-1667) made significant contributions to Anglican spirituality. Lancelot Andrews blended in an admirable way the life of a scholar, pastor, and man of deep prayer. Bouyer refers to him as the spiritual master of Anglicanism. His doctrinal writings and sermons reflect his vast patristic and theological knowledge, and he is one of the principal translators of the Authorized Version of the Bible (King James Bible). The *Preces Privatae (Private Devotions)* is his most popular devotional book.[14] It is a collection of personal prayers and devotions compiled over the course of his life. John Henry Newman remained particularly fond of these prayers throughout his long life. Jeremy Taylor was mainly a moralist, the first in a long line of important Anglican writers who sought to unite moral and ascetic theology. His humanistic religious poetry and other writings are expressive, as many have noted, of a balanced sobriety and a well ordered piety that stresses temperance and moderation in all things. He is the author of *Rules and Exercises of Holy Living* (1650) and *Rules and Exercises of Holy Dying* (1651).[15]

Brief mention should be made of three laymen who gave clear expression of Anglican piety in their lives: Izaak Walton (1593-1683); Sir Thomas Browne (1605-1682); and Nicholas Ferrar

---

[13] For background on Herbert and selections from his writings, see *George Herbert, The Country Parson, The Temple*, edited with an introduction by John N. Wall, Jr. (New York: Paulist Press, 1981).

[14] See *Lancelot Andrews, Private Devotions* (New York: Macmillan, 1961).

[15] See *Jeremy Taylor, Selected Works*, edited with an introduction by Thomas K. Carroll (New York: Paulist Press, 1990).

(1592-1637). Walton is known primarily for his hymns, and Browne's main work was *Religio Medici*. Ferrar's last years were spent living with his extended family in a quasi-monastic community at Little Gidding. In a simple and prayerful lifestyle that reflected the spirit of St. Benedict, the community's way of life was nourished by the *Book of Common Prayer* and Scripture. The poet, T. S. Eliot, commemorated the community at Little Gidding and their experiment in "holy living" in the last of his *Four Quartets*.

Moving some years ahead to include the last Anglican divine we will mention here, we come to William Law (1686-1761). Since he was a Nonjuror, that is an Anglican who believed that the Stuarts were the rightful kings, and thus he would not swear allegiance to the reigning Hanoverian king, Law paid for his convictions by being barred from any university or ecclesiastical position in the Established Church. His most famous book is *A Serious Call to a Devout and Holy Life*. Written in an age that called for a reform and renewal of the Christian life, Law responded with a clear and challenging blueprint describing the way to a Christian reform of life. Stimulated by his reading of such earlier writers as John Tauler, John Ruusbroec, and Thomas à Kempis, Law speaks of a life of devotion as a complete dedication to God. It calls for renunciation, discipline, and single-mindedness of purpose. There is no room in his mind for compromise or equivocation, nor is he sympathetic to those who would speak of different degrees of living the Christian life. It is a way of life that should be lived with complete dedication and generosity. *A Serious Call* was enormously popular during Law's lifetime, and many have been drawn to this spiritual classic and greatly helped by it over the years. On the other hand, it is a work that has not been without its critics. Some have found the work too rigorous and uncompromising, and have criticized its depreciation of human reason, learning, and culture.

A few years after the publication of *A Serious Call*, Law became deeply interested in the esoteric works of the seventeenth-century Protestant mystical writer, Jacob Boehme. This influence was clearly evident in Law's later writings such as *The Spirit of Love* and

The Spirit of Prayer. Law's later attraction and fascination with Boehme's thought disappointed some like John Wesley and Samuel Johnson who had been strong admirers of his earlier work, *A Serious Call.*[16]

3. Puritan Spirituality[17]

The term "Puritan" is one that can be elusive in many ways. It was first given to those in England who believed that the Established Church had not gone far enough in its reform. As spiritual descendants of Calvinism, they wanted to substitute Calvinistic models of ecclesiastical polity and liturgy for the forms that were established in the Anglican Church after the Elizabethan Settlement of 1559. Although they themselves came to be divided into Presbyterians, Independents, and Moderates, they initially intended no separation from the Established Church in England. Since Elizabeth and the first two Stuarts came to believe that political stability required religious uniformity, both Puritans and Catholics fell into disfavor and were looked upon as disloyal subjects and even traitors. Except for the period known as the Commonwealth in which they gained political control of the country for a time, the Puritans suffered oppression in England. As a result, many Puritans emigrated to the English colonies in New England. Those who remained in England eventually separated from the Established Church.

Spirituality and piety were central to the Puritan way of life. It has been noted that "Puritans were to Protestantism what contemplatives and ascetics were to the medieval Church. They

---

[16] For background on Law and selected texts see, William Law, *A Serious Call To A Devout and Holy Life. The Spirit of Love*, edited from the first editions by Paul G. Stanwood, introduction by Austin Warren and Paul G. Stanwood (New York: Paulist Press, 1978).

[17] For Puritan spirituality see Bouyer, *op. cit.*, pp. 134-160; E. Glenn Hinson, "Puritan Spirituality" in *Protestant Spiritual Traditions, op. cit.*, pp. 165-182; and Gordon S. Wakefield, "The Puritans" in *The Study of Spirituality, op. cit.*, pp. 437-445.

parted company with their medieval forbears chiefly in the locus of their efforts. Where monks sought sainthood in monasteries, Puritans sought it everywhere — in homes, schools, town halls, shops as well as churches."[18] A number of characteristics played a part in the formation of Puritan spirituality. First, they looked upon themselves as a pilgrim people on the way to a better country, to "Mount Sion, the Heavenly Jerusalem." Central to this pilgrimage was an election by God in Christ and a conversion that brought one into a covenant with Christ. The covenant with the Lord and with one another was basic to Puritan thought and life, and perseverance in the covenant unto the end was of primary importance.

Following the teaching of John Calvin, Puritans emphasized human sinfulness and divine grace. They tended, however, to be more pessimistic in the way they viewed the world than Calvin was, and so there was present in the discipline they practiced a streak of dour asceticism. Although they shared in the Protestant distrust of Catholic "works," Puritans were conscious of the *duties* that the Covenant imposed upon them and the importance of discipline in maintaining the covenant. Among these practices was the strong emphasis on frequent and ongoing examination of conscience by which they could inquire continually into the security of their "election." They also stressed the ongoing reading and praying over the Bible in order to find God's word to help them lead a holy life. Above all, the practice of prayer and meditation was valued highly. In their methods of meditation, the Puritans were much closer to Post-Reformation Catholic practices than they were to Anglican. The prayer that was valued most of all was the prayer of the heart. A tender and affective love of Christ was expressed in terms that closely resembled those of St. Bernard and St. Francis of Assisi.

Individual Puritan piety was complemented by a strong sacramental and liturgical element. In keeping with their high regard for Scripture, preaching was greatly esteemed, and much was made also of the Lord's Supper. The careful and prayerful keeping of the

---

[18] Hinson, *op. cit.*, p. 165.

Sabbath was of great importance in Puritan life, for it played an important part in maintaining the covenant and the preservation of a true spirit of religion. This true spirit of religion should also manifest itself in one's daily life and in a social concern for others. All of these desires for living a Godly life led the Puritans to bring forth a large number of devotional writings. A look at a few of the most important of these will illustrate the points treated above.

Francis Rous (1579-1669) was Speaker of the House of Parliament under the Commonwealth (the period of Puritan rule in England) and a devout Puritan. Like many other Puritan authors, he wrote a commentary on the Song of Songs. His was entitled, *Mystical Marriage, or Experimental Discourses of the Heavenly Marriage between a Soul and her Savior.* Using the imagery of bridal mysticism, he teaches that because of Christ the human soul can be united with God by a mystical union. The mystical marriage can only be completed in eternity, and so here on earth it is a union of betrothal. In words reminiscent of St. John of the Cross' purifying nights of the soul and traditional Christian mysticism, he treats of the trials and sufferings that must be faced before one can reach the summit of union. In one beautiful phrase Rous writes: "When the wine of natural joy is spent and there is nothing left but the water of affliction, then doth Christ turn this water into wine."[19] The "visitations" of the Bridegroom provide strength and comfort against the times of aridity and seeming absence.

In Richard Goodwin (1600-1680), the chaplain to Oliver Cromwell, we have a Puritan devotion to the Sacred Heart. His book, *The Heart of Christ in Heaven towards Sinners on Earth* was published in 1652. This work antedated by some fifty years the revelations of the Sacred Heart to St. Margaret Mary Alacoque at Paray-le-Monial in France. As Goodwin himself explains: "The purpose of this Discourse is to lay open the Heart of Christ, as now He is in heaven — how it is affected and graciously disposed towards sinners on earth that do come to Him, how willing to receive them,

---

[19] See Bouyer, *op. cit.*, p. 137.

how ready to entertain them, how tender to pity them in all their infirmities, both sins and miseries."[20]

Among the many Puritan writers who developed various methods of meditation, Richard Baxter (1615-1691) has a prominent position. His most popular works were his *Reformed Pastor* and *The Saints' Everlasting Rest*. The latter, published in 1650, seeks to give practical advice and counsel about the central Puritan concern with one's assurance of being among the elect. A major part of the work consists of detailed descriptions and practical suggestions for the practice of meditation that have much in common with St. Ignatius Loyola's *Spiritual Exercises*. It has often been pointed out that with Richard Baxter, Calvinism comes closest to Post-Reformation Catholic spirituality.[21]

The final Puritan writer we will treat here is John Bunyan (1628-1688), the author of the most widely read of all Puritan books, *The Pilgrim's Progress*. A Puritan with Baptist leanings, he was an itinerant preacher and working man who appealed directly to the English masses with his down-to-earth, warm, and practical accounts of the Christian's journey and struggles. He was imprisoned for over twelve years for his refusal to refrain from unlicensed preaching. During his years of imprisonment he composed a number of books. *Grace Abounding to the Chief of Sinners* is a work of spiritual autobiography in the tradition of St. Augustine's *Confessions*. In his struggles and anxieties about his own assurance of salvation, he was greatly helped by the work of an earlier Puritan, Arthur Dent's *The Plain Man's Pathway to Heaven* (1602). His enormously popular *The Pilgrim's Progress from This World to That Which is to Come* (1678), as the full title indicates, is an allegorical account of the Christian's difficult pilgrimage to heaven and the many dangers that must be faced and overcome along the way.

We can fittingly end this treatment of Puritan spirituality with a poem by Richard Baxter that illustrates so well this tradition's tender and unadorned love of Christ:

---

[20] *Ibid.*, p. 140.

[21] *Ibid.*, p. 158.

Christ leads me through no darker rooms
Than he went through before;
And he that to God's kingdom comes
Must enter by this door.
Come Lord, when grace hath made me meet
Thy blessed face to see:
For if thy work on earth be sweet,
What will thy glory be?
My knowledge of that life is small,
The eye of faith is dim;
But 'tis enough that Christ knows all,
And I shall be with him.[22]

4. George Fox and The Friends

During the time of the Civil Wars in seventeenth-century England, a number of dissenting religious sects emerged. Finding little direction or focus from the hopelessly divided religious scene and the traditional Christian sources in this period of political and religious turmoil, many groups of men and women turned inwards to find a more direct inspiration and guidance in their desires for a new Pentecost. These groups were heirs of the persecuted religious sects of the Middle Ages. A number of them had been part of the religious scene on the Continent since the beginnings of the Reformation in the sixteenth century. The most notable of these new sects in England were the Quakers, or the Society of Friends, founded by George Fox around 1647.[23]

George Fox (1624-1691) was a remarkably charismatic person. His *Journal*, a work of spiritual autobiography, describes his

---

[22] Cited by Urban Holmes, *A History of Christian Spirituality* (New York: The Seabury Press, 1980), p. 132 (from *The Hymnal*, 1940, 445).

[23] For Quaker background and spirituality see Bouyer, *op. cit.*, pp. 160-164; Gordon S. Wakefield, "The Quakers," in *The Study of Spirituality, op. cit.*, pp. 445-448; and *Quaker Spirituality, Selected Writings*, edited and introduced by Douglas V. Steere (New York: Paulist Press, 1984).

own religious experiences and the beginnings and growth of the Quaker movement.[24] As he tells us in his *Journal*, Fox spent several years as a wanderer, seeking after "heavenly wisdom." He was unable, however, to find anyone from the Churches, sects, or religious parties of his day who could speak to his condition. Finding himself in deep distress and torment, he was strengthened by an inner voice that told him, "There is only one, Jesus Christ, who can answer thy needs," words that made his heart leap with joy. Experiencing a number of further "openings" or "considerations," his spiritual vision began to clarify, and in 1647 he began his prophetic ministry.

Central to his preaching was his conviction that the God who made heaven and earth does not dwell in temples or churches but in the hearts of his people. There is within each person an "Inner Light" by which God speaks directly to the person who wants to follow the Gospel. The Inner Light alone is enough to bring a person to God and to an understanding of his ways. It is the Inner Light that enables a person to interpret Sacred Scripture and to teach. It is also in the Inner Light that the saints on earth can find unity, a unity that requires treating everyone equally. This emphasis on an Inner Light has its obvious risks, for it can easily lead one to illuminism or to an enthusiastic extreme. But, as Louis Bouyer points out with much insight, what safeguarded Fox and his loyal disciples from this was the conviction that one's feelings should be verified and confirmed in the assembly of the faithful, a gathering that constituted a community of love. He writes that Fox "discovered the meaning of the Church by instinct: as community in love wherein each person is assured that he will hear the Spirit speaking in his heart solely because he is always ready to hear it speaking in others, in a communion of charity with others."[25] Fox continually urged his

---

[24] See *The Journal of George Fox*, edited by J. Nickalls (Cambridge: Cambridge University Press, 1952). There is a good summary of this work by E. Glenn Hinson in *Christian Spirituality, The Essential Guide to the Most Influential Spiritual Writings in the Christian Tradition*, edited by Frank N. Magill and Ian P. McGreal (San Francisco: Harper & Row, 1988), pp. 340-345.

[25] Bouyer, *op. cit.*, p. 162.

followers to see and know God's life and power in one another.

Fox's itinerant and charismatic preaching led to a number of conversions from all walks of life as he urged all who heard him to turn from the way of darkness to the Light of Christ within. His preaching was also accompanied by such social protests as refusing to remove his hat and using the words "thee" and "thou" to everyone regardless of class or station. This led to much opposition and many beatings, sufferings, and frequent imprisonments. His first imprisonment came in 1649 when he disrupted a congregation of worshipers in Nottingham and preached that God does not dwell in a temple made with hands.

In spite of ongoing suffering and opposition from many different quarters, the numbers increased. Fox also had great organizational skills, and in 1654 he sent a number of preachers all over England, urging them to place all their trust in the Light within them. Fox continued his own ministry throughout England, developing in 1667, in addition to the regular meetings, the organizational structure of monthly and quarterly general meetings. With the spread of the Friends in Germany and Holland, he made two trips to the Continent. In the spread of the Quakers, Fox was greatly helped by two outstanding disciples, Robert Barclay and William Penn. Barclay, a Scottish theologian, wrote a work in defense of the Society of Friends, as the Quakers later came to be called, entitled *Apology for the True Christian Religion, as the same is set forth and preached by the People called in Scorn "Quakers."* William Penn, a member of a distinguished family, also defended the Quakers in his spiritual work, *No Cross, No Crown* (1669). He also became famous for founding the Quaker Colony in Pennsylvania and for drawing up a wise and famous constitution that blended freedom and obedience so well.

With its stress on the Inner Light, Quaker worship would be marked by great simplicity. There was no stipulation made for any clergy or ecclesiastical leaders. All had an equal position in the gathering of Friends and were to be treated accordingly. There were no doctrines or confessions of faith outside the Gospel nor was there any bond but the bond of love. There was no liturgical service beyond the gathering that waited together in silence and recollection for the Spirit to inspire the individual to speak to the assembled group with a prophetic voice. Quaker life was also governed by a humble simplicity in all things, obedience to the Gospel, a spirit of non-violence, truthfulness, and a concern and compassion for those in need. Finally, it is interesting to note, as Bouyer also points out, that a number of Catholic mystics such as John of the Cross, Teresa of Avila, and Fénelon found a warm and instinctive welcome in Quaker circles.[26]

Before leaving this treatment of Quaker spirituality, we will move ahead to a Friend who lived in eighteenth-century Colonial America, John Woolman (1720-1772). Born in a rural Quaker community in New Jersey, Woolman sought throughout his life to be faithful to the Light Within. His work of spiritual autobiography, *The Journal of John Woolman*, has become an American spiritual classic.[27] It expresses his strong desire for a simple, unencumbered lifestyle that was completely open to God, as well as his strong awareness of the plight of the poor and oppressed. At this early period when slavery was widely accepted in the colonies, he became acutely aware of its injustice. He spent much of his life traveling throughout the New England and Southern colonies, seeking to persuade his fellow Quakers of the inconsistency of slave holding with the Christian faith.

5. John Wesley and Methodist Spirituality

John Wesley (1703-1791) was the most important figure in the evangelical revival that took place in England in the eighteenth cen-

---

[26] *Ibid.*, p. 163.

[27] For Woolman's Journal see *Quaker Spirituality, Selected Writings, op. cit.*, pp. 161-242.

tury.[28] A number of influences contributed to the formation of John Wesley's synthesis of the Christian life. Born of Anglican parents (his father was the rector at Epworth), he studied at Oxford, was elected Fellow of Lincoln College there in 1726, and ordained an Anglican priest two years later. It was as a young man at Oxford that Wesley began to practice his faith seriously, adopting a disciplined and ascetic way of life and seeking to grow in Christian perfection and perfect love. He became leader of a group whose members sought to grow in the Christian life through mutual support, study of Scripture, a regular liturgical life and frequent reception of the Eucharist, observance of the fasts of the early Church on Wednesdays and Fridays, and service to the poor and the sick. The group became known as the Holy Club, and because of their methodical practices, the members also received the nickname of "Methodists."

During these years at Oxford, Wesley read widely from various sources. His reading included mystics in the Catholic tradition such as Pascal, Fénelon, Mme Guyon, John Tauler, Molinos, the early Western and Eastern Fathers (two favorites were the *Macarian Homilies* and the writings of Ephrem the Syrian), and the Anglican Divines. Of all his readings at this time, however, the most influential authors were Jeremy Taylor, Thomas à Kempis, and William Law.

In 1735 Wesley, together with his brother, Charles, made the decision to leave Oxford and travel to Georgia as missionaries. They intended to work with the Indians and the English colonists at Savannah. During the journey to America, Wesley had frequent contact with some German Moravians, a Pietistic group who were also emigrating to Georgia, and he came to admire many aspects of their

---

[28] For Wesley and Methodist spirituality see *John and Charles Wesley, Selected Writings and Hymns*, edited with an introduction by Frank Whaling (New York: Paulist Press, 1981); Bouyer, *op. cit.*, pp. 187-197; David Lowes Watson, "Methodist Spirituality" in *Protestant Spiritual Traditions*, *op. cit.*, pp. 217-273; and A. Raymond George, "John Wesley and the Methodist Movement" in *The Study of Spirituality*, *op. cit.*, pp. 455-459.

strong faith and their way of life. They taught him German and he later translated into English a number of the German Pietist hymns. Wesley's brief stay in Georgia turned out to be an unsuccessful and disappointing experiment in many respects, and he returned to England, disillusioned and somewhat bewildered spiritually.

Back in England, Wesley continued searching for God's will and his work in life. He had further contact with some Moravians in England and it was at one of their meetings on May 24, 1738, that he had the experience that played an important part in his spiritual development. He went one evening, "unwillingly" as he tells us, to a Moravian meeting at Aldersgate Street in London where he listened to someone read from Luther's preface to Paul's Letter to the Romans. In his journal Wesley writes of this experience:

> About a quarter before nine, while he was describing the change which God works in the heart through faith in Christ, I felt my heart strangely warmed. I felt I did trust in Christ, Christ alone for salvation; and an assurance was given me that he had taken away *my* sins, even *mine*, and saved *me* from the law of sin and death.[29]

Shortly afterwards, with renewed confidence and assurance, Wesley began his great preaching ministry. As the acknowledged leader of the revival, he sought to bring others to the state of peace and assurance of faith that he had finally found. On March 29, 1739, Wesley preached for the first time in the open air, apart from any church building, to about three thousand people. The preaching met with success and the movement was under way that eventually became one of the most effective spiritual and moral revivals in England's religious history. In his preaching he emphasized God's universal love, salvation by faith and a new birth, God's prevenient free grace, and the assurance of faith provided by the Holy Spirit within the believer. His preaching and that of his associates was

---

[29] See *Selected Writings and Hymns, op. cit.,* p. 107.

directed primarily to the poorer classes living in the new settlements and towns that had sprung up in the suburbs as a result of the Industrial Revolution in England. Thus, the preaching and ministry met a direct and concrete need.

Wesley's widespread and successful ministry led to mixed reactions within the Established Church. On the one hand, some regarded him as another enthusiast and feared that another sect was in the making. Some, on the other hand, regarded him as a crypto-Catholic, for his preaching had a closer resemblance to that of Catholic missionaries than anything else being preached at the time in England.[30] Wesley himself had no intention of founding a new denomination. His ministry was aimed at a renewal movement within the Anglican Church, and he himself lived and died as an Anglican priest. He is recognized, however, as the founder and the inspirer of "the people called Methodists," and in time they did form a separate religious denomination.[31]

Much of the ongoing success of Wesley's ministry was due to its subsequent organization. There may have been more effective preachers in the revival movement than Wesley but none surpassed him in organizational ability. Those who responded positively to his preaching were organized into local societies so that they could deepen their own spirituality and pass it on to others. Within the local societies there later developed the smaller "classes" of twelve people with a lay leader, established for the purpose of deeper support and fellowship. The societies became part of the larger circuits, and the circuits came together for the annual conference directed by Wesley himself. It was through the various stages of this structure that Wesley's spirituality was conveyed in a more lasting way to those who were moved by his preaching.

Although Wesley clearly accepted the teaching of justification

---

[30] See Bouyer, *op. cit.*, p. 191.

[31] Although John Wesley's role was the dominant one in the formation of the Methodists, it is important to recognize the other streams within the revival. Frank Whaling in his introduction to *Selected Writings and Hymns, op. cit.*, pp. 26-43, speaks of five main streams that played a part in early Methodism.

by faith, he never separated it from ongoing sanctification. He parted ways with the Moravians because he felt that they tended to a type of Quietism and neglected the means of grace. Wesley emphasized conversion but he never saw it as a guarantee of final perseverance. It was rather the point of departure for the movement towards sanctification and Christian perfection. Thus, Wesley stressed the generosity of one's response to grace and "the means of grace." Among these are prayer, searching the Scripture, the Lord's Supper, fasting, and Christian conference, as well as the prudential means that were provided by the various support meetings in the Methodist organizational structure. There is also a strong social component to Wesley's spirituality for it should apply to all of life. As he writes in one of his sermons: "Christianity is essentially a social religion and to turn it into a solitary religion is indeed to destroy it."

Wesley passed on to his followers the fruit of his extensive reading of the spiritual classics over the course of his life. It is interesting to note that he served as a bridge for Protestants to come in contact with much of the Catholic spiritual and mystical tradition. He did much to make known such writers as Thomas à Kempis, Teresa of Avila, Ignatius of Loyola, Francis de Sales and Fénelon. Also, among the fifty volumes of his *Christian Library* that he published and recommended to his preachers and followers during the years 1750-1756, he included five French and three Spanish writers from the Catholic mystical tradition.

We can fittingly conclude this treatment of John Wesley with a prayer from his covenant service. It is a prayer that echoes clearly the spirit of St. Ignatius of Loyola:

> I am no longer my own, but yours. Put me to what you will, rank me with whom you will; put me to doing, put me to suffering; let me be employed for you or laid aside for you, exalted for you or brought low for you; let me be full, let me be empty; let me have all things, let me have nothing; I freely and heartily yield all things to your pleasure and disposal.
> And now, O glorious and blessed God, Father, Son,

and Holy Spirit, you are mine, and I am yours. So be it. And
the Covenant which I have made on earth, let it be ratified
in heaven.[32]

Charles Wesley (1707-1788), the brother of John, also played
a significant role in the formation of Methodist spirituality. The
lives of the two brothers were closely intertwined throughout their
lives. Like John, Charles was a fervent member of the Holy Club
at Oxford, and he also went with John on the missionary journey
to Georgia in 1735. Both brothers worked closely together as
preachers, organizers, and moving spirits in the Methodist revival
movement. However, it is through his extraordinary hymns that
Charles Wesley made his greatest contribution to the formation and
development of Methodist spirituality. He expresses so beautifully
and movingly in his many hymns the doctrine and spirituality that
John Wesley preached and taught in his writings. The following
provides a flavor of his great gift:

> Love divine, all loves excelling,
>   Joy of heaven, to earth come down,
> Fix in us thy humble dwelling,
>   All thy faithful mercies crown!
> Jesu, thou art all compassion,
>   Pure, unbounded love thou art;
> Visit us with thy salvation!
>   Enter every trembling heart.[33]

6. Continental Pietism

With this discussion of continental Pietism, we move beyond
England and its spiritual developments and back to Germany. The
term "pietism" is for many reasons a complex one. In the course of

---

[32] *Selected Writings and Hymns, op. cit.*, p. 387.

[33] *Ibid.*, p. 227.

history it has taken on many variations, interpretations, and developments. Here we will discuss that significant reform movement that took its origin in German Lutheranism in the seventeenth century, and then went on to become a source of vigorous renewal within the Lutheran and Reformed Churches in a number of other continental countries, England, and the United States.[34]

There were a number of historical events and circumstances that played a significant part in the emergence of Pietism in the German Lutheran Church of the seventeenth century. There were the effects of the devastating Thirty Years War (1618-1648) that left the general populace demoralized and dehumanized in many respects and in great need of human and religious renewal. Many also laid the blame for the poor state of religious and moral life of the times on the system in which the government controlled the territorial Churches, and they sought greater separation between Church and State. Barriers between the clergy and people also had arisen in a climate that stressed the separation of the classes, and the doctrine of the priesthood of the faithful, so important to Martin Luther, was largely a dead letter. Lutheran and Reformed theology at this time was marked by a strong concern for orthodoxy, and many were turned off by the over-intellectual and highly speculative debates that did not address the needs of the people. Theology was also dominated by a polemical thrust, and the writings and preaching of the day clearly reflected this orientation that set the various factions and denominations against one another. In this climate, the practice of the faith was being minimized, and there was a growing desire on the part of many to restore more of a balance between doctrine and life.

This was the climate in which Pietism emerged and in many ways it was a reaction to these prevailing conditions in the Churches. The Pietists, generally speaking, placed a great emphasis on Chris-

---

[34] For general background on the Pietists, see *Pietists-Selected Writings*, edited with an introduction by Peter C. Erb (New York: Paulist Press, 1983); John Weborg, "Pietism: 'The Fire of God which... Flames in the Heart of Germany'," in *Protestant Spiritual Traditions, op. cit.*, pp. 183-216; and Bouyer, *op. cit.*, pp. 169-184.

tian living and the practice of the faith. They were much more concerned with the practice of the faith than they were with doctrinal issues. They held that the study of Scripture should be directed to its application in the life of the believer, and preaching should lead to the edification of the listeners. Pietists placed a strong emphasis also on the experience of a new birth in Christ and the nourishing of this new life through mutual support and encouragement in smaller groups. Thus, the priesthood of the faithful received renewed attention. Pietists were concerned, too, that the education of pastors focus on spiritual and pastoral development and not just on academic preparation. Finally, the Pietists sought to replace the intolerance and polemics so present in the Churches with an ecumenical openness and charity that sought greater unity among Christians.

The sources for Pietist spirituality were numerous. Pietists were influenced by the devotional writings of the English Puritans such as Richard Baxter and John Bunyan, and there were ties with the writings of the Dutch Puritans. The spiritual tradition of Martin Luther played a strong part and the popular Lutheran book of spirituality, *True Christianity* by Johann Arndt, was a special favorite among the Pietists. It was through this devotional classic that the Pietists had contact with such spiritual writers of the Middle Ages as St. Bernard of Clairvaux, John Tauler, and Thomas à Kempis.

Philipp Jakob Spener (1635-1705) is considered the founder of the Pietist movement in Germany. As a Lutheran pastor at Frankfurt am Main, he formed the first *collegia pietatis* (college of piety), a small group or "conventicle" of people who met together to nourish the true Christian life through a prayerful study of Scripture, devotions, and mutual support. In 1675 he published *Pia Desideria* (*Pious Desires*), the work that was to become the most important document for the Pietist movement. He wrote in this book about the new or inner person who is to bring forth the fruit of faith in one's life. As he emphasizes: "Our whole Christian religion consists of the inner man or the new man, whose soul is faith, and whose expressions are the fruits of life, and all sermons should be aimed at this."[35] He also made a number of proposals for reforming and renewing the Church. Among his concrete suggestions were the formation of group meetings for prayer and Bible-reading with a practical point of view in mind. He recommended that they take place in each household with the family gathered around the father. He advocated a new emphasis on the training of future pastors by urging that they have an experiential knowledge of God and be trained in piety so that they could be more effective in awakening a strong faith in the people they served. Preaching, too, should have the practical goal of bringing the listeners to a more authentic living out of the Christian faith. Spener's proposals met with widespread acceptance and implementation but they also faced opposition from many other quarters within the Church. A number took issue with the emphasis that was placed on the subjective and emotional aspects of the religious life.

Another early Pietist who did much to further the movement was August Hermann Franke (1663-1727). The University at Halle became a center of Pietism under his spirited leadership. Franke himself went through a profound conversion experience and in turn came to place a strong emphasis, much more than Spener, on a specific and definite experience itself and its necessity for the reborn and renewed Christian. He described this experience of new birth as a "breakthrough." It was due to Franke's influence that the specific conversion experience that gives assurance of salvation took on added importance in Pietist spirituality. Franke also put his organizational gifts to work at Halle, creating and supervising a number of educational, social, and missionary programs.

The writings of Gottfried Arnold (1666-1705) came to have considerable influence on those who became known as Radical Pietists, those who tended to form separatist groups. In his influential historical study, *Impartial History of the Church and Heresy*, he advocated a different twist on true and false Christians by arguing that heretics and mystics were the bearers of authentic piety rather

---

[35] Cited by Weborg, *op. cit.*, p. 198.

than their persecutors.[36] He also had a strong interest in early mystics and mystical writings, especially those that tended towards a Quietistic thrust. He wrote a history of mystical theology and edited and made available a number of patristic and medieval mystical texts, as well some from the sixteenth and seventeenth centuries. His writings also focus on such themes as the inner voice of the Holy Spirit and the mystical union with Christ. In his work *Mystery of Divine Sophia*, he makes use of a number of themes from the writings of Jacob Boehme.

Foremost among the Pietists in the Duchy of Wurttemberg in southwestern Germany was Johann Albrecht Bengel (1687-1752). His reputation as a biblical scholar and the holiness of his life made him an attractive figure. His approach to Scripture is summed up in one of his phrases: "Te totum applica ad textum, textum totum applica ad te" (Apply yourself totally to the text; apply the text totally to yourself). His scholarly and solid approach to Scripture did not prevent him from engaging in the Pietist fascination with eschatological speculations, and from his study of Scripture he made a prediction that the world would end in 1836.

A group of Pietists which stirred up widespread criticism and opposition was the separatist Moravians under the leadership of Count Nicholas Ludwig von Zinzendorf (1700-1760). He opened his estate at Dresden in 1722 to a group of Moravian refugees (the remnant of the Bohemian Brethren) who built homes there and renamed the place Herrnhut (The Lord's Watch). Close ties were formed in a highly organized form of communal living and the community flourished. Zinzendorf fashioned for his followers a very simplified form of religion which he called "the religion of the heart." He taught that the Christian life should be primarily characterized by an intimate fellowship with Jesus Christ. He believed also that at the level of a religion of the heart, all sincere Christians would be able to unite in a single Church. The movement was also marked by a strong missionary thrust, and evangelists traveled to

---

[36] See the introduction to *Pietists-Selected Writings, op. cit.*, pp. 11-17.

others parts of Europe and to the American Colonies. It will be recalled that John Wesley had extensive contact with Moravians when he went to Georgia in 1735 and later when he returned to England.

From this brief survey it is clear that there were many types of Pietists at this time. The most basic division was between Church Pietists and Radical or Separatist Pietists. The former consisted of those with Pietist leanings who formed conventicles or small groups within the organized Protestant Churches; maintaining unity with these Churches, they became a source of renewal and reform within it. The Radical Pietists severed connections and formed a number of separate denominations. It was in these separatist groups that there developed more pronounced anti-intellectual and anti-institutional elements. As noted earlier, from their beginnings within the Lutheran Church in Germany in the seventeenth century, Pietist concerns spread to other Protestant denominations in various parts of Europe, particularly in the Scandinavian countries. They were then carried to the New World when representatives from these groups migrated to various parts of North America. Pietism had a strong influence on the revivalism that sprung up later in frontier America.

Pietist influence spread to the Reformed Churches in the Netherlands where there was also a strong interest in mystical thought. Fénelon's mystical teaching on pure love and an abandonment in trust to God's will was particularly appreciated.[37] The most noteworthy representative here was Gerhard Tersteegen (1697-1769). Awakening to the presence of God in the depths of the soul was a dominant theme in his mystical thought that was rooted in the Bible. The Holy Spirit has produced in the soul the impression of God. It is through reason (*Vermunft*) that one has the capacity to recognize God and spiritual things. Awakened by the Holy Spirit, this power and capacity for God within us can move from the consideration of the divine Word to acts of contemplative intuition, and then into "a state of contemplation of God living in us, by the fact

---

[37] See Bouyer, *op. cit.*, pp. 197-203.

of our union with Christ and our participation in the spirit that has become fully effective."[38] Bouyer has great praise for Tersteegen, speaking of his spirituality of "rare purity and elevation," and considering him "perhaps the greatest and most complete spiritual writer that Protestantism has produced."[39]

Conclusion

Our main focus in this chapter has been on the spiritual movements and developments that took place in Protestant circles in England and on the continent from the late sixteenth into the eighteenth centuries. Anglican, Puritan, Quaker, Methodist, and Pietist spiritualities all made significant contributions. This would not be the case as the eighteenth century progressed. The later eighteenth century, a time of many profound changes, would witness very little in the way of new developments in spirituality. The French Revolution, the Industrial Revolution, the rise of rationalism, and especially the movement that has come to be known as the Enlightenment did not provide the climate or soil for spirituality to flourish. In the next chapter we will turn primarily to the post-Enlightenment spirituality and important movements and figures of the nineteenth century.

For Further Reading

Bouyer, Louis, *Orthodox Spirituality and Protestant and Anglican Spirituality*. Vol. III of *A History of Christian Spirituality*. New York: The Seabury Press, 1968.

Knox, Ronald A., *Enthusiasm*. New York: Oxford University Press, 1961.

Thornton, Martin, *English Spirituality*. London: S.P.C.K., 1963.

---

[38] *Ibid.*, p. 198.
[39] *Ibid.*

Wakefield, Gordon S., *Puritan Devotion*. London: Epworth, 1967.

Christian Spirituality III: Post-Reformation and Modern. Edited by Louis Dupré and Don E. Saliers. New York: Crossroad, 1989.

The Study of Spirituality. Edited by Cheslyn Jones, Geoffrey Wainwright, Edward Yarnnold, S.J. New York: Oxford University Press, 1986.

Protestant Spiritual Traditions. Edited by Frank C. Senn. New York: Paulist Press, 1986.

John and Charles Wesley, Selected Writings and Hymns. Edited with an introduction by Frank Whaling. New York: Paulist Press, 1981.

The Pietists-Selected Writings. Edited with an introduction by Peter C. Erb. New York: Paulist Press, 1983.

Quaker Spirituality-Selected Writings. Edited and introduced by Douglas V. Steere. New York: Paulist Press, 1984.

11 Post-Enlightenment Spirituality

1. Historical Background

A much more secular society emerged in Europe in the nineteenth century. This was due in no small part to the intellectual movement that was dominant in the eighteenth century that has come to be known as the Enlightenment.[1] It is a term that is used to describe the significant philosophical, scientific, political, and religious developments that took place in eighteenth-century Europe. Its influence extended far beyond Europe, for it spread from England and France to North America and from Portugal and Spain to South America. It was a movement that generated a great deal of hostility towards religion, particularly the Christian religion.

Although there were diverse thinkers in the movement, the Enlightenment was marked by a number of common characteristics.[2] First, there was a great love of liberty and independent thinking, and a corresponding repudiation of anything that smacked of

---

[1] For this period see Gerald R. Cragg, *The Church in the Age of Reason 1648-1789* (New York: Penguin Books, 1960), and his *Reason and Authority in the Eighteenth Century* (Cambridge: University Press, 1964). See also Albert C. Outler, "Pietism and Enlightenment: Alternatives to Tradition" in *Christian Spirituality III: Post-Reformation and Modern*, edited by Louis Dupré and Don E. Saliers (New York: Crossroad, 1989), pp. 240-256.

[2] See Outler, *op. cit.*, p. 249 ff.

tyranny or oppression. Human autonomy was held in great regard and the movement sought to foster the cause of critical thinking and the liberation of human persons from any dependence on an external authority that was not freely chosen. This spirit of free-thinking was summed up in the saying of Immanuel Kant, *Sapere aude!* (Have the courage to think [for yourself]!). Parallel with this emphasis on reason as the final authority was the rejection of the authority of tradition. Philosophers of the Enlightenment such as Voltaire rejected traditional Christianity and were basically secular in their orientation. In their minds, it was unfettered reason and not historical Christianity that offered the best hope of overcoming ignorance and superstition. The human mind should be liberated from such elements of the supernatural as revelation and miracles. Thus, there was a repudiation and often a ridicule of the traditional practices of Christianity, especially those of the Middle Ages.

Closely connected with the emphasis on human autonomy was a renewed confidence in human nature and in human progress. Great faith was placed in science and technology as important means for furthering this autonomy. There was also a great concern for morality, natural rights, and justice. Life, liberty and the pursuit of happiness were looked upon as inalienable rights. The current of Enlightenment thought that was not atheistic in its orientation favored either a providential deism or a purely ethical religion. All of this led to an increasing secularization in attitudes and ideas even in religion. The influence of the Enlightenment was pervasive and it was not the climate for a vibrant Christian spirituality to flourish. The nineteenth century clearly gave witness to this.

2. Orthodox Renaissance in Greece and Russia

The influence of the Enlightenment in the Orthodox world was not as pronounced as it was in the West, although there was still some impact that was felt. This no doubt played a role in the concern on the part of many Orthodox Christians that they not lose touch with their own rich heritage. This desire led to a renewal in Orthodox spirituality in Greece and Russia in the eighteenth and nineteenth centuries. The renewal was associated for the most part with the monastic centers in these countries, and the beginnings fittingly took place at Mount Athos in Greece with the pioneering work of St. Nicodemus the Hagiorite and the publication of the *Philokalia*.[3]

The *Philokalia* that was published at Venice in 1782 consists of passages from the writings of the early Greek Fathers, together with a number of selections from the later Hesychast tradition that reached its peak with St. Gregory Palamas in the fourteenth century.[4] All of these texts focus on the Jesus Prayer and the Hesychast prayer of the heart and are meant to be a guide and a companion for those seeking a life of holiness and union with God. The word *Philokalia* means the love or search for beauty. It is a term that was first used by St. Basil the Great and St. Gregory Nazianzen in the fourth century as a title for their anthology of Origen's spiritual writings. An abridged form of the Greek *Philokalia* was translated into Slavonic and published in Moscow in 1793 under the title of *Dobrotolubiye*. Translations in Russian were published later in the nineteenth century. Thus, the influence of the *Philokalia* and the rediscovery of the whole contemplative tradition of Eastern spirituality spread throughout the Orthodox world. It is important to note that its influence extended far beyond the monastic circles that

---

[3] For background on the Orthodox renaissance see Louis Bouyer, *Orthodox Spirituality and Protestant and Anglican Spirituality* (New York: The Seabury Press, 1982), pp. 39-53; and the essays in *Christian Spirituality III: Post-Reformation and Modern, op. cit.*, pp. 415-476.

[4] Selections of the *Philokalia* in English can be found in *Early Fathers from the Philokalia*, translated from the Russian text *Dobrotolubiye* by E. Kadloubovsky and G.E.H. Palmer (London: Faber & Faber, 1954); and *Writings from the Philokalia on Prayer of the Heart*, translated from the Russian text *Dobrotolubiye* by E. Kadloubovsky and G.E.H. Palmer (London: Faber & Faber, 1973). An English translation of all the original five volumes of the Greek *Philokalia* is presently in progress and is being published by Faber & Faber (edited and translated by G.E.H. Palmer, Philip Sherrard and Kallistos Ware).

were initially responsible for the renewal. All aspects of Orthodox life were nourished by this return to its sources. A closer look at some of the representative figures in the renewal will bring out the developments more fully.

St. Nicodemus the Hagiorite (1749-1809), also known as Nicodemus of the Holy Mountain, was at the center of the Orthodox renaissance.[5] As a monk of Mount Athos in Greece, Nicodemus combined an openness to Western currents of spirituality with a great desire to make available to the entire Orthodox community the treasures of its own traditional spirituality. His literary activity was prodigious and he brought forth many editions of earlier texts as well as writings of his own. It was Nicodemus who, in collaboration with Macarius of Corinth, compiled and published (1782) the vast collection of Patristic and Byzantine texts in five volumes under the title of the *Philokalia*. Bouyer highlights the importance of this work with the words: "The book is centered on the life of prayer, and more exactly on the 'Jesus Prayer' seen as the focus of Christian asceticism and the soul of its mysticism. Nicodemus could hardly have done more to revive the hesychast tradition than by thus showing that it was rooted in the most ancient tradition, while at the same time bringing out its essential content."[6]

Nicodemus also turned to the West and published adaptations of two spiritual writings of post-Reformation Catholicism under the titles of *Spiritual Exercises* and *Unseen Warfare*. The former is a translation into Greek of a series of meditations by an Italian Jesuit, J. Pinamonti (1631-1703), that were based on the *Spiritual Exercises* of St. Ignatius Loyola. Nicodemus added a commentary with a number of references to Scripture and the Church Fathers. The second is a translation and adaptation of two treatises of the Italian Theatine priest, Lorenzo Scupoli, *Spiritual Combat* and *Road to Paradise*. In this work that he called *Unseen Warfare*, Nicodemus added chapters on prayer and Eucharistic communion, and a num-

---

[5] See "St. Nicodemus of the Holy Mountain" in *Christian Spirituality: Post-Reformation and Modern, op. cit.*, 447-557; and Bouyer, *op. cit.*, pp. 39-44.

[6] *Ibid.*, p. 40.

ber of notes for Orthodox readers. Nicodemus' *Unseen Warfare* was published in Venice in 1796 and went on to enjoy great popularity in Orthodox countries. Nicodemus also contributed significantly to the renewed awareness of the importance of the Eucharist in the life of the Church and for growth in personal holiness. He was a strong advocate of the practice of frequent communion and he was instrumental in bringing out in 1783 a new edition of the work *On Frequent Communion* by Macarius of Corinth.[7]

The Hesychast renewal begun by Nicodemus in Greece was furthered in the Slavic speaking countries and Rumania by Paissy Velichkovski (1722-1794), a famous and influential *staretz* or "elder." He was also a major contributor to the monastic revival that took place in Russia in the nineteenth century. Born in the Ukraine, he left his homeland and embraced the monastic life. After spending sixteen years as a monk at Mount Athos, he founded important monastic centers in Moldavia. His work there paralleled in many ways that of Nicodemus. He translated into Slavonic and popularized many of the texts of the Greek Fathers and the Hesychast masters. The most important of these was his translation into Slavonic of selections from the Greek *Philokalia*. It was published a year before his death in 1793 under the title of *Dobrotolubiye*. Like Nicodemus, Paissy was also convinced that the Jesus Prayer and the prayer of the heart should not be confined to the monasteries, and he did much to popularize the practices of Hesychast prayer among the laity. Much of his teaching and influence were also communicated through his letters and the vast correspondence he maintained during his lifetime.

The monastic disciples of Paissy were instrumental in spreading his work and influence into Russia and Rumania after his death. Selections from the *Philokalia* were also translated into Russian, first by Ignatius Brianchaninov (1807-1867) and published in 1857, and

---

[7] For a recent English translation of one of Nicodemus' spiritual treatises with background on his life and writings, see *Nicodemus of the Holy Mountain, A Handbook of Spiritual Counsel,* translation and foreword by Peter A. Chamberas, introduction by George S. Bebis (New York: Paulist Press, 1989).

then in an edition by Theophan the Recluse (1815-1894) that was published in 1877. The nineteenth century thus witnessed a renewal of the monastic life in Russia. The role of the elder or *staretz* took on added importance in Russian monasticism and their influence extended far beyond the monasteries themselves. This was particularly true of the famous Optina monastery where a number of well-known *startzy* lived and worked. They did much to spread what was essentially a monastic spirituality into lay and secular circles.[8] These elders carried on an important ministry of spiritual direction and pastoral assistance for the thousands of pilgrims and visitors who flocked to the Optina monastery from all walks of life. One of the visitors was the novelist Dostoevsky who did much to popularize this spirituality through such monastic figures as Father Zossima in *The Brothers Karamazov* and Bishop Tikhon in *The Possessed*.

Theophan the Recluse was very much in the tradition of the Russian *staretz* or elder. As a young man he studied at the theological Academy at Kiev, and then became a priest and a monk. For eighteen years he held a number of responsible positions before becoming a bishop in 1859. Seven years later he withdrew to the monastery of Vychinsky. His last years were spent in total seclusion, although he kept up a huge correspondence with those who sought his advice and direction. During these years he also devoted himself to study and writing. He was mainly responsible for the translation of the complete Greek *Philokalia* into Russian, although he had the assistance of some of the monks from the Optina monastery. He made some adaptations, for he arranged the material in a different order and he also added a number of Syriac texts. The Russian version of the *Philokalia* was published in five volumes between 1876 and 1890.

Theophan also translated into Russian the *Unseen Warfare* of Nicodemus of the Holy Mountain.[9] Here, too, he made alterations

---

[8] Bouyer writes: "Never perhaps had a monasticism wholly faithful to its purely spiritual vocation been capable of thus fecundating the life of an entire people from the most humble levels to the most exacting intellectuals." *Op. cit.*, p. 47.

[9] This is the version that has been translated into English. See *Unseen Warfare*, translated

to the original text, bringing it more in line with traditional Orthodox spirituality. Theophan has also left eight volumes of his letters most of which were written during his years of solitude. His willingness to be of assistance to the countless numbers who sought his advice and counsel clearly placed him in the tradition that goes back to St. Anthony the hermit. The fruit of solitary prayer should be shared with others, for the love of God finds its expression in a loving concern for one's brothers and sisters.

The work, however, that perhaps did the most to make Russian Orthodox spirituality known on a popular level was that of an anonymous author entitled *The Way of a Pilgrim*.[10] The work first appeared in Russian in 1884 and was entitled *The Sincere Accounts of a Pilgrim to his Spiritual Father*. It is the tale of an unknown pilgrim, traveling with a knapsack that holds only some dry bread, his Bible, and a battered copy of the *Philokalia*. Hearing the words of St. Paul that were addressed to the Thessalonians to "pray without ceasing," he sets out seeking a way to make this a reality in his life. After failing many times to find an answer, he comes to a *staretz* who teaches him the Jesus Prayer ("Lord Jesus Christ, have mercy on me"). This simple but moving account of a sincere spiritual quest did much to make known in Russia and far beyond, through its translation into many languages, the Hesychast way of life and the prayer of the heart.

3. St. Alphonsus Liguori

St. Alphonsus Liguori (1697-1787) was one of the most outstanding religious figures among Roman Catholics in the eighteenth century. His contributions during his long life that spanned most

---

into English from Theophan's Russian text by E. Kadloubovsky and G.E.H. Palmer with an introduction by H.A. Hodges (London: Fabe and Faber, 1952).

[10] For English translations see *The Way of a Pilgrim and The Pilgrim Continues His Way*, translated by R.M. French (New York: Harper, 1952), and *The Pilgrim's Tale*, edited with an introduction by Aleksei Pentkovsky, translated by T. Allan Smith (New York: Paulist Press, 1997).

of this century were monumental. Zealous missionary, founder of the Redemptorists, bishop, theologian, and prolific writer, his influence on nineteenth-century Catholicism was great. In an age in which a spirit of rigorism and a revived Jansenism had taken a firm hold, he did much to inspire in his hearers and readers a renewed awareness of the Divine Love and God's mercy. With his optimistic spirit and his deep pastoral sense, he has often been referred to as an Italian Francis de Sales.

Alphonsus Liguori was born of a noble and ancient Neapolitan family. As a young man he studied at the University of Naples and received a doctorate in both civil and ecclesiastical law. He left his career in law to study theology in preparation for ordination to the priesthood. After joining a community of diocesan priests (Congregation of the Apostolic Missions) and being ordained in 1726, he devoted himself to the pastoral work of preaching popular missions. In 1732 he founded the Congregation of the Most Holy Redeemer (Redemptorists), a congregation of priests and brothers that took as its special apostolate the preaching of missions and meeting the pastoral needs of those living in country and rural areas. The congregation was approved by Benedict XIV in 1749 and Alphonsus was elected Superior General for life. In 1762 he was appointed bishop of Sant' Agata dei Goti and served this diocese until illness forced him to resign in 1775. His last years were spent at the Redemptorist house in Pagani near Salerno where he continued his writing and the work of governing the congregation that would spread throughout the world after his death. Alphonsus was canonized in 1839, declared a doctor of the Church in 1871, and named patron of confessors and moralists in 1950.[11]

St. Alphonsus Liguori was a prolific writer. Between the years 1728 and 1778 over a hundred works of his appeared, and a number of others were published after his death. His writings include

---

[11] For background on St. Alphonsus Liguori see Pourrat, *op. cit.*, vol. 4, pp. 363-395; G. Lieven, "Alphonse de Liguori," in *Dictionnaire de Spiritualité*, vol. 1, col. 357-389; and L. Vereecke, "Alphonsus Liguori," *New Catholic Encyclopedia*, vol. 1, pp. 336-341.

doctrinal, moral, and ascetic works. Some of them are longer studies on particular areas such as *The Holy Eucharist, The Great Means of Salvation and Perfection, The Glories of Mary,* and his important works in moral theology. Others are shorter treatises written for specific needs of lay people, religious, and clergy, such as the *True Spouse of Jesus Christ* and *The Dignity and Duties of the Priest.* His extensive writings in the area of moral theology did much to counteract the prevailing Jansenist rigorism. In all his writings there is a clear and practical pastoral dimension.[12]

St. Alphonsus' spiritual writings are affective in tone but are solidly based on theology. Love of God is at the heart of his spirituality, and holiness consists in the love of God. Since the love of God cannot be pursued apart from Jesus Christ, "the devotion of all devotions is love for Jesus Christ, and frequent meditation on the love which this amiable Redeemer has borne and still bears for us."[13] His devotional books, *The Incarnation, Birth and Infancy of Jesus Christ* and *The Passion and the Death of Jesus Christ,* seek to bring the reader to a deep awareness of Christ's love shown in the mysteries of His life. This approach is also clearly synthesized in his popular book *The Practice of the Love of Jesus Christ,* written in the form of a commentary on St. Paul's hymn on love in 1 Corinthians, chapter 13.[14] The influence of the French School is apparent in these works.

The love of Jesus is also shown in a sublime way in the Holy Eucharist. In his treatment of the Eucharist, St. Alphonsus treats the Holy Sacrifice of the Mass, Holy Communion, and visits to the Blessed Sacrament. One of his most popular devotional books was *Visits to the Blessed Sacrament* published in 1745.[15]

---

[12] An English translation of St. Alphonsus Liguori's complete spiritual writings was published in twelve volumes by the Redemptorist Fathers (Brooklyn, 1934 ff.).

[13] See *The Holy Eucharist* (Brooklyn, 1934), p. 229; also *The Holy Eucharist,* edited and abridged by Msgr. Charles Dollen (New York: Alba House, 1994).

[14] See *The Practice of the Love of Jesus Christ,* edited by N. Fearon (Michigan: Harlo Press, 1974).

[15] This can be found in the English translation of *The Holy Eucharist.*

The Virgin Mary also has a prominent place in the spirituality of St. Alphonsus Liguori. In 1750 he published *The Glories of Mary*, one of the most important studies in Catholic Mariology. He carefully develops the role of Mary in salvation history and provides a theological foundation for devotion to Mary. *The Glories of Mary* enjoyed great popularity in the nineteenth century and played an important role in the significant developments that took place in Marian devotion at this time.

For St. Alphonsus, holiness consists in loving God. But authentic love of God expresses itself in following God's will, in doing the will of God according to one's vocation and in the concrete circumstances of one's life. This conformity to God's will in one's life calls for a detachment and separation from all that would stand in the way of union with the divine will. Among the various means for growing in love and union with God, St. Alphonsus places strong emphasis on the necessity of prayer, a theme that runs through all of his spiritual writings. Thus, he has much to say on the practice of prayer, particularly mental prayer. It is mental prayer that unites us closely with God and enables us to seek the graces we need. It is perseverance in mental prayer that provides a protection against sin, for they cannot exist together. One will either give up meditation or renounce sin. Mental prayer is something that should not be complicated. It should be simple enough for all to practice it. In fact he sees it as simply putting oneself in the presence of God and talking with Him. He developed a method that was a shortened form of the one St. Francis de Sales had developed for general use. It involved the three parts of preparation, meditation, and conclusion.[16]

St. Paul of the Cross (1694-1775) was a contemporary of St. Alphonsus Liguori. His life was marked by a spirit of penance, poverty, and mystical prayer. He was also a missionary preacher of great

---

[16] St. Alphonsus' two treatises on prayer, *The Great Means of Prayer* and *Brief Treatise on the Necessity of Prayer* can be found in vol. 2 of the complete English translation entitled *The Way of Salvation and of Perfection*.

zeal. He founded the Congregation of the Passion (Passionists) at Argentaro in Tuscany in 1721. St. Paul of the Cross did not leave any spiritual writings but his letters and retreat notes are a valuable source for his spiritual thought. The love of the Crucified Christ is at the heart of his spirituality.

A nineteenth-century Italian saint and founder who is well known for his educational work with youth is St. John Bosco (1815-1888). The industrial revolution gave rise to many social problems in urban centers such as Turin in northern Italy. As a young priest in that city, Don Bosco became aware of the social conditions that led many homeless or unemployed youths to end up in prison. His early work with the youth led to his founding a religious congregation in 1859 under the patronage of St. Francis de Sales. The Salesians received papal approval in 1868 and soon spread throughout Italy. In 1872 he founded with St. Maria Mazzarello the Salesian Sisters for similar apostolic work among girls. His preventive system of education that was based on the loving support and guidance of the teachers met with great success. The Salesian system sought to integrate the religious life of the youth with their study, work, and recreation. Don Bosco was also a pioneer in modern vocational training.

4. France After the Revolution

The philosophy of the Enlightenment sank deep roots in eighteenth-century France, and the prevailing spirit of rationalism and skepticism contributed to the ferment and unrest that developed and ultimately led to the violence of the French Revolution. The revolution itself was followed by the Reign of Terror that released strong anti-religious feelings. Persecutions took place and churches, monasteries, and religious houses were closed and their goods confiscated. Large numbers of bishops, priests, and religious men and women were executed, and many others were forced to go into exile. When peace and religious liberty were restored in the early nineteenth century, the Church in France was faced with the huge task of restoration and the re-Christianization of the country.

Thus, the Church in nineteenth-century France needed a time of renewal and restoration. Religious leaders were not lacking and the period witnessed a religious renewal that has rarely been equaled. Churches and monasteries were reopened and new ones were built. Parish missions were preached throughout the country, and a large number of new congregations and institutes of religious men and women were founded to meet the specific needs of the times. A number of outstanding men and women arose who combined in their lives profound holiness and great apostolic activity. Only a representative few will be mentioned in these pages, but the contributions of so many others should be kept in mind. The renewal that took place in France also extended far beyond the confines of France, for no country would have greater influence on Catholic spirituality and thought in other countries than France.

There were still some lingering effects from the eighteenth century that continued to exert some influence on French spirituality in the nineteenth century and these should be kept in mind.[17] The strong influence of rationalism and unbelief had peaked at the time of the French Revolution, but the results were still present. The effects of Jansenism and Quietism were also evident to some extent. Jansenism as a doctrinal teaching had faded away, but it persisted as a habit of mind and a form of Puritan rigorism. A certain heaviness and a psychological pessimism could frequently be found in spiritual writings and even among canonized saints. The condemnation of Quietism as a form of false mysticism in the seventeenth century also resulted in a reaction against all forms of mysticism. An anti-mystical spirit was still very much in evidence in France a century later. The nineteenth century in France and in other European countries was not a period favorable to mystics and the mystical tradition.

---

[17] For these points see Lancelot Sheppard, *Spiritual Writers in Modern Times* (New York: Hawthorn Books, 1967), pp. 15-19.

It is interesting to note that the nineteenth century also witnessed in France and the other countries on the Continent a renewed interest in the extraordinary and the miraculous. There were the apparitions of Our Lady that received ecclesiastical approval such as the ones to St. Catherine Labouré in 1830 that gave birth to the devotion of the "Miraculous Medal," and to St. Bernadette at Lourdes in 1858. Devotion to Our Lady of La Salette also developed from the apparitions there in 1846. There were other apparitions that received only local recognition and there were some that were not recognized at all or condemned. All of these led to a large output of popular devotional writing. Mention should also be made briefly here of the many reported cases during the nineteenth century of people receiving the stigmata, that is the imprint of the wounds of Christ on their bodies. Two well known examples were St. Gemma Galgani (1878-1903) in Italy and the more complicated case of Anna Catherine Emmerich (1774-1824) in Germany.

From the many religious saints and leaders in France from this period, we will briefly mention a few of the representative figures and then focus a little more on three: St. Jean Vianney, St. Thérèse of Lisieux, and Charles de Foucauld. Since the period after the Revolution called for so much rebuilding and activity, French spirituality in the first half of the nineteenth century is found more in works than in writings. From the many new religious congregations that devoted themselves to education and other charitable works, there were St. Madeleine Sophie Barat (1779-1865), foundress of the Religious of the Sacred Heart, and Venerable Jean Claud Colin (1790-1875), the founder of the Society of Mary (Marists). There were devout lay persons such as Pauline Jaricot (1799-1862), who did so much for the foreign missions by founding the Society for the Propagation of the Faith, and Blessed Frederick Ozanam (1813-1853), who founded the charitable organization, the St. Vincent de Paul Society. Henri Dominique Lacordaire (1802-1862) was a famous preacher and spiritual writer who was instrumental in reestablishing the Dominicans in France. The Benedictine abbot, Dom Prosper Gueranger (1805-1875), was responsible for restoring the

Benedictine abbey at Solesmes. He also did much to renew liturgical worship and piety through his great study, *The Liturgical Year*.[18]

St. Jean Baptiste Marie Vianney (1786-1859), the Curé d'Ars,
is the great patron of parish priests. He was ordained in 1815 after
overcoming many difficulties with his preparatory studies. Practically all of his priestly life was spent in the small village of Ars near
Lyons in France, where he lived an austere and prayerful life and
exercised a remarkable priestly ministry. He is a wonderful example
of God's grace working powerfully, not in a learned ecclesiastic or
an eloquent preacher, but through a humble and holy priest.

His greatest fame came as a confessor. Beginning in 1827,
hundreds of thousands of pilgrims came to his confessional in Ars,
and to meet these great demands, he spent most of the day hearing
confessions year after year. His own sensitivity to the enormity of
sin was augmented by these long hours in the confessional, so one
should not be surprised to find a certain sadness and even heaviness in his outlook on life. But there is no question about his great
love of God and the success of the work that he carried out so generously and so patiently in God's service. Jean Vianney was beatified in 1905, canonized in 1925, and in 1929 he was named the patron of parish priests. Devotion to him has always been strong
among the diocesan clergy throughout the world.[19]

St. Thérèse of Lisieux (1873-1897) died at the age of twenty-
four, after spending nine quiet and hidden years in the cloistered
Carmelite monastery at Lisieux in France. Yet her subsequent influence has been enormous, especially through the posthumous
publication of her spiritual autobiography, *The Story of a Soul*.
Countless people throughout the world have been greatly helped
by the account of her "little way," and she has become one of the
most popular and beloved saints of the twentieth century.

---

[18] See Dom Prosper Gueranger, *The Liturgical Year*, translated by Laurence Shepherd,
O.S.B. (Westminster, MD: The Newman Press, 1948).

[19] For the life of Jean Vianney see F. Trochu, *The Curé d'Ars, St. Jean-Marie Baptiste
Vianney*, translated by E. Graf (Westminster, MD: The Newman Press, 1949); and H.
Gheon, *The Secret of the Curé d'Ars*, translated by F.J. Sheed (New York: Sheed and
Ward, 1948).

Marie Françoise Thérèse Martin was the last of nine children born to devout Catholic parents at Alençon in France. She received permission to enter the Carmel in Lisieux in 1888 at the early age of fifteen, and she made her profession two years later, taking as her religious name, Thérèse of the Child Jesus and the Holy Face. She gave herself quietly but fully to the Carmelite way of life during the seven years that remained before her early death from tuberculosis in 1897. There was nothing exceptional about her life as a Carmelite; she did domestic work for three years before being placed in charge of the sacristy, and later she became assistant to the mistress of novices. The account she left of her life was published a year after her death, and its world wide reception was so remarkable that one can easily see the hand of God in the matter. Thérèse was canonized by Pope Pius XI in 1925, and two years later she was named "principal patroness, equal to St. Francis Xavier, of all missionaries, men and women, and of the missions in the whole world." In 1944, Pius XII also named St. Thérèse "secondary patroness of France, equal to St. Joan of Arc." In October of 1997, the centenary of her death, John Paul II declared her a doctor of the Church.

The Story of a Soul, the spiritual autobiography of St. Thérèse, emerged from three separate manuscripts. The first manuscript was written by her in 1895 at the command of the prioress, Mother Agnes, who was also Thérèse's older sister, Pauline. It is the longest of the three documents and is comprised of her childhood memories and early life, and a short account of her first years at Carmel. The second is the brief document she wrote a year later in response to a request from another blood sister, Sister Marie of the Sacred Heart, about her spiritual life. The third manuscript was written by St. Thérèse a few months before her death in 1897. It was addressed to the then prioress, Mother Marie de Gonzague, who had directed Thérèse to write of her life as a religious. Thus, none of these manuscripts of the saint was written with publication in mind. This helps to account for the tone that some have found too effusive. Shortly before her death, however, Thérèse had a premonition of her future mission and asked her sister, Pauline (Mother Agnes of Jesus), to edit the three documents, making whatever changes were necessary. This she did and, in 1898, the year after St. Thérèse's death, the *Histoire d'une Ame* was published in French and immediately became a spiritual classic.[20]

The sense of her future mission came to the fore in Thérèse's mind as she was dying. As she tells us in her famous prediction:

> I feel that my mission is about to begin, my mission of making others love God as I love Him, my mission of teaching my little way to souls. If God answers my requests, my heaven will be spent on earth up until the end of the world. Yes, I want to spend my heaven in doing good on earth.[21]

The "little way" for St. Thérèse is the way of spiritual childhood, the way of trust and a total loving surrender to God. It calls for generous fidelity to the ordinary duties of one's state in life and the willingness to perform hidden acts of sacrifice out of love for God. Love of God is at the heart of her spiritual thought, for she looked upon her vocation as one of love. As she was fond of quoting from John of the Cross: "Love is repaid by love alone." In spite of her extraordinary holiness and her Carmelite vocation, there is something very ordinary about Thérèse of Lisieux. That, no doubt, is why she has so often been proposed as a model for other "little souls."[22]

In many ways the life of Charles de Foucauld (1858-1916) resembled that of the early Desert Fathers. His life was a very un-

---

[20] For the publishing history of the text itself, see the introduction to *Story of A Soul, The Autobiography of St. Thérèse of Lisieux*, translated from the original manuscripts by John Clarke, O.C.D. (Washington, DC: ICS Publications, 1975). This is the most recent English translation. For other recent translations of St. Thérèse's writings, see *Saint Thérèse of Lisieux: General Correspondence*, translated by John Clarke, O.C.D. (Washington, DC: ICS, 1976); and *Saint Thérèse of Lisieux: Her Last Conversations*, translated by John Clarke, O.C.D. (Washington, DC: ICS, 1977). Among the earlier English translations is *Autobiography of St. Thérèse of Lisieux*, translated by Ronald A. Knox (New York: Kenedy, 1958).

[21] See Clarke (tr.), *op. cit.*, p. 263.

[22] For further reading on Thérèse of Lisieux see A. Combes, *Spirituality of Saint Thérèse* (New York: Kenedy, 1955); Hans Urs von Balthasar, *Thérèse of Lisieux* (New York: Sheed and Ward, 1954).

usual one but his example and spirit would bear much fruit in the twentieth century. Born into a devout and aristocratic family, he was orphaned at an early age and brought up by his grandfather, a retired army officer. Charles himself became an officer in the French army and part of his early military career was spent in the Sahara. He resigned from the military so that he could undertake an exploration into the interior of Morocco. This successful work in the desert won for him a gold medal from the French Geographical Society. It also reawakened the faith he had abandoned as a student. Upon his return to France he was reconciled to the Church through Abbé Henri Huvelin. Desiring to live as poor and difficult a life as possible in imitation of the Holy Family at Nazareth, he joined the Trappists. For the next seven years he spent varying lengths of time at Trappist monasteries in Nazareth, Syria, and Algiers, and also began studying for the priesthood in Rome. But even this could not satisfy his desire for a poor and difficult life, and in 1897 he was released from his Trappist vows. He returned to Nazareth and for the next three years he lived as a hermit in a tiny hut near the convent of the Poor Clares and worked for them as a handyman.

But the call of the desert returned. After being ordained in Paris in 1901, he went back to the Sahara and set up a hermitage, first at Beni-Abbes in Algeria and then much deeper into the Sahara desert at Tamanrasset. Here he lived a life of prayer and apostolic charity. In his hermitage he kept the Blessed Sacrament exposed and he spent long hours in prayer before the Eucharistic presence. Charles de Foucauld conceived his missionary vocation among the Moslem tribes as primarily one of presence, preaching the gospel by his example of prayer and loving service. He remained faithful to this heroic way of life until he was murdered by a marauding band of tribesmen in 1916.[23]

Charles de Foucauld had no disciples or followers during his lifetime. His life was indeed a unique and hidden one. The publi-

---

[23] See R. Bazin, *Charles de Foucauld, Hermit and Explorer*, translated by P. Keelan (London: Burns, Oates & Washbourne, 1923); and Alice Freemantle, *Desert Calling* (London: Hollis and Carter, 1950).

cation of his retreat notes and spiritual diaries in 1923, however, as well as subsequent accounts of his life, did much to make known his spirituality and his missionary ideas. In 1933 Father René Voillaume founded the Little Brothers of Jesus in South Oras, Algeria, and in 1939 Sister Madeleine of Jesus founded the Little Sisters of Jesus at Touggourt, Algeria. They live in small fraternities, three to five in number, and they carry on Charles de Foucauld's missionary ideals among non-Christians, the poor, and the abandoned. They go into the "desert" of the slums and factories to make Christ present through the example of their lives.[24]

5. The Oxford Movement

The Oxford Movement was an effort at renewal in the Anglican Church between the years 1833-1845 that sought to revive Catholic doctrine and practice.[25] It was spearheaded by a number of influential Anglican clergymen at Oxford University such as John Keble, Edward Pusey, John Henry Newman, and Hurrell Froude (until his early death). The beginning of this Anglo-Catholic movement is usually dated with the rallying sermon John Keble preached at Oxford on July 14, 1833, entitled "National Apostasy." The leaders were deeply concerned with the spiritual lethargy that was present in the Established Church and they sought to counter the rational and secular tendencies that were sapping it of its spiritual vitality. They wanted to counter the superficial religion of the day with a return to the sources of the Christian Faith — to Sacred Scripture and the teaching of the Fathers. They found their inspiration in Richard Hooker and the other Anglican divines of the seventeenth century who confirmed their interest in the patristic writings and the traditions of the early Church.

---

[24] See René Voillaume, *Seeds of the Desert* (London: Burns & Oates, 1955).

[25] For background on the movement see John Henry Newman, *Apologia Pro Vita Sua*; R.W. Church, *The Oxford Movement: Twelve Years, 1833-1845* (New York: Macmillan, 1891); and Christopher Dawson, *The Spirit of the Oxford Movement.*

The Oxford Movement was primarily a spiritual movement. The main goal that was kept in the forefront was holiness, both personal and corporate. The Tractarians, as the leaders of the movement came to be called after their writings, *Tracts for the Times*, saw the Church as a divine institution that was called to play a prophetic role in its relationship with the State. With their strong sense of the reality of the unseen world, they emphasized that the sacraments were indispensable channels of grace and that a participation in the sacramental and liturgical life of the Church brought one to a participation in the world beyond this one.[26] In their writings and sermons, the Tractarians set themselves in opposition to a watered down Christianity that had accommodated itself to the spirit of the day, and they sought to present the Christian religion in all its fullness and richness.

Later developments brought a revival of Catholic ceremonial rites, practices, and devotions. The Oxford Movement also led to the revival of religious communities in the Anglican Church. The foundation of the Sisterhood of the Holy Cross in London in 1845 was followed by the establishment of a number of religious communities for women. The majority were devoted to teaching or other apostolic works that met the needs of the times, but contemplative communities also came into existence. Some followed the Benedictine and Franciscan way of life while others were native to the Anglican Church. Among the new communities for men, the largest were the Society of St. John the Evangelist (the Cowley Fathers), founded by Richard Meaux Benson at Oxford in 1866, the Community of the Resurrection, founded by the Oxford theologian and later bishop, Charles Gore, and the Society of the Sacred Mission, founded by Herbert Kelly.

With the revival of the Catholic dimension through the Oxford Movement, Anglicanism in the last half of the nineteenth century embraced three branches. The Liberal or Broad Church em-

---

[26] See Paul V. Marshall, "Anglican Spirituality" in *Protestant Spiritual Traditions* (New York: Paulist Press, 1986), p. 147.

phasized the role of human intellect; the Evangelical or Low Church emphasized Protestant teaching and practice; and the Anglo-Catholic or High Church preserved the Catholic tradition.

Thus, the Oxford Movement was a source of renewal on many levels for the Anglican Church. But it also led to the departure of a number of Anglicans for the Roman Catholic Church. Foremost among them was John Henry Newman.

6. John Henry Newman

John Henry Newman (1801-1890) was one of the most outstanding religious figures of modern times.[27] A man richly endowed with intellectual, spiritual, and personal gifts and talents, he blended his great learning and simple and sincere piety in a way that proved to be extremely attractive to others and a source of great influence upon those who came across him personally or through his writings. Throughout his long life which spanned the nineteenth century, he was involved in many activities. He was at various times a parish priest, a teacher, a well-known preacher and lecturer, a writer, an editor of magazines, an organizer and director of a school for boys, the founder and religious superior of the Oratorians in England, the head of a new university, and a cardinal of the Roman Catholic Church. The writings he published include autobiographical works, biographies, poems, novels, tracts, essays, sermons, controversial polemics, dialogues, histories, open letters, lectures, treatises, and prefaces. Newman always brought a special creative quality to his writings and they are all marked by a richness and depth of content and a clarity and brilliance in style.

When the Oxford Movement began in 1833, Newman was an Anglican priest, a Fellow of Oriel College at Oxford, and one of

---

[27] Among the many biographies of Newman see Meriol Trevor, *Newman, The Pillar of the Cloud* (vol. I), and *Newman, Light in Winter* (vol. II) (New York: Doubleday, 1962); and Ian Ker, *John Henry Newman: A Biography* (Oxford: Clarendon Press, 1988).

England's most famous preachers. He assumed a position of leadership in the movement, particularly through the various *Tracts for the Times* he wrote and the preaching he did Sunday after Sunday from the pulpit at St. Mary's Church at Oxford. The "Via Media" Newman attempted to maintain between Protestantism and Roman Catholicism, however, could not be sustained. The passage of time brought strong opposition from certain sections of the Anglican Church and increasing self-doubts about his own position. In 1843 he preached his last sermon as an Anglican, "The Parting of Friends," and two years later, after finishing his *Essay on the Development of Christian Doctrine*, he became a Roman Catholic.

Newman continued his active and productive life as a Catholic. He founded the Oratorians in England, the community of priests begun by St. Philip Neri in the sixteenth century, and in addition to the pastoral and administrative work this involved him in, he continued preaching, lecturing, and writing. In many respects these were not easy years, for many of his projects and undertakings were not as successful as he had hoped. The publication of his *Apologia Pro Vita Sua* in 1863 was a turning point for him. It was warmly received by both Catholics and Anglicans and it restored him to a position of great influence in England. As a recognition of his life of service to the Church, Newman was raised to the cardinalate in 1879 by Pope Leo XIII. He died at the Oratory in Birmingham at the age of 89 on August 11, 1890.

Newman's spirituality does not form any separate segment of his religious thought but is something that is thoroughly integrated with his life and writings.[28] In his own day he was not looked upon as a spiritual writer in the restricted sense. Perhaps his other gifts and activities overshadowed this aspect; perhaps this title was as-

---

[28] For studies on Newman's spirituality see Charles Stephen Dessain, *The Spirituality of John Henry Newman* (Minneapolis: Winston Press, 1977); Hilda Graef, *God and Myself: The Spirituality of John Henry Newman* (New York: Hawthorn Books, 1968); William R. Lamm, *The Spiritual Legacy of Newman* (Milwaukee: The Bruce Publishing Company, 1934); and the chapter on Newman in Charles J. Healey, S.J, *Modern Spiritual Writers, Their Legacies of Prayer* (New York: Alba House, 1989), pp. 173-195.

sociated more with Father Faber and some of the London Oratorians. But spiritual writer he certainly was. Christian spirituality was an abiding concern for him, and his spiritual teaching is found throughout his writings. His published sermons are the richest source of his spirituality, especially the *Parochial and Plain Sermons,* which he preached as an Anglican.[29]

Newman's spiritual thought was nourished above all by Sacred Scripture. From his earliest years he took great delight in reading the Bible, and his knowledge and love of the Bible continued to deepen throughout his life. Secondly, the Fathers of the Church were a rich source of his spirituality. During his early years as a Fellow of Oriel College at Oxford, his systematic reading of the Fathers not only led to the publication of *The Arians of the Fourth Century* in 1833, but also left him with a deep knowledge and profound love for the patristic writings. Finally, there was a strong doctrinal element in Newman's spirituality. He preached the Christian truths as the basis for a life of holiness. In his mind, religion only became a vital and energizing force when a person was aware of Christian truths, not as abstract facts, but as concrete realities that called for a sincere and personal response. In connection with this strong doctrinal element, we might recall the importance he gave to the concept of *realization.* This involved opening both the mind and the heart to a truth and responding with one's entire being.[30]

Certain themes had a place of prominence in Newman's spirituality. There was the emphasis he placed on the reality of God and of the unseen world in his preaching, teaching, and writing. His abiding sense of God's providential love was closely connected with

---

[29] John Henry Newman, *Parochial and Plain Sermons,* 8 volumes (London: Longmans, Green and Co., 1843). These sermons have been frequently republished, most recently in a single volume edition by Ignatius Press, New York, 1987. For a general selection of his sermons with a good introduction see *John Henry Newman, Selected Sermons,* edited with an introduction by Ian Ker (New York: Paulist Press, 1994).

[30] On this point see the introduction to *Realizations, Newman's Selection of His Parochial and Plain Sermons,* edited with an introduction by Vincent Ferrer Blehl, S.J. (London: Darton, Longmans and Todd, 1964).

this as well as his sense of divine mission. This is illustrated in the most beloved of his poems, "Lead, Kindly Light." It also comes through in one of his well-known meditations where he writes:

> God has created me to do Him some definite service; He has committed some work to me which He has not committed to another. I have my mission — I never may know it in this life, but I shall be told it in the next... Therefore I will trust Him. Whatever, wherever, I am, I can never be thrown away. If I am in sickness, my sickness may serve Him; in perplexity, my perplexity may serve Him; if I am in sorrow, my sorrow may serve Him.[31]

Christian repentance was also a very important theme in Newman's spirituality. He knew that this does not come easily for there is a principle of self-seeking that works against the process of letting go and allowing God to change us. He writes in one of his sermons: "What then is it that we who profess religion lack? I repeat it, this: a willingness to be changed, a willingness to suffer (if I may use such a word), to suffer Almighty God to change us. We do not like to let go our old selves."[32] Finally, there is the emphasis he placed on the doctrine of the Indwelling of the Blessed Trinity. He felt that this was a theme that was little understood and often neglected and so he stressed it constantly.

When Newman was raised to the cardinalate in 1879 he took as his motto the expression "cor ad cor loquitur" ("heart speaks to heart"). This theme, so reminiscent of the thought of Francis de Sales, aptly sums up Newman's spirituality, for it is marked by directness, sincerity, and a very personal and concrete approach.

Frederick William Faber (1814-1863), a contemporary of Newman and a fellow Oratorian, became well known as a spiritual

---

[31] See his *Meditations and Devotions* (Westminster, MD: Christian Classics, 1975), p. 301.

[32] See John Henry Newman, *Parochial and Plain Sermons* (London: Longmans, Green and Co.), Vol. V, p. 241.

writer and poet throughout the English-speaking world.[33] He began studying at University College, Oxford, in 1834 and became a Fellow of the same college in 1837. He took an active part in the Oxford Movement and received Anglican orders in 1839. Like Newman he became a Roman Catholic in 1845 and was ordained two years later. When Newman established the Oratorians in England, Faber united the community he had founded with Newman's. Newman sent him from Birmingham to found the London Oratory in 1849. He remained there for the rest of his life and was active as a well-known preacher, spiritual director, and writer.

Faber wrote the eight books that established his reputation as a popular spiritual writer during the years 1853-1860. In his overall approach Faber differed greatly from Newman, for he found his inspiration in the spiritual writings of the Italian and French Schools. Popular devotions in Italy attracted him and he was drawn to such writings as St. Alphonsus Liguori's *Glories of Mary*. Thus there was a strong devotional and affective dimension in Faber's writings. He was basically optimistic and upbeat in his message and his dominant theme was the experience of the love of God. The popularity that Faber's writings enjoyed for many years has taken a sharp decline in recent times, for his exuberant and wordy style has not appealed to contemporary readers. The content, however, still remains solid and insightful.

Faber's books can be conveniently divided into two categories.[34] The first would be those which treat certain Christian mysteries as a means to further the process of personal sanctification. In this category are *The Creator and the Creature*, *Bethlehem*, *The Precious Blood*, *All For Jesus*, and *The Blessed Sacrament*. The influence of Bérulle is discernible, particularly in the study of the In-

---

[33] For a biography of Faber see Ronald Chapman, *Father Faber* (Westminster, MD: Newman Press, 1961). See also J. Verbillion "A New Look at Father Faber," *Cross and Crown* 12 (1960), pp. 164-187.

[34] See Pourrat, *op. cit.*, Vol. IV, p. 452 ff.

carnation in the book *Bethlehem*. A deep love and devotion to Christ is central to Faber's spiritual thought. The book, *At The Foot of the Cross*, is devoted to a treatment of Our Lady's sorrows. The second category includes the two books that focus on spiritual direction and the process of spiritual growth, *Growth in Holiness* and *Spiritual Conferences*. In these practical works Faber shows himself to be a keen psychologist and an astute observer of human nature and the human heart.

Gerard Manley Hopkins (1844-1889) was an Englishman whose religious poetry has won for him a distinguished place in English literature. He converted to Catholicism while he was a student at Oxford and was baptized by John Henry Newman in 1866. He had written to Newman earlier seeking his religious counsel. A year later, while teaching at Newman's school at Birmingham, he decided to enter the Society of Jesus. Throughout his Jesuit years as a student, parish priest, and teacher, he composed a number of poems that explored various religious themes. Influenced by the philosophy of Duns Scotus, he speaks in his poetry of God's presence in terms of perceiving the "inscape" of things as opposed to the "landscape" of things. As he writes at the beginning of his poem *God's Grandeur*, "The world is charged with the grandeur of God," and adding later in the same poem, "And for all this, nature is never spent; There lives the dearest freshness deep down things." Hopkins' poetry, not published until 1918, many years after his death, has won much critical acclaim during the present century.

7. Religious Developments in the United States

Religious developments in the English colonies in America reflected the particular atmosphere and conditions of the emerging new country, as well as the needs of the people who emigrated from England and other European countries. Different forms of Protestantism became firmly established in the New World. Puritanism flourished in the early years of the Massachusetts Bay Colony and left a significant legacy.[35] Anglicanism took firm root in the Virginia colonies, the Quakers settled in Pennsylvania, and early Maryland became a Catholic colony. Later there were large numbers of American Methodists and Baptists, particularly in the southern and rural areas. Jonathan Edwards (1703-1758), Calvinist pastor, preacher, and writer, emerged as the most significant theologian and religious leader of the Colonial period. His preaching and writings prepared the way for the religious revival, known as the First Great Awakening, that took place in New England in the mid-eighteenth century and then spread to the other American colonies.

Popular forms of religion continued to flourish in the nineteenth century. American evangelical spirituality reacted against the rationalism that the Enlightenment gave birth to, and the nineteenth century witnessed the Second Great Awakening and the phenomenal popularity of the revival and camp meetings, especially on the American frontier. Foremost among the popular and successful American evangelists and revival preachers of this time were Charles Finney (1792-1875) and Dwight L. Moody (1837-1899).

The late eighteenth and early nineteenth centuries also witnessed the appearance of a number of utopian and enthusiastic communities in the United States. Among them were the Shakers, founded by Mother Anna Lee, with rural communities in New York, New England, and other areas; the Amana Colonies in Iowa; and the Oneida Creek communities in New York.[36] There were other sects founded that stressed the Second Coming and the imminent end of the world such as the Seventh Day Adventists, founded by William Miller in 1831, and the Jehovah's Witnesses, founded in 1874.

At the end of the eighteenth century Catholics formed only a small minority of the population in the United States. In the early

---

[35] See Charles Hambrick-Stowe, "Puritan Spirituality in America" in *Christian Spirituality: Post-Reformation and Modern*, edited by Louis Dupré and Don E. Saliers (New York: Crossroad, 1989), pp. 338-353.

[36] For background on the Shakers see *The Shakers: Two Centuries of Spiritual Reflection* (New York: Paulist Press, 1983).

Colonial period they were under the jurisdiction of the vicar apostolic of the London district, but this connection ended in 1774 when the Revolutionary War broke out. After the war John Carroll of Baltimore was appointed the first Catholic bishop in 1789. The nineteenth century, however, brought large numbers of Catholic immigrants from the European countries to the United States, thus swelling the Catholic population. The challenges of organization, acculturation, and assimilation did not provide the climate for spiritual writers to emerge, but a number of outstanding religious leaders came forth to meet the many challenges and opportunities of this period. Among them were St. Elizabeth Seton, Isaac Hecker, St. Frances Xavier Cabrini, and St. John Neumann.[37]

St. Elizabeth Bayley Seton (1774-1821) was born in New York into a distinguished colonial family shortly before the outbreak of the American Revolution. A devout Episcopalian, she married a wealthy young merchant in 1794 and they had five children. After the early death of her husband and a period spent in Italy, she returned to New York in 1803 and was received into the Catholic Church. After facing much opposition and many difficulties as a new convert to Catholicism, Mother Seton was asked by Father William DuBourg, the superior of the Sulpicians in Baltimore, to found a school for girls near St. Mary's Seminary in 1807. This work led to her founding the Sisters of Charity, the first native American religious community for women. Two years later she moved to the village of Emmitsburg in northwestern Maryland. Here she adopted as a permanent rule for her community a modification of the rule that St. Vincent de Paul gave to the first Daughters of Charity in France in the seventeenth century. Until her death fourteen years later, Elizabeth Seton did much to lay the foundation for the American parochial school system, worked with the poor and needy, and sent her Sisters to establish orphanages in New York and Philadelphia. Her spirituality was marked by an abiding sense of God's

---

[37] For an account of this growth see James Hennessy, S.J., *American Catholics* (New York: Oxford University Press, 1981).

Providence, a strong desire to be faithful to His Divine Will, and an ardent devotion to the Blessed Sacrament. St. Elizabeth Seton was the first native born American to be beatified and canonized.[38]

Isaac Thomas Hecker (1819-1888), author, missionary, and founder of the Paulists, was born in New York. The son of immigrant Germans, he was a convert to Catholicism and became a Redemptorist in 1845. After studies and ordination in Europe, he returned to the United States and worked among the immigrants with a group of Redemptorist missionaries. Encouraged by Pope Pius IX to found a new congregation for missionary work in the United States, he founded the Missionary Society of St. Paul the Apostle (Paulists). He did much to make known and promote Catholicism in the United States through his many publishing endeavors, public lectures, and writing. In 1865 he inaugurated the monthly publication, the *Catholic World*, and later he established the Catholic Publication Society, the forerunner of the Paulist Press.[39]

St. Frances Xavier Cabrini (1850-1917) and St. John Neumann (1811-1860) were both immigrants themselves to the United States. Mother Cabrini was the first citizen of the United States to be canonized. The foundress of the Missionary Sisters of the Sacred Heart, she came to New York City as a missionary Sister from Italy to work with the Italian immigrants. A woman of great energy although frail in health, she labored heroically in establishing convents, schools, orphanages, and hospitals throughout the United States. St. John Neumann came from Bohemia to New York as a young man of twenty-five. After ordination he did missionary work in New York for four years and then joined the Redemptorists. He

---

[38] For biographies of Mother Seton see Annabelle M. Melville, *Elizabeth Bayley Seton, 1774-1821* (New York: Scribners, 1960, 1976), and Joseph Dirvin, *Mrs. Seton* (New York: Farrar, Straus, Giroux, 1975). See also *Elizabeth Seton, Selected Writings*, edited by Elin Kelly and Annabelle M. Melville (New York: Paulist Press, 1987).

[39] See Vincent F. Holden, *Yankee Paul: Isaac Thomas Hecker* (Chicago: Bruce, 1958) and David J. O'Brien, *Isaac Hecker, An American Catholic* (New York: Paulist Press, 1992).

continued his missionary work in various states until he became bishop of Philadelphia. Gifted with great organizational abilities, he did much to establish a successful diocesan parochial school system. John Neumann was the first bishop in the United States to be canonized.

Conclusion

The increasing secularization of society in the nineteenth century and the profound changes that took place clearly influenced the development of religious life and Christian spirituality at this time. As this chapter sought to indicate, there were, however, religious leaders and movements that arose to meet the challenges and opportunities of this period. A great deal of energy was expended to repair the damages done by the French Revolution and the wars that followed and to cope with the widespread changes that were taking place in all aspects of society. It was a time of rebuilding and re-Christianization in a climate that witnessed many tensions between Church and State. Given the conditions and needs of the time, Christian spirituality was marked by an active and practical thrust and dimension. Little attention was given to the mystical aspect of Christian prayer. The trends and patterns that were established in the nineteenth century continued into the twentieth, providing ongoing challenges and opportunities. It is to these that we will turn in the final chapter.

For Further Reading

Bouyer, Louis, *Orthodox Spirituality and Protestant and Anglican Spirituality.* New York: The Seabury Press, 1982.

Christian Spirituality III: Post-Reformation and Modern. Edited by Louis Dupré and Don E. Saliers. New York: Crossroad, 1989.

John Henry Newman, Selected Sermons. Edited with an introduction by Ian Ker. New York: Paulist Press, 1994.

Early Fathers from the Philokalia. Translated from the Russian text by E. Kadloubovsky and G.E.H. Palmer. London: Faber & Faber, 1954.

Pourrat, Pierre, *Christian Spirituality*, Vol. IV. Translated by Donald Attwater. Westminster, MD: The Newman Press, 1955.

Sheppard, Lancelot, *Spiritual Writers in Modern Times.* New York: Hawthorn Books, 1967.

12 *The Twentieth Century*

The first half of the twentieth century was a period of vast upheavals, changes, and tensions. Two World Wars and the subsequent Cold War brought profound changes in the political, social, and economic spheres throughout the world. Some drew parallels with other calamitous times such as the fourteenth century.[1] On the other hand, it was a time of unprecedented growth as new opportunities and challenges were faced. The Christian Churches sought to cope with these developments, and Christian spirituality continued to express the desire and search for God that was manifested in many different ways.

The twentieth century witnessed a much stronger sense of human solidarity. In sharp contrast to the individualistic thrust that marked so much of the nineteenth century, the twentieth saw a growing awareness and appreciation of the communal dimension. This was reflected on the international level with the establishment of the League of Nations and the United Nations. It was evident religiously in the renewed awareness of the reality of the Church and all that this implies. The liturgical movement, the ecumenical movement, and the missionary expansion throughout the world were all indications of this strong trend. In addition to being the age

---

[1] See for example Barbara Tuchman's *A Distant Mirror, The Calamitous Fourteenth Century* (New York: Alfred A. Knox, 1978).

of the Church, this period was also the age of the Holy Spirit for it witnessed a renewed awakening of the Holy Spirit in the rise of Pentecostal and Charismatic movements. The twentieth century was also much more open to the mystical tradition than the late eighteenth and nineteenth centuries had been, and renewed studies and discussions in this area took place.

Given the vast amount of writings and the developments that have come forth in this period, one must be selective. This chapter will go only to the end of the Second Vatican Council (1965) which brought to a synthesis many of the earlier currents and developments. We will look first at some of the significant movements that have been mentioned and then at some representative spiritual writers of this period.

1. The Pentecostal Movement

The Pentecostal movement that emerged in the early twentieth century had a number of historical roots.[2] There was, of course, the scriptural witness of the outpouring of the Holy Spirit upon the first Christians as described in the early chapters of the Acts of the Apostles. There were also the influences that flowed from the various groups connected with the Pietist tradition as well as the Revivalism that flowered in the United States in the late eighteenth and nineteenth centuries. Perhaps the most important immediate source was that aspect of the Wesleyan tradition that was emphasized in the Holiness Churches that separated from the Methodists in the United States late in the nineteenth century. The Holiness Churches placed a strong emphasis on John Wesley's doctrine of entire sanctification. They distinguished two separate experiences

---

[2] For background on the movement see Steven J. Land, "Pentecostal Spirituality: Living in the Spirit" in *Christian Spirituality III: Post-Reformation and Modern*, edited by Louis Dupré and Don E. Saliers (New York: Crossroad, 1989), pp. 479-499; and Walter J. Hollenweger, "Pentecostals and the Charismatic Movement" in *The Study of Spirituality*, edited by Cheslyln Jones, Geoffrey Wainwright and Edward Yarnold, S.J. (New York: Oxford University Press, 1986), pp. 549-554.

of grace. The first was the experience of conversion or salvation, and the second was for complete holiness or sanctification. They attached great importance to this second experience and sometimes referred to it as the baptism of the Holy Spirit.

The first outpouring of the Spirit in the modern revival seems to have taken place at the Holiness Bible School run by Charles Parham in Topeka, Kansas. On Jan 1, 1901, a number of the students came to the conclusion from their study of Scripture that the sure sign of baptism in the Spirit was the speaking in tongues. One of the students, Agnes Ozman, was prayed over and received the gift of speaking in tongues. The same experience came later to others at the school and word of it quickly spread.

The second and more influential Pentecostal outpouring took place at the Azusa Street Revival Mission in Los Angeles in 1906. The leader was the remarkable black holiness preacher, William J. Seymour, who at one time was a student of Parham. The early prayer meetings had a strong ecumenical and interracial thrust as people from various races and all walks of life came together to hold daily prayer meetings that attracted large crowds. During the next three years, people came to the Azusa Street Mission from all over the United States and many parts of the world. They received the baptism in the Spirit and returned home to spread word of the movement. Thus, in a short time the new Pentecostal spirituality spread rapidly throughout the world and great numbers embraced it.

A large and diverse movement soon came into existence. Because of the ridicule that arose, as well as the opposition and disagreements with the mainline Protestant Churches, those who accepted the Pentecostal way of life gradually began to form new Churches and denominations. They were united in their teaching "that all Christians should seek a post-conversion baptism in the Holy Spirit, see the gifts of the Spirit as being restored to the ordinary Christian life and ministry, and believe that glossolalia is an initial physical evidence of the Spirit baptism."[3] In 1914 the vari-

---

[3] See Land, *op. cit.*, p. 482.

ous Pentecostal groups and denominations merged as an interracial body, although at a later date (1924) the Churches segregated into black and white organizations. The growth and expansion of the Pentecostal Churches since 1900 has been so extensive that historians have often referred to Pentecostalism as representing a "third force" in Christianity together with the Catholic and Protestant Churches.

A new phase of the Pentecostal movement began in the 1950's and continued into the 1960's. It took place among members in mainline Protestant Churches who were drawn to the practice of a Pentecostal spirituality but who had no desire to leave the Church to which they belonged. Committees were set up in the Episcopalian, Lutheran, and Presbyterian Churches to study this new phenomenon that was referred to at the time as neo-Pentecostalism.

The movement came to life in the Catholic Church in the late 1960's and surprisingly it spread more rapidly and with less opposition than in any of the other established Christian denominations. Prayer meetings sprang up spontaneously throughout the United States and Europe at which the experience of the baptism in the Spirit and the appearance of the other charisms were much in evidence. Speaking in tongues (glossolalia) was encouraged but it did not receive the same significance and importance that was attached to it in the regular Pentecostal Churches. The baptism in the Spirit and the exercise of other charisms were interpreted and understood within the Catholic theological tradition. The Charismatic Renewal in the Catholic Church, as it came to be called, did much to renew a spirit of prayer and devotion among Roman Catholics.[4]

---

[4] See Kilian McDonnell, O.S.B., *Charismatic Renewal and the Churches* (New York: Seabury, 1976); Edward D. O'Connor, C.S.C., *The Pentecostal Movement in the Catholic Church* (Notre Dame, IN: Ave Maria Press, 1971); and Francis A. Sullivan, S.J., *Charisms and Charismatic Renewal: A Biblical and Theological Study* (Ann Arbor, MI: Servant Publications, 1982).

2. Ecumenical Spirituality

The concern for unity among Christians took on new significance with the widespread ecumenical activity that took place in the twentieth century.[5] A spirit of sincere prayer has always been at the heart of this activity. As the Second Vatican Council emphasized in its *Decree on Ecumenism*: "This change of heart and holiness of life, along with public and private prayer for the unity of Christians, should be regarded as the soul of the whole ecumenical movement, and can be rightly called 'spiritual ecumenism.'"[6] Spencer Jones, an Anglican clergyman in England, and Father Paul Wattson, the founder of the Society of the Atonement in the United States, joined together to begin the Octave of Prayer for Christian Unity in 1908.[7] The dates chosen, January 18-25, fell between the feast of the Chair of St. Peter and the Conversion of St. Paul. Approved first by Pope Pius X in 1909, its observance was further encouraged for Catholics throughout the world by Benedict XV in 1916. One of the first worldwide Protestant ecumenical groups, the Faith and Order Movement, also included an annual Week of Prayer from its beginning in 1920. Later it changed the dates of its own Week of Prayer for Unity to coincide with the January 18-25 octave. Further cooperation took place in 1966 when the World Council of Churches and the Vatican Secretariat (now the Pontifical Council) for Promoting Christian Unity began to work together in the preparation and planning of the annual Octave of Prayer for Christian Unity.

Meetings that included dialogue, collaborative projects, com-

---

[5] I am indebted to what follows to Geoffrey Wainwright, "Ecumenical Spirituality" in *The Study of Spirituality, op. cit.*, pp. 540-548.

[6] *The Documents of Vatican II*, Walter M. Abbott, S.J., General Editor (New York: America Press, 1966), p. 352.

[7] As an Episcopalian priest, Father Paul James Francis Wattson founded the Society of the Atonement together with Mother Mary Lusana White, an Episcopalian nun, at Graymoor, New York in 1898. The Graymoor community was received corporately into the Catholic Church in 1909. For a life of Father Wattson see D. Gannon, *Father Paul of Graymoor* (New York: 1951).

mon Bible study, and joint prayer took on increased importance as ecumenical activity increased. The rationale for this coming together is summed up in the perceptive words of Cardinal Mercier (1851-1926), the well-known Archbishop of Malines in Belgium: "In order to unite with one another, we must love one another; in order to love one another, we must know one another; in order to know one another, we must go and meet one another."[8] Pioneering ecumenical activity in France between Catholics and Protestants was initiated by the French priest, Paul Couturier (1881-1953), often referred to as "the apostle of unity." He began the annual ecumenical gatherings that took place for the most part at the Trappist monastery at Les Dombes in 1937. Over the years significant documents emerged from the theological discussions, but Couturier was convinced that all of this activity had to be "bathed in prayer," a purifying prayer that brought forth the fruits of charity. A similar ecumenical group was formed in Germany in 1946 and this influential gathering of Catholic and Protestant theologians became known as the Jager-Stahlin circle.

An ecumenically oriented Protestant religious community was formally established at Taizé in France in 1949. Under the leadership of its founding prior and sub-prior, Roger Schultz and Max Thurian, the Taizé community has continued to exercise a worldwide influence through its many activities and through the writings of its leaders and its other publications. Visitors have come to Taizé from all over the world, particularly large groups of young people who have gathered there for youth retreats.

Official Roman Catholic participation in the ecumenical movement became much more active with the summoning of the Second Vatican Council by Pope John XXIII in 1959. One of the Council's main goals was the furthering of Church unity. In June of 1960 John XXIII established the Secretariat for Promoting Christian Unity under the leadership of the Jesuit Scripture scholar, Cardinal Augustin Bea. The Second Vatican Council promulgated its

---

[8] Cited by Wainwright, *op. cit.*, p. 542.

important and influential *Decree on Ecumenism* in November of 1964. Pope Paul VI continued the ecumenical initiatives of John XXIII. In January of 1964 he met with the Ecumenical Patriarch Athenagoras of Constantinople in Jerusalem. Then on December 7, 1965 Paul VI and Athenagoras took the important symbolic step of simultaneously nullifying the mutual anathemas that had been pronounced at the beginning of the Eastern schism in 1054.

It has long been recognized that all ecumenical activity flows from Christ's expressed desire and prayer for the unity of all his followers, "that they may all be one; even as you, Father, are in me, and I in you" (John 16:21). Thus the ecumenical movement is essentially a spiritual movement that is based on the desire for holiness and union with Christ. As Vatican II's *Decree on Ecumenism*, no. 7, so wisely puts it:

> There can be no ecumenism worthy of the name without a change of heart.... Let all Christ's faithful remember that the more purely they strive to live according to the gospel, the more they are fostering and even practicing Christian unity. For they can achieve depth and ease in strengthening mutual brotherhood to the degree that they enjoy profound communion with the Father, the Word, and the Spirit.[9]

3. The Age of the Church

The centuries that preceded the twentieth tended to place more of an emphasis in religion and spirituality, as well as in many other areas, on the individual rather than the community. The twentieth century attempted to redress this imbalance in many ways. In general, a renewed interest in human solidarity followed the disastrous divisions and devastation of the First World War (1914-1918). Theologians and spiritual writers directed a great deal

---

[9] *The Documents of Vatican II*, op. cit., p. 351.

of their attention to the Church as a community and to the communitarian aspects of prayer and worship. This was particularly evident in the case of the liturgical revival in the Catholic Church that culminated with the Second Vatican Council's *Constitution on the Sacred Liturgy*.

Pope Pius X contributed much to early liturgical reform, particularly with his fostering of the frequent reception of Holy Communion in 1905 and his encouragement of more active congregational worship. The Benedictines at Solesmes in France continued the pioneering work in liturgical spirituality that Dom Gueranger had begun there in the nineteenth century. The Benedictine monastery of Maria-Lach in Germany also played a key role in the liturgical revival, and the liturgical writings of Dom Odo Casel (1886-1948) and Pius Parsch (1884-1954) were translated into many languages. All of these liturgical developments received further support with the publication in 1947 of Pope Pius XII's encyclical on the liturgy, *Mediator Dei*.

Much of the work of Catholic theologians after the First World War involved them in a return to the sources — to Scripture, to the Patristic writings, to earlier liturgical documents. Catholic scriptural studies made great strides, especially after the encouragement and direction provided by Pius XII's important encyclical on Sacred Scripture, *Divino Afflante Spiritu*, in 1943. Recognizing that greater attention had been given in the past to the visible and institutional aspects of the Church, a number of Catholic ecclesiologists sought to redress this imbalance with studies on the invisible, spiritual, and communitarian aspects of the Church. The relationship between the human and divine, the visible and the invisible, and the earthly and the heavenly received special attention as they focused on the Church as mystery. The theme of the Church as the Mystical Body of Christ became the dominant one in Catholic theology. This was true, not only in ecclesiology, but also in such areas as Christology, pastoral theology, and spirituality. Pope Pius XII's encyclical, *Mystici Corporis* (1943), was devoted to this theme. As we will see later, it was also central to the spirituality of such popular writers as Dorothy Day and Caryll Houselander.

4. The Revival of Mysticism

The early twentieth century witnessed a renewed interest in the area of mysticism. Much of the discussion centered around such questions as the nature of mysticism, its connection with Christian perfection, and the relationship between asceticism and mysticism (contemplation). Although it resulted in controversies that tended to be speculative and technical in nature, it clearly attested to an interest in mysticism that was lacking in the nineteenth century.

The early Christian tradition looked upon contemplation and mystical prayer as something that was open to all devout Christians. It was seen as the normal outcome of a serious spiritual life and thus was not limited to extraordinary situations and vocations. It was generally accepted that mystical graces were open to all who cooperated fully with God's graces. This view, however, began to change in the seventeenth century. Gradually it was assumed that Christian perfection and holiness were not necessarily tied to mystical prayer. A tendency clearly developed that made much more of a distinction between the ascetical and the mystical aspects of the spiritual life. This view held that all Christians are called to the perfection of charity but all are not called to the higher mystical stages of prayer. Thus, there were two paths that led to Christian holiness; one was through the ordinary ascetic practices and forms of prayer, and the other was linked with extraordinary mystical graces. This latter view continued to remain the dominant one until it began to be challenged in the early twentieth century.

In 1896 Abbé Auguste Saudreau published his influential book, *Les Degrés de la vie spirituelle* (English translation: *The Degrees of the Spiritual Life*), and in 1901 Augustin Poulain, S.J., brought forth his classic study, *Les Grâces d'Oraison (The Graces of Interior Prayer* in English).[10] Although both writers agreed on many aspects of the nature of mystical prayer and did much to coun-

---

[10] See Auguste Saudreau, *The Degrees of the Spiritual Life*, 2 vols. (New York: 1907); and Augustin Poulain, S.J., *The Graces of Interior Prayer* (St. Louis: Herder, 1950).

teract the more narrow earlier view, there were other points that led to expanded controversies as other writers in France, Italy, and Spain responded to their teaching. One controversial point was Poulain's distinction between acquired contemplation (a lower stage which can be achieved by one's own efforts) and infused contemplation (due entirely to God's gratuitous gift and not necessarily linked to perfection). The Dominican, Father Garrigou-Lagrange, followed the teaching of Saudreau and held in his writings that infused contemplation was the normal development of the life of grace.[11] A detailed analysis of these controversial points would not be in order here, but the extent of these speculative writings on mysticism attest to the wide interest in it at this time.[12]

Friedrich von Hügel

Although he did not take a direct part in the above discussions on mysticism, Baron Friedrich von Hügel (1852-1925) made a significant and distinct contribution to the renewal of mysticism with his important study, *The Mystical Element of Religion as Studied in Saint Catherine of Genoa and Her Friends.*[13] Von Hügel was born in Florence during the time his father was Austrian ambassador to Tuscany. His mother was a Scottish gentlewoman, a convert to Catholicism from Presbyterianism. After spending his early years living on the Continent, von Hügel married and settled in England for the rest of his life. As a devout Catholic layman he devoted his life to scholarship and writing, especially in the areas of biblical criti-

---

[11] See. R. Garrigou-Lagrange, O.P., *The Three Ages of the Interior Life*, 2 vols., translated by Sister M. Timothea Doyle, O.P. (St. Louis: Herder, 1947).

[12] On these points one can consult Joseph de Guibert, S.J., *The Theology of the Spiritual Life*, translated by Paul Barrett, O.F.M.Cap. (New York: Sheed and Ward, 1953), p. 340 ff.; Adolphe Tanquerey, S.S., *The Spiritual Life, A Treatise on Ascetical and Mystical Theology*, translated by H. Branderis, S.S. (Philadelphia: The Peter Reilly Company, 1930), p. 727 ff.; and the section "After-thoughts" in the third edition of Dom Cuthbert Butler's *Western Mysticism* (London: Constable, 1967), pp. xxii-lxxi.

[13] Friedrich von Hügel, *The Mystical Element of Religion as Studied in Saint Catherine of Genoa and Her Friends*, 2 vols. (London: Dent, 1908).

cism, the philosophy of religion, and mysticism. In 1905 he founded the London Society for the Study of Religion. Von Hügel was connected with the Modernist movement in the Catholic Church in the early part of the twentieth century, particularly through his friendships with the French biblical scholar, Alfred Loisy, and the English Jesuit, George Tyrrell. He himself was never condemned and his writings since his death in 1925 have exerted much influence.[14]

The Mystical Element of Religion was the great study of von Hügel's lifetime and its publication in 1908 established his reputation as a scholar. In the first part of the book he develops his insightful treatment of the three elements that he sees as required for a fully developed and living religion — the institutional, the intellectual, and the mystical. He emphasizes the necessity of each one of them as well as the need of harmonizing and balancing them. He then concentrates his attention on the mystical element and focuses his extensive reflections around the experience and historical record of one mystic, St. Catherine of Genoa (1447-1510). His study of the life and writings of St. Catherine led him to a detailed analysis of many aspects of mysticism, such as its psycho-physical phenomena, a lengthy treatment of Quietism and the doctrine of pure love, various elements of Catherine's teaching on eschatology, and comparisons with other well known mystics in the Christian tradition. It is true that von Hügel's complex and detailed style of writing makes for challenging reading, but there is no question that he opens up vast new vistas with his great knowledge and careful scholarship.

During the latter part of his life, von Hügel showed himself to be a capable and insightful spiritual director. Much of this direction was carried on as part of the voluminous correspondence that always had a central place in his life. Many people consulted him after reading his writings. For many years he was a spiritual director and guide for Evelyn Underhill whom he assisted in her

---

[14] For further background on Baron von Hügel's life and spirituality see, Michael de la Bedoyere, The Life of Baron von Hügel (London: Dent, 1951); and Joseph P. Whelan, S.J., The Spirituality of Friedrich von Hügel (New York: Paulist Press, 1972).

return to full ecclesial communion. There were also his letters of spiritual guidance to his niece that were published after his death.[15]

Evelyn Underhill (1875-1941) often expressed her appreciation for Baron von Hügel's guidance and assistance in the course of her own spiritual quest and growth.[16] She explored various spiritual paths before returning as a young woman to Christianity in a committed way. Drawn by its mystical and sacramental dimensions, she was initially attracted to Roman Catholicism. Intellectual questions, however, were not resolved and she remained in the Church of England and gradually entered into a full participation. Von Hügel particularly helped her to appreciate the institutional, doctrinal, and liturgical elements of Christianity.

Underhill manifested a strong interest in mysticism throughout her life and she made a distinct contribution to this area through her extensive writings. Her classic work, *Mysticism, A Study in the Development of Man's Spiritual Consciousness* has continued to enjoy widespread popularity since its publication in 1911. In the second part of the book she formulated her treatment of the mystical way according to five stages: awakening, purgation, illumination, surrender, and union. Later she continued to expound her ideas on mysticism in such writings as *The Mystic Way, Practical Mysticism, The Future of Mysticism,* and *The Essentials of Mysticism.* She also published studies on various mystics and made new editions of their writings available. This was particularly true of such medieval mystics as Angela of Foligno and John Ruusbroec (her favorite mystic). She began giving retreats to her fellow Anglicans once she began full practice in the Church of England, and these retreats and other talks and lectures led to the publication of a number of her practical spiritual books. She also involved herself in providing

---

[15] *Letters from Baron von Hügel to a Niece* (London: 1928).

[16] See for example her preface to the twelfth edition of her *Mysticism, A Study in the Nature and Development of Man's Spiritual Consciousness* (New York: Meridian Books, 1955), p. ix.

spiritual direction for others as her many letters attest.[17] In 1936 she published *Worship*, her major and scholarly study of the nature and forms of Christian worship and liturgical practices.

In connection with this revival of mysticism in the early twentieth century, mention should be briefly made once again of the French Catholic priest, Henri Bremond (1865-1933). A voluminous writer, his monumental work was *Histoire littéraire du sentiment religieux en France* (eleven volumes, 1915-32).[18] This wellknown study did much to revive and make known the rich French mystical tradition of the seventeenth century. Bremond was elected a member of the prestigious French Academy in 1923.

5. European Spiritual Writers

One has to be selective in a study such as this when reflecting on the many European spiritual writers of the twentieth century. With this in mind we will focus here on five varied writers who have made distinct and significant contributions through their spiritual writings: the Irish born Benedictine monk, Columba Marmion; the German Lutheran pastor, Dietrich Bonhoeffer; the English Catholic laywoman, Caryll Houselander; the French Jesuit, Pierre Teilhard de Chardin; and the Anglican religious writer, C.S. Lewis.[19]

---

[17] See *The Letters of Evelyn Underhill*, edited with an introduction by Charles Williams (Westminster, MD: Christian Classics, 1989). For further background on her life see the biography by Christopher Armstrong, *Evelyn Underhill: An Introduction to Her Life and Writings* (Grand Rapids, MI: Eerdmans, 1975). This study has a full bibliography of her many writings.

[18] As mentioned earlier, the first three volumes are available in the English translation, *A Literary History of Religious Thought in France*, translated by K.L. Montgomery (New York: Macmillan, 1930).

[19] See Charles J. Healey, S.J., *Modern Spiritual Writers, Their Legacies of Prayer* (New York: Alba House, 1989).

Columba Marmion

Dom Columba Marmion (1858-1923) served as a diocesan priest in his native Ireland before joining the Benedictines at the abbey of Maredsous in Belgium. He subsequently became its abbot and an illustrious twentieth century witness of the rich Benedictine tradition he inherited. His trilogy of books, *Christ the Life of the Soul* (1918), *Christ in His Mysteries* (1919), and *Christ the Ideal of the Monk* (1922), met with widespread acceptance and established his reputation as a spiritual master. Written originally in French, they were soon translated into many languages and went through many editions. He was also the author of *Christ the Ideal of the Priest* (1951), published many years after his death. All of these writings flowed from the retreat conferences and other talks he gave to priests, religious, and monks during his years as abbot of Maredsous.

Marmion's legacy is a rich one because it draws deeply from the scriptural and doctrinal founts of the Christian faith. But his theology is also integrated with his spirituality for there is a spirit of faith and prayer that permeates all of his spiritual conferences and writings. Marmion was writing at a time when the biblical and liturgical movements were beginning to have positive effects upon spirituality and so his writings met a distinct need on the part of those who were seeking solid spiritual guidance. Marmion also had a particular gift for explaining profound truths of the Christian faith with great simplicity and directness. St. Paul was a particular favorite and the Pauline influence is clearly apparent in all of Marmion's spiritual conferences. In *Christ the Life of the Soul*, he begins with the opening passage of Paul's Letter to the Ephesians that stresses God's plan of our divine adoption in Christ Jesus. The influence of the French Berullian school is also evident in Marmion's Christology and his emphasis on the mysteries of Christ.

The main theme in Marmion's writings is clearly that of divine adoption in Christ. He seeks to bring his readers to a renewed awareness of God's love and goodness as shown in the divine plan of our adoption in Jesus Christ. For Marmion, this is the foundation of our relationship with God and the source of our holiness. God wills to share the divine life, the life of the Triune God, with those He has created. Marmion writes: "To these mere creatures God will give the condition and sweet name of children. By nature God has only one Son; by love, He wills to have an innumerable multitude: that is *the grace of supernatural adoption.*"[20] Supernatural adoption and participation in the divine life are brought about by the grace that has been gained through the redemptive work of Christ.

The centrality of Christ, then, is at the heart of Marmion's spirituality. It is in Jesus Christ and through Jesus Christ that we receive the divine adoption. He is the only Way, the only Truth, the only Life. He is the source of our holiness, and we can only be saints according to the measure in which the life of Christ is in us. As Marmion stresses: "Our holiness is nothing else but this: the more we participate in the divine life through the communication Jesus Christ makes to us of the grace of which He ever possesses the fullness, the higher is the degree of our holiness."[21] The practical aim of Marmion, then, is to lead others from an awareness and realization of the Divine Plan of adoption to an actual living it out in their lives, that is, to live out what they are, adopted children of God in Jesus Christ. This status as children of God through the grace of Christ also determines one's fundamental attitude in prayer.

Dietrich Bonhoeffer

Dietrich Bonhoeffer (1906-1945) began a promising career as a theologian and Lutheran pastor at the University of Berlin in 1931. The political events occurring in Germany in the early 1930's, however, soon brought about many profound changes in his life. Bonhoeffer's opposition to the Nazi party led to his decision to

---

[20] Columba Marmion, *Christ the Life of the Soul* (St. Louis: B. Herder Book Co., 1925), p. 24.

[21] *Ibid.*, p. 38.

abandon his academic career when Hitler came to power in 1933. Hitler's subsequent policies led to divisions in the German Lutheran Church, and Bonhoeffer became an active member of the Confessing Church that was formed in opposition to Hitler's totalitarian government. This Church commissioned Bonhoeffer to direct one of the underground seminaries that were established for the training of young pastors. His two main spiritual writings, *The Cost of Discipleship*, and *Life Together*, reflect the prayerful vision and spirit of his work at this seminary. This important activity continued until the seminary was closed by the Nazi authorities in September of 1937.

The late 1930's brought further changes for Bonhoeffer. As the German war operation expanded, he was drawn more and more into active opposition against Hitler's government. Convinced of the righteousness of the cause, he eventually became involved in the conspiracy to overthrow Hitler. He was arrested by the Gestapo on April 5, 1943, and spent the next two years in prison. Another attempt to overthrow Hitler in 1945 led to the execution of a number of political prisoners only weeks before the end of the war. Bonhoeffer, only thirty-nine years old at the time, was among them.

The theme of Christian discipleship was a prominent one in Bonhoeffer's spirituality. It is the main theme of his popular book, *The Cost of Discipleship*. His reflections on discipleship flowed from his exposition of the Sermon on the Mount. For Bonhoeffer, Christ is central to the call to discipleship. We are summoned to follow Jesus, not as a teacher or the model of the good life, but as the Christ, the Son of God. It is a call that demands a complete response in faith and obedience. It is a call that also involves the Cross, for suffering applies not only to Jesus but to His disciples as well. The lives of the disciples of Christ should also be marked with a spirit of love that is unconditional. But such a love can only be the fruit of grace, that grace which must be sought and which is costly. He writes:

> Costly grace is the gospel which must be *sought* again and again, the gift of which must be *asked* for, the door at which a man must *knock*. Such grace is costly because it calls us to

follow *Jesus Christ*. It is costly because it costs a man his life, and it is grace because it gives a man the only true life.[22]

Christian community is another important theme in Bonhoeffer's spirituality. It is a topic that is developed in *Life Together*, the book that emerged from his years of seminary work. For Bonhoeffer, Christian community is a grace, a gift of God that should not be taken for granted. It is Christ who should be at the center of every Christian community, for He alone is the source of unity. Corporate prayer at the beginning and end of the day should also be central to the Christian community, but there should also be time for silence and solitude, and individual prayer. Recognizing the need for balance he stresses: "Let him who cannot be alone beware of community" and "Let him who is not in community beware of being alone."[23] In *Life Together* Bonhoeffer also provides a number of insightful and practical suggestions for the ministry of service to one another within the community.

A final theme that can be mentioned briefly here is that of Christian involvement in, and identification with, the world. Bonhoeffer's interest in this theme intensified with his increasing political activity and involvement in 1939. It played a major part in the letters he sent from prison that were published after his death as *Letters and Papers from Prison*.[24] From the confinement of his cell, he attempted to reshape his theology and struggled with the role of the Christian in the modern world. As a number of his commentators have emphasized, these letters during his last months should be integrated with the fullness of Bonhoeffer's thought.[25]

---

[22] Dietrich Bonhoeffer, *The Cost of Discipleship* (New York: Macmillan, 1963), p. 47.

[23] Bonhoeffer, *Life Together* (New York: Harper and Row, 1954), p. 77.

[24] D. Bonhoeffer, *Letters and Papers from Prison*, edited by Eberhard Bethge (New York: Macmillan, 1962).

[25] See Eberhard Bethge, *Dietrich Bonhoeffer, Man of Vision, Man of Courage* (New York: Harper and Row, 1970); and Mary Bosanquet, *The Life and Death of Dietrich Bonhoeffer* (New York: Harper and Row, 1968).

Caryll Houselander

Although Caryll Houselander (1901-1954) was gifted in such areas as poetry, art, and counseling, it is primarily as a spiritual writer that this English Catholic laywoman is best known. Much of her spiritual writing flowed from her own prayerful experience, particularly her basic message that we must learn to see Christ in everyone. The indwelling presence of Jesus Christ in each of us was at the center of all her spiritual writings. For her "the core of happiness in every human relationship is our realization of the indwelling presence of Christ in one another."[26]

There was much sadness in Caryll Houselander's early life and it left its mark upon her as a young woman. A broken home, frequent attacks of sickness, and an education away from home at different boarding schools left her shy, ill at ease with conventional society, and somewhat critical and rebellious. Although she drifted away from the Catholic Church as a young art student, she continued to search for some spiritual meaning in her life. After much struggling and searching, she returned to full communion in the Catholic Church and sought to respond generously to the grace of God that was working so powerfully in her life.[27]

Although she first supported herself by her artistic work in churches, she gradually devoted more and more of her time to writing. Her first spiritual book was published during the Second World War and was entitled *This War is the Passion* (1941). The second book, *The Reed of God* (1944), a devotional work on the Blessed Virgin Mary, met with great success and firmly established her reputation as an insightful spiritual writer. This was followed by such works as *The Comforting of Christ*, *The Passion of the Infant Christ*, and *The Risen Christ*.

---

[26] Caryll Houselander, "Christ in Men," *Integrity* (Sept., 1952), p. 2.

[27] For an account of her early years and her return to the Catholic Church, see Caryll Houselander's autobiographical work *A Rocking-Horse Catholic* (New York: Sheed and Ward, 1955). For a biography of her see Maisie Ward, *Caryll Houselander, The Divine Eccentric* (New York: Sheed and Ward, 1962).

In addition to the emphasis placed on Christ's indwelling presence and the doctrine of the Mystical Body of Christ, the theme of suffering has a prominent place in Caryll Houselander's writings. Suffering was certainly a part of her own life and she was acutely sensitive to the suffering of others. This sensitivity and empathy for those who were suffering from mental and emotional problems led a number of doctors to seek out her assistance with their patients. It seems that her own neurotic sufferings left her with an unusual gift for reaching out with a healing touch to a wide range of distraught people. This work, along with her own study and research, led eventually to the publication of her book *Guilt*, in which she explores the relationship between the spiritual and the psychological.

Caryll Houselander died of cancer in 1954 at the age of fifty-three. We can conclude this brief treatment of her with a passage from her book, *The Risen Christ*, that poignantly sums up her great faith in eternal life.

> Everything falls away from us, even memories — even the weariness of self. This is the breaking of the bread, the supreme moment in the prayer of the body, the end of the liturgy of our mortal lives, when we are broken for and in the communion of Christ's love to the whole world. But it is not the end of the prayer of the body. To that there is no end. Our dust pays homage to God, until the endless morning of resurrection wakens our body, glorified.[28]

Pierre Teilhard de Chardin

As a Jesuit priest and scientist, Teilhard de Chardin (1881-1955) continually sought to integrate his deep Christian faith with his lifelong scientific work. He was convinced that the Christian could be united with God through the world precisely because the Risen Christ was at the center of the world. For Teilhard, the Lordship of Christ embraces the whole world. Thus, a personal relation-

---

[28] Caryll Houselander, *The Risen Christ* (New York: Sheed and Ward, 1958), pp. 73-74.

ship with the Risen Christ is at the heart of his spirituality. There is in his writings a profound awareness of the Christian's role in the world united with the Risen Christ. Teilhard was a mystic and an apostle who had a vision of the world that he passionately sought to share with others. He sought to disclose the presence of Christ in all things and to proclaim Christ in all His fullness.

Since he was a pioneer in many ways in articulating his vision, there was a certain amount of suspicion and controversy connected with Teilhard's life. There is a complexity to his thought, and the newness of his language make some aspects of his thought difficult at times to grasp. Still, there is a power and attraction to his message that has drawn many to a spirituality that seeks to reconcile faith in God and faith in the world.[29]

There were three important themes that Teilhard de Chardin sought to integrate in his religious thought and spirituality: his evolutionary theory and eschatology; his theology of Christ at the center of the world; and his emphasis on the Christian's involvement in the world. He saw the world in a process of development that had a definite purpose and direction. For Teilhard, given the finitude of human persons, there has to be an ultimate point of the whole evolutionary process. He calls this final point of all human effort and progress the Omega Point, and he equates it with the Second Coming of Christ at the end time. Thus, the Parousia or the Second Coming of Christ is the central Christian mystery in his theology which has such a strong eschatological focus. The universe is converging towards its ultimate goal, Jesus Christ, and towards the final reconciliation of all things in Him. The influence of St. Paul, particularly his letters to the Ephesians and to the Colossians, is very apparent in Teilhard's Christology.

It should be noted that the Eucharist has a special place in Teilhard's theological framework. Although Christ is the focal point towards which the whole world is heading, the Risen Christ

---

[29] For Teilhard's spirituality and religious thought see Robert Faricy, S.J., *The Spirituality of Teilhard de Chardin* (Minneapolis: Winston Press, 1981); and Henri deLubac, *The Religion of Teilhard de Chardin* (New York: Image Books, 1968).

is present now in a special way through the Eucharistic presence. The Eucharist is a powerful source of unity, and from the Eucharist the love of Christ radiates out into the world. Many of Teilhard's thoughts on the Eucharist are developed in his long and beautiful prayer, "The Mass on the World."[30]

Teilhard unites to his Christology what can be referred to as a mysticism of involvement in the world. Since the Risen Lord is the focal point of all human effort and progress, Teilhard is convinced that all human activity carried out in Jesus has great value. In his spiritual classic, *The Divine Milieu*, Teilhard highlights the importance and significance of human activity. Through this activity the Christian is called to cooperate with God's plan to unite progressively all things in Christ. As Teilhard writes:

> To repeat: by virtue of the Creation and, still more, of the Incarnation, *nothing* here below is *profane* for those who know how to see. On the contrary, everything is sacred to the men who can distinguish that portion of chosen being which is subject to Christ's drawing power in the process of consummation. Try, with God's help, to perceive the connection — even physical and natural — which binds your labor with the building of the kingdom of heaven.[31]

C.S. Lewis

C.S. Lewis (1898-1963) spent practically all his life in the academic circles of Oxford and Cambridge universities in England. There he distinguished himself as a classical and English scholar and teacher. His greatest fame, however, followed upon the publication of his many religious books that achieved a huge public response and reception. These writings continue nearly forty years after his death to enjoy a widespread popularity.

---

[30] See Teilhard de Chardin "The Mass on the World" in *Hymn of the Universe* (New York: Harper and Row, 1965), p. 19.

[31] Teilhard de Chardin, *The Divine Milieu* (New York: Harper Torchbooks, 1965), p. 66.

C.S. Lewis was a young Oxford don in 1930 when he was converted from atheism to Christianity and became a practicing member of the Church of England. Years later (1955), he wrote an account of his religious conversion entitled *Surprised By Joy*. His long and careful search ended with the experience he described so vividly:

> You must picture me alone in that room at Magdalen, night after night, feeling, whenever my mind lifted even for a second from my work, the steady, unrelenting approach of Him whom I so earnestly desired not to meet. That which I greatly feared had at last come upon me. In the Trinity Term of 1929 I gave in, and admitted that God was God, and knelt and prayed: perhaps, that night, the most dejected and reluctant convert in all England.[32]

Lewis' strong Christian faith would become the catalyst that would unite two particular gifts that he possessed: first, a clear, insightful, and logical mind; and second, a creative and soaring imagination. Because of these two strands of his thought, he has often been described as a "romantic rationalist." The marks of a romanticist and a realist are both manifested in his life and writings. In general, his religious books stress one or the other of these two characteristics. For example, his clear and logical reasoning powers are very much in evidence in such books as *Mere Christianity* and *The Problem of Pain*, while his fictional writings give wide scope to his spirit of creativity and romanticism.

It was as a Christian apologist that C.S. Lewis achieved much fame and popularity. His own conversion from atheism to a committed Christian faith left him with a strong desire to share the fruits of that experience. It also made him sensitive and sympathetic to the difficulties of nonbelievers. His many literary gifts, particularly

---

[32] C.S. Lewis, *Surprised by Joy, The Shape of My Early Life* (London: Collins, Fontana Books, 1959), p. 182. For an informative biography of Lewis see Roger Lancelyn Green and Walter Hooper, *C.S. Lewis: A Biography* (New York: Harcourt, Brace, Jovanovich, 1974).

that of a clear, logical, and concrete writing style, aptly equipped him for the role of an apologist. His first book on a specific religious area was *The Problem of Pain* (1940). The publication of his enormously popular *The Screwtape Letters* a year later firmly established his reputation as a religious writer. This was followed by such varied works as *The Abolition of Man, The Great Divorce, Miracles, Mere Christianity,* and *The Four Loves.*

In his book, *Mere Christianity,* Lewis is at his best as an apologist. This work emerged from the radio broadcasts he was invited to give for the BBC by the Director of Religious Broadcasting in 1941. He readily accepted the invitation and decided to explain the basics of Christianity, for he was convinced that "many people were under the impression that they had rejected Christianity when in truth, they had never had it."[33] The first four of the fifteen-minute talks were entitled "Right and Wrong: A Clue to the Meaning of the Universe." These were followed by five talks on "What Christians Believe"; eight talks on "Christian Behavior"; and seven final talks entitled "Beyond Personality: The Christian View of God." Although these enormously popular radio talks were published in sections shortly after their delivery, they were later gathered together in a revised edition and published under the title of *Mere Christianity.*[34]

Lewis' fictional writings were also the means of developing many of his religious ideas. Among them was his space trilogy that began with the imaginative *Out of the Silent Planet* (1938). There were also the highly successful children's stories, known as *The Chronicles of Narnia.* The first of them, *The Lion, The Witch, and the Wardrobe,* was published in 1950 and was soon followed by six other titles. Finally, mention should be made of his wide correspondence, for Lewis carried on a fruitful ministry as a pastoral guide and counselor in his letters to the many who sought his advice.[35]

---

[33] Green and Hooper, *op. cit.,* p. 202.

[34] C.S. Lewis, *Mere Christianity* (New York: Macmillan, 1960).

[35] See *Letters of C.S. Lewis,* edited with a memoir by W.H. Lewis (New York: Harcourt, Brace & World, 1966).

7. American Spiritual Writers

Thomas Merton

The publication of the *The Seven Storey Mountain* in 1948 brought the Trappist monk and spiritual writer, Thomas Merton (1915-1968), to the public eye in a dramatic way. This spiritual autobiography went on to have an enormous influence and has since been recognized as a spiritual classic. He traces in this work his early years in France and England, his conversion experience during the years of study at Columbia University that culminated with his baptism in the Catholic Church in 1938, and the vocational discernment that led him to embrace the monastic life. Merton was twenty-seven when he entered the Cistercian (Trappist) Abbey of Our Lady of Gethsemani in Kentucky in December of 1941. The next twenty-seven years were spent as a monk at Gethsemani, and during these years he became a prolific spiritual writer and clearly the most famous monk of the times. Ironically, death came to him on his first extended trip away from the monastery on December 10, 1968. While attending an international meeting on the monastic life in Bangkok, he suffered a fatal shock that was caused by the defective wiring of an electric fan.[36]

Merton's vocation as a monk was central to his life and writings. Questions might arise for him concerning the particular form it should take (his last three years were spent as a hermit), but there was always a basic conviction and commitment to the way of life he had embraced. One will never understand Merton and his life unless this is realized.

His early monastic years at Gethsemani provided him with the opportunity for growth in many areas. For the first time in his life

---

[36] For a full account of Merton's life see the authorized biography by Michael Mott, *The Seven Mountains of Thomas Merton* (Boston: Houghton Mifflin, 1984). For an informative overview of the man see the excellent introduction by Lawrence S. Cunningham to *Thomas Merton: Spiritual Master, The Essential Writings*, edited with an introduction by Lawrence S. Cunningham (New York: Paulist Press, 1992), pp. 15-60.

he was able to sink roots in one particular place and devote himself to a structured and disciplined life of prayer and work. The opportunity for regular spiritual direction and guidance helped him to resolve such difficulties as the tension he experienced between his vocation as a monk and his ongoing desire to write. He was also able to experience God's love and forgiveness in a way that brought a deep sense of peace and freedom. As he writes so simply of this period: "It was true. I was hidden in the secrecy of His protection. He was surrounding me constantly with the work of His love, His wisdom and His mercy. And so it would be, day after day, year after year."[37] This growth brought a change in the way he looked upon the world and greatly expanded his concerns and interests. All of this is reflected in the subsequent writings that flowed from his pen.

Merton's output as a writer was vast, for writing was something that was always an important part of his life.[38] Many books have been published posthumously, for he left behind a large amount of material in manuscript form. This is particularly true of his letters and journals that have been published in recent times in multiple volumes. His writings cover a number of areas, for his interests ranged far and wide. There was, however, a basic unity and an integrating element. He points this out in the statement he prepared for the opening of the Thomas Merton Collection at the Bellarmine College library in Louisville in November, 1963. Merton writes:

> Whatever I may have written, I think it all can be reduced in the end to this one root truth: that God calls human persons to union with Himself and with one another in Christ, in the Church which is His Mystical Body. It is also a witness to the fact that there is and must be, in the Church, a contemplative life which has no other function than to re-

---

[37] Thomas Merton, *The Seven Storey Mountain* (New York: Signet Books, 1952), p. 112.

[38] For a bibliography of Merton's writings see Marquita Breit and Robert E. Daggy, *Thomas Merton: A Comprehensive Bibliography*, new edition (New York: Garland, 1986).

alize these mysterious things, and to return to God all the
thanks and praise that human hearts can give Him.[39]

Merton's autobiographical works form an extremely important part of his writings. Included in this category would be such
books as *The Seven Storey Mountain, The Sign of Jonas, Conjectures
of a Guilty Bystander, A Vow of Conversation,* and his many other
published journals and volumes of letters. These writings flowed
from his own experience as a monk and a man of prayer. He has a
way of writing about his own graced experiences of God that easily
invite his readers to reflect on their own experiences of God and their
own searching. This is also true of his spiritual writings which have
always enjoyed widespread popularity. In this category would be
such Merton favorites as *New Seeds of Contemplation, No Man is
An Island, Thoughts in Solitude, Wisdom of the Desert, Life and
Holiness,* and *Contemplative Prayer.*

What can be referred to as the monastic writings also form a
significant group of books. Merton did much to make the monastic
life known to a wide audience through the publication of *The Seven
Storey Mountain* and the other writings on monasticism (such as *The
Waters of Siloe*) that followed. In fact, these publications played an
influential role in the surge that took place in monastic vocations in
the late 1940's and 1950's. Then during the 1960's, a period of reform and renewal in many areas, Merton had much to say about
monastic renewal and the place of monasticism in the modern
world. The books in this area include *Contemplation in a World of
Action, The Monastic Journey,* and his many letters on the subject
of monasticism in *The School of Charity.*

The late 1950's and the 1960's also found Merton expanding
the scope of his interests and concerns in his writings. He wrote a
number of essays dealing with many of the important social and
political issues of the day, and they were subsequently collected in
such books as *Disputed Questions, Seeds of Destruction, Raids on the*

---

[39] This statement can be found in the booklet, *The Thomas Merton Reference Studies Center* (Santa Barbara: Unicorn Press, 1971), pp. 14-15.

Unspeakable, and *Faith and Violence.* Merton always recognized the intimate connection between a vibrant social awareness and prayer and contemplation. Such terms as "a contemplative critic" and "a solitary explorer" have often been used to describe this orientation of his. His ongoing interest in mystical prayer also led him to explore Eastern forms of prayer and spirituality in works such as *The Way of Chuang Tzu, Mystics and Zen Masters,* and *Zen and the Birds of Appetite.*

Merton's work as a poet should not be overlooked, for during his lifetime he published nine books of poetry.[40] He began writing poetry before he entered the monastery, and his early years as a monk saw the publication of some of his best poems. In fact, his first published work in 1944 was a collection of some of these early poems. Included in this work entitled *Thirty Poems* were such well-known poems as "Song for Our Lady of Cobre" and the poignant "For My Brother: Reported Missing in Action, 1943." Merton's later poetry underwent many changes as the subject matter broadened in scope and the style became more and more experimental.

In one of his early journals Merton recalled the time his first abbot put a copy of the newly published *Seven Storey Mountain* in his hands and urged him to continue writing and to help others "penetrate the mystery of the love of God." This was something Merton sought to do in his writings throughout his life. Since his early and tragic death in 1968, his popularity and influence have continued to grow in an unprecedented way and so his message is still widely heard. It is a simple but insistent message. He continually and powerfully reminds his readers of the reality of God and the central place God should have in their lives. He reminds them of the need of prayer, solitude, and a contemplative orientation if they are to remain open to themselves, open to God, and fully alive to God's presence in the world. Above all, he emphasizes that we are called to union with God and union with one another in the love

---

[40] These have been collected in the large volume, *The Collected Poems of Thomas Merton* (New York: New Directions, 1977).

of Christ. Merton's legacy to the twentieth century has been a rich one.

Dorothy Day

When Dorothy Day (1897-1980) turned seventy-five on November 8, 1972, *America* magazine devoted a special issue to her and the Catholic Worker Movement she had inspired for the previous forty years. Recognizing her unique contributions to Church and society, the introductory editorial stressed: "By now, if one had to choose a single individual to symbolize the best in the aspiration and action of the American Catholic community during the last forty years, that one person would surely be Dorothy Day."[41] Her long and ongoing pilgrimage to that point had indeed been marked by a life of service to others and a persevering spirit of faith, hope, and love.[42]

Dorothy Day has provided us with two autobiographical accounts of her spiritual journey. The first, *From Union Square to Rome*, was written a few years after her conversion to Catholicism and the beginnings of the Catholic Worker Movement, and a fuller narrative, *The Long Loneliness*, was published in 1952. She describes her first twenty-five years as floundering ones, years in which she sought to find a cause that would give meaning and direction to her life. She experienced for many years an ongoing struggle to reconcile her growing religious sentiment with her social activism and concerns. Her long period of searching and waiting came to an end with her baptism and entrance into the Catholic Church in December, 1927. The next five years were a time of spiritual growth as well as a period of further searching as she sought to integrate her strong Christian faith with her social interests and human concerns.

---

[41] *America* (November 11, 1972), p. 378.

[42] For a biography of Dorothy Day see William D. Miller, *Dorothy Day: A Biography* (San Francisco: Harper and Row, 1982). For her spirituality see William D. Miller, *All is Grace: The Spirituality of Dorothy Day* (Garden City, NY: Doubleday, 1987).

In 1932 she met Peter Maurin and together they launched the Catholic Worker Movement. The publication of the *Catholic Worker* was one of their first undertakings, and Dorothy Day began writing the column "On Pilgrimage" that would continue until her death. The first house of hospitality was opened in May, 1934, and volunteer workers came to assist them in the many corporal and spiritual works of mercy that were so much a part of the movement. Dorothy Day was intimately connected with this movement until her death in 1980 and served as a guiding light and inspiration for so many others.[43]

Certain aspects of Dorothy Day's spirituality can be briefly mentioned here. First of all there was a strong sense of mission. Peter Maurin provided the focus and direction for this mission. She felt that he had provided her with "a way of life and instruction" and for this she was always grateful. As she writes in her autobiography: "Peter made you feel a sense of his mission as soon as you met him.... He made you feel that you and all men had great and generous hearts with which to love God. If you once recognized this fact in yourself you would expect and find it in others."[44] Her abiding trust in God's providence was closely connected with this sense of mission. It is interesting to note that her first spiritual director gave her a copy of de Caussade's *Abandonment to Divine Providence*, a book that spoke to her directly.

Central to Dorothy Day's spirituality was the emphasis she gave to the basic gospel message of love of neighbor, especially those in most need. This flowed from her deep awareness of Christ's presence in others and her deep conviction of Christ's Mystical Body. Her life was marked by a service to the poor that was carried out in a spirit of voluntary poverty and selfless love. It was a love in action that was difficult and demanding for it called for great generosity

---

[43] For an account of the early years of the Catholic Worker Movement and its purpose and philosophy, see Dorothy Day's book *Loaves and Fishes* (New York: Curtis Books, 1972). See also William D. Miller, *A Harsh and Dreadful Love: Dorothy Day and the Catholic Worker Movement* (New York: Liveright, 1973).

[44] Dorothy Day, *The Long Loneliness* (New York: Curtis Books, 1972), pp. 195-196.

and constancy. She was fond of recalling the words of Fr. Zossima in Dostoevsky's novel, *The Brothers Karamazov*, that "love in action is a harsh and dreadful thing compared with love in dreams." But she never wavered in her conviction that love was the final word. As she writes at the end of her autobiography, *The Long Loneliness*: "We cannot love God unless we love each other, and to love we must know each other.... We have all known the long loneliness and we have learned that the only solution is love and that love comes with community."[45]

8. The Spirituality of Vatican Council II

The Second Vatican Council (1962-1965) was the twenty-first ecumenical council in the Catholic Church's history and the first since Vatican I in 1869-70. In his opening address for this event that was to have such great importance and significance, Pope John XXIII stressed that the Council's goal was to eradicate the seeds of discord and promote peace and unity among all. It was also a Council that was convoked for *aggiornamento*, that is for the updating and renewal of the Church. This Council was able to build upon and develop many of the earlier theological studies and movements of the twentieth century in such areas as ecclesiology, ecumenism, Scripture, and liturgy. Much could be said of the significant teaching that came forth from this important Council. We will limit ourselves here, however, to some of the themes that are more intimately connected with what can be referred to as the spirituality of Vatican II.

The mystery of the Church was at the heart of all sixteen documents that emerged from the deliberations of the Council Fathers. The *Constitution on the Church* (*Lumen Gentium*) developed this concept in its opening chapter as it began its reflections on the nature and mission of the Church. Pope Paul VI had earlier spoken

---

[45] *Ibid.*, pp. 317-318.

of the Church as a mystery in his opening talk at the second session (September 29, 1963). He stressed that "the Church is a mystery. It is a reality imbued with the hidden presence of God. It lies, therefore, within the very nature of the Church to be always open to new and greater exploration." *Lumen Gentium* also speaks of the Church as a unified reality that is comprised of a divine and human element, and thus is in need of ongoing purification and renewal. "The Church, embracing sinners in her bosom, is at the same time holy and always in need of being purified and incessantly pursues the path of penance and renewal."[46]

Although it makes use of many images to describe the mystery of the Church, it is the image of the Church as the people of God that receives the most attention in this document. The pilgrim people of God share in Christ's threefold mission of prophet, priest, and king. It is in the celebration of the Sacred Liturgy that the people of God express in a special way the mystery of Christ and the real nature of the true Church. As the *Constitution on the Sacred Liturgy* teaches: "The liturgy is the summit toward which the activity of the Church is directed; at the same time it is the fountain from which all her power flows."[47] For it is in the celebration of the liturgy that the people of God come together "to praise God in the midst of His Church, to take part in her sacrifice, and to eat the Lord's supper."[48]

The outward thrust of the Church's mission also received significant attention in the teaching that came forth from the Second Vatican Council. As noted earlier when discussing ecumenical spirituality, the Council's *Decree on Ecumenism* sought to promote the restoration of unity among all Christians through change of heart, prayer, and dialogue. Recognizing the dignity of the human person, the *Declaration on Religious Freedom* declared that the human

---

[46] *Constitution on the Church*, # 8. See *The Documents of Vatican II*, Walter M. Abbott, S.J., General Editor (New York: America Press, 1966), p. 24.

[47] *Constitution on the Sacred Liturgy*, # 10. *Ibid.*, p. 142.

[48] *Ibid.*, # 2, p. 137.

person has a right to religious freedom. It supported civil tolerance for all faiths and rejected any coercion in the sphere of belief. The *Declaration on Non-Christian Religions* encouraged dialogue and collaboration with adherents of other religions stating that the Catholic Church rejects nothing that is true and holy in these religions. The *Pastoral Constitution on the Church in the Modern World* emphasized the intimate bond between the Church and the whole human family. As the opening words indicate: "The joys and the hopes, the griefs and the anxieties of the men of this age, especially those who are poor or in any way afflicted, these too are the joys and hopes, the griefs and anxieties of the followers of Christ."[49] This document provides a synthesis of Catholic social teaching as it focuses on the social mission of the Church in the world of today.

The importance of Sacred Scripture in the life of the Church also received a good deal of renewed attention at the Second Vatican Council. Four of the six chapters in the *Dogmatic Constitution on Divine Revelation (Dei Verbum)* focused explicitly on Scripture. This important document built upon the significant developments that had taken place in biblical studies in the Catholic Church, especially the encouragement and guidance provided for this movement by Pope Pius XII's encyclical *Divino Afflante Spiritu* (1943). Vatican II's *Dei Verbum* emphasized the close coordination and interplay of Scripture, Tradition, and the Magisterium, the teaching office of the Church. It stressed that all the preaching of the Church should be nourished and ruled by Sacred Scripture. The study of the sacred page should be the soul of sacred theology, and all forms of the ministry of the Word should take wholesome nourishment and yield fruits of holiness by the same word of Scripture. Those officially engaged in the ministry of the Word should immerse themselves in the Scriptures through a reading and studying that is accompanied by prayer. Suitable translations were also encouraged so that the riches of Scripture might be readily accessible to all the Christian faithful.

---

[49] *Documents of Vatican II,* pp. 199-200.

The Second Vatican Council stressed the active role the laity should have in the life of the Church and thus gave renewed attention to the priesthood of the faithful. This role was developed in a special way in the fourth chapter of *Lumen Gentium*. The apostolate of the laity is a participation in the saving mission of the Church. All are commissioned to that apostolate by Christ Himself through baptism and confirmation. The soul of that apostolate is the love of God and one's neighbor and it is communicated and nourished through the sacraments, especially the Holy Eucharist (see #33).

Finally, in a significant and important chapter in the *Constitution on the Church*, the Council Fathers treated the call of the whole Church to holiness. They emphasized that all Christians in any state or walk of life are called to the fullness of Christian life and to the perfection of love (#40). Holiness of life does not pertain to only segments of the faithful but to all followers of Christ. Since love is the bond of perfection, the true measure of holiness is a sincere and efficacious love of God and neighbor. The goal is the same for all but each person must seek it according to his or her personal gifts and particular duties and responsibilities. "All of Christ's followers, therefore, are invited and bound to pursue holiness and the perfect fulfillment of their proper state."[50]

For Further Reading

Christian Spirituality III: Post-Reformation and Modern. Edited by Louis Dupré and Don E. Saliers. New York: Crossroad, 1989.

The Study of Spirituality. Edited by Cheslyn Jones, Geoffrey Wainwright and Edward Yarnold, S.J. New York: Oxford University Press, 1986.

The Documents of Vatican II. Walter M. Abbott, S.J., General Editor. New York: America Press, 1966.

---

[50] *Constitution on the Church,* # 42, p. 72.

Callahan, Annice, *Spiritual Guides For Today*. New York: Crossroad, 1992.

Healey, Charles J., *Modern Spiritual Writers, Their Legacies of Prayer*. New York: Alba House, 1989.

Underhill, Evelyn, *Mysticism, A Study in the Nature and Development of Man's Spiritual Consciousness*. New York: Meridian Books, 1955.

Woods, Richard, *Christian Spirituality, God's Presence Through the Ages*. Chicago: Thomas More Press, 1989.

Thomas Merton: Spiritual Master, The Essential Writings. Edited with an Introduction by Lawrence S. Cunningham. New York: Paulist Press, 1992.

Epilogue

We come to the end of this study with the treatment of the spirituality of the Second Vatican Council. The events and trends that followed during the last third of the twentieth century lie beyond the scope of this present work. Since the focus in this book has been on the legacy of Christian spirituality, it seems best to leave this contemporary period with its many new and diverse movements and trends to other studies. Only a brief mention of some of the key characteristics of contemporary Christian spirituality will be offered here.[51]

This period witnessed a strong and continued interest in reviving and retrieving the classical spiritual writings of the Christian tradition. This was particularly true for the classical mystical writers, for a renewed interest in the mystical tradition was surprisingly widespread. Numerous studies of these classics were undertaken, and translations in modern English were made available.[52] This fresh return to the sources was also carried out in such influential schools of spirituality as the Benedictine, Franciscan, Dominican, Ignatian, and Carmelite.

---

[51] For a treatment of some contemporary trends see Michael Downey, *Understanding Christian Spirituality* (New York: Paulist Press, 1997), pp. 90-114.

[52] An extremely helpful series is the *Classics of Western Spirituality* published by Paulist Press.

A renewed interest in prayer took many different directions. Various retreat experiences were developed to meet the spiritual needs of many people seeking opportunities for silence, solitude, and renewal, and many types of houses of prayer sprang up. Directed retreats in the Ignatian tradition became popular. Contemplative forms of prayer such as the method of "centering prayer" came to the fore. Such practices of Eastern Christian spirituality as the Jesus Prayer and praying with icons have become well known in the West. The writings of the Indian Jesuit, Anthony De Mello, attained much popularity with their practical and creative suggestions for prayer. The writings of the Dutch-born priest, Henri Nouwen, have reached a wide and appreciative audience. A major renewal also took place in the practice of spiritual direction.

The social apostolate and the thrust for social justice have also been an important focus for contemporary spirituality. The intimate connection between the service of faith and the promotion of justice has been clearly recognized. A number of movements for peace and human rights have sought to foster these goals. A spirituality of liberation has arisen in Latin American countries in the struggle against political and economic oppression. The emergence of *communidades de base* (base communities) in Central and South America has done much to revitalize Christian living in these areas and in other parts of the world.

Contemporary Christian spirituality emphasizes a *holistic* and integrative approach that takes into account the whole person. Interpersonal, relational, and communitarian dimensions receive a great deal of attention. A central place is given to a person's experience of God in the concrete circumstances of his or her life. There is a recognition and appreciation of individual differences and the various ways people are drawn to God in prayer and service. Present also is a distinct awareness of the experiences and contributions of various groups and classes, especially those who have been neglected or marginalized. This is particularly true regarding women's experience, and studies in feminist spirituality have sought to do justice to the unique contributions of women. Although it is not as extensive as the feminist spirituality movement, there has likewise emerged a men's movement that has sought to articulate a distinctive masculine spirituality.

The influence of psychology upon contemporary Christian spirituality has been significant, and the relationship between human development and spiritual development has received much attention. Programs and studies that focus on recognizing various types of personalities and promoting self-understanding such as the Myers-Briggs and the Enneagram have enjoyed widespread popularity. The influence of the Twelve Steps of Alcoholics Anonymous has also had a significant impact on contemporary spirituality.

An openness to elements from other religions has further broadened the scope of contemporary Christian spirituality. For example, many have incorporated in their spiritual practices various forms of Zen and yoga from Eastern religions. Others have borrowed insights from Native American spirituality, especially a greater awareness of the sacredness of the earth. This has led to a greater ecological concern and an appreciation of all aspects of God's creation.

This brief listing of some contemporary trends and emphases in Christian spirituality indicates the great diversity that marks the present scene. Strengths and limitations exist together, and careful and prayerful discernment is always needed to sift the wheat and the chaff. It may be helpful to recall once again in this context Friedrich von Hügel's emphasis on the three elements of religion: the institutional, intellectual, and mystical, and the ongoing need to maintain a healthy and vital tension among them.

We might also recall, as we conclude, that Christ is the fullness of God's revelation — the way, the truth, and the life. He is the source of unity for He is the same yesterday, today, and tomorrow. The words of St. Cyprian from the third century are still applicable today as Christian men and women seek to follow Him and continue the journey:

> It is with Christ that we journey, and we walk with our steps in His footprints. He it is who is our guide and the burning

flame which illumines our paths; pioneer of salvation, He it is who draws us towards Heaven, towards the Father, and promises success to those who seek in faith. We shall one day be that which He is in glory, if by faithful imitation of his example, we become true Christians, other Christs.[53]

---

[53] St. Cyprian, *De idolorum vanitate*, c. 15; cited in Columba Marmion, *Christ the Life of the Soul* (St. Louis: B. Herder Book Co., 1925), p. 17.

Selected Bibliography

A. General Works

Dictionnaire de Spiritualité Ascétique et Mystique, Doctrine et Histoire. 16 volumes. Edited by Marcel Viller, F. Cavallera, and J. De Guibert. Paris: Beauchesne, 1937-1995. (An extremely rich source for treatments of individual persons, themes, schools, etc.)

Christian Spirituality. 3 volumes. New York: Crossroad. (Vols. 16, 17, 18 of World Spirituality Series). Vol. I *From the Apostolic Fathers to the 12th Century* (1985); Vol. II *High Middle Ages and Reformation* (1987); and Vol. III *Post-Reformation and Modern* (1989).

Christian Spirituality, The Essential Guide to the Most Influential Writings of the Christian Tradition. Ed. by F. Magill and Ian McGeal. Harper, 1988. (Contains summaries of Christian spiritual classics.)

The Classics of Western Spirituality. A Library of the Great Spiritual Masters. 90 + vols. New York: Paulist Press, 1978-. (A very valuable source for individual studies.)

The New Dictionary of Catholic Spirituality. Ed. by Michael Downey. Collegeville, MN: A Michael Glazier Book, The Liturgical Press, 1993.

The Study of Spirituality. Edited by Cheslyn Jones, Geoffrey Wainwright, Edward Yarnold. New York: Oxford University Press, 1986.

The Westminster Dictionary of Christian Spirituality. Ed. by Gordon S. Wakefield. Philadelphia: Westminster, 1983.

Aumann, Jordan, *Christian Spirituality in the Catholic Tradition.* San Francisco: Ignatius Press, 1985.

409

Bouyer, L., Leclercq, J., and Vadenbroucke, F., *A History of Christian Spirituality.* 3 vols. New York: Seabury, 1982. 1. *The Spirituality of the New Testament and the Fathers*; 2. *The Spirituality of the Middle Ages*; 3. *Orthodox Spirituality and Protestant and Anglican Spirituality.* (The original French edition of this series also included Louis Cognet, *La Spiritualite Moderne* as part 2 of vol. 3. Paris: Aubier, 1966.)

Cunningham, Lawrence S. and Egan, Keith J., *Christian Spirituality, Themes From the Tradition.* New York: Paulist Press, 1996.

De Cea, Emeterio, O.P., (ed.) *Compendium of Spirituality.* 2 vols. Translated by Jordan Aumann, O.P. New York: Alba House, 1997.

Dupre, L. & Wiseman, J. (eds.), *Light from Light, An Anthology of Christian Mysticism.* New York: Paulist Press, 1988.

Egan, Harvey, SJ, *Christian Mysticism, the Future of a Tradition.* New York: Pueblo, 1987.

_____. *An Anthology of Christian Mysticism.* Collegeville: A Pueblo Book, The Liturgical Press, 1991.

Gannon, Thomas and Traub, George, *The Desert and the City, An Interpretation of Christian Spirituality.* New York: Macmillan, 1969.

Holmes, Urban T., *A History of Christian Spirituality, An Analytical Introduction.* New York: The Seabury Press, 1980.

Holt, Bradley, *Thirsty For God, A Brief History of Christian Spirituality.* Minneapolis: Ausburg, 1994.

McGinn, Bernard, *The Presence of God: A History of Western Christian Mysticism.* 3 vols. New York: Crossroad. 1. *The Origins of Mysticism* (1992); 2. *The Growth of Mysticism* (1994); 3. *The Flowering of Mysticism* (1998).

O'Brien, Elmer, S.J., *Varieties of Mystic Experience. An Anthology and Interpretation.* New York: A Mentor-Omega Book, 1964.

Pourrat, P. *Christian Spirituality.* 4 vols. Westminster, MD: Newman Press, 1953-1955; also London: Burns, Oates, 1922-1923, 3 vols.

Sheldrake, Philip, *Spirituality and History, Questions of Interpretation and Method.* New York: Crossroad, 1992.

Williams, Rowan, *The Wound of Knowledge: Christian Spirituality from the New Testament to St. John of the Cross.* London: Darton, Longmans & Todd, 1979; Boston: Cowley, 1991.

Woods, Richard, O.P., *Christian Spirituality, God's Presence Through the Ages*. Chicago: The Thomas More Press, 1989.

B. Early Church

Ancient Christian Writers, The Works of the Fathers in Translation. Ed. by J. Quasten and Joseph Plumpe. Westminster, MD: Newman Press, Paulist Press, 1946 ff.

The Fathers of the Church, Series of the Fathers in Translation. Washington, DC: The Catholic University of America Press, 1947 ff.

The Ante-Nicene Fathers. Edited by Philip Schaff. Grand Rapids: Eerdmans Publishing Co., 1950 (reprinted).

A Select Library of Nicene and Post-Nicene Fathers of the Christian Church. First Series. Edited by Philip Schaff. Grand Rapids: Eerdmans Publishing Co., 1978 (reprinted).

A Select Library of Nicene and Post-Nicene Fathers of the Christian Church. Second Series. Grand Rapids: Eerdmans Publishing Co., 1979 (reprinted).

Athanasius, The Life of Anthony and the Letter to Marcellinus. Translation and introduction by Robert Gregg. New York: Paulist Press, 1980.

Augustine of Hippo, Selected Writings. Translation and introduction by Mary T. Clark. New York: Paulist Press, 1985.

Augustine, Saint, *The Confessions of St. Augustine*. John K. Ryan, ed. New York: Doubleday Image Books, 1960.

Basil, Saint, *Ascetical Works*. Trans. by Sr. M. Monica Wagner. Washington, DC: Catholic University Press, 1962.

Benedict, Saint, *The Rule of St. Benedict*. A. Meisel & M.L. del Mastro, eds., New York: Image Books, 1975.

_____. *RB 1980, The Rule of Benedict in Latin and English with Notes*. Timothy Fry, O.S.B., general editor. Collegeville: The Liturgical Press, 1981.

Bouyer, Louis, *The Spirituality of the New Testament and the Fathers*. New York: The Seabury Press, 1982.

Brown, Peter, *Augustine of Hippo: A Biography*. Berkeley: University of California Press, 1969.

Chadwick, Owen, *John Cassian, A Study in Primitive Monasticism*. Cambridge: Cambridge University Press, 1968.

_____ (ed.). *Western Monasticism, Selected Translations*. Philadelphia: Westminster, 1958.

Chitty, Derwas, *The Desert, A City. An Introduction to the Study of Egyptian and Palestinian Monasticism under the Christian Empire*. Oxford: Blackwell, 1966.

Clark, Elizabeth, *Jerome, Chrysostom and Friends*. New York, 1979.

_____. (ed.) *A Lost Tradition, Women Writers of the Early Church*. University of America Press, 1981.

Christian Spirituality, Origins to the Twelfth Century. Edited by Bernard McGinn, John Meyendorff, and Jean Leclercq. New York: Crossroad, 1989.

Daniélou, Jean, *From Glory to Glory, Texts from Gregory of Nyssa's Mystical Writings*. New York: Charles Scribner's Sons, 1961.

_____. *Origen*. Trans. by Walter Mitchell. New York: Sheed and Ward, 1955.

Dudden, Frederick H., *Gregory the Great, His Place in History and Thought*. 2 vols. New York: Russell and Russell, 1967.

Ephrem the Syrian, Hymns. Translation and introduction by Kathleen E. McVey. New York: Paulist Press, 1982.

Evagrius Ponticus, *The Praktikos and Chapters on Prayer*. Trans. with an introduction and notes by John Eudes Bamberger O.C.S.O. Kalamazoo, MI: Cistercian Publications, 1981.

Gingras, George E. (ed.) *Egeria, Diary of A Pilgrimage*. New York: The Newman Press, 1970.

Gregory of Nyssa, St., The Life of Moses. Translated with introduction and notes by Abraham J. Malherbe and Everett Ferguson. New York: Paulist Press, 1978.

_____. *Ascetical Works*. Translated by V. Callahan. Washington, DC: Catholic University Press,

Gregory the Great, St. *Forty Gospel Homilies*. Kalamazoo: Cistercian Publications, 1990.

_____. *Pastoral Care*. New York: Newman Press, 1950.

Harney, Martin, *The Legacy of St. Patrick*. Boston: St. Paul's Editions, 1972.

Hausherr, Irenee, *Doctrine of Compunction in the Christian East*. Kalamazoo: Cistercian Publications, 1982.

_____. *Spiritual Direction in the Early Christian East*. Kalamazoo: Cistercian Publications, 1990.

John Cassian, Conferences. Translation and preface by Colm Luibheid. New York: Paulist Press, 1985.

John Cassian, *The Conferences*. Translated and annotated by Boniface Ramsey, O.P. New York: Paulist Press, 1998.

John Chrysostom, Saint, *The Priesthood*. Translation by W.A. Jurgens. New York: Paulist Press, 1963.

_____. *Baptismal Instruction*. Translation by Paul W. Harkins. New York: Paulist Press, 1963.

John Climacus, The Ladder of Divine Ascent. Translation by Colm Luibheid and Norman Russell, and introduction by Kallistos Ware. New York: Paulist Press, 1982.

Kelly, J.N.D. *Golden Mouth, The Story of John Chrysostom - Ascetic, Preacher, Bishop*. London: Duckworth, and Ithaca, NY: Cornell University Press, 1995.

_____. *Jerome, His Life, Writings, and Controversies*. New York: Harper and Row, 1984.

Louth, Andrew, *The Origins of the Christian Mystical Tradition. From Plato to Denys*. Oxford: Clarendon Press, 1981.

_____. *Denys the Areopagite*. Wilton, CT: Morehouse-Barlow, 1989.

Maximus the Confessor, Selected Writings. Trans. and notes by George C. Berthold, and introduction by Jaroslav Pelikan. New York: Paulist Press, 1985.

Merton, Thomas, *The Wisdom of the Desert*. New York: New Directions, 1960.

Musurillo, Herbert, S.J., (ed.), *The Fathers of the Primitive Church*. New York: Mentor-Omega Books, 1966.

Nouwen, Henri, *The Way of the Heart, Desert Spirituality and Contemporary Ministry*. New York: The Seabury Press, 1981.

Origen, An Exhortation to Martyrdom, Prayer and Selected Works. Translation and Introduction by Rowan A. Greer. New York: Paulist Press, 1979.

Psuedo-Dionysius, The Complete Works. Trans. by Colm Luibheid. Foreword, notes and translation collaboration by Paul Rorem. New York: Paulist Press, 1987.

Psuedo-Macarius, The Fifty Spiritual Homilies and the Great Letter. Trans. and edited by George Maloney, S.J. New York: Paulist Press, 1992.

Quasten, Johannes. *Patrology*, 3 vols. Westminster, MD: The Newman Press, 1953. Vol. 4, edited by Angelo DiBeradino. Christian Classics, 1986.

Ramsey, Boniface, *Beginning to Read the Fathers.* New York: Paulist Press, 1985.

Richardson, Cyril C. (ed.), *Early Christian Fathers.* New York: Macmillan, 1970.

Squire, Aelred, *Asking the Fathers.* New York: Morehouse-Barlow, 1973.

Waddell, Helen, *The Desert Fathers.* New York: Sheed and Ward, 1942.

Ward, Benedicta (ed.), *The Desert Christian, The Sayings of the Desert Fathers.* New York: Macmillan, 1975.

C. The Middle Ages

Aelred of Rievaulx, *Spiritual Friendship.* Translated by Mary Eugenia Laker, S.S.N.D. Introduction by Douglas Roby. Kalamazoo: Cistercian Publications, 1977.

Albert and Thomas, Selected Writings. Translated, edited and introduced by Simon Tugwell, O.P. New York: Paulist Press, 1988.

Anchorite Spirituality, Ancrenne Wisse and Associated Works. Translated and introduced by Anne Savage and Nicholas Watson. New York: Paulist Press, 1991.

Angela of Foligno, Complete Works. Translation with introduction by Paul Lachance, O.F.M. New York: Paulist Press, 1993.

The Prayers and Meditations of St. Anselm with the Proslogion. Translated with an introduction by Benedicta Ward. New York: Penguin, 1973.

Bernard of Clairvaux, *On the Song of Songs.* 4 vols. Trans. by Kilian Walsh, O.C.S.O. and Irene Edmunds. Kalamazoo: Cistercian Publications, 1976.

Bernard of Clairvaux, Selected Works. Translation and foreword by G.R. Evans, introduction by Jean Leclercq, O.S.B. New York: Paulist Press, 1987.

Birgitta of Sweden, Life and Selected Revelations. Edited with a preface by Marguerite Tjader Harris. New York: Paulist Press, 1990.

Bonaventure, *The Soul's Journey Into God, The Tree of Life, The Life of St. Francis.* Translation and introduction by Ewert Cousins. New York: Paulist Press, 1978.

Bouyer, Louis, *The Cistercian Heritage.* Westminster, MD: Newman Press, 1958.

Bowie, Fiona (ed.), *Beguine Spirituality, Mystical Writings of Mechthild of Magdebourg, Beatrice of Nazareth and Hadewijch of Brabant.* New York: Crossroad, 1990.

Butler, Cuthbert, *Western Mysticism.* 3rd edition. London, 1967.

_____. *Benedictine Monachism.* 2nd edition. London: Longmans, 1924.

Bynum, Caroline Walker, *Jesus as Mother, Studies in the Spirituality of the High Middle Ages.* Berkeley: University of California Press, 1982.

Catherine of Genoa: Purgation and Purgatory, The Spiritual Dialogue. Translation and notes by Serge Hughes. New York: Paulist Press, 1979.

Catherine of Siena, The Dialogue. Translation and introduction by Suzanne Nofke, O.P. New York: Paulist Press, 1980.

_____. *The Prayers of Catherine of Siena.* Suzanne Nofke, O.P., ed. New York: Paulist Press, 1983.

_____. *The Letters of St. Catherine of Siena*, vol. 1. Suzanne Nofke, O.P., ed. Binghamton, NY: 1988.

The Cloud of Unknowing. Edited with an introduction by James Walsh, S.J. New York: Paulist Press, 1981.

Davies, Oliver, *God Within, The Mystical Tradition of Northern Europe.* New York: Paulist Press, 1988.

Dechanet, J.M., *William of St. Thierry: The Man and His Work.* Translated by R. Strachan. Kalamazoo: Cistercian Publications, 1972.

Devotio Moderna, Basic Writings. Translated and introduced by John Van Engen. New York: Paulist Press, 1988.

Early Dominicans, Selected Writings. Edited with an introduction by Simon Tugwell, O.P. New York: Paulist Press, 1982.

Meister Eckhart, The Essential Sermons, Commentaries, Treatises, and Defense. Translation and introduction by Edmund Colledge, O.S.A. and Bernard McGinn. New York: Paulist Press, 1981.

Meister Eckhart, Teacher and Preacher. Edited by Bernard McGinn. New York: Paulist Press, 1986.

Elkins, Sharon, *Holy Women of Twelfth-Century England*. Chapel Hill: University of North Carolina Press, 1988.

Francis and Clare, The Complete Works. Translated by Regis Armstrong and Ignatius Brady. New York: Paulist Press, 1982.

Hadewijch, The Complete Works. Translation and introduction by Mother Columba Hart, O.S.B. New York: Paulist Press, 1980.

Gertrude of Helfta, The Herald of Divine Love. Translated and edited by Margaret Winkworth. New York: Paulist Press, 1993.

Gilson, Etienne, *The Mystical Theology of St. Bernard.* London: Sheed and Ward, 1940.

Guigo II, *The Ladder of Monks and Twelve Meditations.* Translated with an introduction by Edmund Colledge, O.S.A. and James Walsh, S.J. Kalamazoo: Cistercian Publications, 1981.

Henry Suso, The Exemplar With Two German Sermons. Translated, edited and introduced by Frank Tobin. New York: Paulist Press, 1989.

Hildegaard of Bingen, Scivias. Translated by Mother Columba Hart and Jane Bishop, introduction by Barbara J. Newman. New York: Paulist Press, 1990.

Hinnebusch, William A., *The History of the Dominican Order.* 2 vols. New York: Alba House, 1973.

Jacopone da Todi, The Lauds. Translated by Serge and Elizabeth Hughes. New York: Paulist Press, 1982.

Jantzen, Grace M., *Julian of Norwich, Mystic and Theologian.* New York: Paulist Press, 1988.

Johnston, William, S.J., *The Mysticism of the Cloud of Unknowing.* St. Meinrad: The Abbey Press, 1975.

John Tauler, Sermons. Translation by Maria Shrady. Introduction by Josef Schmidt. New York: Paulist Press, 1985.

Julian of Norwich, Showings. Translated from the critical edition with an introduction by Edmund Colledge, O.S.A. and James Walsh, S.J. New York: Paulist Press, 1978.

The Book of Margery Kempe, The Autobiography of the Madwoman of God. A new translation by Tony D. Triggs. Liguori, MO: Triumph Books, 1995.

Knowles, David, *The English Mystical Tradition.* New York: 1961. (First published in 1927 as *The English Mystics*).

_____. *The Monastic Order in England.* 2nd edition. Cambridge: Cambridge University Press, 1963.

_____. *From Pachomius to Ignatius.* Oxford, 1966.

Leclerq, Jean, O.S.B., *The Love of Learning and the Desire for God.* New York: Mentor Omega Books, 1962.

Leclercq, J., Vandenbroucke, F., and Bouyer, L., *The Spirituality of the Middle Ages.* New York: The Seabury Press, 1968.

Lull, Ramon, *The Book of the Lover and Beloved.* Edited by Kenneth Leech, translation by W. Alison Peers. London: Sheldon Press, 1978.

McDonnell, Ernest, *The Beguines and Begherds in Medieval Culture: With Special Emphasis on the Belgian Scene.* New Brunswick, NJ: Rutgers University Press, 1954.

McGinn, Bernard, *The Growth of Mysticism.* Vol. II of *The Presence of God: A History of Western Mysticism.* New York: Crossroad, 1994. Vol. III, *The Flowering of Mysticism,* 1998.

Mechthild of Magdeburg, The Flowing Light of the Godhead. Translated and introduced by Frank Tobin. New York: Paulist Press, 1998.

Molinari, Paul, S.J., *Julian of Norwich, The Teaching of a 14th Century Mystic.* London: Longmans, Green and Co., 1958.

Moorman, John R.H., *A History of the Franciscan Order, From its Origins to the Year 1517.* London: Oxford University Press, 1968.

Petroff, Elizabeth Alvilda, *Body and Soul, Essays on Medieval Women and Mysticism.* New York: Oxford University Press, 1994.

_____. (ed.), *Medieval Women's Visionary Literature.* New York: Oxford University Press, 1986.

The Pursuit of Wisdom and Other Works by the Author of the Cloud of Unknowing. Translated, edited and annotated by James A. Walsh, S.J. New York: Paulist Press, 1988.

Raitt, Jill (ed.), *Christian Spirituality: High Middle Ages and Reformation.* New York: Crossroad, 1989.

Richard of St. Victor, The Twelve Patriarchs, The Mystical Ark, Book Three of the Trinity. Translation and introduction by Grover A. Zinn. New York: Paulist Press, 1979.

Richard Rolle, *The Fire of Love.* Translated into modern English with an introduction by Clifton Wolters. New York: Penguin Books, 1972.

Richard Rolle, The English Writings. Translated, edited and introduced by Rosamund S. Allen. New York: Paulist Press, 1988.

John Ruusbroec, The Spiritual Espousals and Other Works. Introduction and translation by James A. Wiseman, O.S.A. New York: Paulist Press, 1985.

Ryan, John, *Irish Monasticism, Origins and Early Development.* New York: Colgate University Press, 1972. (First edition, Dublin, 1931).

Schmitt, Miriam, O.S.B. and Kulzer, Linda, O.S.B. (editors), *Medieval Women Monastics, Wisdom's Wellsprings.* Collegeville: The Liturgical Press, 1996.

Sitwell, Gerard, *Spiritual Writers of the Middle Ages.* New York: Hawthorn, 1961.

Squire, Aelred, *Aelred of Rievaulx, A Study.* Kalamazoo: Cistercian Publications, 1969.

The Theologica Germanica of Martin Luther. Translation, introduction and commentary by Bengt Hoffman. New York: Paulist Press, 1980.

Thomas à Kempis, *The Imitation of Christ.* Edited with introduction by Harold Gardiner, S.J. New York: Image Books, 1955.

Von Hügel, Friedrich, *The Mystical Element of Religion as Studied in Saint Catherine of Genoa and Her Friends.* London: J.M. Dent, 1908.

Walter Hilton, The Scale of Perfection. Translated with an introduction and notes by John Clark and Rosemary Dorward. New York: Paulist Press, 1991.

Ward, Benedicta, S.L.G., *The Venerable Bede.* Kalamazoo: Cistercian Publications, 1998.

William of St. Thierry, *The Golden Epistle.* Translated by Theodore Berkeley, O.C.S.O. Kalamazoo: Cistercian Publications, 1971.

Wilson, Katharina (ed.), *Medieval Women Writers.* Athens: University of Georgia Press, 1984.

Woods, Richard, O.P., *Eckhart's Way.* Wilmington, DE: Michael Glazier, 1986.

Zum Brunn, Emilie and Epiney-Burgard, *Women Mystics in Medieval Europe.* New York: Paragon House, 1989.

D. Byzantine, Reformation and Counter-Reformation

Andrews, Lancelot, *Private Devotions*. New York: Macmillan, 1961.

Johann Arndt, True Christianity. Translation and introduction by Peter Erb. New York: Paulist Press, 1979.

Bangert, William, S.J., *A History of the Society of Jesus*. St. Louis: The Institute of Jesuit Sources, 1962.

Bedoyere, Michael de la, *The Archbishop and the Lady, The Story of Fénelon and Madame Guyon*. London: Collins, 1956.

Benoit of Canfield, *La Règle de Perfection - The Rule of Perfection*. Critical edition by Jean Orcibal. Paris: Presses Universitaires de France, 1982.

Bernardino of Laredo, *The Ascent of Mount Sion*. Translated by E. Allison Peers. London: Faber and Faber, 1952.

Bérulle and the French School, Selected Writings. Edited with an introduction by William M. Thompson. New York: Paulist Press, 1989.

Jacob Boehme, The Way to Christ. Translation and introduction by Peter Erb. New York: Paulist Press, 1978.

Bouyer, Louis, *Orthodox Spirituality and Protestant and Anglican Spirituality*. New York: The Seabury Press, 1982.

Bremond, Henri, *Histoire litteraire du sentiment religieux en France*. 11 volumes. Paris: Libraire Armand Colin, 1916-1936. The first three volumes have been translated into English, *A Literary History of Religious Thought in France*. New York: Macmillan, 1930.

Brodrick, James, S.J., *The Origins of the Jesuits*. London: Longmans, Green, 1940.

_____. *The Progress of the Jesuits*. London: Longmans, Green, 1947.

Caussade, Jean Pierre de, *Abandonment to Divine Providence*. Newly translated with an introduction by John Beevers. New York: Image Books, 1975.

Christian Spirituality II, High Middle Ages and Reformation. Edited by Jill Raitt. New York: Crossroad, 1987.

Cognet, Louis, *Post-Reformation Spirituality*. Translated by P. Hepburne Scott. New York: Hawthorn Books, 1959.

Davis, Charles (ed.), *English Spiritual Writers*. New York: Sheed and Ward, 1961.

Denville, Raymond, *The French School of Spirituality, An Introduction and Reader*. Translated by Agnes Cunningham, S.S.C.M. Pittsburgh: Duquesne University Press, 1994.

John Donne, Selections from Divine Poems, Sermons, Devotions and Prayers. Edited and introduced by John Booty. New York: Paulist Press, 1990.

Early Anabaptist Spirituality, Selected Writings. Translated, edited, with an introduction by Daniel Liechty. New York: Paulist Press, 1994.

Egan, Harvey, S.J., *Ignatius Loyola the Mystic*. Wilmington, DE: Michael Glazier, 1987.

Fleming, David L., S.J., *The Spiritual Exercises of St. Ignatius, A Literal Translation and a Contemporary Reading*. St. Louis: The Institute of Jesuit Sources, 1978.

Fox, George, *The Journal of George Fox*. Rufus M. Jones, ed. New York: Capricorn Books, 1963.

Fremantle, Alice (ed.), *The Protestant Mystics*. New York: Mentor Books, 1965.

Francisco de Osuna, The Third Spiritual Alphabet. Translation and introduction by Mary E. Giles. New York: Paulist Press, 1981.

Francis de Sales, *Introduction to the Devout Life*. Translated and edited by John K. Ryan. New York: Image Books, 1972.

_____. *On the Love of God*. 2 vols. Translated by John K. Ryan. New York: Image Books, 1963.

Francis de Sales and Jane de Chantal, Letters of Spiritual Direction. Selected and introduced by Wendy M. Wright and Joseph F. Power, O.S.F.S. New York: Paulist Press, 1988.

Gregory Palamas, The Triads. Edited with an introduction by John Meyendorff. New York: Paulist Press, 1983.

Guibert, Joseph de, S.J., *The Jesuits, Their Spiritual Doctrine and Practice. A Historical Study*. Translated by William J. Young, S.J. St. Louis: The Institute of Jesuit Sources, 1972.

George Herbert, The Country Parson, The Temple. Edited with introduction by John N. Wall, Jr. New York: Paulist Press, 1981.

Ignatius of Loyola, Spiritual Exercises and Selected Works. Edited by George E. Ganss, S.J. New York: Paulist Press, 1991.

John of the Cross, Selected Writings. Edited with an introduction by Kieran Kavanaugh, O.C.D. New York: Paulist Press, 1987.

The Collected Works of St. John of the Cross. Translated by Kieran Kavanaugh, O.C.D. and Otilo Rodriguez, O.C.D. Washington, DC: The Institute of Carmelite Studies, 1973.

Kadloubovsky, E. and Palmer, G.H. (editors), *Early Fathers from the Philokalia.* Translated from the Russian text *Dobrotolubiye.* London: Faber and Faber, 1954.

_____. *Writings From the Philokalia on Prayer of the Heart.* Translated from the Russian text *Dobrotolubiye.* London: Faber and Faber, 1973.

Knox, Ronald, *Enthusiasm, A Chapter in the History of Religion.* New York: Oxford University Press, 1961.

William Law, A Serious Call to a Devout Life, The Spirit of Love. Edited by Paul G. Stanwood. New York: Paulist Press, 1978.

Luis Ponce de Leon, The Name of Christ. Translation and introduction by Manuel Duran and William Klubach. New York: Paulist Press, 1984.

Marie of the Incarnation, Selected Writings. Edited by Irene Mahoney, O.S.U. New York: Paulist Press, 1989.

McDougal, Alan (ed.), *The Spiritual Doctrine of Father Louis Lallemant of the Society of Jesus.* Westminster, MD: Newman Book Shop, 1946.

Meyendorff, John, *St. Gregory Palamas and Orthodox Spirituality.* Crestwood, New York: St. Vladimir's Seminary Press, 1974.

O'Malley, John, S.J., *The First Jesuits.* Cambridge: Harvard University Press, 1993.

Padberg, John W., S.J., (General Editor), *The Constitutions of the Society of Jesus and Their Complementary Norms.* St. Louis: The Institute of Jesuit Sources, 1996.

Palmer, G.E.H., Sherrard, Philip, and Ware, Kallistos (editors), *Philokalia, The Complete Text.* Translated from the original five volumes of the Greek *Philokalia.* London: Faber and Faber, 1979 ff.

Pascal, Blaise, *Pensées.* Translated by A.J. Krailsheimer. New York: Penguin Classics, 1966.

Peers, E. Allison, *Studies of the Spanish Mystics.* 3 vols. London: Sheldon Press, 1927-1930.

The Pietists, Selected Writings. Edited with an introduction by Peter C. Erb. New York: Paulist Press, 1983.

Quaker Spirituality, Selected Writings. Edited and introduced by Douglas V. Steere. New York: Paulist Press, 1984.

Richard, Lucien Joseph, *The Spirituality of John Calvin.* Atlanta, Georgia: John Knox Press, 1974.

Robert Bellarmine, Spiritual Writings. Translated with an introduction by John Patrick Donnelly and Roland J. Teske. New York: Paulist Press, 1989.

Senn, Frank C. (ed.) *Protestant Spiritual Traditions.* New York: Paulist Press, 1986.

Stopp, Elisabeth, *Madame de Chantal, Portrait of a Saint.* Westminster, MD: Newman Press, 1963.

St. Symeon the New Theologian, *Hymns of Divine Love.* Introduction and translation by George A. Maloney, S.J. Denville, NJ: Dimension Books, 1976.

Symeon the New Theologian, The Discourses. Translation by C.J. Catanzaro. Introduction by George A. Maloney, S.J. New York: Paulist Press, 1980.

Jeremy Taylor, Selected Works. Edited with an introduction by Thomas K. Carroll. New York: Paulist Press, 1990.

Teresa of Avila, The Interior Castle. Translation by Kieran Kavanaugh, O.C.D. and Otilo Rodriguez, O.C.D. New York: Paulist Press, 1979.

The Collected Works of St Teresa of Avila. Translated by Kieran Kavanaugh, O.C.D. and Otilo Rodriguez, O.C.D., 3 vols. Washington, DC: Institute of Carmelite Studies, 1976, 1980, 1985.

Theatine Spirituality, Selected Writings. Translated with an introduction by William V. Hudon. New York: Paulist Press, 1976.

Thornton, Martin, *English Spirituality.* London: SPCK, 1963.

Vincent de Paul and Louise de Marillac, Rules, Conferences, and Writings. Edited by Frances Ryan, D.C. and John E. Rybolt, C.M. New York: Paulist Press, 1996.

Walsh, James, S.J. (ed.), *Pre-Reformation English Spirituality.* London: Burns & Oates.

John and Charles Wesley, Selected Writings and Hymns. Edited with an introduction by Frank Whaling. New York: Paulist Press, 1981.

Wicks, Jared, S.J., *Luther and His Spiritual Legacy.* Wilmington, DE: Michael Glazier, 1983.

Williams, George H., *The Radical Reformation*. Philadelphia: Westminster Press, 1963. 3rd revised edition, Kirksville: Sixteenth Century Journal Pub., 1992.

Wright, Wendy, *Bond of Perfection, Jeanne de Chantal and Francois de Sales*. New York: Paulist Press, 1985.

E. Modern Period

Abbott, Walter, S.J. (General Editor), *The Documents of Vatican II*. New York: America Press, 1966.

Alphonsus de Liguori, Selected Writings. Edited by Frederick M. Jones, C.Ss.R. New York: Paulist Press, 1998.

Armstrong, Christopher, *Evelyn Underhill, An Introduction to Her Life and Writings*. Grand Rapids: Eerdmans, 1975.

Bedoyere, Michael de la, *The Life of Baron von Hügel*. London: Dent, 1951.

Bethge, Eberhard, *Dietrich Bonhoeffer, Man of Vision, Man of Courage*. New York: Harper & Row, 1970.

Blehl, Vincent Ferrer, S.J. (ed.), *Realization, Newman's Selection of His Parochial and Plain Sermons*. London: Darton, Longmans and Todd, 1964.

Bonhoeffer, Dietrich, *The Cost of Discipleship*. New York: Macmillan, 1963.

_____. *Life Together*. New York: Harper & Row, 1954.

Bosanquet, Mary, *The Life and Death of Dietrich Bonhoeffer*. New York: Harper & Row, 1968.

Callahan, Annice, R.S.C.J., *Spiritual Guides For Today*. New York: Crossroad, 1992.

Chapman, Ronald, *Father Faber*. Westminster, MD: Newman Press, 1961.

Christian Spirituality III, Post-Reformation and Modern. Edited by Louis Dupre and Donald Saliers. New York: Crossroad, 1989.

Cragg, Gerald R., *The Church in the Age of Reason (1648-1789)*. New York: Penguin, 1964.

Day, Dorothy, *The Long Loneliness*. New York: Curtis Books, 1972.

Dessain, Charles Stephen, *The Spirituality of John Henry Newman*. Minneapolis: Winston Press, 1977.

Downey, Michael, *Understanding Christian Spirituality*. New York: Paulist Press, 1977.

Elizabeth Seton, Selected Writings. Edited by Elin Kelly and Annabelle M. Melville. New York: Paulist Press, 1987.

Faricy, Robert, S.J., *The Spirituality of Teilhard de Chardin*. Minneapolis: Winston Press, 1981.

Freemantle, Alice, *Desert Calling, The Life of Charles de Foucauld*. London: Hollis and Carter, 1950.

Gannon, David, *Father Paul of Graymoor*. New York: Macmillan, 1959.

Graef, Hilda, *God and Myself, The Spirituality of John Henry Newman*. New York: Hawthorn Books, 1968.

Green, Roger Lancelyn and Hooper, Walter, *C.S. Lewis, A Biography*. New York: Harcourt, Brace, Jovanovich, 1974.

Gueranger, Dom Prosper, *The Liturgical Year*. Translated by Laurence Shepherd, O.S.B. Westminster, MD: The Newman Press, 1948.

Healey, Charles J., S.J., *Modern Spiritual Writers, Their Legacies of Prayer*. New York: Alba House, 1989.

Hennesey, James, S.J., *American Catholics*. New York: Oxford University Press, 1981.

Holden, Vincent F., *Yankee Paul, Isaac Thomas Hecker*. Chicago: Bruce, 1958.

Houselander, Caryll, *A Rocking-Horse Catholic*. New York: Sheed and Ward, 1955.

Kaschmitter, William A., *The Spirituality of Vatican II: Conciliar Texts Concerning the Spiritual Life of All Christians*. Huntington, IN: Our Sunday Visitor, 1975.

Ker, Ian, *John Henry Newman, A Biography*. Oxford: Clarendon Press, 1988.

Leech, Kenneth, *Soul Friend, The Practice of Christian Spirituality*. San Francisco: Harper & Row, 1977.

Lewis, C.S., *Surprised by Joy, The Shape of My Early Life*. London: Collins, Fontana Books, 1959.

Marmion, Columba, *Christ the Life of the Soul*. St. Louis: B. Herder Books, Co., 1925.

McDonnell, Kilian, O.S.B., *Charismatic Renewal and the Churches*. New York: Seabury Press, 1976.

Melville, Annabelle M., *Elizabeth Bayley Seton 1774-1821*. New York: Scribners, 1960.

Merton, Thomas, *The Seven Storey Mountain*. New York: Signet Books, 1952.

_____. Lawrence S. Cunningham, ed., *Thomas Merton: Spiritual Master, The Essential Writings*. New York: Paulist Press, 1992.

Miller, William D., *Dorothy Day, A Biography*. San Francisco: Harper & Row, 1982.

_____. *All is Grace. The Spirituality of Dorothy Day*. Garden City, New York: Doubleday, 1987.

Mott, Michael, *The Seven Mountains of Thomas Merton*. Boston: Houghton Mifflin, 1984.

Newman, John Henry, *Parochial and Plain Sermons*. San Francisco: Ignatius Press, 1987.

John Henry Newman, Selected Sermons. Edited with an introduction by Ian Ker. New York: Paulist Press, 1994.

Nicodemus of the Holy Mountain, A Handbook of Spiritual Counsel. Translation and foreword by Peter A. Chamberas. New York: Paulist Press, 1989.

O'Brien, David J., *Isaac Hecker, An American Catholic*. New York: Paulist Press, 1992.

The Pilgrim's Tale. Edited with an introduction by Aleksei Pentkovsky. New York: Paulist Press, 1997.

Poulain, Augustin, S.J., *The Graces of Interior Prayer*. St. Louis: Herder, 1950.

Sheppard, Lancelot, *Spiritual Writers in Modern Times*. New York: Hawthorn Books, 1967.

Thérèse of Lisieux, Saint, *Autobiography of St. Thérèse of Lisieux*. New York: Kenedy, 1958.

_____. *Story of a Soul, The Autobiography of St. Thérèse of Lisieux*. Translated from the original manuscripts by John Clarke, O.C.D. Washington, DC: ICS Publications, 1975.

Teilhard de Chardin, Pierre, S.J., *The Divine Milieu*. New York: Harper & Row, 1960.

Trevor, Meriol, *Newman, The Pillar of the Cloud* (vol. I) and *Newman, Light in Winter* (vol. II). New York: Doubleday, 1962.

Trochu, F., *The Curé d'Ars, St. Jean-Marie Baptiste Vianney.* Translated by E. Graf. Westminster, MD: Newman Press, 1949.

Underhill, Evelyn, *Mysticism, A Study in the Nature and Development of Man's Spiritual Consciousness.* New York: Meridian Books, 1955.

Ward, Maisie, *Caryll Houselander, The Divine Eccentric.* New York: Sheed and Ward, 1962.

Whelan, Joseph P., S.J., *The Spirituality of Friedrich von Hügel.* New York: Paulist Press, 1972.

INDEX